# The Idea of Justice

AMARTYA SEN

# The Idea of Justice

ALLEN LANE
*an imprint of*
PENGUIN BOOKS

*In memory of*

# John Rawls

ALLEN LANE

Published by the Penguin Group

Penguin Books Ltd, 80 Strand, London WC2R 0RL, England

Penguin Group (USA) Inc., 375 Hudson Street, New York, New York 10014, USA

Penguin Group (Canada), 90 Eglinton Avenue East, Suite 700, Toronto, Ontario, Canada M4P 2Y3
(a division of Pearson Penguin Canada Inc.)

Penguin Ireland, 25 St Stephen's Green, Dublin 2, Ireland
(a division of Penguin Books Ltd)

Penguin Group (Australia), 250 Camberwell Road, Camberwell, Victoria 3124, Australia
(a division of Pearson Australia Group Pty Ltd)

Penguin Books India Pvt Ltd, 11 Community Centre, Panchsheel Park, New Delhi – 110 017, India

Penguin Group (NZ), 67 Apollo Drive, Rosedale, North Shore 0632, New Zealand
(a division of Pearson New Zealand Ltd)

Penguin Books (South Africa) (Pty) Ltd, 24 Sturdee Avenue, Rosebank, Johannesburg 2196, South Africa

Penguin Books Ltd, Registered Offices: 80 Strand, London WC2R 0RL, England

www.penguin.com

First published 2009

5

Copyright © Amartya Sen, 2009

The moral right of the author has been asserted

Set in 10.5/14 pt PostScript Linotype Sabon
Typeset by Rowland Phototypesetting Ltd, Bury St Edmunds, Suffolk
Printed in England by Clays Ltd, St Ives plc

ISBN: 978-1-846-14147-8

www.greenpenguin.co.uk

Mixed Sources
Product group from well-managed
forests and other controlled sources
www.fsc.org  Cert no. SA-COC-1592
© 1996 Forest Stewardship Council
FSC

Penguin Books is committed to a sustainable future
for our business, our readers and our planet.
The book in your hands is made from paper
certified by the Forest Stewardship Council.

# Contents

CONTENTS

PART III

## The Materials of Justice

PART IV

## Public Reasoning and Democracy

# Preface

'In the little world in which children have their existence', says Pip in Charles Dickens's *Great Expectations*, 'there is nothing so finely perceived and finely felt, as injustice.'[1] I expect Pip is right: he vividly recollects after his humiliating encounter with Estella the 'capricious and violent coercion' he suffered as a child at the hands of his own sister. But the strong perception of manifest injustice applies to adult human beings as well. What moves us, reasonably enough, is not the realization that the world falls short of being completely just – which few of us expect – but that there are clearly remediable injustices around us which we want to eliminate.

This is evident enough in our day-to-day life, with inequities or subjugations from which we may suffer and which we have good reason to resent, but it also applies to more widespread diagnoses of injustice in the wider world in which we live. It is fair to assume that Parisians would not have stormed the Bastille, Gandhi would not have challenged the empire on which the sun used not to set, Martin Luther King would not have fought white supremacy in 'the land of the free and the home of the brave', without their sense of manifest injustices that could be overcome. They were not trying to achieve a perfectly just world (even if there were any agreement on what that would be like), but they did want to remove clear injustices to the extent they could.

The identification of redressable injustice is not only what animates us to think about justice and injustice, it is also central, I argue in this book, to the theory of justice. In the investigation presented here, diagnosis of injustice will figure often enough as the starting point for critical discussion.[2] But, it may be asked, if this is a reasonable starting point, why can't it also be a good ending point? What is the need to go beyond our sense of justice and injustice? Why must we have a theory of justice?

To understand the world is never a matter of simply recording our immediate perceptions. Understanding inescapably involves reasoning. We have to 'read' what we feel and seem to see, and ask what those perceptions indicate and how we may take them into account without being overwhelmed by them. One issue relates to the reliability of our feelings and impressions. A sense of injustice could serve as a signal that moves us, but a signal does demand critical examination, and there has to be some scrutiny of the soundness of a conclusion based mainly on signals. Adam Smith's conviction of the importance of moral sentiments did not stop him from seeking a 'theory of moral sentiments', nor from insisting that a sense of wrong-doing be critically examined through reasoned scrutiny to see whether it can be the basis of a sustainable condemnation. A similar requirement of scrutiny applies to an inclination to praise someone or something.*

We also have to ask what kinds of reasoning should count in the assessment of ethical and political concepts such as justice and injustice. In what way can a diagnosis of injustice, or the identification of what would reduce or eliminate it, be objective? Does this demand impartiality in some particular sense, such as detachment from one's own vested interests? Does it also demand re-examination of some attitudes even if they are not related to vested interests, but reflect local preconceptions and prejudices, which may not survive reasoned confrontation with others not restricted by the same parochialism? What is the role of rationality and of reasonableness in understanding the demands of justice?

These concerns and some closely related general questions are addressed in the first ten chapters, before I move on to issues of

---

* Smith's classic book, *The Theory of Moral Sentiments*, was published exactly 250 years ago in 1759, and the last revised edition – the 6th – in 1790. In the new anniversary edition of *The Theory of Moral Sentiments*, to be published by Penguin Books later this year (2009), I discuss, in the Introduction, the nature of Smith's moral and political engagement and its continuing relevance to the contemporary world.

application, involving critical assessment of the grounds on which judgements about justice are based (whether freedoms, capabilities, resources, happiness, well-being or something else), the special relevance of diverse considerations that figure under the general headings of equality and liberty, the evident connection between pursuing justice and seeking democracy seen as government by discussion, and the nature, viability and reach of claims of human rights.

## WHAT KIND OF A THEORY?

What is presented here is a theory of justice in a very broad sense. Its aim is to clarify how we can proceed to address questions of enhancing justice and removing injustice, rather than to offer resolutions of questions about the nature of perfect justice. In this there are clear differences with the pre-eminent theories of justice in contemporary moral and political philosophy. As will be discussed more fully in the Introduction that follows, three differences in particular demand specific attention.

First, a theory of justice that can serve as the basis of practical reasoning must include ways of judging how to reduce injustice and advance justice, rather than aiming only at the characterization of perfectly just societies – an exercise that is such a dominant feature of many theories of justice in political philosophy today. The two exercises for identifying perfectly just arrangements, and for determining whether a particular social change would enhance justice, do have motivational links but they are nevertheless analytically disjoined. The latter question, on which this work concentrates, is central to making decisions about institutions, behaviour and other determinants of justice, and how these decisions are derived cannot but be crucial to a theory of justice that aims at guiding practical reasoning about what should be done. The assumption that this comparative exercise cannot be undertaken without identifying, first, the demands of perfect justice, can be shown to be entirely incorrect (as is discussed in Chapter 4, 'Voice and Social Choice').

Second, while many comparative questions of justice can be successfully resolved – and agreed upon in reasoned arguments – there could well be other comparisons in which conflicting considerations are not fully resolved. It is argued here that there can exist several distinct reasons of justice, each of which survives critical scrutiny, but yields divergent conclusions.* Reasonable arguments in competing directions can emanate from people with diverse experiences and traditions, but they can also come from within a given society, or for that matter, even from the very same person.†

There is a need for reasoned argument, with oneself and with others, in dealing with conflicting claims, rather than for what can be called 'disengaged toleration', with the comfort of such a lazy resolution as: 'you are right in your community and I am right in mine'. Reasoning and impartial scrutiny are essential. However, even the most vigorous of critical examination can still leave conflicting and competing arguments that are not eliminated by impartial scrutiny. I shall have more to say on this in what follows, but I emphasize here that the necessity of reasoning and scrutiny is not compromised in any way by the possibility that some competing priorities may survive despite the confrontation of reason. The plurality with which we will then end up will be the result of reasoning, not of abstention from it.

Third, the presence of remediable injustice may well be connected with behavioural transgressions rather than with institutional shortcomings (Pip's recollection, in *Great Expectations*, of his coercive sister was just that, not an indictment of the family as an institution). Justice is ultimately connected with the way people's lives go, and not merely with the nature of the institutions surrounding them. In contrast, many of the principal theories of justice concentrate over-

---

* The importance of valuational plurality has been extensively – and powerfully – explored by Isaiah Berlin and Bernard Williams. Pluralities can survive even within a given community, or even for a particular person, and they need not be reflections of values of 'different communities'. However, variations of values between people in different communities can also be significant (as has been discussed, in different ways, in important contributions by Michael Walzer, Charles Taylor and Michael Sandel, among others).

† For example, Marx expounded the case both for eliminating the exploitation of labour (related to the justness of getting what can be seen as the product of one's efforts) and for allocation according to needs (related to the demands of distributive justice). He went on to discuss the inescapable conflict between these two priorities in his last substantial writing: *The Critique of the Gotha Programme* (1875).

whelmingly on how to establish 'just institutions', and give some derivative and subsidiary role to behavioural features. For example, John Rawls's rightly celebrated approach of 'justice as fairness' yields a unique set of 'principles of justice' that are exclusively concerned with setting up 'just institutions' (to constitute the basic structure of the society), while requiring that people's behaviour complies entirely with the demands of proper functioning of these institutions.[3] In the approach to justice presented in this work, it is argued that there are some crucial inadequacies in this overpowering concentration on institutions (where behaviour is assumed to be appropriately compliant), rather than on the lives that people are able to lead. The focus on actual lives in the assessment of justice has many far-reaching implications for the nature and reach of the idea of justice.*

The departure in the theory of justice that is explored in this work has a direct bearing, I argue, on political and moral philosophy. But I have also tried to discuss the relevance of the arguments presented here with some of the ongoing engagements in law, economics and politics, and it might, if one were ready to be optimistic, even have some pertinence to debates and decisions on practical policies and programmes.†

The use of a comparative perspective, going well beyond the limited – and limiting – framework of social contract, can make a useful contribution here. We are engaged in making comparisons in terms of the advancement of justice whether we fight oppression (like slavery, or the subjugation of women), or protest against systematic medical neglect (through the absence of medical facilities in parts of Africa or Asia, or a lack of universal health coverage in most countries in

* The recent investigation of what has come to be called the 'capability perspective' fits directly into the understanding of justice in terms of human lives and the freedoms that the persons can respectively exercise. See Martha Nussbaum and Amartya Sen (eds), *The Quality of Life* (Oxford: Clarendon Press, 1993). The reach and limits of that perspective will be examined in Chapters 11–14.

† For example, the case for what is called here 'open impartiality', which admits voices from far as well as near in interpreting the justice of laws (not only for the sake of fairness to others, but also for the avoidance of parochialism, as discussed by Adam Smith in *The Theory of Moral Sentiments* and in *Lectures on Jurisprudence*), has direct relevance to some of the contemporary debates in the Supreme Court of the United States, as is discussed in the concluding chapter of this book.

the world, including the United States), or repudiate the permissibility of torture (which continues to be used with remarkable frequency in the contemporary world – sometimes by pillars of the global establishment), or reject the quiet tolerance of chronic hunger (for example in India, despite the successful abolition of famines).* We may often enough agree that some changes contemplated (like the abolition of apartheid, to give an example of a different kind) will reduce injustice, but even if all such agreed changes are successfully implemented, we will not have anything that we can call perfect justice. Practical concerns, no less than theoretical reasoning, seem to demand a fairly radical departure in the analysis of justice.

## PUBLIC REASONING AND DEMOCRACY AND GLOBAL JUSTICE

Even though in the approach presented here principles of justice will not be defined in terms of institutions, but rather in terms of the lives and freedoms of the people involved, institutions cannot but play a significant instrumental role in the pursuit of justice. Together with the determinants of individual and social behaviour, an appropriate choice of institutions has a critically important place in the enterprise of enhancing justice. Institutions come into the reckoning in many different ways. They can contribute directly to the lives that people are able to lead in accordance with what they have reason to value. Institutions can also be important in facilitating our ability to scrutinize the values and priorities that we can consider, especially through opportunities for public discussion (this will include considerations of freedom of speech and right to information as well as actual facilities for informed discussion).

In this work, democracy is assessed in terms of public reasoning

---

* I was privileged to address the Indian Parliament on 'The Demands of Justice' on 11 August 2008 at the invitation of the Speaker. This was the first Hiren Mukerjee Memorial Lecture, which is going to be an annual parliamentary event. The full version of the address is available in a brochure printed by the Indian Parliament, and a shortened version is published in *The Little Magazine*, vol. 8, issues 1 and 2 (2009), under the title 'What Should Keep Us Awake at Night'.

(Chapters 15–17), which leads to an understanding of democracy as 'government by discussion' (an idea that John Stuart Mill did much to advance). But democracy must also be seen more generally in terms of the capacity to enrich reasoned engagement through enhancing informational availability and the feasibility of interactive discussions. Democracy has to be judged not just by the institutions that formally exist but by the extent to which different voices from diverse sections of the people can actually be heard.

Furthermore, this way of seeing democracy can have an impact on the pursuit of it at the global level – not just within a nation-state. If democracy is not seen simply in terms of the setting up of some specific institutions (like a democratic global government or global elections), but in terms of the possibility and reach of public reasoning, the task of *advancing* – rather than perfecting – both global democracy and global justice can be seen as eminently understandable ideas that can plausibly inspire and influence practical actions across borders.

## THE EUROPEAN ENLIGHTENMENT AND OUR GLOBAL HERITAGE

What can I say about the antecedents of the approach I am trying to present here? I will discuss this question more fully in the Introduction that follows, but I should point out that the analysis of justice I present in this book draws on lines of reasoning that received particular exploration in the period of intellectual discontent during the European Enlightenment. Having said that, however, I must immediately make a couple of clarificatory points to prevent possible misunderstanding.

The first clarification is to explain that the connection of this work with the tradition of European Enlightenment does not make the intellectual background of this book particularly 'European'. Indeed, one of the unusual – some will probably say eccentric – features of this book compared with other writings on the theory of justice is the extensive use that I have made of ideas from non-Western societies, particularly from Indian intellectual history, but also from elsewhere. There are powerful traditions of reasoned argument, rather than reliance on faith and unreasoned convictions, in India's intellectual past, as there are in the thoughts flourishing in a number of other non-Western societies. In confining attention almost exclusively to Western literature, the contemporary – and largely Western – pursuit of political philosophy in general and of the demands of justice in particular has been, I would argue, limited and to some extent parochial.*

It is not, however, my claim that there is some radical dissonance between 'Western' and 'Eastern' (or generally, non-Western) thinking on these subjects. There are many differences in reasoning within the West, and within the East, but it would be altogether fanciful to think of a united West confronting 'quintessentially eastern' priorities.† Such views, which are not unknown in contemporary discussions, are quite distant from my understanding. It is my claim, rather, that similar – or closely linked – ideas of justice, fairness, responsibility, duty, goodness and rightness have been pursued in many different parts of the world, which can expand the reach of arguments that have been considered in Western literature and that the global presence of such reasoning is often overlooked or marginalized in the dominant traditions of contemporary Western discourse.

Some of the reasoning of, for example, Gautama Buddha (the agnostic champion of the 'path of knowledge'), or of the writers in the

---

* Kautilya, the ancient Indian writer on political strategy and political economy, has sometimes been described in the modern literature, when he has been noticed at all, as 'the Indian Machiavelli'. This is unsurprising in some respects, since there are some similarities in their ideas on strategies and tactics (despite profound differences in many other – often more important – areas), but it is amusing that an Indian political analyst from the fourth century BC has to be introduced as a local version of an European writer born in the fifteenth century. What this reflects is not, of course, any kind of crude assertion of a geographical pecking order, but simply the lack of familiarity with non-Western literature of Western intellectuals (and in fact intellectuals all across the modern world because of the global dominance of Western education today).

† Indeed, I have argued elsewhere that there are no quintessentially eastern priorities, not even quintessentially Indian ones, since arguments in many different directions can be seen in the intellectual history of these countries (see my *The Argumentative Indian* (London and Delhi: Penguin, and New York: FSG, 2005), and *Identity and Violence: The Illusion of Destiny* (New York: Norton, and London and Delhi: Penguin, 2006).

Lokayata school (committed to relentless scrutiny of every traditional belief) in India in sixth-century BC, may sound closely aligned, rather than adversarial, to many of the critical writings of the leading authors of the European Enlightenment. But we do not have to get all steamed up in trying to decide whether Gautama Buddha should be seen as an anticipating member of some European Enlightenment league (his acquired name does, after all, mean 'enlightened' in Sanskrit); nor do we have to consider the far-fetched thesis that the European Enlightenment may be traceable to long-distance influence of Asian thought. There is nothing particularly odd in the recognition that similar intellectual engagements have taken place in different parts of the globe in distinct stages of history. Since somewhat different arguments have often been advanced in dealing with similar questions, we may miss out on possible leads in reasoning about justice if we keep our explorations regionally confined.

One example of some interest and relevance is an important distinction between two different concepts of justice in early Indian jurisprudence – between *niti* and *nyaya*. The former idea, that of *niti*, relates to organizational propriety as well as behavioural correctness, whereas the latter, *nyaya*, is concerned with what emerges and how, and in particular the lives that people are actually able to lead. The distinction, the relevance of which will be discussed in the Introduction, helps us to see clearly that there are two rather different, though not unrelated, kinds of justness for which the idea of justice has to cater.*

My second explanatory remark relates to the fact that the Enlightenment authors did not speak in one voice. As I will discuss in the Introduction, there is a substantial dichotomy between two different lines of reasoning about justice that can be seen among two groups of leading philosophers associated with the radical thought of the

---

* The distinction between *nyaya* and *niti* has significance not only within a polity, but also across the borders of states, as is discussed in my essay 'Global Justice', presented at the World Justice Forum in Vienna, July 2008, sponsored by the American Bar Association, along with the International Bar Association, Inter-American Bar Association, Inter-Pacific Bar Association, and Union Internationale des Avocats. This is part of the American Bar Association's 'World Justice Program', and will be published in a volume entitled *Global Perspectives on the Rule of Law*.

Enlightenment period. One approach concentrated on identifying perfectly just social arrangements, and took the characterization of 'just institutions' to be the principal – and often the only identified – task of the theory of justice. Woven in different ways around the idea of a hypothetical 'social contract', major contributions were made in this line of thinking by Thomas Hobbes in the seventeenth century, and later by John Locke, Jean-Jacques Rousseau and Immanuel Kant, among others. The contractarian approach has been the dominant influence in contemporary political philosophy, particularly since a pioneering paper ('Justice as Fairness') in 1958 by John Rawls which preceded his definitive statement on that approach in his classic book, *A Theory of Justice*.[4]

In contrast, a number of other Enlightenment philosophers (Smith, Condorcet, Wollstonecraft, Bentham, Marx, John Stuart Mill, for example) took a variety of approaches that shared a common interest in making comparisons between different ways in which people's lives may be led, influenced by institutions but also by people's actual behaviour, social interactions and other significant determinants. This book draws to a great extent on that alternative tradition.* The analytical – and rather mathematical – discipline of 'social choice theory', which can be traced to the works of Condorcet in the eighteenth century, but which has been developed in the present form by the pioneering contributions of Kenneth Arrow in the mid-twentieth century, belongs to this second line of investigation. That approach, suitably adapted, can make a substantial contribution, as I will discuss, to addressing questions about the enhancement of justice and the removal of injustice in the world.

---

* This will not, however, prevent me from drawing on insights from the first approach, from the enlightenment we get from the writings, for example, of Hobbes and Kant, and in our time, from John Rawls.

# THE PLACE OF REASON

Despite the differences between the two traditions of the Enlightenment – the contractarian and the comparative – there are many points of similarity as well. The common features include reliance on reasoning and the invoking of the demands of public discussion. Even though this book relates mainly to the second approach, rather than to contractarian reasoning developed by Immanuel Kant and others, much of the book is driven by the basic Kantian insight (as Christine Korsgaard puts it): 'Bringing reason to the world becomes the enterprise of morality rather than metaphysics, and the work as well as the hope of humanity.'[5]

To what extent reasoning can provide a reliable basis for a theory of justice is, of course, itself an issue that has been subject to controversy. The first chapter of the book is concerned with the role and reach of reasoning. I argue against the plausibility of seeing emotions or psychology or instincts as independent sources of valuation, without reasoned appraisal. Impulses and mental attitudes remain important, however, since we have good reasons to take note of them in our assessment of justice and injustice in the world. There is no irreducible conflict here, I argue, between reason and emotion, and there are very good reasons for making room for the relevance of emotions.

There is, however, a different kind of critique of the reliance on reasoning that points to the prevalence of unreason in the world and to the unrealism involved in assuming that the world will go in the way reason dictates. In a kind but firm critique of my work in related fields, Kwame Anthony Appiah has argued, 'however much you extend your understanding of reason in the sorts of ways Sen would like to do – and this is a project whose interest I celebrate – it isn't going to take you the whole way. In adopting the perspective of the individual reasonable person, Sen has to turn his face from the pervasiveness of unreason.'[6] As a description of the world, Appiah is clearly right, and his critique, which is not addressed to building a theory of justice, presents good grounds for scepticism about the practical effectiveness of reasoned discussion of confused social

PREFACE

subjects (such as the politics of identity). The prevalence and resilience of unreason may make reason-based answers to difficult questions far less effective.

This particular scepticism of the reach of reasoning does not yield – nor (as Appiah makes clear) is it intended to yield – any ground for not using reason to the extent one can, in pursuing the idea of justice or any other notion of social relevance, such as identity.* Nor does it undermine the case for our trying to persuade each other to scrutinize our respective conclusions. It is also important to note that what may appear to others as clear examples of 'unreason' may not always be exactly that.† Reasoned discussion can accommodate conflicting positions that may appear to others to be 'unreasoned' prejudice, without this being quite the case. There is no compulsion, as is some- times assumed, to eliminate every reasoned alternative except exactly one.

However, the central point in dealing with this question is that prejudices typically ride on the back of some kind of reasoning – weak and arbitrary though it might be. Indeed, even very dogmatic persons tend to have some kinds of reasons, possibly very crude ones, in support of their dogmas (racist, sexist, classist and caste-based preju- dices belong there, among varieties of other kinds of bigotry based on coarse reasoning). Unreason is mostly not the practice of doing with- out reasoning altogether, but of relying on very primitive and very defective reasoning. There is hope in this, since bad reasoning can be confronted by better reasoning. So the scope for reasoned engagement does exist, even though many people may refuse, at least initially, to enter that engagement, despite being challenged.

What is important for the arguments in this book is not anything

* There is, in fact, considerable evidence that interactive public discussions can help to weaken the refusal to reason. See the empirical material on this presented in *Development as Freedom* (New York: Knopf, and Oxford: Clarendon Press, 1999), and *Identity and Violence: The Illusion of Destiny* (New York: Norton, and London: Penguin, 2006).
† As James Thurber notes, while those who are superstitious may avoid walking under ladders, the scientific minds who 'want to defy the superstition' may choose to 'look for ladders and delight in passing under them'. But 'if you keep looking for and walking under the ladders long enough, something is going to happen to you' (James Thurber, 'Let Your Mind Alone!' *New Yorker*, 1 May 1937).

like the omnipresence of reason in everyone's thinking right now. No such presumption can be made, and it is not needed. The claim that people would agree on a particular proposition if they were to reason in an open and impartial way does not, of course, assume that people are already so engaged, or even that they are eager to be so. What matters most is the examination of what reasoning would demand for the pursuit of justice – allowing for the possibility that there may exist several different reasonable positions. That exercise is quite compatible with the possibility, even the certainty, that at a particular time not everyone is willing to undertake such scrutiny. Reasoning is central to the understanding of justice even in a world which contains much 'unreason'; indeed, it may be particularly important in such a world.

# Acknowledgements

In acknowledging the help I have received from others in the work presented here, I must begin by recording that my greatest debt is to John Rawls, who inspired me to work in this area. He was also a marvellous teacher over many decades and his ideas continue to influence me even when I disagree with some of his conclusions. This book is dedicated to his memory, not only for the education and affection I received from him, but also for his encouragement to pursue my doubts.

My first extensive contact with Rawls was in 1968–9, when I came from Delhi University to Harvard as a visiting professor and taught a joint graduate seminar with him and Kenneth Arrow. Arrow has been another powerful influence on this book, as on many of my past works. His influence has come not only through extensive discussions over many decades, but also through the use I make of the analytical framework of modern social choice theory that he initiated.

The work presented here was done at Harvard where I have been mostly based since 1987, and at Trinity College, Cambridge, particularly during the six years between 1998 and 2004 when I went back there to serve as the Master of the great college where, fifty years ago, I had started thinking about philosophical issues. I was influenced in particular by Piero Sraffa and C. D. Broad, and encouraged by Maurice Dobb and Dennis Robertson to pursue my inclinations.

This book has been slow in coming, since my doubts and constructive thoughts have developed over a long period of time. During these decades, I have been privileged to receive comments, suggestions, questions, dismissals and encouragement from a large number of people, all of which have been very useful for me and my acknowledge-ment list is not going to be short.

I must first note the help and advice I have received from my wife, Emma Rothschild, whose influence is reflected throughout the book. The influence of Bernard Williams on my thinking on philosophical issues will be apparent to readers familiar with his writings. This influence came over many years of 'chatty friendship' and also from a productive period of joint work in planning, editing and introducing a collection of essays on the utilitarian perspective and its limitations (*Utilitarianism and Beyond*, 1982)

I have been very fortunate in having colleagues with whom I have had instructive conversations on political and moral philosophy. I must acknowledge my extensive debt – in addition to Rawls – to Hilary Putnam and Thomas Scanlon for many illuminating conver-sations over the years. I also learned a great deal from talking with W. V. O. Quine and Robert Nozick, both of whom are now, alas, gone. Holding joint classes at Harvard has also been for me a steady source of dialectical education, coming both from my students and of course from my co-teachers. Robert Nozick and I taught joint courses every year for nearly a decade, on a number of occasions with Eric Maskin, and they have both influenced my thinking. At various times I have also taught courses with Joshua Cohen (from the not-so-distant Massachusetts Institute of Technology), Christine Jolls, Philippe Van Parijs, Michael Sandel, John Rawls, Thomas Scanlon and Richard Tuck, and with Kaushik Basu and James Foster when they visited Harvard. Aside from my sheer enjoyment of these joint classes, they were also tremendously useful for me in developing my ideas, often in arguments with my co-teachers.

In all my writings I benefit a lot from the critiques of my students, and this book is no exception. Regarding the ideas in this particular book, I would like to acknowledge my interactions especially with Prasanta Pattanaik, Kaushik Basu, Siddiqur Osmani, Rajat Deb, Ravi Kanbur, David Kelsey and Andreas Papandreou, over many decades, and later with Stephan Klasen, Anthony Laden, Sanjay Reddy, Jonathan Cohen, Felicia Knaul, Clemens Puppe, Bertil Tungodden, A. K. Shiva Kumar, Lawrence Hamilton, Douglas Hicks, Jennifer Prah Ruger, Sousan Abadian, among others.

The joys and benefits of interactive teaching go back for me to the 1970s and 1980s when I taught joint classes – 'riotous' ones, a student told me – at Oxford with Ronald Dworkin and Derek Parfit, later joined by G. A. Cohen. My warm memories of those argumentative discussions were recently revived by the kindness of Cohen who arranged a hugely engaging seminar at University College London in January 2009 on the main approach of this book. The gathering was agreeably full of dissenters, including Cohen (of course), but also Jonathan Wolff, Laura Valentis, Riz Mokal, George Letsas and Stephen Guest, whose different critiques have been very helpful for me (Laura Valentis kindly sent me further comments in communications after the seminar).

Even though a theory of justice must belong primarily to philosophy, the book uses ideas presented in a number of other disciplines as well. A major field of work on which this book draws heavily is social choice theory. Although my interactions with others working in this broad area are too numerous to capture in a short statement here, I would like particularly to acknowledge the benefit I have received from working with Kenneth Arrow and Kotaro Suzumura, with whom I have been editing the *Handbook of Social Choice Theory* (the first volume is out, the second overdue), and also to note my appreciation of the leadership role that has been played in this field by Jerry Kelly, Wulf Gaertner, Prasanta Pattanaik and Maurice Salles, particularly through their visionary and tireless work for the emergence and flourishing of the journal *Social Choice and Welfare*. I would also like to acknowledge the benefits I have had from my long association and extended discussions on social choice problems in one form or another with (in addition to the names already mentioned) Patrick Suppes, John Harsanyi, James Mirrlees, Anthony Atkinson, Peter Hammond, Charles Blackorby, Sudhir Anand, Tapas Majundar, Robert Pollak, Kevin Roberts, John Roemer, Anthony Shorrocks, Robert Sugden, John Weymark and James Foster.

A long-standing influence on my work on justice, particularly related to freedom and capability, has come from Martha Nussbaum. Her work, combined with her strong commitment to the development of the 'capability perspective', has deeply influenced many of its recent advances, including the exploration of its linkage with the classical

Aristotelian ideas on 'capacity' and 'flourishing', and also with works on human development, gender studies and human rights.

The relevance and use of the capability perspective has been powerfully explored in recent years by the research of a group of remarkable scholars. Even though their writings have greatly influenced my thinking, a full list would be far too long to include here. I must, however, mention the influence coming from the works of Sabina Alkire, Bina Agarwal, Tania Burchardt, Enrica Chiappero-Martinetti, Flavio Comim, David Crocker, Séverine Deneulin, Sakiko Fukuda-Parr, Reiko Gotoh, Mozaffar Qizilbash, Ingrid Robeyns and Polly Vizard. There is also a close connection between the capability perspective and the new area of human development, which was pioneered by my late friend Mahbub ul Haq, and also bears the impact of the influence of Paul Streeten, Frances Stewart, Keith Griffin, Gustav Ranis, Richard Jolly, Meghnad Desai, Sudhir Anand, Sakiko Fukuda-Parr, Selim Jahan, among others. The *Journal of Human Development and Capabilities* has a strong involvement with work on the capability perspective, but the journal *Feminist Economics* has also taken a special interest in this area, and it has always been stimulating for me to have conversations with its editor, Diana Strassman, on the relation between the feminist perspective and the capability approach.

At Trinity I have had the excellent company of philosophers, legal thinkers and others interested in problems of justice, and had the opportunity of interacting with Garry Runciman, Nick Denyer, Gisela Striker, Simon Blackburn, Catharine Barnard, Joanna Miles, Ananya Kabir, Eric Nelson, and occasionally with Ian Hacking (who sometimes came back to his old college where we had first met and talked as fellow students in the 1950s). I have also had the marvellous possibility of conversing with outstanding mathematicians, natural scientists, historians, social scientists, legal theorists and scholars in humanities.

I have benefited substantially also from my conversations with several other philosophers, including (in addition to those I have already mentioned) Elizabeth Anderson, Kwame Anthony Appiah, Christian Barry, Charles Beitz, the late Isaiah Berlin, Akeel Bilgrami, Hilary Bok, Sissela Bok, Susan Brison, John Broome, Ian Carter, Nancy Cartwright, Deen Chatterjee, Drucilla Cornell, Norman

Daniels, the late Donald Davidson, John Davis, Jon Elster, Barbara
Fried, Allan Gibbard, Jonathan Glover, James Griffin, Amy Gutmann,
Moshe Halbertal, the late Richard Hare, Daniel Hausman, Ted Hond-
erich, the late Susan Hurley, Susan James, Frances Kamm, the late Stig
Kanger, Erin Kelly, Isaac Levi, Christian List, Sebastiano Maffetone,
Avishai Margalit, David Miller, the late Sidney Morgenbesser,
Thomas Nagel, Sari Nusseibeh, the late Susan Moller Okin, Charles
Parsons, Herlinde Pauer-Struder, Fabienne Peter, Philip Pettit,
Thomas Pogge, Henry Richardson, Alan Ryan, Carol Rovane, Debra
Satz, John Searle, the late Judith Shklar, Quentin Skinner, Hillel
Steiner, Dennis Thompson, Charles Taylor and Judith Thomson.

In legal thinking I have much benefited from discussions with (in
addition to those already cited) Bruce Ackerman, Justice Stephen
Breyer, Owen Fiss, the late Herbert Hart, Tony Honoré, Anthony
Lewis, Frank Michelman, Martha Minow, Robert Nelson, Justice
Kate O'Regan, Joseph Raz, Susan Rose-Ackerman, Stephen Sedley,
Cass Sunstein and Jeremy Waldron. Even though my work for this
book effectively began with my John Dewey Lectures (on 'Well-being,
Agency and Freedom') to the Philosophy Department of Columbia
University in 1984, and came largely to an end with another set of
philosophy lectures at Stanford University (on 'Justice') in 2008, I
also tried out my arguments about theories of justice at various law
schools. In addition to several lectures and seminars at the Law
Schools of Harvard, Yale and Washington University, I also gave the
Storrs Lectures (on 'Objectivity') at the Yale Law School in September
1990, the Rosenthal Lectures (on 'The Domain of Justice') at the
Northwestern University Law School in September 1998, and a special
lecture (on 'Human Rights and the Limits of Law') in the Cardozo
Law School in September 2005.*

In economics, which is my original field of concentration, and which
has considerable relevance to the idea of justice, I have benefited
greatly from regular discussions over many decades with (in addition
to the names already mentioned) George Akerlof, Amiya Bagchi,

* The Dewey lectures were arranged primarily by Isaac Levi, the Storrs Lectures by
Guido Calabresi, the Rosenthal Lectures by Ronald Allen, and the Cardozo School
lecture by David Rudenstine. I benefited greatly from discussions with them and their
colleagues.

Jasodhara Bagchi, the late Dipak Banerjee, Nirmala Banerjee, Pranab Bardhan, Alok Bhargava, Christopher Bliss, Samuel Bowles, Samuel Brittan, Robert Cassen, the late Sukhamoy Chakravarty, Partha Dasgupta, Mrinal Datta-Chaudhuri, Angus Deaton, Meghnad Desai, Jean Drèze, Bhaskar Dutta, Jean-Paul Fitoussi, Nancy Folbre, Albert Hirschman, Devaki Jain, Tapas Majumdar, Mukul Majumdar, Stephen Marglin, Dipak Mazumdar, Luigi Pasinetti, the late I. G. Patel, Edmund Phelps, K. N. Raj, V. K. Ramachandran, Jeffrey Sachs, Arjun Sengupta, Rehman Sobhan, Barbara Solow, Robert Solow, Nicholas Stern, Joseph Stiglitz and Stefano Zamagni.

I have also had very useful conversations with Isher Ahluwalia, Montek Ahluwalia, Paul Anand, the late Peter Bauer, Abhijit Banerjee, Lourdes Beneria, Timothy Besley, Ken Binmore, Nancy Birdsall, Walter Bossert, François Bourguignon, Satya Chakravarty, Kanchan Chopra, Vincent Crawford, Asim Dasgupta, Claude d'Aspremont, Peter Diamond, Avinash Dixit, David Donaldson, Esther Duflo, Franklin Fisher, Marc Fleurbaey, Robert Frank, Benjamin Friedman, Pierangelo Garegnani, the late Louis Gevers, the late W. M. Gorman, Jan Graaff, Jean-Michel Grandmont, Jerry Green, Ted Groves, Frank Hahn, Wahidul Haque, Christopher Harris, Barbara Harris White, the late John Harsanyi, James Heckman, Judith Heyer, the late John Hicks, Jane Humphries, Nurul Islam, Rizwanul Islam, Dale Jorgenson, Daniel Kahneman, Azizur Rahman Khan, Alan Kirman, Serge Kolm, Janos Kornai, Michael Kramer, the late Jean-Jacques Laffont, Richard Layard, Michel Le Breton, Ian Little, Anuradha Luther, the late James Meade, John Muellbauer, Philippe Mongin, Dilip Mookerjee, Anjan Mukherji, Khaleq Naqvi, Deepak Nayyar, Rohini Nayyar, Thomas Piketty, Robert Pollak, Anisur Rahman, Debraj Ray, Martin Ravallion, Alvin Roth, Christian Seidl, Michael Spence, T. N. Srinivasan, David Starrett, S. Subramanian, Kotaro Suzumura, Madhura Swaminathan, Judith Tendler, Jean Tirole, Alain Trannoy, John Vickers, the late William Vickrey, Jorgen Weibull, Glen Weyl and Menahem Yaari.

I have also benefited a great deal from conversations over the years on a variety of other subjects closely related to justice with Alaka Basu, Dilip Basu, Seyla Benhabib, Sugata Bose, Myra Buvinic, Lincoln Chen, Martha Chen, David Crocker, Barun De, John Dunn, Julio

Frenk, Sakiko Fukuda-Parr, Ramachandra Guha, Geeta Rao Gupta, Geoffrey Hawthorn, Eric Hobsbawm, Jennifer Hochschild, Stanley Hoffmann, Alisha Holland, Richard Horton, Ayesha Jalal, Felicia Knaul, Melissa Lane, Mary Kaldor, Jane Mansbridge, Michael Marmot, Barry Mazur, Pratap Bhanu Mehta, Uday Mehta, the late Ralph Miliband, Christopher Murray, Elinor Ostrom, Carol Richards, David Richards, Jonathan Riley, Mary Robinson, Elaine Scarry, Gareth Stedman Jones, Irene Tinker, Megan Vaughan, Dorothy Wedderburn, Leon Wieseltier and James Wolfensohn. The part of the book that deals with democracy in its relation to justice (Chapters 15–17) draws on my three lectures on 'Democracy' at the School of Advanced International Studies (SAIS) of the Johns Hopkins University at their campus in Washington DC in 2005. Those lectures were the result of an initiative of Sunil Khilnani, endorsed by Francis Fukuyama, from both of whom I received very useful suggestions. The lectures themselves yielded other discussions in these SAIS meetings that were also very useful for me.

The new Harvard 'Program on Justice, Welfare and Economics', which I directed for five years from January 2004 to December 2008, also gave me a wonderful opportunity to interact with students and colleagues interested in similar problems from different fields. The new Director, Walter Johnson, is continuing – and enlarging – these interactions with great leadership, and I took the liberty of presenting the main thrust of this book in my farewell presentation to the group, receiving many excellent questions and comments.

Erin Kelly and Thomas Scanlon have been immensely helpful in reading through much of the manuscript and have made a number of critically important suggestions. I am most grateful to them both.

The expenses of research, including assistance, have been partly met by a five-year project on democracy at the Centre for History and Economics at King's College, Cambridge, jointly supported by the Ford Foundation, the Rockefeller Foundation and the Mellon Foundation, during 2003 to 2008, and subsequently from a new project supported by the Ford Foundation on 'India in the Global World' with a particular focus on the relevance of Indian intellectual history to contemporary issues. I am very grateful for this support, and also appreciative of the wonderful work of coordination of these projects by Inga Huld Markan. I have also had the good fortune of having extremely able and imaginative research assistants, who have taken a deep interest in the book and made a number of very productive comments that have helped me to improve my arguments and presentation. For this I am much beholden to Pedro Ramos Pintos, who worked with me for over a year and left his lasting influence on this book, and currently to Kirsty Walker and Afsan Bhadelia for their outstanding help and intellectual input.

The book is being published both by Penguin, and for North America by Harvard University Press. My Harvard editor, Michael Aronson, has made a number of excellent general suggestions. The two anonymous reviewers of the manuscript gave me remarkably helpful comments, and since my detective work has revealed that they were Frank Lovett and Bill Talbott, I can even thank them by name. The production and copy-editing at Penguin Books have been carried through excellently, under huge pressure of time, by the swift and tireless work of Richard Duguid (the managing editor), Jane Robertson (the copy-editor) and Phillip Birch (assistant editor). To them all I am most grateful.

It is impossible for me to express adequately my gratitude to the editor of this work, Stuart Proffitt of Penguin Books, who has made invaluable comments and suggestions on every chapter (indeed, almost on every page of every chapter) and has led me to rewrite many sections of the manuscript to make it clearer and more accessible. His advice on the general organization of the book has also been indispensable. I can well imagine the relief that he will experience when this book, at long last, leaves his hands.

Amartya Sen

# Introduction

## An Approach to Justice

About two and a half months before the storming of the Bastille in Paris, which was effectively the beginning of the French Revolution, the political philosopher and orator, Edmund Burke, said in Parliament in London: 'An event has happened, upon which it is difficult to speak, and impossible to be silent.' This was on 5 May 1789. Burke's speech had nothing much to do with the developing storm in France. The occasion, rather, was the impeachment of Warren Hastings, who was then commanding the British East India Company, which was setting up British rule in India, beginning with the Company's victory in the Battle of Plassey (on 23 June 1757).

In impeaching Warren Hastings, Burke invoked the 'eternal laws of justice' which, Burke claimed, Hastings had 'violated'. The impossibility of remaining silent on a subject is an observation that can be made about many cases of patent injustice that move us to rage in a way that is hard for our language to capture. And yet any analysis of injustice would also demand clear articulation and reasoned scrutiny.

Burke did not, in fact, give much evidence of being lost for words: he spoke eloquently not on one misdeed of Hastings but on a great many, and proceeded from there to present simultaneously a number of separate and quite distinct reasons for the need to indict Warren Hastings and the nature of the emerging British rule in India:

I impeach Warren Hastings, Esquire, of high crimes and misdemeanours.
I impeach him in the name of the Commons of Great Britain in Parliament assembled, whose Parliamentary trust he has betrayed.
I impeach him in the name of all the Commons of Great Britain, whose national character he has dishonoured.

I impeach him in the name of the people of India, whose laws, rights, and liberties he has subverted; whose properties he has destroyed, whose country he has laid waste and desolate.

I impeach him in the name and by virtue of those eternal laws of justice which he has violated.

I impeach him in the name of human nature itself, which he has cruelly outraged, injured, and oppressed, in both sexes, in every age, rank, situation, and condition of life.[1]

No argument is separated out here as *the* reason for impeaching Warren Hastings – as an isolated knock-out punch. Instead, Burke presents a collection of distinct reasons for impeaching him.* Later on in this work, I will examine the procedure of what can be called 'plural grounding', that is, of using a number of different lines of condemnation, without seeking an agreement on their relative merits. The underlying issue is whether we have to agree on one specific line of censure for a reasoned consensus on the diagnosis of an injustice that calls for urgent rectification. What is important to note here, as central to the idea of justice, is that we can have a strong sense of injustice on many different grounds, and yet not agree on one particular ground as being *the* dominant reason for the diagnosis of injustice.

Perhaps a more immediate, and more contemporary, illustration of this general point about congruent implications can be given by considering a recent event, involving the decision of the US government to launch a military invasion of Iraq in 2003. There are diverse ways of judging decisions of this kind, but the point to be considered here is that it is possible that a number of distinct and divergent

---

* I am not commenting here on the factual veracity of Burke's claims, but only on his general approach of presenting plural grounds for indictment. Burke's particular thesis about Hastings's personal perfidy was actually rather unfair to Hastings. Oddly enough, Burke had earlier defended the wily Robert Clive, who was a great deal more responsible for lawless plunder of India under the Company's dominance – something that Hastings did try to stem through a greater emphasis on law and order (as well as through bringing in a measure of humanity in the Company's administration which was badly missing earlier). I have discussed these historical events in a Commemorative Speech at the London City Hall, on the occasion of the 250th anniversary of the Battle of Plassey ('The Significance of Plassey'), in June 2007. The lecture was published, in an extended version, as 'Imperial Illusions: India, Britain and the wrong lessons', *The New Republic*, December 2007.

arguments can still lead to the same conclusion – in this case, that the policy chosen by the US-led coalition in starting the war in Iraq in 2003 was mistaken.

Consider the different arguments that have been presented, each with considerable plausibility, as critiques of the decision to go to war in Iraq.\* First, the conclusion that the invasion was a mistake can be based on the necessity for more global agreement, particularly through the United Nations, before one country could justifiably land its army on another country. A second argument can focus on the importance of being well informed, for example on the facts regarding the presence or absence of weapons of mass destruction in pre-invasion Iraq, before taking such military decisions, which would inevitably place a great many people in danger of being slaughtered or mutilated or displaced. A third argument may be concerned with democracy as 'government by discussion' (to use that old phrase often linked with John Stuart Mill, but which was used earlier by Walter Bagehot), and concentrate instead on the political significance of informational distortion in what is presented to the people of the country, including cultivated fiction (such as the imaginary links of Saddam Hussein with the events on 9/11 or with al-Qaeda), making it harder for the citizens of America to assess the executive proposal to go to war. A fourth argument could see the principal issue to be none of the above, but instead the actual *consequences* of the intervention: would it bring peace and order in the country invaded, or in the Middle East, or in the world, and could it have been expected to reduce the dangers of global violence and terrorism, rather than intensifying them?

These are all serious considerations and they involve very different evaluative concerns, none of which could be readily ruled out as being irrelevant or unimportant for an appraisal of actions of this kind. And in general, they may not yield the same conclusion. But if it is shown, as in this specific example, that all of the sustainable criteria lead to the same diagnosis of a huge mistake, then that specific conclusion

\* Arguments were of course also presented in favour of intervention. One was the belief that Saddam Hussein was responsible for the terrorism on 9/11, and another that he was hand-in-glove with al-Qaeda. Neither accusation proved to be correct. It is true that Hussein was a brutal dictator, but then there were – and are – many others across the world with the same qualification.

need not await the determination of the relative priorities to be attached to these criteria. Arbitrary reduction of multiple and potentially conflicting principles to one solitary survivor, guillotining all the other evaluative criteria, is not, in fact, a prerequisite for getting useful and robust conclusions on what should be done. This applies as much to the theory of justice as it does to any other part of the discipline of practical reason.

## REASONING AND JUSTICE

The need for a theory of justice relates to the discipline of engagement in reasoning about a subject on which it is, as Burke noted, very difficult to speak. It is sometimes claimed that justice is not a matter of reasoning at all; it is one of being appropriately sensitive and having the right nose for injustice. It is easy to be tempted to think along these lines. When we find, for example, a raging famine, it seems natural to protest rather than reason elaborately about justice and injustice. And yet a calamity would be a case of injustice only if it could have been prevented, and particularly if those who could have undertaken preventive action had failed to try. Reasoning in some form cannot but be involved in moving from the observation of a tragedy to the diagnosis of injustice. Furthermore, cases of injustice may be much more complex and subtle than the assessment of an observable calamity. There could be different arguments suggesting disparate conclusions, and evaluations of justice may be anything but straightforward.

The avoidance of reasoned justification often comes not from indignant protesters but from placid guardians of order and justice. Reticence has appealed throughout history to those with a governing role, endowed with public authority, who are unsure of the grounds for action, or unwilling to scrutinize the basis of their policies. Lord Mansfield, the powerful English judge in the eighteenth century, famously advised a newly appointed colonial governor: 'consider what you think justice requires and decide accordingly. But never give your reasons; for your judgement will probably be right, but your reasons will certainly be wrong.'[2] This may well be a good advice for tactful governance, but it is surely no way of guaranteeing that the right things are done. Nor does it help to ensure that the people affected can see that justice is being done (which is, as will be discussed later, part of the discipline of making sustainable decisions regarding justice).

The requirements of a theory of justice include bringing reason into play in the diagnosis of justice and injustice. Over hundreds of years, writers on justice in different parts of the world have attempted to provide the intellectual basis for moving from a general sense of injustice to particular reasoned diagnoses of injustice, and from there to the analyses of ways of advancing justice. Traditions of reasoning about justice and injustice have long – and striking – histories across the world, from which illuminating suggestions on reasons of justice can be considered (as will be examined presently).

## THE ENLIGHTENMENT AND A BASIC DIVERGENCE

Even though the subject of social justice has been discussed over the ages, the discipline received an especially strong boost during the European Enlightenment in the eighteenth and nineteenth centuries, encouraged by the political climate of change and also by the social and economic transformation taking place then in Europe and America. There are two basic, and divergent, lines of reasoning about justice among leading philosophers associated with the radical thought of that period. The distinction between the two approaches has received far less attention than, I believe, it richly deserves. I will begin with this dichotomy since that will help to locate the particular understanding of the theory of justice that I am trying to present in this work.

One approach, led by the work of Thomas Hobbes in the seventeenth century, and followed in different ways by such outstanding thinkers as Jean-Jacques Rousseau, concentrated on identifying just institutional arrangements for a society. This approach, which can be called 'transcendental institutionalism', has two distinct features. First, it concentrates its attention on what it identifies as perfect justice, rather than on relative comparisons of justice and injustice. It tries only to identify social characteristics that cannot be transcended in terms of justice, and its focus is thus not on comparing feasible societies, all of which may fall short of the ideals of perfection. The inquiry is aimed at identifying the nature of 'the just', rather than finding some criteria for an alternative being 'less unjust' than another.

Second, in searching for perfection, transcendental institutionalism concentrates primarily on getting the institutions right, and it is not directly focused on the actual societies that would ultimately emerge. The nature of the society that would result from any given set of institutions must, of course, depend also on non-institutional features, such as actual behaviours of people and their social interactions. In elaborating the likely consequences of the institutions, if and when a transcendental institutionalist theory goes into commenting on them, some specific behavioural assumptions are made that help the working of the chosen institutions.

Both these features relate to the 'contractarian' mode of thinking that Thomas Hobbes had initiated, and which was further pursued by John Locke, Jean-Jacques Rousseau and Immanuel Kant.[3] A hypothetical 'social contract' that is assumed to be chosen is clearly concerned with an ideal alternative to the chaos that might otherwise characterize a society, and the contracts that were prominently discussed by the authors dealt primarily with the choice of institutions. The overall result was to develop theories of justice that focused on transcendental identification of the ideal institutions.*

It is important, however, to note here that transcendental institutionalists in search of perfectly just institutions have sometimes also presented deeply illuminating analyses of moral or political imperatives regarding socially appropriate behaviour. This applies particu-

* Even though the social contract approach to justice initiated by Hobbes combines transcendentalism with institutionalism, it is worth noting that the two features need not necessarily be combined. We can, for example, have a transcendental theory that focuses on social realizations rather than on institutions (the search for the perfect utilitarian world with people blissfully happy would be a simple example of pursuing 'realization-based transcendence'). Or we can focus on institutional assessments in comparative perspectives rather than undertaking a transcendental search for the perfect package of social institutions (preferring a greater – or indeed lesser – role for the free market would be an illustration of comparative institutionalism).

larly to Immanuel Kant and John Rawls, both of whom have participated in transcendental institutional investigation, but have also provided far-reaching analyses of the requirements of behavioural norms. Even though they have focused on institutional choices, their analyses can be seen, more broadly, as 'arrangement-focused' approaches to justice, with the arrangements including right behaviour by all as well as right institutions.* There is, obviously, a radical contrast between an arrangement-focused conception of justice and a realization-focused understanding: the latter must, for example, concentrate on the actual behaviour of people, rather than presuming compliance by all with ideal behaviour.

In contrast with transcendental institutionalism, a number of other Enlightenment theorists took a variety of comparative approaches that were concerned with social realizations (resulting from actual institutions, actual behaviour and other influences). Different versions of such comparative thinking can be found, for example, in the works of Adam Smith, the Marquis de Condorcet, Jeremy Bentham, Mary Wollstonecraft, Karl Marx, John Stuart Mill, among a number of other leaders of innovative thought in the eighteenth and nineteenth centuries. Even though these authors, with their very different ideas of the demands of justice, proposed quite distinct ways of making social comparisons, it can be said, at the risk of only a slight exaggeration, that they were all involved in comparisons of societies that already existed or could feasibly emerge, rather than confining their analyses to transcendental searches for a perfectly just society. Those focusing on realization-focused comparisons were often interested primarily in the removal of manifest injustice from the world that they saw.

The distance between the two approaches, *transcendental institutionalism*, on the one hand, and *realization-focused comparison*, on the other, is quite momentous. As it happens, it is the first tradition – that of transcendental institutionalism – on which today's mainstream political philosophy largely draws in its exploration of the theory of justice. The most powerful and momentous exposition of this

---

* As Rawls explains: 'The other limitation on our discussion is that for the most part I examine the principles of justice that would regulate a well-ordered society. Everyone is presumed to act justly and to do his part in upholding just institutions.' (*A Theory of Justice* (Cambridge, MA: Harvard University Press, 1971), pp. 7–8.)

approach to justice can be found in the work of the leading political philosopher of our time, John Rawls (whose ideas and far-reaching contributions will be examined in Chapter 2 'Rawls and Beyond').\* Indeed, Rawls's 'principles of justice' in his *A Theory of Justice* are defined entirely in relation to perfectly just institutions, though he also investigates – very illuminatingly – the norms of right behaviour in political and moral contexts.†

Also a number of the other pre-eminent contemporary theorists of justice have, broadly speaking, taken the transcendental institutional route – I think here of Ronald Dworkin, David Gauthier, Robert Nozick, among others. Their theories, which have provided different, but respectively important, insights into the demands of a 'just society', share the common aim of identifying just rules and institutions, even though their identifications of these arrangements come in very different forms. The characterization of perfectly just institutions has become the central exercise in the modern theories of justice.

## THE POINT OF DEPARTURE

In contrast with most modern theories of justice, which concentrate on the 'just society', this book is an attempt to investigate realization-based comparisons that focus on the advancement or retreat of justice. It is, in this respect, not in line with the strong and more philosophically celebrated tradition of transcendental institutionalism that emerged in the Enlightenment period (led by Hobbes and developed by Locke, Rousseau and Kant, among others), but more in the 'other'

---

\* He explained in *A Theory of Justice* (1971): 'My aim is to present a conception of justice which generalizes and carries to a higher level of abstraction the familiar theory of the social contract as found, say, in Locke, Rousseau, and Kant' (p. 10). See also his *Political Liberalism* (New York: Columbia University Press, 1993). The 'contractarian' routes of Rawls's theory of justice had already been emphasized by him in his early – pioneering – paper, 'Justice as Fairness', *Philosophical Review*, 67 (1958).

† In suggesting the need for what he calls a 'reflective equilibrium', Rawls builds into his social analysis the necessity to subject one's values and priorities to critical scrutiny. Also, as was briefly mentioned earlier, the 'just institutions' are identified in Rawlsian analysis with the assumption of compliance of actual conduct with the right behavioural rules.

tradition that also took shape in about the same period or just after (pursued in various ways by Smith, Condorcet, Wollstonecraft, Bentham, Marx, Mill, among others). The fact that I share a point of departure with these diverse thinkers does not, of course, indicate that I agree with their substantive theories (that should be obvious enough, since they themselves differed so much from each other), and going beyond the shared point of departure, we have to look also at some points of eventual arrival.* The rest of the book will explore that journey.

Importance must be attached to the starting point, in particular the selection of some questions to be answered (for example, 'how would justice be advanced?'), rather than others (for example, 'what would be perfectly just institutions?'). This departure has the dual effect, first, of taking the comparative rather than the transcendental route, and second, of focusing on actual realizations in the societies involved, rather than only on institutions and rules. Given the present balance of emphases in contemporary political philosophy, this will require a radical change in the formulation of the theory of justice.

Why do we need such a dual departure? I begin with transcendentalism. I see two problems here. First, there may be no reasoned agreement at all, even under strict conditions of impartiality and open-minded scrutiny (for example, as identified by Rawls in his 'original position') on the nature of the 'just society': this is the issue of the *feasibility* of finding an agreed transcendental solution. Second, an exercise of practical reason that involves an actual choice demands a framework for comparison of justice for choosing among the feasible alternatives and not an identification of a possibly unavailable perfect situation that could not be transcended: this is the issue of the *redundancy* of the search for a transcendental solution. I shall presently discuss these problems with the transcendental focus (both feasibility and redundancy), but before that let me comment briefly on the institutional concentration involved in the approach of transcendental institutionalism.

* Also these authors use the word 'justice' in many different ways. As Adam Smith noted, the term 'justice' has 'several different meanings' (*The Theory of Moral Sentiments*, 6th edn (London: T. Cadell, 1790), VII. ii. 1. 10 in the Clarendon Press edition (1976), p. 269). I shall examine Smith's ideas on justice in the broadest sense.

This second component of the departure concerns the need to focus on actual realizations and accomplishments, rather than only on the establishment of what are identified as the right institutions and rules. The contrast here relates, as was mentioned earlier, to a general – and much broader – dichotomy between an *arrangement-focused* view of justice, and a *realization-focused* understanding of justice. The former line of thought proposes that justice should be conceptualized in terms of certain organizational arrangements – some institutions, some regulations, some behavioural rules – the active presence of which would indicate that justice is being done. The question to ask in this context is whether the analysis of justice must be so confined to getting the basic institutions and general rules right? Should we not also have to examine what emerges in the society, including the kind of lives that people can actually lead, given the institutions and rules, but also other influences, including actual behaviour, that would inescapably affect human lives?

I shall consider the arguments for the two respective departures in turn. I start with the problems of transcendental identification, beginning with the question of feasibility, and shall take up the issue of redundancy later.

## FEASIBILITY OF A UNIQUE TRANSCENDENTAL AGREEMENT

There can be serious differences between competing principles of justice that survive critical scrutiny and can have claims to impartiality. This problem is serious enough, for example, for John Rawls's assumption that there will be a unanimous choice of a unique set of 'two principles of justice' in a hypothetical situation of primordial equality (he calls it 'the original position'), where people's vested interests are not known to the people themselves. This presumes that there is basically only one kind of impartial argument, satisfying the demands of fairness, shorn of vested interests. This, I would argue, may be a mistake.

There can be differences, for example, in the exact comparative weights to be given to distributional equality, on the one hand, and overall or aggregate enhancement, on the other. In his transcendental identification, John Rawls pinpoints one such formula (the lexico-graphic maximin rule, to be discussed in Chapter 2), among many that are available, without convincing arguments that would eliminate all other alternatives that might compete with Rawls's very special formula for impartial attention.* There can be many other reasoned differences involving the particular formulae on which Rawls concentrates in his two principles of justice, without showing us why other alternatives would not continue to command attention in the impartial atmosphere of his original position.

If a diagnosis of perfectly just social arrangements is incurably problematic, then the entire strategy of transcendental institutionalism is deeply impaired, even if every conceivable alternative in the world were available. For example, the two principles of justice in John Rawls's classic investigation of 'justice as fairness', which will be more fully discussed in Chapter 2, are precisely about perfectly just institutions in a world where all alternatives are available. However, what we do not know is whether the plurality of reasons for justice would allow one unique set of principles of justice to emerge in the original position. The elaborate exploration of Rawlsian social justice, which proceeds step by step from the identification and establishment of just institutions, would then get stuck at the very base.

In his later writings, Rawls makes some concessions to the recognition that 'citizens will of course differ as to which conceptions of political justice they think most reasonable'. Indeed, he goes on to say in *The Law of Peoples* (1999):

The content of public reason is given by a family of political conceptions of justice, and not by a single one. There are many liberalisms and related views, and therefore many forms of public reason specified by a family of reasonable political conceptions. Of these, justice as fairness, whatever its merits, is but one.[4]

---

* Different types of impartial rules of distribution are discussed in my *On Economic Inequality* (Oxford: Clarendon Press, 1973; extended edn, with a new Annexe, jointly with James Foster, 1997). See also Alan Ryan (ed.), *Justice* (Oxford: Clarendon Press, 1993), and David Miller, *Principles of Social Justice* (Cambridge, MA: Harvard University Press, 1999).

It is not, however, clear how Rawls would deal with the far-reaching implications of this concession. The specific institutions, firmly chosen for the basic structure of society, would demand one specific resolution of the principles of justice, in the way Rawls had outlined in his early works, including *The Theory of Justice* (1971).* Once the claim to uniqueness of the Rawlsian principles of justice is dropped (the case for which is outlined in Rawls's later works), the institutional programme would clearly have serious indeterminacy, and Rawls does not tell us much about how a particular set of institutions would be chosen on the basis of a set of competing principles of justice that would demand different institutional combinations for the basic structure of the society. Rawls could, of course, resolve that problem by abandoning the transcendental institutionalism of his earlier work (particularly of *The Theory of Justice*), and this would be the move that would appeal most to this particular author.† But I am afraid I am not able to claim that this was the direction in which Rawls himself was definitely heading, even though some of his later works raise that question forcefully.

## THREE CHILDREN AND A FLUTE: AN ILLUSTRATION

At the heart of the particular problem of a unique impartial resolution of the perfectly just society is the possible sustainability of plural and competing reasons for justice, all of which have claims to impartiality and which nevertheless differ from – and rival – each other. Let me

---

* Rawls discusses the difficulties in arriving at a unique set of principles to guide institutional choice in the original position in his later book *Justice as Fairness: A Restatement*, edited by Erin Kelly (Cambridge, MA: Harvard University Press, 2001), pp. 132–4. I am most grateful to Erin Kelly for discussing with me the relation between Rawls's later writings and his earlier formulations of the theory of justice as fairness.
† John Gray's scepticism about the Rawlsian theory of justice is much more radical than mine, but there is an agreement between us in the rejection of the belief that questions of value can have only one right answer. I also agree that the 'diversity of ways of life and regimes is a mark of human freedom, not of error' (*Two Faces of Liberalism* (Cambridge: Polity Press, 2000), p. 139). My inquiry concerns reasoned agreements that can nevertheless be reached on how injustice can be reduced, despite our different views on 'ideal' regimes.

illustrate the problem with an example in which you have to decide which of three children – Anne, Bob and Carla – should get a flute about which they are quarrelling. Anne claims the flute on the ground that she is the only one of the three who knows how to play it (the others do not deny this), and that it would be quite unjust to deny the flute to the only one who can actually play it. If that is all you knew, the case for giving the flute to the first child would be strong.

In an alternative scenario, it is Bob who speaks up, and defends his case for having the flute by pointing out that he is the only one among the three who is so poor that he has no toys of his own. The flute would give him something to play with (the other two concede that they are richer and well supplied with engaging amenities). If you had heard only Bob and none of the others, the case for giving it to him would be strong.

In another alternative scenario, it is Carla who speaks up and points out that she has been working diligently for many months to make the flute with her own labour (the others confirm this), and just when she had finished her work, 'just then', she complains, 'these expropriators came along to try to grab the flute away from me'. If Carla's statement is all you had heard, you might be inclined to give the flute to her in recognition of her understandable claim to something she has made herself.

Having heard all three and their different lines of reasoning, there is a difficult decision that you have to make. Theorists of different persuasions, such as utilitarians, or economic egalitarians, or no-nonsense libertarians, may each take the view that there is a straight-forward just resolution staring at us here, and there is no difficulty in spotting it. But almost certainly they would respectively see totally different resolutions as being obviously right.

Bob, the poorest, would tend to get fairly straightforward support from the economic egalitarian if he is committed to reducing gaps in the economic means of people. On the other hand, Carla, the maker of the flute, would receive immediate sympathy from the libertarian. The utilitarian hedonist may face the hardest challenge, but he would certainly tend to give weight, more than the libertarian or the economic egalitarian, to the fact that Anne's pleasure is likely to be stronger because she is the only one who can play the flute (there is also the general dictum of 'waste not, want not'). Nevertheless, the utilitarian should also recognize that Bob's relative deprivation could make his incremental gain in happiness from getting the flute that much larger. Carla's 'right' to get what she has made may not resonate immediately with the utilitarian, but deeper utilitarian reflection would nevertheless tend to take some note of the requirements of work incentives in creating a society in which utility-generation is sustained and encouraged through letting people keep what they have produced with their own efforts.*

The libertarian's support for giving the flute to Carla will not be conditional in the way it is bound to be for the utilitarian on the working of incentive effects, since a libertarian would take direct note of a person's right to have what people have produced themselves. The idea of the right to the fruits of one's labour can unite right-wing libertarians and left-wing Marxists (no matter how uncomfortable each might be in the company of the other).†

The general point here is that it is not easy to brush aside as foundationless any of the claims based respectively on the pursuit of human fulfilment, or removal of poverty, or entitlement to enjoy the products of one's own labour. The different resolutions all have serious arguments in support of them, and we may not be able to identify, without some arbitrariness, any of the alternative arguments as being the one that must invariably prevail.‡

I also want to draw attention here to the fairly obvious fact that the

* We are, of course, considering here a simple case in which who has produced what can be readily identified. This may well be easy enough with the single-handed making of a flute by Carla. That kind of diagnosis could, however, raise deep problems when various factors of production, including non-labour resources, are involved.

† As it happens, Karl Marx himself became rather sceptical of the 'right to one's labour', which he came to see as a 'bourgeois right', to be ultimately rejected in favour of 'distribution according to needs', a point of view he developed with some force in his last substantial work, *The Critique of the Gotha Program* (1875). The importance of this dichotomy is discussed in my book, *On Economic Inequality* (Oxford: Clarendon Press, 1973), Chapter 4. See also G. A. Cohen, *History, Labour and Freedom: Themes from Marx* (Oxford: Clarendon Press, 1988).

‡ As Bernard Williams has argued, 'Disagreement does not necessarily have to be overcome.' Indeed, it 'may remain an important and constitutive feature of our relations to others, and also be seen as something that is merely to be expected in the light of the best explanations we have of how such disagreement arises' (*Ethics and the Limits of Philosophy* (London: Fontana, 1985), p. 133).

differences between the three children's justificatory arguments do not represent divergences about what constitutes individual advantage (getting the flute is taken to be advantageous by each of the children and is accommodated by each of the respective arguments), but about the principles that should govern the allocation of resources in general. They are about how social arrangements should be made and what social institutions should be chosen, and through that, about what social realizations would come about. It is not simply that the vested interests of the three children differ (though of course they do), but that the three arguments each point to a different type of impartial and non-arbitrary reason.

This applies not only to the discipline of fairness in the Rawlsian original position, but also to other demands of impartiality, for example Thomas Scanlon's requirement that our principles satisfy 'what others could not reasonably reject'.[5] As was mentioned earlier, theorists of different persuasions, such as utilitarians, or economic egalitarians, or labour right theorists, or no-nonsense libertarians, may each take the view that there is one straightforward just resolution that is easily detected, but they would each argue for totally different resolutions as being obviously right. There may not indeed exist any identifiable perfectly just social arrangement on which impartial agreement would emerge.

## A COMPARATIVE OR A TRANSCENDENTAL FRAMEWORK?

The problem with the transcendental approach does not arise only from the possible plurality of competing principles that have claims to being relevant to the assessment of justice. Important as the problem of the non-existence of an identifiable perfectly just social arrangement is, a critically important argument in favour of the comparative approach to the practical reason of justice is not just the infeasibility of the transcendental theory, but its redundancy. If a theory of justice is to guide reasoned choice of policies, strategies or institutions, then the identification of fully just social arrangements is neither necessary nor sufficient.

To illustrate, if we are trying to choose between a Picasso and a Dali, it is of no help to invoke a diagnosis (even if such a transcendental diagnosis could be made) that the ideal picture in the world is the *Mona Lisa*. That may be interesting to hear, but it is neither here nor there in the choice between a Dali and a Picasso.[6] Indeed, it is not at all necessary to talk about what may be the greatest or most perfect picture in the world, to choose between the two alternatives that we are facing. Nor is it sufficient, or indeed of any particular help, to know that the *Mona Lisa* is the most perfect picture in the world when the choice is actually between a Dali and a Picasso.

This point may look deceptively simple. Would not a theory that identifies a transcendental alternative also, through the same process, tell us what we want to know about comparative justice? The answer is no – it does not. We may, of course, be tempted by the idea that we can rank alternatives in terms of their respective closeness to the perfect choice, so that a transcendental identification may indirectly yield also a ranking of alternatives. But that approach does not get us very far, partly because there are different dimensions in which objects differ (so that there is the further issue of assessing the relative importance of distances in distinct dimensions), and also because descriptive closeness is not necessarily a guide to valuational proximity (a person who prefers red wine to white may prefer either to a mixture of the two, even though the mixture is, in an obvious descriptive sense, closer to the preferred red wine than pure white wine would be).

It is, of course, possible to have a theory that does both comparative assessments between pairs of alternatives, and a transcendental identification (when that is not made impossible through the surviving plurality of impartial reasons that have claims on our attention). That would be a 'conglomerate' theory, but neither of the two different types of judgements follows from each other. More immediately, the standard theories of justice that are associated with the approach of transcendental identification (for example, those of Hobbes, Rousseau, Kant or, in our time, Rawls or Nozick) are not, in fact, conglomerate theories. It is, however, true that in the process of developing their respective transcendental theories, some of these authors have presented particular arguments that happen to carry over to the comparative exercise. But in general the identification of a transcendental alternative does not offer a solution to the problem of comparisons between any two non-transcendental alternatives.

Transcendental theory simply addresses a different question from those of comparative assessment – a question that may be of considerable intellectual interest, but which is of no direct relevance to the problem of choice that has to be faced. What is needed instead is an agreement, based on public reasoning, on rankings of alternatives that can be realized. The separation between the transcendental and the comparative is quite comprehensive, as will be more fully discussed in Chapter 4 ('Voice and Social Choice'). As it happens, the comparative approach is central to the analytical discipline of 'social choice theory', initiated by the Marquis de Condorcet and other French mathematicians in the eighteenth century, mainly working in Paris.[7] The formal discipline of social choice was not much used for a long time, though work continued in the specific sub-area of voting theory. The discipline was revived and established in its present form by Kenneth Arrow in the middle of the twentieth century.[8] This approach has become, in recent decades, quite an active field of analytical investigation, exploring ways and means of basing comparative assessments of social alternatives on the values and priorities of the people involved.* Since the literature of social choice theory is typically quite technical and largely mathematical, and since many of the results in the field cannot be established except through fairly extensive mathematical reasoning,† its basic approach has received relatively little attention,

---

* On the general characteristics of the social choice approach which motivates and supports the analytical results, see my Alfred Nobel Lecture in Stockholm in December 1998, later published as 'The Possibility of Social Choice', *American Economic Review*, vol. 89 (1999), and in *Les Prix Nobel 1998* (Stockholm: The Nobel Foundation, 1999).

† The mathematical formulations are, however, of some importance for the content of the arguments presented through axioms and theorems. For discussion of some of the linkages between formal and informal arguments, see my *Collective Choice and Social Welfare* (San Francisco, CA: Holden-Day; republished, Amsterdam: North-Holland, 1979), in which the mathematical and informal chapters alternate. See also my critical survey of the literature in 'Social Choice Theory', in Kenneth Arrow and Michael Intriligator (eds) *Handbook of Mathematical Economics* (Amsterdam: North-Holland, 1986).

especially from philosophers. And yet the approach and its underlying reasoning are quite close to the commonsense understanding of the nature of appropriate social decisions. In the constructive approach I try to present in this work, insights from social choice theory will have a substantial role to play.*

## REALIZATIONS, LIVES
## AND CAPABILITIES

I turn now to the second part of the departure, to wit the need for a theory that is not confined to the choice of institutions, nor to the identification of ideal social arrangements. The need for an accomplishment-based understanding of justice is linked with the argument that justice cannot be indifferent to the lives that people can actually live. The importance of human lives, experiences and realizations cannot be supplanted by information about institutions that exist and the rules that operate. Institutions and rules are, of course, very important in influencing what happens, and they are part and parcel of the actual world as well, but the realized actuality goes well beyond the organizational picture, and includes the lives that people manage – or do not manage – to live.

In noting the nature of human lives, we have reason to be interested not only in the various things we succeed in doing, but also in the freedoms that we actually have to choose between different kinds of lives. The freedom to choose our lives can make a significant contribution to our well-being, but going beyond the perspective of well-being, the freedom itself may be seen as important. Being able to reason and choose is a significant aspect of human life. In fact, we are under no obligation to seek only our own well-being, and it is for us to decide what we have good reason to pursue (this question will be further discussed in Chapters 8 and 9). We do not have to be a Gandhi, or a Martin Luther King Jr., or a Nelson Mandela, or a Desmond Tutu, to recognize that we can have aims or priorities that differ from

* The connections between social choice theory and the theory of justice are particularly explored in Chapter 4, 'Voice and Social Choice'.

the single-minded pursuit of our own well-being only.* The freedoms and capabilities we enjoy can also be valuable to us, and it is ultimately for us to decide how to use the freedom we have.

It is important to emphasize, even in this brief account (a fuller exploration is pursued later in the book, particularly in Chapters 11–13), that if social realizations are assessed in terms of capabilities that people actually have, rather than in terms of their utilities or happiness (as Jeremy Bentham and other utilitarians recommend), then some very significant departures are brought about. First, human lives are then seen inclusively, taking note of the substantive freedoms that people enjoy, rather than ignoring everything other than the pleasures or utilities they end up having. There is also a second significant aspect of freedom: it makes us accountable for what we do.

Freedom to choose gives us the opportunity to decide what we should do, but with that opportunity comes the responsibility for what we do – to the extent that they are chosen actions. Since a capability is the power to do something, the accountability that emanates from that ability – that power – is a part of the capability perspective, and this can make room for demands of duty – what can be broadly called deontological demands. There is an overlap here between agency-centred concerns and the implications of capability-based approach; but there is nothing immediately comparable in the utilitarian perspective (tying one's responsibility to one's own happiness).† The perspective of social realizations, including the actual capabilities that people can have, takes us inescapably to a large variety of further issues that turn out to be quite central to the analysis of justice in the world, and these will have to be examined and scrutinized.

---

* Adam Smith argued that even for selfish people, 'there are evidently some principles in his nature, which interest him in the fortune of others' and went on to suggest: 'The greatest ruffian, the most hardened violator of the laws of society, is not altogether without it' (*The Theory of Sentiments*, 1.i.1.1. in the 1976 edn, p. 9).
† This issue will be further discussed in Chapters 9, 'Plurality of Impartial Reasons', and 13, 'Happiness, Well-being and Capabilities'.

# A CLASSICAL DISTINCTION IN
# INDIAN JURISPRUDENCE

In understanding the contrast between an arrangement-focused and a realization-focused view of justice, it is useful to invoke an old distinction from the Sanskrit literature on ethics and jurisprudence. Consider two different words – *niti* and *nyaya* – both of which stand for justice in classical Sanskrit. Among the principal uses of the term *niti* are organizational propriety and behavioural correctness. In contrast with *niti*, the term *nyaya* stands for a comprehensive concept of realized justice. In that line of vision, the roles of institutions, rules and organization, important as they are, have to be assessed in the broader and more inclusive perspective of *nyaya*, which is inescapably linked with the world that actually emerges, not just the institutions or rules we happen to have.*

To consider a particular application, early Indian legal theorists talked disparagingly of what they called *matsyanyaya*, 'justice in the world of fish', where a big fish can freely devour a small fish. We are warned that avoiding *matsyanyaya* must be an essential part of justice, and it is crucial to make sure that the 'justice of fish' is not allowed to invade the world of human beings. The central recognition here is that the realization of justice in the sense of *nyaya* is not just a matter of judging institutions and rules, but of judging the societies themselves. No matter how proper the estab-

---

* The most famous of the ancient Indian legal theorists, viz. Manu, was extensively concerned, as it happens, with *niti*s; indeed, often of the most severe kind (I have heard Manu being described in contemporary Indian discussions, with some modicum of veracity, as 'a fascist law-giver'). But Manu too could not escape being drawn into realizations and *nyaya*, in justifying the rightness of particular *niti*s; for example, we are told: it is better to be scorned than to scorn, 'for the man who is scorned sleeps happily, awakes happily, and goes about happily in this world; but the man who scorns perishes' (Chapter 2, instruction 163). Similarly, 'where women are not revered all rites are fruitless', since 'where the women of the family are miserable, the family is soon destroyed, but it always thrives where women are not miserable' (Chapter 3, instructions 56 and 57). The translations are taken from Wendy Doniger's excellent translation, *The Laws of Manu* (London: Penguin, 1991).

lished organizations might be, if a big fish could still devour a small fish at will, then that must be a patent violation of human justice as *nyaya*.

Let me consider an example to make the distinction between *niti* and *nyaya* clearer. Ferdinand I, the Holy Roman emperor, famously claimed in the sixteenth century: 'Fiat justitia, et pereat mundus', which can be translated as 'Let justice be done, though the world perish'. This severe maxim could figure as a *niti* – a very austere *niti* – that is advocated by some (indeed, Emperor Ferdinand did just that), but it would be hard to accommodate a total catastrophe as an example of a just world, when we understand justice in the broader form of *nyaya*. If indeed the world does perish, there would be nothing much to celebrate in that accomplishment, even though the stern and severe *niti* leading to this extreme result could conceivably be defended with very sophisticated arguments of different kinds.

A realization-focused perspective also makes it easier to understand the importance of the prevention of manifest injustice in the world, rather than seeking the perfectly just. As the example of *matsyanyaya* makes clear, the subject of justice is not merely about trying to achieve – or dreaming about achieving – some perfectly just society or social arrangements, but about preventing manifestly severe injustice (such as avoiding the dreadful state of *matsyanyaya*). For example, when people agitated for the abolition of slavery in the eighteenth and nineteenth centuries, they were not labouring under the illusion that the abolition of slavery would make the world perfectly just. It was their claim, rather, that a society with slavery was totally unjust (among the authors mentioned earlier, Adam Smith, Condorcet and Mary Wollstonecraft were quite involved in presenting this perspective). It was the diagnosis of an intolerable injustice in slavery that made abolition an overwhelming priority, and this did not require the search for a consensus on what a perfectly just society would look like. Those who think, reasonably enough, that the American Civil War, which led to the abolition of slavery, was a big strike for justice in America would have to be reconciled to the fact that not much can be said in the perspective of transcendental institutionalism (when the only contrast is that between the perfectly just and the rest) about the enhancement of justice through the abolition of slavery.*

## THE IMPORTANCE OF PROCESSES AND RESPONSIBILITIES

Those who tend to see justice in terms of *niti* rather than *nyaya*, no matter what they call that dichotomy, may be influenced by their fear that a concentration on actual realizations would tend to ignore the significance of social processes, including the exercise of individual duties and responsibilities. We may do the right thing and yet we may not succeed. Or, a good result may come about not because we aimed at it, but for some other, perhaps even an accidental, reason, and we may be deceived into thinking that justice has been done. It could hardly be adequate (so the argument would run) to concentrate only on what actually happens, ignoring altogether the processes and efforts and conducts. Philosophers who emphasize the role of duty and other features of what is called a deontological approach may be particularly suspicious of the fact that the distinction between arrangements and realizations could look quite like the old contrast between deontological and consequential approaches to justice.

This worry is important to consider, but it is, I would argue, ultimately misplaced. A full characterization of realizations should have room to include the exact processes through which the eventual states of affairs emerge. In a paper in *Econometrica* about a decade ago, I called this the 'comprehensive outcome' which includes the processes involved, and which has to be distinguished from only the 'culmination outcome',[9] for example, an arbitrary arrest is more than the

---

* It is interesting that Karl Marx's diagnosis of 'the one great event of contemporary history' made him attribute that distinction to the American Civil War leading to the abolition of slavery (see *Capital*, vol. I (London: Sonnenschein, 1887), Chapter X, Section 3, p. 240). While Marx argued that capitalist labour arrangements are exploitative, he was keen on pointing out what a huge improvement wage labour was compared with a system of slave labour; on this subject, see also Marx's *Grundrisse* (Harmondsworth: Penguin Books, 1973). Marx's analysis of justice went well beyond his fascination, much discussed by his critics, with 'the ultimate stage of communism'.

capture and detention of someone – it is what it says, an arbitrary arrest. Similarly, the role of human agency cannot be obliterated by some exclusive focus on what happens only at the culmination; for example, there is a real difference between some people dying of starvation due to circumstances beyond anyone's control and those people being starved to death through the design of those wanting to bring about that outcome (both are, of course, tragedies, but their connection with justice cannot be the same). Or, to take another type of case, if a presidential candidate in an election were to argue that what is really important for him or her is not just to win the forthcoming election, but 'to win the election fairly', then the outcome sought must be something of a comprehensive outcome.

Or consider a different kind of example. In the Indian epic *Mahabharata*, in the particular part of it called *Bhagavadgita* (or *Gita*, for short), on the eve of the battle that is the central episode of the epic, the invincible warrior, Arjuna, expresses his profound doubts about leading the fight which will result in so much killing. He is told by his adviser, Krishna, that he, Arjuna, must give priority to his duty, that is, to fight, irrespective of the consequences. That famous debate is often interpreted as one about deontology versus consequentialism, with Krishna, the deontologist, urging Arjuna to do his duty, while Arjuna, the alleged consequentialist, worries about the terrible consequences of the war.

Krishna's hallowing of the demands of duty is meant to win the argument, at least as seen in the religious perspective. Indeed, the *Bhagavadgita* has become a treatise of great theological importance in Hindu philosophy, focusing particularly on the 'removal' of Arjuna's doubts. Krishna's moral position has also been eloquently endorsed by many philosophical and literary commentators across the world. In the *Four Quartets*, T. S. Eliot summarizes Krishna's view in the form of an admonishment: 'And do not think of the fruit of action./ Fare forward.' Eliot explains, so that we do not miss the point: 'Not fare well,/ But fare forward, voyagers'.[10] I have argued elsewhere (in *The Argumentative Indian*) that if we leave the narrow confines of the end of the debate in the part of *Mahabharata* that is called *Bhagavadgita*, and look at the earlier sections of *Gita* in which Arjuna presents his argument, or look at *Mahabharata* as a whole, the limitations of Krishna's perspective are also quite evident.[11] Indeed, after the total desolation of the land following the successful end of the 'just war', towards the end of the *Mahabharata*, with funeral pyres burning in unison and women weeping about the death of their loved ones, it is hard to be convinced that Arjuna's broader perspective was decisively vanquished by Krishna. There may remain a powerful case for 'faring well', and not just 'forward'.

While that contrast may well fit broadly into the differentiation between the consequentialist and the deontological perspectives, what is particularly relevant here is to go beyond that simple contrast to examine what the totality of Arjuna's concerns were about the prospect of his *not* faring well. Arjuna is not concerned only about the fact that, if the war were to occur, with him leading the charge on the side of justice and propriety, many people would get killed. That too, but Arjuna also expresses concern, in the early part of *Gita* itself, that he himself would inescapably be doing a lot of the killing, often of people for whom he has affection and with whom he has personal relations, in the battle between the two wings of the same family, in which others, well known to the two sides, had also joined. Indeed, the actual event that Arjuna worries about goes well beyond the process-independent view of consequences. An appropriate understanding of social realization – central to justice as *nyaya* – has to take the comprehensive form of a process-inclusive broad account.[12] It would be hard to dismiss the perspective of social realizations on the grounds that it is narrowly consequentialist and ignores the reasoning underlying deontological concerns.

## TRANSCENDENTAL INSTITUTIONALISM AND GLOBAL NEGLECT

I end this introductory discussion with a final observation on a particularly restrictive aspect of the prevailing concentration in mainstream political philosophy on transcendental institutionalism. Consider any of the great many changes that can be proposed for reforming the institutional structure of the world today to make it less unfair and unjust (in terms of widely accepted criteria). Take, for example, the

reform of the patent laws to make well-established and cheaply pro-
ducible drugs more easily available to needy but poor patients (for
example, those who are suffering from AIDS) – an issue clearly of
some importance for global justice. The question that we have to ask
here is: what international reforms do we need to make the world a
bit less unjust?

However, that kind of discussion about enhancement of justice in
general, and enlargement of global justice in particular, would appear
to be merely 'loose talk' to those who are persuaded by the Hobbesian
– and Rawlsian – claim that we need a sovereign state to apply the
principles of justice through the choice of a perfect set of institutions:
this is a straightforward implication of taking questions of justice
within the framework of transcendental institutionalism. Perfect
global justice through an impeccably just set of institutions, even if
such a thing could be identified, would certainly demand a sovereign
global state, and in the absence of such a state, questions of global
justice appear to the transcendentalists to be unaddressable.

Consider the strong dismissal of the relevance of 'the idea of global
justice' by one of the most original, most powerful and most humane
philosophers of our time, my friend Thomas Nagel, from whose work
I have learned so much. In a hugely engaging article in *Philosophy
and Public Affairs* in 2005, he draws exactly on his transcendental
understanding of justice to conclude that global justice is not a viable
subject for discussion, since the elaborate institutional demands
needed for a just world cannot be met at the global level at this time.
As he puts it, 'It seems to me very difficult to resist Hobbes's claim
about the relation between justice and sovereignty', and 'if Hobbes is
right, the idea of global justice without a world government is a
chimera'.[13]

In the global context, Nagel concentrates, therefore, on clarifying
other demands, distinguishable from the demands of justice, such as
'minimal humanitarian morality' (which 'governs our relation to all
other persons'), and also to long-term strategies for radical change in
institutional arrangements ('I believe the most likely path toward some
version of global justice is through the creation of patently unjust and
illegitimate global structures of power that are tolerable to the interests
of the most powerful current nation-states').[14] The contrast that is

involved here is between seeing institutional reforms in terms of their role in taking us towards transcendental justice (as outlined by Nagel), and assessing them in terms of the improvement that such reforms actually bring about, particularly through the elimination of what are seen as cases of manifest injustice (which is an integral part of the approach presented in this book).

In the Rawlsian approach too, the application of a theory of justice requires an extensive cluster of institutions that determines the basic structure of a fully just society. Not surprisingly, Rawls actually abandons his own principles of justice when it comes to the assessment of how to think about global justice, and he does not go in the fanciful direction of wanting a global state. In a later contribution, *The Law of Peoples*, Rawls invokes a kind of 'supplement' to his national (or, within-one-country) pursuit of the demands of 'justice as fairness'. But this supplement comes in a very emaciated form, through a kind of negotiation between the representatives of different countries on some very elementary matters of civility and humanity – what can be seen as very limited features of justice. In fact, Rawls does not try to derive 'principles of justice' that might emanate from these negotiations (indeed, none would emerge that can be given that name), and concentrates instead on certain general principles of humanitarian behaviour.[15]

Indeed, the theory of justice, as formulated under the currently dominant transcendental institutionalism, reduces many of the most relevant issues of justice into empty – even if acknowledged to be 'well-meaning' – rhetoric. When people across the world agitate to get *more* global justice – and I emphasize here the comparative word 'more' – they are not clamouring for some kind of 'minimal humanitarianism'. Nor are they agitating for a 'perfectly just' world society, but merely for the elimination of some outrageously unjust arrangements to enhance global justice, as Adam Smith, or Condorcet or Mary Wollstonecraft did in their own time, and on which agreements can be generated through public discussion, despite a continuing divergence of views on other matters.

The aggrieved people might, instead, find their voice well reflected in an energizing poem by Seamus Heaney:

History says, Don't hope
On this side of the grave,
But then, once in a lifetime
The longed-for tidal wave
Of justice can rise up,
And hope and history rhyme.[16]

Hugely engaging as this longing is for hope and history to rhyme together, the justice of transcendental institutionalism has little room for that engagement. This limitation provides one illustration of the need for a substantial departure in the prevailing theories of justice. That is the subject matter of this book.

# PART I

# The Demands of Justice

# I

# Reason and Objectivity

Ludwig Wittgenstein, one of the great philosophers of our time, wrote in the Preface to his first major book in philosophy, *Tractatus Logico-Philosophicus*, published in 1921: 'What can be said at all can be said clearly; and whereof one cannot speak thereof one must be silent.'* Wittgenstein would re-examine his views on speech and clarity in his later work, but it is a relief that, even as he was writing the *Tractatus*, the great philosopher did not always follow his own exacting commandment. In a letter to Paul Engelmann, written in 1917, Wittgenstein made the wonderfully enigmatic remark: 'I work quite diligently and wish that I were better and smarter. And these both are one and the same.'[1] Really? One and the same thing – being a *smarter* human being and a *better* person?

I am, of course, aware that modern transatlantic usage has drowned the distinction between 'being good' as a moral quality and 'being well' as a comment on a person's health (no aches and pains, fine blood pressure, and so on), and I have long ceased worrying about the manifest immodesty of those of my friends who, when asked how they are, reply with apparent self-praise, 'I am very good.' But Wittgenstein was not an American, and 1917 was well before the conquest of the world by vibrant American usage. When Wittgenstein

---

* It is interesting to note that Edmund Burke also talked about the difficulty of speaking in some circumstances (see Introduction, where I cited Burke on this issue), but Burke proceeded to speak on the subject nevertheless, since it was, he argued, 'impossible to be silent' on a grave matter of the kind he was dealing with (the case for impeaching Warren Hastings). Wittgenstein's counsel for silence when we cannot speak clearly enough would appear to be, in many ways, the opposite of Burke's approach.

said that being 'better' and being 'smarter' were 'one and the same thing', he must have been making a substantial assertion.

Underlying the point may be the recognition, in some form, that many acts of nastiness are committed by people who are deluded, in one way or another, about the subject. Lack of smartness can certainly be one source of moral failing in good behaviour. Reflecting on what would really be a smart thing to do can sometimes help one act better towards others. That this can easily be the case has been brought out very clearly by modern game theory.[2] Among the prudential reasons for good behaviour may well be one's own gain from such behaviour. Indeed, there could be great gain for all members of a group by following rules of good behaviour which can help everyone. It is not particularly smart for a group of people to act in a way that ruins them all.[3]

But maybe that is not what Wittgenstein meant. Being smarter can also give us the ability to think more clearly about our goals, objectives and values. If self-interest is, ultimately, a primitive thought (despite the complexities just mentioned), clarity about the more sophisticated priorities and obligations that we would want to cherish and pursue would tend to depend on our power of reasoning. A person may have well-thought-out reasons other than the promotion of personal gain for acting in a socially decent way.

Being smarter may help the understanding not only of one's self-interest, but also how the lives of others can be strongly affected by one's own actions. Proponents of so-called 'Rational Choice Theory' (first proposed in economics and then enthusiastically adopted by a number of political and legal thinkers) have tried hard to make us accept the peculiar understanding that rational choice consists only in clever promotion of self-interest (which is how, oddly enough, 'rational choice' is defined by the proponents of brand-named 'rational choice theory'). Nevertheless, our heads have not all been colonized by that remarkably alienating belief. There is considerable resistance to the idea that it must be patently irrational – and stupid – to try to do anything for others except to the extent that doing good to others would enhance one's own well-being.[4]

'What we owe to each other' is an important subject for intelligent reflection.[5] That reflection can take us beyond the pursuit of a very narrow view of self-interest, and we can even find that our own well-reflected goals demand that we cross the narrow boundaries of exclusive self-seeking altogether. There can also be cases in which we have reason to restrain the exclusive pursuit of our own goals (whether or not these goals are themselves exclusively self-interested), because of following rules of decent behaviour that allow room for the pursuit of goals (whether or not self-interested) by other people who share the world with us.*

Since there were precursors to brand-named 'rational choice theory' even in Wittgenstein's days, perhaps his point was that being smarter helps us to think more clearly about our social concerns and responsibilities. It has been argued that some children carry out acts of brutality on other children, or animals, precisely because of their inability to appreciate adequately the nature and intensity of the pains of others, and that this appreciation generally accompanies the intellectual development of maturity.

We cannot, of course, really be sure about what Wittgenstein meant.† But there is certainly much evidence that he himself devoted a great deal of his time and intellect to thinking about his own responsibilities and commitments. The result was not invariably very intelligent or wise. Wittgenstein was absolutely determined to go to Vienna in 1938, just as Hitler was holding his triumphant procession through the city, despite his own Jewishness and his inability to be silent and diplomatic; he had to be restrained from going there by his colleagues in his Cambridge college.‡ There is, however, much

---

* Some commentators find it puzzling that we can reasonably allow the compromising of a single-minded pursuit of our own goals through making room for others to pursue their goals (some even see in this some kind of a 'proof' that what we took to be our goals were not in fact the actual goals we had), but there is no puzzle here when the reach of practical reasoning is adequately appreciated. These issues will be discussed in Chapters 8 'Rationality and Other People' and 9, 'Plurality of Impartial Reasons'.

† Tibor Machan has illuminatingly pursued this interpretational issue in 'A Better and Smarter Person: A Wittgensteinian Idea of Human Excellence', presented at the 5th International Wittgenstein Symposium, 1980.

‡ Piero Sraffa, the economist, who had a significant influence on Ludwig Wittgenstein in his re-examination of his earlier philosophical position in the *Tractatus Logico-Philosophicus* (thereby helping to pave the way towards Wittgenstein's later works, including *Philosophical Investigations* (Oxford: Blackwell, 1953)), played a leading role in dissuading Wittgenstein from going to Vienna and delivering a severe lecture

evidence from what we know from Wittgenstein's conversations that he did think that his intellectual capacity should definitely be used to make the world a better place.\*

## CRITIQUE OF THE ENLIGHTENMENT TRADITION

If that is indeed what Wittgenstein meant, then he was, in an important sense, within the powerful tradition of European Enlightenment, which saw clear-headed reasoning as a major ally in the desire to make societies better. Social improvement through systematic reasoning was a prominent strand in the arguments that were integral to the intellectual animation of the European Enlightenment, especially in the eighteenth century.

It is, however, difficult to generalize about any overwhelming dominance of reason in the thinking prevalent in what is seen as the Enlightenment period. As Isaiah Berlin has shown, there were also different kinds of counter-rational strands during the 'Age of Enlightenment'.[6] But certainly a strong – and somewhat self-conscious – reliance on reason was one of the major departures of Enlightenment thought from the traditions prevailing earlier. And it has become quite common in contemporary political discussions to argue that the Enlightenment oversold the reach of reason. Indeed, it has also been argued that the over-reliance on reason, which the Enlightenment tradition helped to instil in modern thinking, has contributed to the propensity towards atrocities in the post-Enlightenment world. Jonathan Glover, the distinguished philosopher, adds his voice, in his powerfully argued 'Moral History of the Twentieth Century', to this

---

to the triumphant Hitler. Their intellectual and personal relationships are reviewed in my essay, 'Sraffa, Wittgenstein and Gramsci', *Journal of Economic Literature*, 41 (December 2003). Sraffa and Wittgenstein were close friends and also colleagues, as Fellows of Trinity College, Cambridge. See Chapter 5, 'Impartiality and Objectivity', for a discussion of Sraffa's intellectual engagement with, first, Antonio Gramsci, and then, Wittgenstein, and the relevance of the contents of these tripartite exchanges for some of the themes of this work.
\* This commitment relates to what his biographer Ray Monk calls 'the duty of genius' (*Ludwig Wittgenstein: The Duty of Genius*, London: Vintage, 1991).

line of reproach, arguing that 'the Enlightenment view of human psychology' has increasingly looked 'thin and mechanical', and 'Enlightenment hopes of social progress through the spread of humanitarianism and the scientific outlook' now appear rather 'naive'.[7] He goes on to link modern tyranny with that perspective (as have other critics of the Enlightenment), arguing that not only were 'Stalin and his heirs' altogether 'in thrall to the Enlightenment', but also that Pol Pot 'was indirectly influenced by it'.[8] But since Glover does not wish to seek his solution through the authority of religion or of tradition (he notes that, in this respect, 'we cannot escape the Enlightenment'), he concentrates his fire on forcefully held beliefs, to which overconfident use of reasoning substantially contributes. 'The crudity of Stalinism', he argues, 'had its origin in the beliefs.'[9]

It would be hard to dispute Glover's pointer to the power of strong beliefs and terrible convictions, or indeed to challenge his thesis of 'the role of ideology in Stalinism'. The question to be asked here does not relate to the nasty power of bad ideas, but rather to the diagnosis that this is somehow a criticism of the reach of reason in general and the Enlightenment perspective in particular.[10] Is it really right to place the blame for the propensity towards premature certainties and the unquestioned beliefs of gruesome political leaders on the Enlightenment tradition, given the pre-eminent importance that so many Enlightenment authors attached to the role of reasoning in making choices, particularly against reliance on blind belief? Surely, 'the crudity of Stalinism' could be opposed, as indeed it was by dissidents through a reasoned demonstration of the huge gap between promise and practice, and by showing the brutality of the regime despite its pretensions – a brutality that the authorities had to conceal from scrutiny through censorship and expurgation.

Indeed, one of the main points in favour of reason is that it helps us to scrutinize ideology and blind belief.* Reason was not, in fact,

---

* It is, of course, true that many crude beliefs originate in some kinds of reason – possibly of rather primitive kinds (for example, racist and sexist prejudices survive often enough on the basis of the perceived 'reason' that non-whites or women are biologically or intellectually inferior). The case for reliance on reason does not involve any denial of the easily recognized fact that people do give reasons of some kind or other in defence of their beliefs (no matter how crude). The point of *reasoning* as a

Pol Pot's main ally. Frenzy and unreasoned conviction played that role, with no room for reasoned scrutiny. The interesting and important issues that Glover's critique of the Enlightenment tradition forcefully raises include the question: where is the remedy to bad reasoning to be found? There is also the related question: what is the relationship between reason and emotions, including compassion and sympathy? And beyond that, it must also be asked: what is the ultimate justification for reliance on reason? Is reason cherished as a good tool, and if so, a tool for pursuing what? Or is reason its own justification, and if so, how does it differ from blind and unquestioning belief? These issues have been discussed over the ages, but there is a special need to face them here, given the focus on reasoning in the exploration of the idea of justice in this work.

## AKBAR AND THE NECESSITY OF REASON

W. B. Yeats wrote on the margin of his copy of Nietzsche's *The Genealogy of Morals*, 'But why does Nietzsche think the night has no stars, nothing but bats and owls and the insane moon?'[11] Nietzsche's scepticism about humanity and his chilling vision of the future were presented just before the beginning of the twentieth century (he died in 1900). The events of the century that followed, including world wars, holocausts, genocides and other atrocities, give us reason enough to worry whether Nietzsche's scepticism about humankind might not have been just right.* Indeed, in investigating Nietzsche's concerns at the end of the twentieth century, Jonathan Glover concludes that we 'need to look hard and clearly at some monsters inside us', and consider ways and means of 'caging and taming them'.[12]

---

discipline is to subject the prevailing beliefs and alleged reasons to critical examination. These issues will be further discussed in Chapters 8, 'Rationality and Other People', and 9, 'Plurality of Impartial Reasons'.

* As Javed Akhtar, the Urdu poet, puts it in a ghazal: 'Religion or war, caste or race, these things it does not know/ Before our savagery how do we judge the wild beast' (Javad Akhtar, *Quiver: Poems and Ghazals*, translated by David Matthews (New Delhi: HarperCollins, 2001), p. 47).

Occasions such as the turn of a century have appeared to many people to be appropriate moments to engage in critical examinations of what is happening and what needs to be done. The reflections are not always as pessimistic and sceptical of human nature and the possibility of reasoned change as those of Nietzsche (or of Glover). An interesting contrast can be seen in the much earlier deliberations of the Mughal emperor, Akbar, in India, at a point of even 'millennial', rather than merely centurial, interest. As the first millennium of the Muslim Hijri calendar came to an end in 1591–2 (it was a thousand lunar years after Muhammad's epic journey from Mecca to Medina in AD 622),* Akbar engaged in a far-reaching scrutiny of social and political values and legal and cultural practice. He paid particular attention to the challenges of inter-community relations and the abiding need for communal peace and fruitful collaboration in the already multicultural India of the sixteenth century. We have to recognize how unusual Akbar's policies were for the time. The Inquisitions were in full swing and Giordano Bruno was burnt at the stake for heresy in Rome in 1600 even as Akbar was making his pronouncements on religious tolerance in India. Not only did Akbar insist that the duty of the state included making sure that 'no man should be interfered with on account of his religion, and any one was to be allowed to go over to any religion he pleased',[13] he also arranged systematic dialogues in his capital city of Agra between Hindus, Muslims, Christians, Jains, Parsees, Jews and others, even including agnostics and atheists.

Taking note of the religious diversity of his people, Akbar laid the foundations of secularism and religious neutrality of the state in a variety of ways; the secular constitution that India adopted in 1949, after independence from British rule, has many features already championed by Akbar in the 1590s. The shared elements include interpreting secularism as the requirement that the state be equidistant from different religions and must not treat any religion with special favour.

Underlying Akbar's general approach to the assessment of social

---

* A lunar year has a mean length of 354 days, 8 hours and 48 minutes, and thus moves ahead significantly faster than a solar year.

custom and public policy was his overarching thesis that 'the pursuit of reason' (rather than what he called 'the marshy land of tradition') is the way to address difficult problems of good behaviour and the challenges of constructing a just society.[14] The question of secularism is only one of a great many cases in which Akbar insisted that we should be free to examine whether reason does or does not support any existing custom, or provides justification for ongoing policy; for example, he abolished all special taxes on non-Muslims on the ground that they were discriminatory since they did not treat all citizens as equal. In 1582 he resolved to release 'all the Imperial slaves', since 'it is beyond the realm of justice and good conduct' to benefit from 'force'.[15]

Illustrations of Akbar's criticisms of prevailing social practice are also easy to find in the arguments he presented. He was, for example, opposed to child marriage, which was then quite conventional (and alas, not even fully eradicated now in the subcontinent), since, he argued, 'the object that is intended' in marriage 'is still remote, and there is immediate possibility of injury'. He also criticized the Hindu practice of not allowing the remarriage of widows (a practice that would be reformed only several centuries later) and added that 'in a religion that forbids the remarriage of the widow', the hardship of permitting child marriage 'is much greater'. On the inheritance of property, Akbar noted that 'in the Muslim religion, a smaller share of inheritance is allowed to the daughter, though owing to her weakness, she deserves to be given a larger share'. A very different kind of example of reasoning can be seen in his allowing religious rituals of which he himself took a very sceptical view. When his second son, Murad, who knew that Akbar was opposed to all religious rituals, asked him whether these rituals should be banned, Akbar immediately opposed that, on the ground that 'preventing that insensitive simpleton, who considers body exercise to be divine worship, would amount to preventing him from remembering God [at all]'.

While Akbar himself remained a practising Muslim, he argued for the need for everyone to subject their inherited beliefs and priorities to critical scrutiny. Indeed, perhaps the most important point that Akbar made in his defence of a secular and a tolerant multicultural society concerned the role that he gave to reasoning in this entire enterprise. Akbar took reason to be supreme, since even in disputing reason we would have to give reasons for that disputation. Attacked by strong traditionalists within his own religious affiliation, who argued in favour of unquestioning and instinctive faith in the Islamic tradition, Akbar told his friend and trusted lieutenant, Abul Fazl (a formidable scholar in Sanskrit as well as Arabic and Persian): 'The pursuit of reason and rejection of traditionalism are so brilliantly patent as to be above the need of argument.'[16] He concluded that the 'path of reason' or 'the rule of the intellect' (*rahi aql*) must be the basic determinant of good and just behaviour as well as of an acceptable framework of legal duties and entitlements.*

## ETHICAL OBJECTIVITY AND REASONED SCRUTINY

Akbar was right to point to the indispensability of reason. As will be presently argued, even the importance of emotions can be appreciated within the reach of reason. Indeed, the significant place of emotions for our deliberations can be illustrated by the reasons for taking them seriously (though not uncritically). If we are strongly moved by some particular emotion, there is good reason to ask what that tells us. Reason and emotion play complementary roles in human reflection, and the complex relationship between them will be considered more fully later on in this chapter.

It is not hard to see that ethical judgements demand *rahi aql* – the use of reason. The question that remains, however, is this: why should we accept that reason has to be the ultimate arbitrator of ethical beliefs? Is there some special role for reasoning – perhaps reasoning of a particular kind – that must be seen as overarching and crucial for ethical judgements? Since reasoned support can hardly be in itself a value-giving quality, we have to ask: why, precisely, is reasoned

* Akbar would have endorsed Thomas Scanlon's diagnosis (in his illuminating study of the role of reason in determining 'what we owe to each other') that we should not 'regard the idea of reason as mysterious, or one that needs, or can be given, a philosophical explanation in terms of some other, more basic notion' (*What We Owe to Each Other* (Cambridge, MA: Harvard University Press, 1998), p. 3).

support so critical? Can it be claimed that reasoned scrutiny provides some kind of a guarantee of reaching the truth? This would be hard to maintain, not only because the nature of truth in moral and political beliefs is such a difficult subject, but mainly because the most rigorous of searches, in ethics or in any other discipline, could still fail.

Indeed, sometimes a very dubious procedure could end up, accidentally, yielding a more correct answer than extremely rigorous reasoning. This is obvious enough in epistemology: even though a scientific procedure may have a better probability of success among alternative procedures, even a crazy procedure could happen to produce the correct answer in a particular case (more correct, in such a case, than more reasoned procedures). For example, a person who relies on a stopped watch to check the time will get the time exactly right twice a day, and if he happened to be looking for the time precisely at one of those moments, his unmoving watch might beat all other moving clocks to which he had access. However, as a procedure to be chosen, relying on the motionless timepiece rather than on a clock that moves approximately close to the actual time does not have much to commend it, despite the fact that the moving clock would be beaten twice a day by the stationary timepiece.*

It is plausible to think that a similar argument exists for choosing the best reasoned procedure, even though there is no guarantee that it would be invariably right, and not even any guarantee that it would be always more right than some other, less reasoned, procedure (even if we could judge the correctness of judgements with any degree of confidence). The case for reasoned scrutiny lies not in any sure-fire way of getting things exactly right (no such way may exist), but on being as objective as we reasonably can.† What lies behind the case for relying on reasoning in making ethical judgements are, I would

* Leela Majumdar, the Bengali writer (and aunt of the great film director Satyajit Ray), recollected in a children's story, that when she was a feisty college student in Calcutta, she had stopped and asked a passing stranger – just to annoy and confuse him – 'Oh, hello, when did you come from Chittagong?' The man replied, in sheer amazement, 'Yesterday, how did you know?'
† See Bernard Williams's powerful discussion about seeing reasoned belief as 'aiming at' truth ('Deciding to believe', in *Problems of the Self* (Cambridge: Cambridge University Press, 1973). See also Peter Railton, *Facts, Values and Norms: Essays Toward a Morality of Consequence* (Cambridge: Cambridge University Press, 2003).

argue, also the demands of objectivity, and they call for a particular discipline of reasoning. The important role given to reasoning in this work relates to the need for objective reasoning in thinking about issues of justice and injustice.

Since objectivity is itself a rather difficult issue in moral and political philosophy, the subject demands some discussion here. Does the pursuit of ethical objectivity take the form of the search for some ethical *objects*? While a good deal of complex discussion on the objectivity of ethics has tended to proceed in terms of ontology (in particular, the metaphysics of 'what ethical objects exist'), it is difficult to understand what these ethical objects might be like. Instead, I would go along with Hilary Putnam's argument that this line of investigation is largely unhelpful and misguided.* When we debate the demands of ethical objectivity, we are not crossing swords on the nature and content of some alleged ethical 'objects'.

There are, of course, ethical statements that presume the existence of some identifiable objects that can be observed (this would be a part of the exercise, for example, in looking for observable evidence to decide whether a person is courageous or compassionate), whereas the subject matter of other ethical statements may not have that association (for example, a judgement that a person is altogether immoral or unjust). But despite some overlap between description and evaluation, ethics cannot be simply a matter of truthful description of specific objects. Rather, as Putnam argues, 'real ethical questions are a species of practical question, and practical questions don't only involve valuings, they involve a complex mixture of philosophical beliefs, religious beliefs, and factual beliefs as well'.[17] The actual procedures used in pursuit of objectivity may not be always clear, nor

* Hilary Putnam, *Ethics without Ontology* (Cambridge, MA: Harvard University Press, 2004). Putnam is concerned not only with the unhelpfulness of the ontological approach to the objectivity of ethics but also with the mistake it makes in looking for something that is far removed from the nature of the subject. 'I see the attempt to provide an ontological explanation of the objectivity of mathematics as, in effect, an attempt to provide *reasons which are not part of mathematics for the truth of mathematical statements* and the attempt to provide an ontological explanation of the objectivity of ethics as a similar attempt to provide *reasons which are not part of ethics for the truth of ethical statements*, and I see both attempts as deeply misguided' (p. 3).

spelt out, but as Putnam argues, this can be done with clarity if the underlying issues are adequately scrutinized.*

The reasoning that is sought in analysing the requirements of justice will incorporate some basic demands of impartiality, which are integral parts of the idea of justice and injustice. At this point there is some merit in summoning the ideas of John Rawls and his analysis of moral and political objectivity, which he presented in his defence of the objectivity of 'justice as fairness' (a subject to which the next chapter will be devoted).† Rawls argues: 'The first essential is that a conception of objectivity must establish a public framework of thought sufficient for the concept of judgement to apply and for conclusions to be reached on the basis of reasons and evidence after discussion and due reflection.' He goes on to argue: 'To say that a political conviction is objective is to say that there are reasons, specified by a reasonable and mutually recognizable political conception (satisfying those essentials), sufficient to convince all reasonable persons that it is reasonable.'[18]

There can be an interesting discussion as to whether this criterion of objectivity, which has some clearly normative elements (particularly in the identification of 'reasonable persons'), would tend to coincide

---

* In my book *Development as Freedom* (New York: Knopf, 1999), I abstained from any serious discussion of ethical methodology, and based the claim of acceptability of some general developmental priorities on rather commonsense grounds. Hilary Putnam has analysed, with clarity and definitiveness, the underlying methodology of that work in development economics, and has discussed how the particular methodology of that work fits, happily for me, into his general approach to objectivity; see his *The Collapse of the Fact/Value Dichotomy and Other Essays* (Cambridge, MA: Harvard University Press, 2002). See also Vivian Walsh, 'Sen after Putnam', *Review of Political Economy*, 15 (2003).

† I should emphasize here that there exist substantial differences between the way in which Putnam sees the problem of objectivity, which makes room for his scepticism about 'universal principles' (*Ethics without Ontology*, 'few real problems can be solved by treating them as mere instances of a universal generalization', p. 4), and the way Rawls gets at the problem, with his use of universal principles along with investigation of the specificities of particular ethical problems (*Political Liberalism*, pp. 110–18). Neither Rawls nor Putnam, however, is tempted to see objectivity of ethics in terms of ontology, or in terms of a search for some actual objects. In this work I draw on both Putnam's and Rawls's analyses, but do not explore further the specific issues on which their differences rest.

with what is likely to survive open and informed public discussion. In contrast with Rawls, Jürgen Habermas has focused on the latter, largely procedural, route, rather than relying on some procedure-independent identification of what would convince people who are 'reasonable' persons and who would find some political conviction to be 'reasonable' as well.[19] I see the force of Habermas's point and the correctness of the categorical distinction he makes, even though I am not fully persuaded that Rawls's and Habermas's approaches are, in fact, radically different in terms of the respective strategies of reasoning.

In order to get the kind of political society that he tends to concentrate on, Habermas also imposes many exacting demands on public deliberation. If people are capable of being reasonable in taking note of other people's points of view and in welcoming information, which must be among the essential demands of open-minded public dialogue, then the gap between the two approaches would tend to be not necessarily momentous.*

I will not make a big distinction between those whom Rawls categorizes as 'reasonable persons' and other human beings, despite Rawls's frequent reference to – and the evident use of – the category of 'reasonable persons'. I have tried to argue elsewhere that, by and large, all of us are capable of being reasonable through being open-minded about welcoming information and through reflecting on arguments coming from different quarters, along with undertaking interactive deliberations and debates on how the underlying issues should be seen.[20] I do not see this presumption to be fundamentally different from Rawls's own idea of 'free and equal persons' who all

---

* Habermas also argues that the kind of agreement that would emerge in the system he describes will be substantively different from Rawls's more 'liberal' rules and priorities ('Reconciliation through the Public Use of Reason: Remarks on John Rawls's Political Liberalism', *The Journal of Philosophy* (1995)). What has to be determined is whether those differences between Habermasian and Rawlsian conclusions in substantive outcomes are really the result of the two distinct procedures used respectively by Habermas and Rawls, rather than resulting from their respective beliefs about how open and interactive deliberations could be expected to proceed in free democratic exchanges. See also Jürgen Habermas, *Justification and Application: Remarks on Discourse Ethics*, translated by Ciaran Cronin (Cambridge, MA: MIT Press, 1993).

have 'moral powers'.* Rawls's analysis seems, in fact, to focus more on the *characterization* of deliberating human beings rather than on the *categorization* of some 'reasonable persons' while excluding others.† The role of unrestricted public reasoning is quite central to democratic politics in general and to the pursuit of social justice in particular.‡

## ADAM SMITH AND THE IMPARTIAL SPECTATOR

Public reasoning is clearly an essential feature of objectivity in political and ethical beliefs. If Rawls presents one way of thinking about objectivity in the assessment of justice, Adam Smith's invoking of the impartial spectator provides another. This 'ancient' approach (as I write these lines it is almost exactly 250 years since the first publication of Smith's *Theory of Moral Sentiments* in 1759) has a very long reach. It also has both procedural and substantive contents. In seeking resolution by public reasoning, there is clearly a strong case for not leaving out the perspectives and reasonings presented by anyone whose assessments are relevant, either because their interests are involved, or because their ways of thinking about these issues throw light on particular judgements – a light that might be missed in the absence of giving those perspectives an opportunity to be aired.

While Rawls's primary focus seems to be on variations of personal

---

* Rawls refers in particular to 'two moral powers', viz. 'the capacity for a sense of justice', and 'a capacity for a conception of the good' (*Justice as Fairness: A Restatement*, edited by Erin Kelly (Cambridge, MA: Harvard University Press, 2001), pp. 18–19).

† Indeed, we do not hear much from Rawls about how those who could be seen as 'unreasonable persons' come to terms with ideas of justice, and how they would be integrated into the social order.

‡ See Joshua Cohen, 'Deliberation and Democratic Legitimacy', in Alan Hamlin and Phillip Pettit (eds), *The Good Polity: Normative Analysis of the State* (Oxford: Blackwell, 1989), and *Politics, Power and Public Relations*, Tanner Lectures at the University of California, Berkeley, 2007. See also Seyla Benhabib (ed.), *Democracy and Difference: Contesting the Boundaries of the Political* (Princeton, NJ: Princeton University Press, 1996).

interests and personal priorities, Adam Smith was also concerned with the need to broaden the discussion to avoid local parochialism of values, which might have the effect of ignoring some pertinent arguments, unfamiliar in a particular culture. Since the invoking of public discussion can take a counter-factual form ('what would an impartial spectator from a distance say about that?'), one of Smith's major methodological concerns is the need to invoke a wide variety of viewpoints and outlooks based on diverse experiences from far and near, rather than remaining contented with encounters – actual or counterfactual – with others living in the same cultural and social milieu, and with the same kind of experiences, prejudices and convictions about what is reasonable and what is not, and even beliefs about what is feasible and what is not. Adam Smith's insistence that we must *inter alia* view our sentiments from 'a certain distance from us' is motivated by the object of scrutinizing not only the influence of vested interest, but also the impact of entrenched tradition and custom.*

Despite the differences between the distinct types of arguments presented by Smith, Habermas and Rawls, there is an essential similarity in their respective approaches to objectivity to the extent that objectivity is linked, directly or indirectly, by each of them to the ability to survive challenges from informed scrutiny coming from diverse quarters. In this work too, I will take reasoned scrutiny from different perspectives to be an essential part of the demands of objectivity for ethical and political convictions.

However, I must add here – indeed, assert here – that the principles that survive such scrutiny need not be a unique set (for reasons that were already presented in the Introduction). This is, in fact, a larger departure from John Rawls than from Hilary Putnam.† Indeed, any approach to justice, like Rawls's, that proposes to follow up the choice of principles of justice by the rigidity of a unique institutional structure

---

* See also Simon Blackburn's discussion of the role of 'the common point of view', and in particular the contributions of Adam Smith and David Hume in developing that perspective (*Ruling Passions: A Theory of Practical Reasoning* (Oxford: Clarendon Press, 1998), especially Chapter 7).

† It is not a departure at all from Bernard Williams, see *Ethics and the Limits of Philosophy* (London: Fontana, 1985) Chapter 8. See also John Gray, *Two Faces of Liberalism* (London: Polity Press, 2000).

(this is part of transcendental institutionalism discussed in the Introduction), and which proceeds to tell us, step by step, an *as if* history of the unfolding of justice, cannot easily accommodate the co-survival of competing principles that do not speak in one voice. As discussed in the Introduction, I am arguing for the possibility that there may remain contrary positions that simultaneously survive and which cannot be subjected to some radical surgery that reduces them all into one tidy box of complete and well-fitted demands, which, in Rawls's theory, take us to some unique institutional route to fulfil these requirements (to be implemented by a sovereign state).

While there are differences between the distinct approaches to objectivity considered here, the overarching similarity among them lies in the shared recognition of the need for reasoned encounter on an impartial basis (the approaches differ largely on the domain of the required impartiality, as will be discussed further in Chapter 6). Reason can, of course, take distinct forms which have many different uses.* But to the extent that we look for ethical objectivity, the reasoning that is necessary has to satisfy what can be seen as the requirements of impartiality. Reasons of justice may differ from, to use one of Smith's expressions, reasons of 'self-love', and also from reasons of prudence, but reasons of justice still constitute a large expanse. A lot of what follows in this work will be concerned with exploring that huge territory.

# THE REACH OF REASON

Reasoning is a robust source of hope and confidence in a world darkened by murky deeds – past and present. It is not hard to see why this is so. Even when we find something immediately upsetting, we can question that response and ask whether it is an appropriate reaction and whether we should really be guided by it. Reasoning can be concerned with the right way of viewing and treating other people, other cultures, other claims, and with examining different grounds

---

* I shall consider some of these differences in Chapters 8, 'Rationality and Other People', and 9, 'Plurality of Impartial Reasons'.

for respect and tolerance. We can also reason about our own mistakes and try to learn not to repeat them, in the way Kenzaburo Oe, the great Japanese writer, hopes the Japanese nation will remain committed to 'the idea of democracy and the determination never to wage a war again', aided by an understanding of its own 'history of territorial invasion'.*

No less importantly, intellectual probing is needed to identify deeds that are not intended to be injurious, but which have that effect; for example, horrors like terrible famines can remain unchecked on the mistaken presumption that they cannot be averted without increasing the total availability of food, which can be hard to organize rapidly enough. Hundreds of thousands, indeed, millions, can die from calamitous inaction resulting from unreasoned fatalism masquerading as composure based on realism and common sense.† As it happens, famines are easy to prevent, partly because they affect only a small proportion of the population (rarely more than 5 per cent and hardly ever more than 10 per cent), and redistribution of existing food can be arranged through immediate means such as emergency employment creation, thereby giving the indigent an immediate income for purchasing food. Obviously, having more food would make things easier (it can help the public distribution of food and also more food available in markets can help to keep prices lower than they would otherwise be), but having more food is not an absolute necessity for successful famine relief (as is often taken for granted and seen as a

---

* Kenzaburo Oe, *Japan, the Ambiguous, and Myself* (Tokyo and New York: Kodansha International, 1995), pp. 118–19. See also Onuma Yasuaki, 'Japanese War Guilt and Postwar Responsibilities of Japan', *Berkeley Journal of International Law*, 20 (2002). Similarly, in post-war Germany, learning from past mistakes, particularly from the Nazi period, has been an important issue in contemporary German priorities.
† I have discussed the causes of famines and the policy requirement for famine prevention in *Poverty and Famines: An Essay on Entitlement and Deprivation* (Oxford: Clarendon Press, 1981), and jointly with Jean Drèze, in *Hunger and Public Action* (Oxford: Clarendon Press, 1989). This is one illustration of the general problem that a mistaken theory can have fatal consequences. On this, see my *Development as Freedom* (New York: Knopf and Oxford: Clarendon Press, 1999) and Sabina Alkire, 'Development: A Misconceived Theory Can Kill', in Christopher W. Morris (ed.), *Amartya Sen* (Cambridge: Cambridge University Press, forthcoming, 2009). See also Cormac Ó Gráda, *Famine: A Short History* (Princeton, NJ: Princeton University Press, 2009).

justification for inaction in arranging immediate relief). The relatively small redistribution of the food supply that is needed to avoid starvation can be brought about through the creation of purchasing power for those deprived of all incomes, through one calamity or another, which is typically the primary cause of starvation.*

Consider another subject, which is beginning, at long last, to receive the attention it deserves, that is, the neglect and deterioration of the natural environment. It is, as is increasingly clear, a hugely serious problem and one that is closely linked with the negative effects of human behaviour, but the problem does not arise from any desire of people today to hurt those yet to be born, or even to be deliberately callous about the future generations' interests. And yet, through lack of reasoned engagement and action, we do still fail to take adequate care of the environment around us and the sustainability of the requirements of good life. To prevent catastrophes caused by human negligence or callous obduracy, we need critical scrutiny, not just goodwill towards others.[21]

Reasoning is our ally in this, not a threat that endangers us. So why does it look so different to those who find reliance on reasoning to be deeply problematic? One of the issues to consider is the possibility that the critics of relying on reason are influenced by the fact that some people are easily *over*-convinced by their own reasoning, and ignore counter-arguments and other grounds that may yield the opposite conclusion. This is perhaps what Glover is really worried about, and it can indeed be a legitimate worry. But the difficulty here surely comes from precipitate and badly reasoned certitude, rather than from

* Further, since most famine victims suffer from and often die from standard diseases (helped by debilitation and the spread of infection caused by a growing famine), much can be done through healthcare and medical facilities. More than four-fifths of the death toll resulting from the Great Bengal famine of 1943 was directly connected with diseases common to the region, with pure starvation death accounting for no more than a fifth of the total (see Appendix D in my *Poverty and Famines* (Oxford: Clarendon Press, 1981)). A similar picture emerges from many other famines. See particularly Alex de Waal, *Famine that Kills: Darfur, Sudan, 1984–1985* (Oxford: Clarendon Press, 1989); also his *Famine Crimes: Politics and the Disaster Relief Industry in Africa* (London: African Rights and the International African Institute, 1997). This issue is assessed in my entry on 'Human Disasters' in *The Oxford Textbook of Medicine* (Oxford: Oxford University Press, 2008).

making use of reason. The remedy for bad reasoning lies in better reasoning, and it is indeed the job of reasoned scrutiny to move from the former to the latter. It is also possible that in some statements of 'Enlightenment authors' the need for reassessment and caution was not sufficiently emphasized, but it would be hard to derive from that any general indictment of the Enlightenment outlook, and even more, an arraignment of the general role of reason in just behaviour or good social policy.

## REASON, SENTIMENTS AND THE ENLIGHTENMENT

There is, however, the further issue of the relative importance of instinctive sentiments and cool calculation, on which several Enlightenment authors themselves had much to say. Jonathan Glover's arguments for the need for a 'new human psychology' draws on his recognition that politics and psychology are interwoven. It is hard to think that reasoning, based on the available evidence about human behaviour, would not lead to the acceptance of this interconnection. In avoiding atrocities, there is surely a huge preventive role that can be played by instinctive revulsion to cruelty and to insensitive behaviour, and Glover rightly emphasizes the importance, among other things, of 'the tendency to respond to people with certain kinds of respect' and 'sympathy: caring about the miseries and the happiness of others'.

However, there need be no conflict here with reason, which can endorse precisely those priorities. Good reasoning has clearly played that role in Glover's own investigation of the dangers of one-sided and overconfident belief (Akbar's point that even to dispute reason one has to give a reason for that disputation is surely relevant here). Nor need reasoning withhold the understanding, if justified, that a total reliance only on cool calculation may not be a good – or reasonable – way of ensuring human security.

Indeed, in celebrating reason, there is no particular ground for denying the far-reaching role of instinctive psychology and spontaneous responses.[22] They can supplement each other, and in many cases an understanding of the broadening and liberating role of our feelings can constitute good subject matter for reasoning itself. Adam Smith, a central figure in Scottish Enlightenment (and very influential in the French Enlightenment as well), discussed extensively the central role of emotions and psychological response in his *The Theory of Moral Sentiments*.* Smith may not have gone as far as David Hume in asserting that 'reason and sentiment concur in almost all moral determinations and conclusions',[23] but both saw reasoning and feeling as deeply interrelated activities. Both Hume and Smith were, of course, quintessential 'Enlightenment authors', no less so than Diderot or Kant.

However, the need for reasoned scrutiny of psychological attitudes does not disappear even after the power of emotions is recognized and the positive role of many instinctive reactions (such as a sense of revulsion about cruelty) is celebrated. Smith in particular – perhaps even more than Hume – gave reason a huge role in assessing our sentiments and psychological concerns. In fact, Hume often seems to take passion to be more powerful than reason. As Thomas Nagel puts it in his strong defence of reason in his book *The Last Word*, 'Hume famously believed that because a "passion" immune to rational assessment must underlie every motive, there can be no such thing as specifically practical reason, nor specifically moral reason either.'† Smith did not take that view, even though he, like Hume, took emotions to be both important and influential, and argued that our 'first perceptions' of right and wrong 'cannot be the object of reason, but of immediate sense and feeling'. But Smith also argued that even these instinctive reactions to particular conduct cannot but rely – if only implicitly – on our reasoned understanding of causal connections between conduct and consequences in 'a vast variety of instances'. Furthermore, first perceptions may also change in response to critical

* See also Martha Nussbaum, *Upheavals of Thought: The Intelligence of Emotions* (Cambridge: Cambridge University Press, 2001).
† Thomas Nagel, *The Last Word* (New York: Oxford University Press, 1997), p. 102. However, Hume seems to vary on the priority issue. While he does give passion an elevated standing that seems to be more dominant than the role of reason, Hume also argues: 'The moment we perceive the falsehood of any supposition, or the insufficiency of any means our passions yield to our reason without any opposition' (David Hume, *A Treatise of Human Nature*, edited by L. A. Selby-Bigge (Oxford: Clarendon Press, 1888; 2nd edn 1978) p. 416).

examination, for example on the basis of causal empirical investigation that may show, Smith notes, that a certain 'object is the means of obtaining some other'.[24]

Adam Smith's argument for recognizing the abiding need for reasoned scrutiny is well illustrated by his discussion about how to assess our attitudes to prevailing practices. This is obviously important for Smith's powerful advocacy of reform, for example the case for abolishing slavery, or for lessening the burden of arbitrary bureaucratic restrictions on the commerce between different countries, or for relaxing the punitive restrictions imposed on the indigent as a condition for the economic support provided through the Poor Laws.*

While it is certainly true that ideology and dogmatic belief can emerge from sources other than religion and custom, and have frequently done so, that does not deny the role of reason in assessing the rationale behind instinctive attitudes, any less than in the appraisal of arguments presented to justify deliberate policies. What Akbar called the 'path of reason' does not exclude taking note of the value of instinctive reactions, nor ignore the informative role that our mental reactions often play. And all this is quite consistent with not giving our unscrutinized instincts an unconditional final say.

---

* In his well-argued essay, 'Why Economies Need Ethical Theory', John Broome argues: 'Economists do not like to impose their ethical opinion on people, but there is no question of that. Very few economists are in a position to impose their opinion on anyone . . . The solution is for them to get themselves good arguments, and work out the theory. It is not to hide behind the preferences of other people when those preferences may not be well founded, when the people themselves may be looking for help from economists in forming better preferences.' (*Arguments for a Better World: Essays in Honor of Amartya Sen*, edited by Kaushik Basu and Ravi Kanbur, Vol.1 (Oxford: Oxford University Press, 2009), p. 14). This is, of course, exactly what Smith tried to do.

# 2

# Rawls and Beyond

This chapter is mainly a critique of the theory of justice presented by the leading political philosopher of our time, John Rawls. I will discuss where I have to differ from Rawls, but I cannot begin this critique without acknowledging, first, how my own understanding of justice – and of political philosophy in general – has been influenced by what I have learned from him, and without mentioning also the very large debt that we all owe to Rawls for reviving philosophical interest in the subject of justice. Indeed, Rawls has made the subject what it is today, and I start this critique by recollecting, first, the thrill of seeing him transform contemporary political philosophy in a truly radical way. In addition to benefiting from Rawls's writings, I had the privilege of having this wonderful person as a friend and a colleague – his kindness was astonishing, and his insightful comments, criticisms and suggestions have constantly enlightened me and radically influenced my own thinking.

I was lucky in terms of timing. Moral and political philosophy took huge steps, under Rawls's leadership, just when I was beginning to become interested in the subject, as an observer from other disciplines (first from mathematics and physics, and then from economics). His 1958 paper, 'Justice as Fairness', threw a shaft of light of a kind that would be hard for me to describe adequately today, just as his earlier papers in the 1950s on the nature of 'decision procedures' and on different concepts of 'rules', which I read as an undergraduate, illuminated my thinking in a way that was quite thrilling.[1]

And then, in 1971, came Rawls's path-breaking book, *A Theory of Justice*.[2] Rawls, Kenneth Arrow and I had in fact used an earlier draft of the book in a joint class we taught on political philosophy while I was visiting Harvard for the academic year 1968–9 (from my then home base at Delhi University). I was writing my own book on social choice (including its treatment of justice), *Collective Choice and Social Welfare* (1970), and I benefited immensely from Rawls's incisive comments and suggestions. Slightly later I had the privilege of commenting formally on the final text of *A Theory of Justice* for Harvard University Press. It may sound a little 'over the top', but I did think that I could grasp the feeling to which Wordsworth gave expression: 'Bliss was it in that dawn to be alive,/ But to be young was very heaven!'

That sense of excitement has not dimmed over the years merely because I now think that some of the main planks of the Rawlsian theory of justice are seriously defective. I will discuss my dissensions presently, but first I must take the opportunity to acknowledge the firm footing on which Rawls placed the whole subject of the theory of justice.[3] Some of the basic concepts that Rawls identified as essential continue to inform my own understanding of justice, despite the different direction and conclusions of my own work.

## JUSTICE AS FAIRNESS: THE RAWLSIAN APPROACH

Perhaps the most far-reaching example of what is essential for an adequate understanding of justice is Rawls's foundational idea that justice has to be seen in terms of the demands of fairness. Even though every summary is ultimately an act of barbarism, it is still useful to describe briefly (at the risk of some oversimplification) Rawls's theory of 'justice as fairness', in order to focus on some basic features that are helpful in understanding Rawls's approach, and also for attempting further work on justice.* In this approach, the notion of fairness is

---

* I should note here that the idea of justice figures in Rawls's works in at least three different contexts. First, there is the derivation of his 'principles of justice' based on the idea of fairness, and this in turn identifies the institutions needed, on grounds of justice, for the basic structure of the society. This theory, which Rawls elaborates in considerable detail, proceeds step by step from there to the legislation and implementation of what Rawls sees as the demands of 'justice as fairness'. There is a second sphere – that of reflection and the development of a 'reflective equilibrium' – in which

taken to be foundational, and is meant to be, in some sense, 'prior' to the development of the principles of justice. I would argue that we have good reason to be persuaded by Rawls that the pursuit of justice has to be linked to – and in some sense derived from – the idea of fairness. This central understanding is not only important for Rawls's own theory, it is also deeply relevant to most analyses of justice, including what I am trying to present in this book.*

So what *is* fairness? This foundational idea can be given shape in various ways, but central to it must be a demand to avoid bias in our evaluations, taking note of the interests and concerns of others as well, and in particular the need to avoid being influenced by our respective vested interests, or by our personal priorities or eccentricities or prejudices. It can broadly be seen as a demand for impartiality. Rawls's specification of the demands of impartiality is based on his constuctive idea of the 'original position', which is central to his theory of 'justice as fairness'. The original position is an imagined situation of primordial equality, when the parties involved have no knowledge of their personal identities, or their respective vested interests, within the group as a whole. Their representatives have to choose under this 'veil of ignorance', that is, in an imagined state of selective ignorance (in particular, ignorance about the distinct personal interests and actual views of a good life – what Rawls calls 'comprehensive preferences'), and it is in that state of devised ignorance that the principles of justice are chosen unanimously. The principles of justice, in a Rawlsian formulation, determine the basic social institutions that should govern the society they are, we imagine, about to 'create'.

The deliberations in this imagined original position on the principles

---

ideas of justice can figure, but the focus here is on our respective personal assessments of goodness and rightness. The third context is what Rawls calls 'overlapping consensus', which deals with the complex patterns of our agreements and disagreements on which the stability of social orders depend. It is with the principles of justice – the first issue – that I am primarily concerned here.

* The impact of Rawls's thinking can be seen in other contemporary works on justice, for example, those of Ronald Dworkin, Thomas Nagel, Robert Nozick, Thomas Pogge, Joseph Raz, Thomas Scanlon and many others, whose analyses of the problems of justice have clearly been strongly influenced by Rawlsian theory, though in some cases, as with Robert Nozick, in a rather combatively dialectical way (see Nozick's *Anarchy, State and Utopia* (New York: Basic Books, 1974)).

of justice demand the impartiality needed for fairness. Rawls puts the point in this way, in *A Theory of Justice* (1971, p. 17):

the original position is the appropriate initial status quo which insures that the fundamental agreements reached in it are fair. This fact yields the name 'justice as fairness.' It is clear, then, that I want to say that one conception of justice is more reasonable than another, or justifiable with respect to it, if rational persons in the initial situation would choose those principles over those of the other for the role of justice. Conceptions of justice are to be ranked by their acceptability to persons so circumstanced.

In his later works, particularly in *Political Liberalism* (1993), based on his Dewey Lectures at Columbia University, Rawls gave an even fuller defence of how the process of fairness is supposed to work.* Justice as fairness is seen as being a quintessentially 'political conception of justice', right 'from the outset' (p. xvii). A basic question that Rawls addresses is how people can cooperate with each other in a society despite subscribing to 'deeply opposed though reasonable comprehensive doctrines' (p. xviii). This becomes possible 'when citizens share a reasonable political conception of justice', which gives them 'a basis on which public discussion of fundamental political questions can proceed and be reasonably decided, not of course in all cases but we hope in most cases of constitutional essentials and matters of basic justice' (pp. xx–xxi). They may differ, for example, in their religious beliefs and general views of what constitutes a good and worthwhile life, but they are led by the deliberations to agree, in Rawls's account, on how to take note of those diversities among the members and to arrive at one set of principles of justice fair to the entire group.

---

* The extraordinary reach of Rawls's reasoning can be further confirmed thanks to the recent publication of a veritable feast of Rawls's published and unpublished writings, which consolidate and extend his earlier writings. See John Rawls, *Collected Papers*, edited by Samuel Freeman (Cambridge, MA: Harvard University Press, 1999); *The Law of Peoples* (Cambridge, MA: Harvard University Press, 1999); *Lectures on the History of Moral Philosophy*, edited by Barbara Herman (Cambridge, MA: Harvard University Press, 2000); *A Theory of Justice* (Cambridge, MA: Harvard University Press, revised edn, 2000); *Justice as Fairness: A Restatement*, edited by Erin Kelly (Cambridge, MA: Harvard University Press, 2001).

# FROM FAIRNESS TO JUSTICE

The fairness exercise, thus structured, is aimed at identifying appropriate principles that would determine the choice of just institutions needed for the basic structure of a society. Rawls identifies some very specific principles of justice (to be discussed presently), and makes the strong claim that these principles would be the unanimous choice that would emerge from the political conception of justice as fairness. He argues that since these principles would be chosen by all in the original position, with its primordial equality, they constitute the appropriate 'political conception' of justice, and that people growing up in a well-ordered society governed by these principles would have good reason to affirm a sense of justice based on them (irrespective of each person's particular conception of a 'good life' and personal 'comprehensive' priorities). So the unanimous choice of these principles of justice does quite a bit of work in the Rawlsian system, which includes the choice of *institutions* for the basic structure of the society, as well as the determination of a *political conception* of justice, which Rawls presumes will correspondingly influence individual behaviours in conformity with that shared conception (I will return to this issue later on in this chapter).

The choice of basic principles of justice is the first act in Rawls's multi-staged unfolding of social justice. This first stage leads to the next, 'constitutional', stage in which actual institutions are selected in line with the chosen principle of justice, taking note of the conditions of each particular society. The working of these institutions, in turn, leads to further social decisions at later stages in the Rawlsian system, for example through appropriate legislation (in what Rawls calls 'the legislative stage'). The imagined sequence moves forward step by step on firmly specified lines, with an elaborately characterized unfolding of completely just societal arrangements.

The whole process of this unfolding is based on the emergence of what he describes as 'two principles of justice' in the first stage that influence everything else that happens in the Rawlsian sequence. I have to express considerable scepticism about Rawls's highly specific claim about the unique choice, in the original position, of one particular set of principles for just institutions, needed for a fully just society. There are genuinely plural, and sometimes conflicting, general concerns that bear on our understanding of justice.[4] They need not differ in the convenient way – convenient for choice, that is – that only one such set of principles really incorporates impartiality and fairness, while the others do not.* Many of them share features of being unbiased and dispassionate, and represent maxims that their proponents can 'will to be a universal law' (to use Immanuel Kant's famous requirement).[5]

Indeed, plurality of unbiased principles can, I would argue, reflect the fact that impartiality can take many different forms and have quite distinct manifestations. For example, in the illustration with the competing claims of three children over a flute, considered in the Introduction, underlying each child's claim there is a general theory of how to treat people in an unbiased and impartial way, focusing, respectively, on effective use and utility, economic equity and distributional fairness, and the entitlement to the fruits of one's unaided efforts. Their arguments are perfectly general, and their respective reasonings about the nature of a just society reflect different basic ideas that can each be defended impartially (rather than being parasitic on vested interests). And if there is no unique emergence of a given set of principles of justice that together identify the institutions needed for the basic structure of the society, then the entire procedure of 'justice as fairness', as developed in Rawls's classic theory, would be hard to use.†

---

* The alternative theories of justice that John Roemer compares and contrasts in his *Theories of Distributive Justice* (Cambridge, MA: Harvard University Press, 1996) all have some claims to impartiality, and the choice between them has to be based on other reasons.

† My scepticism of Rawls's claim about a unanimous choice of a social contract in the 'original position' is, I am afraid, not a fresh thought. My first doubts about it, shared with my friend Garry Runciman, are reflected in a joint paper, 'Games, Justice and the General Will', *Mind*, 74 (1965). This was, of course, before the publication of Rawls's *A Theory of Justice* (Cambridge, MA: Harvard University Press, 1971), but it was based on Rawls's account of the 'original position' in his pioneering paper, 'Justice as Fairness', *Philosophical Review*, 67 (1958). See also my book *Collective Choice and Social Welfare* (San Francisco, CA: Holden-Day, 1970; republished, Amsterdam: North-Holland, 1979).

As was discussed in the Introduction, Rawls's basic claim of the emergence of a unique set of principles of justice in the original position (discussed and defended in his *A Theory of Justice*) is considerably softened and qualified in his later writings. Indeed, in his *Justice as Fairness: A Restatement*, Rawls notes that 'there are indefinitely many considerations that may be appealed to in the original position and each alternative conception of justice is favored by some consideration and disfavored by others', and also that 'the balance of reasons itself rests on judgment, though judgment informed and guided by reasoning'.[6] When Rawls goes on to concede that 'the ideal cannot be fully attained', his reference is to his ideal theory of justice as fairness. However, there need not be anything particularly 'non-ideal' in a theory of justice that makes room for surviving disagreement and dissent on some issues, while focusing on many solid conclusions that would forcefully emerge from reasoned agreement on the demands of justice.

What is clear, however, is that if Rawls's second thoughts are really saying what they seem to be saying, then his earlier stage-by-stage theory of justice as fairness would have to be abandoned. If institutions have to be set up on the basis of a unique set of principles of justice emanating from the exercise of fairness, through the original position, then the absence of such a unique emergence cannot but hit at the very root of the theory. There is a real tension here within Rawls's own reasoning over the years. He does not abandon, at least explicitly, his theory of justice as fairness, and yet he seems to accept that there are incurable problems in getting a unanimous agreement on one set of principles of justice in the original position, which cannot but have devastating implications for his theory of 'justice as fairness'.

My own inclination is to think that Rawls's original theory played a huge part in making us understand various aspects of the idea of justice, and even if that theory has to be abandoned – for which there is, I would argue, a strong case – a great deal of the enlightenment from Rawls's pioneering contribution would remain and continue to enrich political philosophy. It is possible to be at once deeply appreciative and seriously critical of a theory, and nothing would make me happier than having Rawls's own company, if that were to come, in this 'dual' assessment of the theory of justice as fairness.

# APPLICATION OF RAWLSIAN PRINCIPLES OF JUSTICE

Be that as it may, let me proceed with the outlining of Rawls's theory of justice as fairness. Rawls never abandoned it, and it has been about the most influential theory of justice in modern moral philosophy. Rawls argued that the following 'principles of justice' will emerge in the original position with unanimous agreement (*Political Liberalism*, 1993, p. 291):

a. Each person has an equal right to a fully adequate scheme of equal basic liberties which is compatible with a similar scheme of liberties for all.

b. Social and economic inequalities are to satisfy two conditions. First, they must be attached to offices and positions open to all under conditions of fair equality of opportunity; and second, they must be to the greatest benefit of the least advantaged members of society.

It is important to note that the principles of justice identified by Rawls include the priority of liberty (the 'first principle') giving precedence to maximal liberty for each person subject to similar liberty for all, compared with other considerations, including those of economic or social equity. Equal personal liberty is given priority over the demands of the second principle which relates to the equality of certain general opportunities and to equity in the distribution of general-purpose resources. That is to say, liberties that all can enjoy cannot be violated on grounds of, say, the furtherance of wealth or income, or for a better distribution of economic resources among the people. Even though Rawls puts liberty on an absolute pedestal that towers indisputably over all other considerations (and there is clearly some extremism here), the more general claim that lies behind all this is that liberty cannot be reduced to being only a facility that complements other facilities (such as economic opulence); there is something very special about the place of personal liberty in human lives. It is that more general – and not necessarily extreme – claim from which I will take part of my cue in the constructive part of this book.

Other issues of institutional choice are taken up in the Rawlsian principles of justice through a compound set of requirements that are combined in the 'second principle'. The first part of the second principle is concerned with the institutional requirement of making sure that public opportunities are open to all, without anyone being excluded or handicapped on grounds of, say, race or ethnicity or caste or religion. The second part of the second principle (called the 'Difference Principle') is concerned with distributive equity as well as overall efficiency, and it takes the form of making the worst-off members of the society as well off as possible.

Rawls's analysis of equity in the distribution of resources invokes an index of what he calls 'primary goods', which are general-purpose means to achieve a variety of ends (whatever resources would be generally helpful in getting what people want, varied as these wants might be). Rawls sees primary goods as including such things as 'rights, liberties and opportunities, income and wealth, and the social bases of self-respect'.[7] Note that liberties enter here again, this time only as a facility that complements other facilities, such as income and wealth.

In addition to what is included among the distributional concerns, there is significance in Rawls's exclusion of certain distributive claims that have been emphasized by other theorists. Indeed, it is important to note the kind of consideration that is *not* brought into direct valuational reckoning by Rawls, such as claims based on entitlements related to ideas of merits and deserts, or on ownership of property. Rawls provides reasoned justification for these exclusions as well as his inclusions.*

Productivities do, however, get indirect recognition through their role in advancing efficiency and equity, so that inequalities related to them are allowed and defended in the Rawlsian distributive theory if those inequalities help the worst-off people to be better off as a result, for example through the operation of incentives. Obviously in a world in which individual behaviour is not solely moulded by the 'conception of justice' in the original position, there is no way of avoiding incentive problems.

---

* See also Liam Murphy and Thomas Nagel, *The Myth of Ownership: Taxes and Justice* (New York: Oxford University Press, 2002), which applies general ideas of justice to the ideologically loaded battle over tax policy, (p. 4).

On the other hand, if in the original position inequalities based on the demands of incentives were judged to be wrong and unjust (they can be seen as something like bribes given to people to make them diligent at their work and appropriately productive), then should not the principles adopted at the original position eliminate the need for incentives? If a just economy should not have inequality arising from incentives, should not the principles emerging in that state of impartiality take the form of people agreeing to do their respective bits without the need to be bribed? And, on the basis of Rawlsian reasoning that, in the post-contract world, each person will behave in conformity with the conception of justice emanating from the original position, should we then not expect, in that duty-oriented world, spontaneous compliance by everyone with their respective productive duties (as a part of that conception of justice), without any need for incentives?

The idea that people will spontaneously do what they agreed to do in the original position is Rawls's own.* And yet Rawls seems to go 'this far, and no further', and it is not absolutely clear that a line can be drawn in a way that incentive-based inequalities are seen as acceptable (even in a world in which behavioural norms emerging from the original position are uniformly effective), while other grounds for inequality are rejected.[8]

This problem can generate two different kinds of response. One is the argument that has been forcefully presented by G. A. Cohen in his book *Rescuing Justice and Equality* (2008), that the accommodation of inequality for reasons of incentives limits the reach of the Rawlsian theory of justice.[9] The concession to incentives may make good practical sense, but can it be a part of a plausible theory, specifically, of justice? In a world in which justice is only about transcendental justice, Cohen's point would seem to be a legitimate critique.

A different take on the same issue is that it is hard to imagine that the need for incentives can be made to go away on the basis of the expectation that the conception of justice in the original position will make everyone spontaneously play their full productive role with no

* Cf. 'Everyone is presumed to act justly and to do his part in upholding just institutions' (Rawls, *A Theory of Justice*, p. 8).

incentive arrangements. Cohen may well be right that a society that can be seen as perfectly just should not have the impediment of incentive-based inequality, but that is one more reason for not concentrating so much on transcendental justice in developing a theory of justice. Rawls's halfway house may not be quite transcendental enough for Cohen, but there are other problems of transcendental concentration (for reasons already discussed) that Rawls has to face, even in the absence of taking a leaf from Cohen's book. In a world of comparative justice, Cohen's just world may stand above the one that Rawls outlines in justice as fairness, but the main use of the theory of comparative justice would be in making comparisons between feasible possibilities less exalted – in terms of justice – than both Cohen's and Rawls's 'just' worlds.

## SOME POSITIVE LESSONS FROM THE RAWLSIAN APPROACH

It is not hard to see that there are some contributions of great importance in the Rawlsian approach to justice as fairness and in the way Rawls has presented and explicated its implications. First, the idea that fairness is central to justice, which is illuminatingly defended by Rawls, is a major avowal that takes us well beyond the understanding generated by the previous literature on the subject of justice (for example, the justificatory basis of the Benthamite utilitarian theory). Even though I do not believe that the impartiality captured in the reflective device of the 'original position' (on which Rawls greatly relies) is adequate for the purpose, this is in no way a rebellion against the basic Rawlsian idea of the foundational priority of fairness in developing a theory of justice.

Second, I must reiterate a point I have already made concerning the far-reaching importance of Rawls's thesis about the nature of objectivity in practical reason, in particular his argument that 'The first essential is that a conception of objectivity must establish a public framework of thought sufficient for the concept of judgement to apply and for conclusions to be reached on the basis of reasons and evidence after discussion and due reflection.'[10] The issue was discussed fairly extensively in Chapter 1 ('Reason and Objectivity') and I will not belabour it further here.

Third, aside from clarifying the need for the idea of fairness as preceding justice, Rawls makes another basic contribution in pointing to 'the moral powers' that people have, related to their 'capacity for a sense of justice' and 'for a conception of the good'. This is a far cry from the imagined world, on which exclusive attention is showered on some versions of 'rational choice theory' (to be more fully discussed in Chapter 8, 'Rationality and Other People'), in which human beings only have a sense of self-interest and prudence but evidently not any capacity or inclination to consider ideas of fairness and justice.[11] Aside from enriching the concept of rationality, Rawls also pursues the distinction between being 'rational' and being 'reasonable' in a very useful way,[12] and that is a distinction that will be used fairly extensively in this work.

Fourth, Rawls's prioritization of liberty, admittedly in the rather extreme form of its total priority, does draw attention to the strong case for seeing liberty as a separate and, in many ways, overriding concern in the assessment of the justice of social arrangements. Liberty also, of course, works alongside other concerns in determining a person's overall advantage: it is included in the list of 'primary goods' specified by Rawls as a part of the picture of individual advantage for use in his difference principle. But going much beyond that shared role with other concerns as a primary good, liberty also has, more selectively, an additional status, which has an importance of its own. Giving a special place – a general pre-eminence – to liberty goes well beyond taking note of the importance of liberty as one of many influences on a person's overall advantage. While personal liberty is indeed useful, like income and other primary goods, that is not all that is involved in its importance. It is a central concern both in a person's freedom, touching the most private aspects of personal life, and it is also a basic necessity (for example, in the form of freedom of speech) for the practice of public reasoning, which is so crucial to social evaluation.* The reasoned perception of the importance of

---

* On the various ways in which liberty, including freedom of expression, is crucially important for justice, see also Thomas Scanlon, *The Difficulty of Tolerance* (Cambridge: Cambridge University Press, 2003).

personal liberty has, not surprisingly, moved people to defend and fight for it over the centuries. By separating out the importance of liberty shared by all, Rawls draws attention to a distinction – between liberty and other helpful facilities – that is really important to note and pursue.[13]

Fifth, by insisting on the need for procedural fairness under the first part of the second principle, Rawls provided a significant enrichment of the literature on inequality in the social sciences, which has often tended to concentrate too exclusively on disparities in social *status* or economic *outcomes*, while ignoring disparities in the processes of operation, for example, those associated with excluding people from offices on grounds of their race or colour or gender.*

Sixth, after giving liberty its due and after recognizing the need to have openness in allowing people to compete equitably for offices and positions, the difference principle indicates the importance of equity in social arrangements so that attention is drawn particularly to the predicament of the worst-off people.[14] The removal of poverty measured in terms of the deprivation of primary goods is given a big place in Rawls's theory of justice, and this Rawlsian focus has indeed been powerfully influential on the analysis of public policy for poverty removal.

Finally (though this is very much my own reading, which others may or may not find to be a good interpretation of Rawls), by focusing on 'primary goods' (that is, on the general-purpose means for the pursuit of one's comprehensive goals), Rawls gives indirect acknowledgement to the importance of human freedom in giving people real – as distinct from only formally recognized – opportunity to do what they would like with their own lives. I shall argue later on, in Chapters 11 and 12, that the fit between a person's holding of primary goods and the substantive freedoms that the person can in fact enjoy, can be very imperfect, and that this problem can be addressed through focusing instead on the actual capabilities of people.[15] And yet by

---

* One of the reasons for the extraordinarily positive response that the election of Barack Obama to the presidency of the United States has received across the world is its demonstration of the weakening of the racial barrier in the politics of the country. This is a distinct issue from the evident suitability of Obama himself as a visionary leader, irrespective of his racial background.

instrumentally highlighting the importance of human freedom, Rawls has, I would argue, given a definitive place to freedom-related thinking within the main corpus of his theory of justice.*

## PROBLEMS THAT CAN BE ADDRESSED EFFECTIVELY

There are, however, problems and difficulties as well. Let me begin with a couple of problems that are important, but which can be, I believe, accommodated without going against Rawls's basic approach, and which have already been receiving considerable attention in the literature.

First, it has been argued that the total priority of liberty is too extreme. Why should we regard hunger, starvation and medical neglect to be invariably less important than the violation of any kind of personal liberty? That question was first raised powerfully by Herbert Hart shortly after Rawls's *Theory of Justice* was published,[16] and in his later works (particularly in his *Political Liberalism*), Rawls himself has gone some distance towards making the priority, in effect, less extreme.[17] It is indeed possible to accept that liberty must have some kind of priority, but total unrestrained priority is almost certainly an overkill. There are, for example, many different types of weighting schemes that can give partial priority to one concern over another.†

Second, in the difference principle, Rawls judges the opportunities

* Similarly, Philippe Van Parijs's powerful arguments for a basic income for everyone draws on its role in advancing each person's freedom; see his *Real Freedom for All: What (If Anything) Can Justify Capitalism* (Oxford: Clarendon Press, 1995).

† There is a mathematical issue of 'weighting' that might have had a role in influencing Rawls in the direction of the total lexicographic priority he gives to liberty. Rawls clearly found it wrong to put no more emphasis on liberty than on other facilities for human flourishing. This, it would appear, made him give liberty irresistible priority in every case of conflict, which seems much too strong, if my reading of Rawls's intention is right. In fact, the mathematics of weighting allows many intermediate positions of higher weighting of liberty (with varying degrees of intensity). Some of the methods of using weights much more flexibly are discussed in my *Choice, Welfare and Measurement* (1982), particularly in essays 9–12. There are many different ways of attaching some priority to one concern over another, without making that priority totally unbeatable under any circumstances (as implied by the 'lexical' form chosen by Rawls).

that people have through the means they possess, without taking into account the wide variations they have in being able to *convert* primary goods into good living. For example, a disabled person can do far less with the same level of income and other primary goods than can an able-bodied human being. A pregnant woman needs, among other things, more nutritional support than another person who is not bearing a child. The conversion of primary goods into the capability to do various things that a person may value doing can vary enormously with differing inborn characteristics (for example, propensities to suffer from some inherited diseases), as well as disparate acquired features or the divergent effects of varying environmental surroundings (for example, living in a neighbourhood with endemic presence, or frequent outbreaks, of infectious diseases). There is, thus, a strong case for moving from focusing on primary goods to actual assessment of freedoms and capabilities.* However, if my reading of Rawls's motivation in using primary goods is right (that is, to focus indirectly on human freedom), then I would argue that a move from primary goods to capabilities would not be a foundational departure from Rawls's own programme, but mainly an adjustment of the strategy of practical reason.†

## DIFFICULTIES THAT NEED FRESH INVESTIGATION

The problems discussed in the last section have received considerable attention, and continue to do so. While they have not been fully

---

* On this, see my 'Equality of What?' in S. McMurrin (ed.), *Tanner Lectures on Human Values*, vol. I (Cambridge: Cambridge University Press, and Salt Lake City, UT: University of Utah Press, 1980); *Commodities and Capabilities* (Amsterdam: North-Holland, 1985); *Inequality Reexamined* (Cambridge, MA: Harvard University Press, and Oxford: Oxford University Press, 1992); jointly with Martha Nussbaum (eds)., *The Quality of Life* (Oxford: Clarendon Press, 1993). The underlying issues are taken up in Chapters 11, 'Lives, Freedoms and Capabilities', and 12, 'Capabilities and Resources' of this work.
† See Philippe Van Parijs, *Real Freedom for All* (1995) on the strategic advantage in making use of the instrument of income even when the basic objective is to advance freedom. See also Norman Daniels, *Just Health* (2008).

resolved, there is reason to think that their central points are, by now, reasonably clear and understood. They will not be neglected in the rest of the book, but I will suggest that more immediate attention is needed to clarify some other problems with the Rawlsian approach that have not figured much in the ongoing literature.

## (1) The Inescapable Relevance of Actual Behaviour

First, the exercise of fairness through the approach of social contract is geared, in the Rawlsian case, to identifying only the 'just institutions', through arriving at 'an agreement on the principles that are to regulate the institutions of the basic structure itself from the present into the future'.[18] In the Rawlsian system of justice as fairness, direct attention is bestowed almost exclusively on 'just institutions', rather than focusing on 'just societies' that may try to rely on both effective institutions and on actual behavioural features.

Samuel Freeman, who with Erin Kelly has done a great job of gathering together and editing Rawls's extensive writings, summarizes Rawls's strategy in 'justice as fairness' in the following way:

Rawls applies the idea of a hypothetical social agreement to argue for principles of justice. These principles apply in the first instance to decide the justice of the institutions that constitute *the basic structure of the society*. Individuals and their actions are just insofar as they conform to the demands of just institutions . . . How [these institutions] are specified and integrated into a social system deeply affects people's characters, desires and plans, and their future prospects, as well as the kind of persons they aspire to be. Because of the profound effects of these institutions on the kinds of persons we are, Rawls says that the basic structure of society is 'the primary subject of justice'.[19]

We can see how different this *niti*-centred approach is from any *nyaya*-based approach to justice, for example that of social choice theory (see the contrast drawn in the Introduction). The latter would tend to ground the assessment of combinations of social institutions and public behaviour patterns on the social consequences and realizations they yield (taking note *inter alia* of any intrinsic importance that particular institutions and behaviour patterns may have within the social realizations to be assessed).

Two issues in particular in this comparison deserve special attention. First, the understanding of justice as *nyaya* cannot neglect the actual social realizations that may be expected to emerge from any choice of institutions, given other social features (including actual behaviour patterns). What really happens to people cannot but be a central concern of a theory of justice, in the alternative perspective of *nyaya* (without ignoring any intrinsic valuation that may be reasonably attached to having institutions and behaviour norms that are also seen as important on their own).

Second, even if we do accept that the choice of basic social institutions through a unanimous agreement would yield some identification of 'reasonable' behaviour (or 'just' conduct), there is still a large question about how the chosen institutions would work in a world in which everyone's actual behaviour may or may not come fully into line with the identified reasonable behaviour. The unanimous choice of the principles of justice is ground enough, Rawls argues, for their forming a 'political conception' of justice that all accept, but that acceptance may still be a far cry from the actual patterns of behaviour that emerge in any actual society with those institutions. Since no one has argued more powerfully and more elaborately than John Rawls for the need for 'reasonable' behaviour by individuals for a society to function well, he is clearly very aware of the difficulty in presuming any kind of spontaneous emergence of universal reasonable behaviour on the part of all members of a society.

The question to ask, then, is this: if the justice of what happens in a society depends on a combination of institutional features and actual behavioural characteristics, along with other influences that determine the social realizations, then is it possible to identify 'just' institutions for a society without making them contingent on actual behaviour (not necessarily the same as 'just' or 'reasonable' behaviour)? The mere acceptance of some principles as forming the right 'political conception of justice' does not resolve this issue if the theory of justice sought has to have any kind of applicability in guiding the choice of institutions in actual societies.

Indeed, we have good reasons for recognizing that the pursuit of justice is partly a matter of the gradual formation of behaviour patterns – there is no immediate jump from the acceptance of some principles of justice and a total redesign of everyone's actual behaviour in line with that political conception of justice. In general, the institutions have to be chosen not only in line with the nature of the society in question, but also co-dependently on the actual behaviour patterns that can be expected even if – and even after – a political conception of justice is accepted by all. In the Rawlsian system, the choice of the two principles of justice is meant to ensure both the right choice of institutions as well as the emergence of appropriate actual behaviour on the part of everyone, making individual and social psychology thoroughly dependent on a kind of political ethics. Rawls's approach, developed with admirable consistency and skill, does involve a formulaic and drastic simplification of a huge and multi-faceted task – that of combining the operation of the principles of justice with the actual behaviour of people – which is central to practical reasoning about social justice. This is unfortunate since it can be argued that the relationship between social institutions and actual – as opposed to ideal – individual behaviour cannot but be critically important for any theory of justice that is aimed at guiding social choice towards social justice.*

## (2) Alternatives to the Contractarian Approach

Rawls's method of investigation invokes 'contractarian' reasoning, involving the question: what 'social contract' would be accepted by everyone unanimously in the original position? The contractarian method of reasoning is broadly in the Kantian tradition,[20] and has been very influential in contemporary political and moral philosophy – to a great extent led by Rawls. Justice as fairness, as a theory, is situated by Rawls broadly within that tradition, and he describes his

---

* As I shall presently discuss, the relationship between these two features in the pursuit of justice was a major bone of contention in early Indian political thinking, for example between Kautilya on the one side and Ashoka on the other (see Chapter 3, 'Institutions and Persons'). This is also the subject matter of one of Adam Smith's central engagements in his investigation of political philosophy and jurisprudence; see *The Theory of Moral Sentiments* (T. Cadell, 1790; republished, edited by D. D. Raphael and A. L. Macfie, Oxford: Clarendon Press, 1976), and *Lectures on Jurisprudence, The Glasgow Edition of the Works and Correspondence of Adam Smith*, vol. 5, edited by R. L. Meek, D. D. Raphael and P. G. Stein (Oxford: Clarendon Press, 1978).

theory, as was noted in the Introduction, as an attempt 'to generalize and carry to a higher order of abstraction the traditional theory of social contract as represented by Locke, Rousseau, and Kant'.[21]

Rawls compares this mode of reasoning that yields a social contract with the utilitarian tradition that focuses on producing 'the most good summed over all its members, where this good is a complete good specified by a comprehensive doctrine'.[22] This is an interesting and important comparison, and yet Rawls's exclusive focus on this particular contrast allows him to neglect the exploration of other approaches that are neither contractarian nor utilitarian. To consider again the example of Adam Smith, he invokes the device of what he calls the 'impartial spectator' to base judgements of justice on the demands of fairness. This is neither a model of social contract, nor one of maximization of the sum-total of utilities (or indeed the maximization of any other aggregate indicator of the 'complete good').

The idea of addressing the issue of fairness through the device of the Smithian impartial spectator allows some possibilities that are not readily available in the contractarian line of reasoning used by Rawls. We need to examine the respects in which the Smithian line of reasoning, involving the impartial spectator, may be able to take note of possibilities that the social contract approach cannot easily accommodate, including:

(1) dealing with comparative assessment and not merely identifying a transcendental solution;
(2) taking note of social realizations and not only the demands of institutions and rules;
(3) allowing incompleteness in social assessment, but still providing guidance in important problems of social justice, including the urgency of removing manifest cases of injustice; and
(4) taking note of voices beyond the membership of the contractarian group, either to take note of their interests, or to avoid our being trapped in local parochialism.

I have already commented briefly, in the Introduction, on each of these problems that limit the contractarian approach and Rawls's theory of 'justice as fairness', and which demand more constructive engagement.

## (3) The Relevance of Global Perspectives

The use of the social contract in the Rawlsian form inescapably limits the involvement of participants in the pursuit of justice to the members of a given polity, or 'people' (as Rawls has called that collectivity, broadly similar to that of a nation-state in standard political theory). The device of the original position leaves one with little option here, short of seeking a gigantic global social contract, as Thomas Pogge and others have done in a 'cosmopolitan' extension of the Rawlsian original position.[23] The possibility of proceeding, in this case, through the Rawlsian sequence of setting up just institutions for the global society, i.e demanding a world government, is, however, deeply problematic, and in the Introduction I have already had occasion to comment on the scepticism that has prompted authors like Thomas Nagel to deny the very possibility of global justice.

And yet the world beyond a country's borders cannot but come into the assessment of justice in a country for at least two distinct reasons which were briefly identified earlier. First, what happens in this country, and how its institutions operate, cannot but have effects, sometimes huge consequences, on the rest of the world. This is obvious enough when we consider the operation of world terrorism or attempts to overcome their activities, or events such as the US-led invasion in Iraq, but the influences that go beyond national borders are altogether omnipresent in the world in which we live. Second, each country, or each society, may have parochial beliefs that call for more global examination and scrutiny, because it can broaden the class and type of questions that are considered in that scrutiny, and because the factual presumptions that lie behind particular ethical and political judgements can be questioned with the help of the experiences of other countries or societies. Globally sensitive questioning can be more important in a fuller assessment than local discussions on, say, the facts and values surrounding women's unequal position, or the acceptability of torture or – for that matter

– of capital punishment. The fairness exercise in Rawlsian analysis addresses other issues, in particular varying personal interests and priorities of individuals *within* a given society. The ways and means of dealing with the limitations of both vested interests and local parochialism will have to be investigated in the chapters that follow.

## JUSTITIA AND JUSTITIUM

I end this chapter by considering a different, and perhaps less momentous, issue. In the Rawlsian theory of 'justice as fairness', the idea of fairness relates to *persons* (how to be fair between them) whereas the Rawlsian principles of justice apply to the choice over *institutions* (how to identify just institutions). The former leads to the latter in Rawls's analysis (an analysis about which I have expressed some scepticism), but we must take note of the fact that fairness and justice are very distinct concepts in Rawlsian reasoning. Rawls explains the distinction between the two ideas with much care, and I have commented on that earlier in this chapter.

But how fundamental is the distinction between fairness and justice – a distinction that is clearly indispensable for Rawls's theory of 'justice as fairness'? I got a characteristically enlightening reply from John Rawls when I asked him to comment on a particular criticism of his approach that was put to me, in conversation, by Isaiah Berlin. 'Justice as fairness', Berlin had told me, can hardly be such a fundamental idea since some of the major languages in the world do not even have clearly distinguished words for the two. French, for example, does not have specialized terms for one without the other: 'justice' has to serve both the purposes.* Rawls replied that the actual existence of sufficiently distinguished specialized words is really of little significance; the main issue is whether people speaking in a language that lacks a distinction based on a single word can

* The English word 'fair' has Germanic roots, and comes from the old High German *fagar*, from which the Old English *faeger* originated. Their uses were originally mostly aesthetic, meaning 'pleasing' or 'attractive'. The use of 'fair' as 'equitable' begins much later, in Middle English.

nevertheless differentiate between the separate concepts, and go on to articulate the contrast using as many words as they need. I believe this is indeed the right answer to Berlin's question.* Words have their significance but we must not become too imprisoned by them.

There is an interesting contrast related to the word 'justice' itself to which my attention was drawn by W. V. O. Quine when he commented on an essay of mine. In his letter, dated 17 December 1992, Quine wrote to me:

I got thinking about the word *justice*, alongside *solstice*. Clearly, the latter, *solstitium*, is *sol* + a reduced *stit* from *stat-*, thus 'solar standstill'; so I wondered about *justitium*: originally a legal standstill? I checked in Meillet, and he bore me out. Odd! It meant a court vacation. Checking further, I found that *justitia* is unrelated to *justitium*. *Justitia* is *just* (um) + *-itia*, thus 'just-ness', quite as it should be, whereas *justitium* is *jus* + *stitium*.

After receiving Quine's letter, I was sufficiently worried about our heritage of democracy to look up immediately, with some anxiety, the *Magna Carta*, that classic document on democratic governance. Happily, I was reassured to find: 'Nulli vendemus, nulli negabimus aut differemus, rectum aut justitiam', which can indeed be translated: 'To no man will we sell, or deny, or delay, right or justice.' We have reason to celebrate the fact that the leaders of that great anti-authoritarian agitation not only knew what they were doing, they also knew which words to use (even though I can well imagine that the sitting judges in office across the world might be alarmed by the absence of any guarantee of 'court vacation' in the *Magna Carta*).

John Rawls's major contributions to the ideas of fairness and justice call for celebration, and yet there are other ideas that are present in his theory of justice that demand, as I have argued, critical scrutiny

---

* Even though, I must confess, it was amusing to speculate, when the French translation of Rawls's book on the virtues of 'justice as fairness' was about to come out, how the Parisian intellectual would cope with the challenging task of coming to grips with 'justice comme justice'. I should hasten to add that Rawls's French translator retained the distinction with well-chosen descriptions, and through emphasizing the basic idea as 'la justice comme équité' (see John Rawls, *Théorie de la justice*, translated by Catherine Audard (Paris: Editions du Seuil, 1987). See also John Rawls, *La justice comme équité: Une Reformulation de Théorie de la justice*, translated by Bertrand Guillaume (Paris: Éditions La Découverte, 2008).

and modification. Rawls's analysis of fairness, justice, institutions and behaviour has illuminated our understanding of justice very profoundly and has played – and is still playing – a hugely constructive part in the development of the theory of justice. But we cannot make the Rawlsian mode of thinking on justice into an intellectual 'standstill'. We have to benefit from the richness of the ideas we have got from Rawls – and then move on, rather than taking a 'vacation'. We do need 'justitia', not 'justitium'.

# 3

# Institutions and Persons

The belief that goodness has much to do with smartness, suggested by Wittgenstein (see Chapter 1), is not quite as novel as it might first appear. Indeed, a great many thinkers have pronounced on this issue over a long time, even though they may not have made the connection with the starkness of Wittgenstein's remark. To take an interesting example, Ashoka, the emperor of India in the third century BC and the author of numerous inscriptions on good and just behaviour, carved on durable stone tablets and pillars across the country and abroad, commented on this connection in one of his more famous inscriptions.

Ashoka argued against intolerance and in favour of the understanding that even when one social or religious sect of people find themselves opposed to other ones, 'other sects should be duly honoured in every way on all occasions'. Among the reasons he gave for this behavioural advice was the broadly epistemic one that 'the sects of other people all deserve reverence for one reason or another'. But he went on to say: 'he who does reverence to his own sect while disparaging the sects of others wholly from attachment to his own sect, in reality inflicts, by such conduct, *the severest injury on his own sect*'.[1] Ashoka was clearly pointing to the fact that intolerance of other people's beliefs and religions does not help to generate confidence in the magnanimity of one's own tradition. So there is a claim here that the lack of smartness in not knowing what may inflict 'the severest injury' on one's own sect – the very sect that one is trying to promote – may be stupid and counter-productive. That kind of behaviour would be, on this analysis, both 'not good' and 'not smart'.

Ashoka's thinking on social justice included not only his conviction that advancing the welfare and freedom of people in general is an important role for the state as well as of the individuals in society, but also that this social enrichment could be achieved through the voluntary good behaviour of the citizens themselves, without being compelled through force. Ashoka spent a good bit of his life trying to promote good, spontaneous behaviour in people towards each other, and the inscriptions that he erected across the country were a part of this effort.*

In contrast with Ashoka's focus on human behaviour, Kautilya, who was the principal adviser to Ashoka's grandfather Chandragupta (the Mauryan emperor who established the dynasty and was the first king to rule over nearly all of India) and author of the celebrated fourth-century BC treatise *Arthasastra* (broadly translatable as 'Political Economy'), put his emphasis on building up and making use of social institutions. Kautilya's political economy was based on his understanding of the role of institutions both in successful politics and in efficient economic performance, and he saw institutional features, including restrictions and prohibitions, as major contributors to good conduct and necessary restraints on behavioural licence. This is clearly a no-nonsense institutional view of advancing justice, and very little concession was made by Kautilya to people's capacity for doing good things voluntarily without being led there by well-devised material incentives and, when needed, restraint and punishment. Many economists today do, of course, share Kautilya's view of a venal humanity, but these views contrast sharply with Ashoka's optimistic belief in making people behave dramatically better by persuading them to reflect more, and by encouraging them to understand that dumb thought tends to yield coarse behaviour, with terrible consequences for all.

Ashoka almost certainly overestimated what can be done through

* The remarkable record of Ashoka's unusual social commitments, along with his widespread attempts at enhancing social welfare facilities for the people over whom he ruled, led to H. G. Wells's claim in *The Outline of History* that 'among the tens of thousands names of monarchs that crowd the columns of history, their majesties and graciousnesses and serenities and royal highnesses and the like, the name of Ashoka shines, and shines almost alone, a star' (H. G. Wells, *The Outline of History: Being a Plain History of Life and Mankind* (London: Cassell, 1940), p. 389).

behavioural reform alone. He had started as a severe and stern emperor, but underwent a major moral and political conversion after being revolted by the barbarity he saw in his own victorious war against a remaining unconquered territory in India (Kalinga, what is today's Orissa). He decided to change his moral and political priorities, embraced the non-violent teachings of Gautama Buddha, gradually disbanded his army and went about liberating the slaves and indentured labourers, and took on the role of a moral teacher rather than that of a strong ruler.[2] Sadly, Ashoka's vast empire dissolved into fragments of fractured territory not long after his own death, but there is some evidence that this did not happen during his own lifetime partly because of the awe in which he was held by the people at large, but also because he had not, in fact, fully dismantled the Kautilyan administrative system of disciplined rule (as Bruce Rich has discussed).[3]

While Ashoka was evidently not quite justified in his optimism about the domain and reach of moral behaviour, was Kautilya correct in being so sceptical about the feasibility of producing good results through social ethics? It seems plausible to argue that the perspectives of both Ashoka and Kautilya were incomplete in themselves, but both need attention in thinking of ways and means of advancing justice in society.

## THE CONTINGENT NATURE OF INSTITUTIONAL CHOICE

The interdependent roles of institutions and behavioural patterns in achieving justice in society are of relevance not only in assessing ideas of governance from the remote past, such as those of Kautilya and Ashoka, but also in their application, obviously enough, to contemporary economies and political philosophy.* One question that can be asked about John Rawls's formulation of justice as fairness is this:

* See Edmund S. Phelps's fine analysis of the interdependence in Friedrich Hayek's view of capitalism: 'Hayek and the Economics of Capitalism: Some Lessons for Today's Times', 2008 Hayek Lecture, Friedrich August von Hayek Institute, Vienna, January 2008.

77

if behaviour patterns vary between different societies (and there is evidence that they do), how can Rawls use the same principles of justice, in what he calls the 'constitutional phase', to establish basic institutions in different societies?

In answering this question, it must be noted that Rawls's principles for just institutions do not, in general, specify particular, physical institutions, but identify rules that should govern the choice of actual institutions. The choice of actual institutions can, therefore, take as much notice as may be needed of the actual parameters of standard social behaviour. Consider, for example, Rawls's second principle of justice:

Social and economic inequalities are to satisfy two conditions: first, they are to be attached to offices and positions open to all under conditions of fair equality of opportunity; and second, they are to be to the greatest benefit of the least advantaged members of society.[4]

Even though the first part may suggest that this is a straightforward demand for non-discriminatory institutions, which need not be conditional on behavioural norms, it is plausible to think that the requirements of 'fair equality of opportunity' could give a much greater role to behavioural features (for example, what kind of selection criteria would be effective given behavioural characteristics, and so on) in determining the appropriate choice of institutions.

When we turn to the second part of this principle for institutional choice (the important requirement that goes by its own name of 'the Difference Principle'), we have to examine how the different potential institutional arrangements would mesh with, and interact with, behavioural norms standard in the society. Indeed, even the language of the difference principle reflects the involvement of this criterion with what would actually happen in the society (that is, whether inequalities will work out to be of 'the greatest benefit of the least-advantaged members of society'). Again, this gives Rawls much more room to build in sensitivity to behavioural differences.

# BEHAVIOURAL RESTRICTION THROUGH CONTRACTARIAN REASONING

There is, however, also a second issue that is relevant in discussing the relation between actual behaviour and the choice of institutions. This issue, which was introduced in the last chapter, concerns Rawls's presumption that once the social contract has been arrived at, people would abandon any narrow pursuit of self-interest and follow instead the rules of behaviour that would be needed to make the social contract work. Rawls's idea of 'reasonable' behaviour extends to the actual conduct that can be presumed once those chosen institutions – unanimously chosen in the original position – have been put in place.[5]

Quite demanding assumptions are made by Rawls on the nature of *post-contract* behaviour. He puts the issue thus in *Political Liberalism*:

Reasonable persons . . . desire for its own sake a social world in which they, as free and equal, can cooperate with others on terms all can accept. They insist that reciprocity should hold within that world so that each benefits along with others. By contrast, people are unreasonable in the same basic aspect when they plan to engage in cooperative schemes but are unwilling to honour, or even to propose, except as a necessary public pretense, any general principles or standards for specifying fair terms of cooperation. They are ready to violate such terms as suits their interests when circumstances allow.[6]

By assuming that actual behaviour in the post-social contract world would incorporate the demands of reasonable behaviour in line with the contract, Rawls makes the choice of institutions that much simpler, since we are told what to expect in the behaviour of individuals once the institutions are set in place.

Rawls cannot, then, be accused in any way of either inconsistency or incompleteness in presenting his theories. The question that remains, however, is how this consistent and coherent political model will translate into guidance about judgements of justice in the world in which we live, rather than in the imagined world with which Rawls is here primarily concerned. Rawls's focus does indeed make sense, if the intention is to outline how to achieve the perfectly just social arrangements and, with the additional help of reasonable behaviour, a totally just society.* But this makes the distance between transcendental thinking and comparative judgements of social justice, on which I commented in the Introduction, that much larger and more problematic.

There is a real similarity here between Rawlsian presumptions about reasonable behaviour following the presumed agreements in the original position, and Ashoka's vision of a society led by right behaviour (or *dharma*), except that in Rawls's critical hands we get a much fuller picture of how things are supposed to work out in a world that we can try to get to, taking note of the dual role of institutions and behaviour. This can be seen as an important contribution to thinking about transcendental justice seen on its own. Rawls outlines his idealized transcendental vision for institutions and behaviours with force and clarity:

Thus very briefly: i) besides a capacity for a conception of the good, citizens have a capacity to acquire conceptions of justice and fairness and a desire to act as these conceptions require; ii) when they believe that institutions and social practices are just, or fair (as these conceptions specify), they are ready and willing to do their part in those arrangements provided they have reasonable assurance that others will also do their part; iii) if other persons with evident intention strive to do their part in just or fair arrangements, citizens tend to develop trust and confidence in them; iv) this trust and confidence becomes stronger and more complete as the success of cooperative arrangements is sustained over a longer time; and v) the same is true as the basic institutions framed to secure our fundamental interests (the basic rights and liberties) are more firmly and willingly recognized.[7]

* There is, however, an important issue here with regard to the adequacy of Rawlsian theory for the characterization of transcendental justice because of the concession that Rawls makes to inequalities needed to cater for the demands of incentives. If we accept G. A. Cohen's argument, presented in *Rescuing Justice and Equality* (Cambridge, MA: Harvard University Press, 2008), that this makes Rawls's theory quite unsatisfactory as a theory for perfect justice since there should be no concession to inequality to cajole people to behave right (what they should do even without personal incentives, in a just world), then surely the substantive content of the Rawlsian theory of perfect justice would be undermined. As was discussed in the last chapter, there is an important issue of theory here, since Rawls does make strong behavioural demands on individual conduct in the post-contract world, but exempts the need for ideal behaviour without incentives by accommodating incentives in the social contract itself.

This vision is both illuminating and in many ways hugely inspiring. And yet if we are trying to wrestle with injustices in the world in which we live, with a combination of institutional lacunae and behavioural inadequacies, we also have to think about how institutions should be set up here and now, to advance justice through enhancing the liberties and freedoms and well-being of people who live today and will be gone tomorrow. And this is exactly where a realistic reading of behavioural norms and regularities becomes important for the choice of institutions and the pursuit of justice. Demanding more from behaviour today than could be expected to be fulfilled would not be a good way of advancing the cause of justice. This basic realization must play a part in the way we think about justice and injustice today, and it will figure in the constructive work that follows in the rest of the book.

## POWER AND THE NEED
## FOR COUNTERVAILING

This is perhaps also the place where we must take note of a basic insight of John Kenneth Galbraith on the nature of appropriate social institutions that society may need. Galbraith was very aware of the negative influence of unchecked power, both because institutional balance is very important for society, but also because power corrupts. He argued for the importance of distinct social institutions that could exercise 'countervailing power' over each other. This requirement and its relevance are spelt out in Galbraith's 1952 book, *American Capitalism*, which also provides an unusual and illuminating account of how the success of American society is deeply dependent on the operation of the power of a multiplicity of institutions that check and balance the force and possible domination that might otherwise be exercised by one institution.[8]

Galbraith's analysis has much to offer on what has tended to go rather badly wrong in recent years in the USA as the executive branch has tried to exercise more unrestrained power than the American Constitution would seem to have intended. But even more strikingly, it also tells us a lot about what goes wrong in one-party states with commanding central control, like the former Soviet Union. Despite the early political enthusiasm and justice-related expectations that the October Revolution generated, huge political and economic failures soon came to characterize the USSR (including the purges, the show trials, the Gulags as well as its bureaucracy-dominated non-functioning economic and social institutions). The origin of these failures can, at least partly, be traced, I would argue, to the complete absence of countervailing powers in the Soviet institutional structure. The issue relates obviously to the absence of democracy, a subject to which I will return later on (in Chapter 15 'Democracy as Public Reason'). The issue of democratic practice can be closely linked with the existence and use of countervailing power in a society with a plurality of sources of voice and strength.

## INSTITUTIONS AS FOUNDATIONS

Any theory of justice has to give an important place to the role of institutions, so that the choice of institutions cannot but be a central element in any plausible account of justice. However, for reasons already discussed, we have to seek institutions that *promote* justice, rather than treating the institutions as themselves manifestations of justice, which would reflect a kind of institutionally fundamentalist view. Even though the arrangement-centred perspective of *niti* is often interpreted in ways that make the presence of appropriate institutions themselves adequate to satisfy the demands of justice, the broader perspective of *nyaya* would indicate the necessity of examining what social realizations are actually generated through that institutional base. Of course, the institutions themselves can sensibly count as *part* of the realizations that come through them, but they can hardly be the entirety of what we need to concentrate on, since people's lives are also involved.*

* Justice Stephen Breyer has brought out with much force and clarity the importance of paying 'attention to purpose and consequence' in interpreting a democratic constitution, emphasizing the role of 'consequences as an important yardstick to measure a given interpretation's faithfulness to these democratic purposes' (*Active Liberty: Interpreting Our Democratic Constitution* (New York: Knopf, 2005), p. 115).

There is a long tradition in economic and social analysis of identifying the realization of justice with what is taken to be the right institutional structure. There are a great many examples of such a concentration on institutions, with powerful advocacy for alternative institutional visions of a just society, varying from the panacea of wonderfully performing free markets and free trade to the Shangri-La of socially owned means of production and magically efficient central planning. There are, however, good evidential reasons to think that none of these grand institutional formulae typically deliver what their visionary advocates hope, and that their actual success in generating good social realizations is thoroughly contingent on varying social, economic, political and cultural circumstances.[9] Institutional fundamentalism may not only ride roughshod over the complexity of societies, but quite often the self-satisfaction that goes with alleged institutional wisdom even prevents critical examination of the actual consequences of having the recommended institutions. Indeed, in the purely institutional view, there is, at least formally, no story of justice beyond establishing the 'just institutions'. Yet, whatever good institutions may be associated with, it is hard to think of them as being basically good in themselves, rather than possibly being effective ways of realizing acceptable or excellent social achievements.

All this would seem to be easy enough to appreciate. And yet institutionalist fundamentalism is very often implied by the nature of the chosen institution-focused advocacy, even in political philosophy. For example, in his deservedly famous exploration of 'morals by agreement', David Gauthier relies on agreements between different parties that take the form of accord on institutional arrangements, and this is supposed to take us all the way to social justice. The institutions are given an overwhelming priority – a priority that may seem immune to the nature of the actual consequences generated by the agreed institutions. As it happens, Gauthier relies heavily on the market economy doing its job in producing efficient arrangements, on which the parties seeking agreement are imagined to focus, and once the 'right' institutions have been set up, we are supposed to be in the secure hands of these institutions. Gauthier argues lucidly that the setting up of the right institutions liberates the parties from having to be constantly constrained by morality as well. The chapter of

Gauthier's book where all this is explained is aptly named 'The Market: Freedom from Morality'.[10]

Giving such a foundational role to institutions for the assessment of social justice, in the way that David Gauthier does, may be somewhat exceptional, but there are many other philosophers who have been clearly tempted in that direction. There is evidently considerable attraction in assuming institutions to be inviolable once they are imagined to be rationally chosen by some hypothetical just agreement, irrespective of what the institutions actually achieve. The general point at issue here is whether we can leave matters to the choice of institutions (obviously chosen with an eye to results to the extent that they enter the negotiations and agreements) but without questioning the status of the agreements and of the institutions *once* the arrangements have been chosen, no matter what the actual consequences prove to be.*

There are some theories, which do not take the form of being institutionally fundamentalist in the way that Gauthier's theory is, but which share the priority of chosen institutions over the nature of the outcomes and realizations. For example, when Robert Nozick argues for the necessity, for reasons of justice, of guaranteeing individual liberties, including the rights of property ownership, free exchange, free transfer and free inheritance, he makes the institutions needed for these rights (the legal as well as the economic framework) essential requirements of his vision of a just society.[11] And he is ready to leave matters in the hands of these institutions rather than calling for any revision based on an assessment of outcomes (no 'patterning' of outcome is allowed in his theory, at least in its pure form). Formally, there is still a difference between valuing the institutions themselves and seeing an institution as being essential to justice because of its being necessary for the realization of something else, such as the 'rights' of people, as in the Nozickian system. The distinction is, however, rather formal, and it would not be entirely misleading to see Nozick's theory to be derivatively fundamentalist about institutions.

* The advocacy for a market economy need not, however, ignore the conditional nature of the support; see, for example, John Gray's strong defence of the market as an institution which takes a consequence-contingent form (*The Moral Foundations of Market Institutions* (London: IEA Health and Welfare Unit, 1992)).

But what if the collectivity of what are taken to be 'just institutions' generates terrible results for the people in that society (without actually violating their immediate concerns, such as the guarantee of libertarian rights, as in Nozick's case)?* Nozick did recognize that there could be a problem here. Indeed, he proceeded to make a possible exception to the case in which the system advocated by him, with complete priority of libertarian rights, would lead to what he called 'catastrophic moral horror'.† The institutional requirements might well be dropped in those extreme cases. But once such an exception is made, it is not clear what remains of the basic priorities in his theory of justice, and the fundamental place that is given to the necessary institutions and rules within that theory. If catastrophic moral horrors are adequate for abandoning the reliance on the allegedly right institutions altogether, could it be the case that bad social consequences that are not absolutely catastrophic but still quite nasty might be adequate grounds for second-guessing the priority of institutions in less drastic ways?

The more general issue, of course, is the basic unreliability of not being constantly sensitive to what actually happens in the world, no matter how excellent the institutions are taken to be. Even though John Rawls is quite clear in motivating the discussion on institutions in terms of the social structure they promote, nevertheless, through defining his 'principles of justice' entirely in institutional terms, Rawls too goes some distance towards a purely institutional view of justice.‡

---

* It can be shown that economic and political forces that generate even gigantic famines can work to yield that result without violating anyone's libertarian rights. On this, see my *Poverty and Famines: An Essay and Entitlement and Deprivation* (Oxford; Oxford University Press, 1981). See also Chapter 1, 'Reason and Objectivity'. See Cormac Ó Gráda, *Ireland's Great Famine: Interdisciplinary Perspectives* (Dublin: University College Dublin Press, 2006).

† Nozick does, however, leave the question open: 'the question of whether these side constraints reflecting rights are absolute, or whether they may be violated in order to avoid catastrophic moral horror, and if the latter, what the resulting structure might look like, is one I hope largely to avoid' (Robert Nozick, *Anarchy, State and Utopia* (Oxford: Blackwell, 1974), p. 30).

‡ It is, of course, true that in the Rawlsian system of 'justice as fairness' institutions are chosen with an eye to results. But once they are chosen through 'the principles of justice', there is no procedure within the system to check whether the institutions are, in fact, generating the anticipated results.

So do a number of other leading theorists of justice through their ultimate reliance on the soundness of the institutions they recommend on the basis of how they are expected to operate.

And here we do come to a parting of ways. In contrast with such institutional approaches, there are theories of justice and of social choice that take extensive note of the social states that actually emerge in order to assess how things are going and whether the arrangements can be seen as just. Utilitarianism takes such a view (even though its assessment of social states is confined to the limited perspective of utilities generated, ignoring everything else), but much more generally, so does social choice theory as an approach to evaluation and justice, as explored in a framework established by Kenneth Arrow, broadly in line with the normative approaches explored by Condorcet and Adam Smith, among others. There is no necessity here to rely only on utilities for the assessment of states of affairs, or, for that matter, only on 'end states' (as Robert Nozick calls them), ignoring the huge significance of the processes used. Rather, the comprehensive states of affairs that actually emerge are seen to be critically important in assessing whether we are doing the right thing, or could do better.

In the inclusive perspective of *nyaya*, we can never simply hand over the task of justice to some *niti* of social institutions and social rules that we see as exactly right, and then rest there, and be free from further social assessment (not to mention anything like 'freedom from morality', to use David Gauthier's colourful phrase). To ask how things are going and whether they can be improved is a constant and inescapable part of the pursuit of justice.

# 4

# Voice and Social Choice

As Alexander the Great roamed around north-west India in 325 BC, he engaged in a series of battles against the local kings in and around Punjab and won them all. But he was not able to generate enthusiasm among his soldiers to take on the powerful Nanda imperial family that ruled over the bulk of India from their capital city Pataliputra in eastern India (now called Patna). Alexander was not, however, ready to return quietly to Greece, and as a good student of Aristotle spent some considerable time holding relaxed conversations with Indian philosophers and theorists – religious as well as social.*

In one of the more vigorous debates, the world conquerer asked a group of Jain philosophers why they were neglecting to pay any attention to him. To this question, he received the following broadly democratic reply:

King Alexander, every man can possess only so much of the earth's surface as this we are standing on. You are but human like the rest of us, save that you are always busy and up to no good, travelling so many miles from your home, a nuisance to yourself and to others! . . . You will soon be dead, and then you will own just as much of the earth as will suffice to bury you.[1]

---

* India was full of intellectual heterodoxy at that time, roughly the period when the great epics, the *Ramayana* (in particular the *Valmiki Ramayana*) and the *Mahabharata*, were composed, which are dated between the seventh and the fifth centuries BC. The huge heterodoxy of beliefs and reasonings within the epics is discussed in my Foreword to the new Clay Sanskrit Library edition of the *Valmiki Ramayana*, edited by Richard Gombrich and Sheldon Pollock (to be published by New York University Press). This was also the time when the rebellious teachings of Gautama Buddha and Mahavira Jain, from the sixth century BC, offered a huge challenge to the dominant religious orthodoxy.

We learn from his biographer, Arrian, that Alexander responded to this stern egalitarian reproach with the same kind of intense admiration that he had shown in his encounter with Diogenes, expressing huge respect for the interlocutor and conceding the argument made against him. But his own personal conduct, Arrian also noted, remained altogether unchanged: 'the exact opposite of what he then professed to admire'.[2]

Clearly, debates and discussions are not always effective. But they can be. Indeed, even in the case of Alexander, it is possible that these apparently idle chats – with Diogenes, with the Jains, and with many others – did have some effect on the expanding reach and liberality of his thinking and on his firm rejection of intellectual parochialism. But no matter what happened to Alexander himself, the channels of communication that his visit to India established had profound effects, over the centuries, on Indian literature, drama, mathematics, astronomy, sculpture and many other pursuits, deeply influencing the face of India in many radical ways.*

Understanding the demands of justice is no more of a solitarist exercise than any other human discipline. When we try to assess how we should behave, and what kind of societies should be understood to be patently unjust, we have reason to listen and pay some attention to the views and suggestions of others, which might or might not lead us to revise some of our own conclusions. We also attempt, frequently enough, to make others pay some attention to our priorities and our ways of thought, and in this advocacy we sometimes succeed, while at other times we fail altogether. Not only are dialogue and communi-

---

* As will be discussed later (in Chapter 15, 'Democracy as Public Reason'), it is also under Greek influence that the Indians would start their own experiments with democratic governance in municipal administration. On the other side, the Greeks also became much engaged in Indian ideas and philosophy, often in a somewhat romanticized form. On the similarities between Greek and Indian philosophies of that period, see the excellent study by Thomas McEvilley, *The Shape of Ancient Thought: Comparative Studies in Greek and Indian Philosophies* (New York: Allworth Press, 2002). Some of the similarities may have been independently generated, but there are also huge areas of influence and interaction as well. An important study, regrettably unpublished, is John Mitchener, 'India, Greece and Rome: East–West Contacts in Classical Times', mimeographed (Office of the UK Deputy High Commissioner, Kolkata, India, 2003).

cation part of the subject matter of the theory of justice (we have good reason to be sceptical of the possibility of 'discussionless justice'), it is also the case that the nature, robustness and reach of the theories proposed themselves depend on contributions from discussion and discourse.

A theory of justice that rules out the possibility that our best efforts could still leave us locked into some mistake or other, however hidden it might be, makes a pretension that would be hard to vindicate. Indeed, it is not defeatist for an approach to allow incompleteness of judgements, and also to accept the absence of once-and-for-all finality. It is particularly important for a theory of practical reason to accommodate a framework for reasoning within the body of a capacious theory – that, at any rate, is the approach to the theory of justice that this work pursues.

Theories of justice are not, however, taken by most mainstream practitioners to be anything like as general and underspecified as a framework of reasoning. Rather, these specialists seem determined to take us straightaway to some fairly detailed formula for social justice and to firm identification, with no indeterminacy, of the nature of just social institutions. Rawls's theory of justice illustrates this very well. As we have just seen, there is a lot of critical reasoning, involving respectively the pre-eminence of fairness, the conception of the original position, the nature of representation that is involved in the exercise and the type of unanimity that is expected in the choice of institutional principles in the original position. All such general reasoning takes us, we are assured, to quite clear-cut rules to follow as unambiguous principles of justice, with singular institutional implications. In the case of Rawlsian justice, these principles primarily include (as discussed in Chapter 2) the priority of liberty (the first principle), some requirements of procedural equality (first part of the second principle) and some demands of equity, combined with efficiency, in the form of giving precedence to promoting the interests and advantages of the worst-off group (the second part of the second principle). With all this particularized delineation in Rawlsian theory, there need be no great fear of being accused of indecisiveness.

But is there too much decisiveness here? If the reasoning presented so far is correct, then this degree of specification requires us to close our eyes to a number of relevant, indeed vitally important, considerations. The nature and content of the Rawlsian 'principles of justice' and the process through which they are derived may have the effect of leading to some seriously problematic exclusions, including:

(1) ignoring the discipline of answering comparative questions about justice, by concentrating only on the identification of the demands of a perfectly just society;

(2) formulating the demands of justice in terms of principles of justice that are exclusively concerned with 'just institutions', ignoring the broader perspective of social realizations;

(3) ignoring the possibly adverse effects on people beyond the borders of each country from the actions and choices in this country, without any institutional necessity to hear the voices of the affected people elsewhere;

(4) failure to have any systematic procedure for correcting the influence of parochial values to which any society may be vulnerable when detached from the rest of the world;

(5) not allowing the possibility that even in the original position different persons could continue to take, even after much public discussion, some very different principles as appropriate for justice, because of the plurality of their reasoned political norms and values (rather than because of their differences in vested interests); and

(6) giving no room to the possibility that some people may not always behave 'reasonably' despite the hypothetical social contract, and this could affect the appropriateness of all social arrangements (including, of course, the choice of institutions), made drastically simpler through forceful use of the sweeping assumption of compliance with a specific kind of 'reasonable' behaviour by all.*

* Some of these limitations have already been discussed, and others will be taken up in the chapters to follow. The last item in this list of omissions and commissions has received some attention in the standard literature, in a somewhat stylized form, through the recognition of the need for theories that deal with 'non-ideal' conditions. The other items, however, are not helpfully understood in terms of the distinction between 'ideal' and 'non-ideal' theories, and must not be brushed under the same carpet. The reach and limits of 'ideal theory' are instigated in an illuminating symposium on 'Social Justice: Ideal Theory, Non-Ideal Circumstances' in *Social Theory and Practice*, 34 (July 2008), led by Ingrid Robeyns and Adam Swift.

If these invitations to close our eyes to significant issues related to justice are to be resisted, then the identification and pursuit of the demands of justice may have to take a much broader and more contingent form. The importance of a framework for public reasoning – much emphasized by John Rawls himself – is particularly important in that larger exercise.

Perhaps the nature of the task can be clarified a little with the help of social choice theory, and I turn now to that line of inquiry.

## SOCIAL CHOICE THEORY AS AN APPROACH

Discussions about ethics and politics are not new. Aristotle wrote on these subjects in the fourth century BC with great reach and clarity, particularly in *Nicomachean Ethics* and *Politics*; his contemporary Kautilya in India wrote on them with a rather more rigidly institutional approach in his famous treatise on political economy, *Arthasastra* (as was discussed in the last chapter). But the exploration of the formal procedures of public decisions and their underlying – often hidden – normative presumptions began much later. One of the ways of going into those issues can be found in social choice theory, which, as a systematic discipline, first came into its own at the time of the French Revolution.

That subject was pioneered by French mathematicians working mostly in Paris in the late eighteenth century, such as Jean-Charles de Borda and the Marquis de Condorcet, who addressed the problem of arriving at aggregate assessments based on individual priorities in rather mathematical terms. They initiated the formal discipline of social choice theory through their investigation of the discipline of aggregation over individual judgements of a group of different persons.[3] The intellectual climate of the period was much influenced by the European Enlightenment, and in particular by the French Enlightenment (as well as the French Revolution), with its interest in reasoned construction of social order. Indeed, some of the early social choice theorists, most notably Condorcet, were also among the intellectual leaders of the French Revolution.

The motivation that moved the early social choice theorists included the avoidance of both arbitrariness and instability in procedures of social choice. Their work focused on the development of a framework for rational and democratic decisions for a group, paying attention to the preferences and interests of all its members. However, their theoretical investigations typically yielded rather pessimistic results. Condorcet showed, for example, that majority rule can be thoroughly inconsistent, with A defeating B by a majority, B defeating C also by a majority, and C in turn defeating A, by a majority as well (a demonstration that is sometimes called the 'Condorcet Paradox'). On the nature of these difficulties, a good deal of exploratory work (often, again, with further pessimistic results) continued in Europe through the nineteenth century. Indeed, some very creative people worked in this area and wrestled with the difficulties of social choice, for example Lewis Carroll, the author of *Alice in Wonderland*, who wrote on social choice under his real name, C. L. Dodgson.[4]

When the subject of social choice theory was revived in its modern form by Kenneth Arrow around 1950 (Arrow also gave the subject its name), he too was very concerned with the difficulties of group decisions and the inconsistencies to which they may lead. Arrow put the discipline of social choice in a structured and analytical form, with explicitly stated and examined axioms, demanding that social decisions satisfy certain minimal conditions of reasonableness, from which the appropriate social rankings and choices of social states would emerge.[5] This led to the birth of the modern discipline of social choice theory, replacing the somewhat haphazard approach of Condorcet, Borda and others with a recognition of the need to state explicitly which conditions must be satisfied by any social decision procedure in order to be acceptable, and allowing other contributors to vary Arrow's own axioms and demands, after reasoned critique.

That was the positive and constructive avenue that Arrow's pioneering work opened up. However, so far as his own axioms were concerned, Arrow dramatically deepened the pre-existing gloom by establishing an astonishing – and hugely pessimistic – result of apparently ubiquitous reach, which is now known as 'Arrow's impossibility theorem' (Arrow himself gave it the more cheerful name of 'General Possibility Theorem').[6] This is a mathematical result of remarkable elegance and power, which shows that even some very mild conditions of reasonable sensitivity of social decisions to what the members of a society want cannot be simultaneously satisfied by any social choice procedure that can be described as rational and democratic (as Arrow characterized these requirements, with some plausibility). Two centuries after the flowering of the ambitions of social rationality in Enlightenment thinking and in the writings of the theorists of the French Revolution, the subject of rational democratic decisions seemed to be inescapably doomed, just at a time when a peaceful world, full of new democratic commitment, was emerging from the gore of the Second World War.[7]

Arrow's pessimistic theorem, and a cluster of new mathematical results that followed his pioneering lead, together with the wide-ranging general discussions that were generated by this largely technical literature, eventually had a major constructive impact on the discipline of social choice.* It forced the theorists of group decisions to look deeply into what caused the apparently reasonable requirements of sensitive democratic practice to yield these impossibility results. It also emerged that while impossibilities and impasses of this kind can arise with considerable frequency and amazing reach, they can also be, in most cases, largely resolved by making the social decision procedures more informationally sensitive.[8] Information on interpersonal comparisons of well-being and relative advantages turns out to be particularly crucial in this resolution.[9]

Most of the mechanical procedures of political choice (like voting and elections) or economic assessment (like the evaluation of national income) can accommodate rather little information, except in the discussions that may accompany these exercises. A voting result, in itself, reveals nothing much except that one candidate got more votes

* The motivational as well as analytical connections between the impossibility theorems and the constructive departures that emerged are discussed in my Nobel Lecture 'The Possibility of Social Choice', *American Economic Review*, 89 (1999), and in *Le Prix Nobel 1998* (Stockholm: The Nobel Foundation, 1999). The mathematical relations involved are scrutinized in my *Choice, Welfare and Measurement* (Oxford: Blackwell; Cambridge, MA: Harvard University Press, 1997), and 'Social Choice Theory', in K. J. Arrow and M. Intriligator (eds), *Handbook of Mathematical Economics*, vol. 3 (Amsterdam: North-Holland, 1986).

than another. Similarly, the economic procedure of national income aggregation draws only on information about what was bought and sold at what prices, and nothing else. And so on. When all the information that we can put into the system of evaluation or decision-making takes such an emaciated form, then we have to be reconciled to those pessimistic results. But for an adequate understanding of the demands of justice, the needs of social organization and institutions, and the satisfactory making of public policies, we have to seek much more information and scrutinized evidence.

Kenneth Arrow himself joined others in pursuing ways and means of broadening the informational basis of social choice.[10] In fact, Condorcet too had already pointed in that direction in the 1780s in very general terms.[11] There is a close motivational link here with Condorcet's passionate advocacy of public education and particularly women's education: Condorcet was one of the first to emphasize the special importance of the schooling of girls. There is also a close connection with Condorcet's deep interest in enriching societal statistics, and with his commitment to the necessity of continuing public discussion, since they all help to advance the use of more information in the procedures of public choice and in the exploration of social justice.[12]

I shall return to these issues after considering the nature and implications of the huge difference between the formulations of social choice theory, with its focus on arriving at a ranking of alternative social realizations, and the form of mainstream theories of justice that concentrate not on the discipline of assessing improvements or declines of justice, but on the identification of the perfectly just social arrangements in the form of 'just institutions'.

## THE REACH OF SOCIAL CHOICE THEORY

Because of the apparent remoteness of formal social choice theory from matters of immediate interest, many commentators have tended to see its applicability as being extremely limited. The uncompromisingly mathematical nature of formal social choice theory has also contributed to this sense of the remoteness of the discipline of social choice from applicable practical reason. Certainly, actual interactions between the theory of social choice and the pursuit of practical concerns have tended to be significantly discouraged by what is seen as a big gulf between exacting formal and mathematical methods, on one side, and readily understandable public arguments, on the other.

Not surprisingly, social choice theory is seen by many commentators as being at some disadvantage, in terms of practical relevance, compared with philosophical analysis of social justice. Even though the writings of Hobbes or Kant or Rawls demand arduous deliberation and intricate reflection, their central messages have appeared, in general, to be much easier to absorb and use, compared with what emerges from the discipline of social choice theory. The mainstream philosophical theories of justice, therefore, appear to many to be much closer to the world of practice than social choice theory can aspire to be.

Is this conclusion right? I would argue that not only is this conclusion wrong, almost the exact opposite may be true, at least in an important sense. There are many features of social choice theory from which a theory of justice can draw a great deal, as will be discussed later, but I begin here by pointing to what is certainly one of the most important contrasts between social choice theory and mainstream theories of justice. As an evaluative discipline, social choice theory is deeply concerned with the rational basis of social judgements and public decisions in choosing between social alternatives. The outcomes of the social choice procedure take the form of ranking different states of affair from a 'social point of view', in the light of the assessments of the people involved.* This is very different from a search for the supreme alternative among all possible alternatives, with which

* As will be discussed presently, the individual rankings that serve as informational inputs in the process can be interpreted in many different ways, and that versatility is important for the reach of social choice theory and its ability to adapt the social choice format to varying problems of social assessment. See *Social Choice Re-examined*, edited by Kenneth J. Arrow, Amartya Sen and Kotaro Suzumura (London: Macmillan, 1997); *Handbook of Social Choice and Welfare*, vol. 1, edited by Kenneth J. Arrow, Amartya Sen and Kotaro Suzumura (Amsterdam and Oxford: Elsevier, 2002; vol. 2 forthcoming); *The Handbook of Rational and Social Choice*, edited by Paul Anand, Prasanta K. Pattanaik and Clemens Puppe (Oxford: Oxford University Press, 2009).

theories of justice from Hobbes to Rawls and Nozick are concerned.[13]

The distinction is important, for reasons that have already been discussed in earlier chapters. A transcendental approach cannot, on its own, address questions about advancing justice and compare alternative proposals for having a more just society, short of the utopian proposal of taking an imagined jump to a perfectly just world. Indeed, the answers that a transcendental approach to justice gives – or can give – are quite distinct and distant from the type of concerns that engage people in discussions on justice and injustice in the world (for example, iniquities of hunger, poverty, illiteracy, torture, racism, female subjugation, arbitrary incarceration or medical exclusion as social features that need remedying).

## THE DISTANCE BETWEEN THE TRANSCENDENTAL AND THE COMPARATIVE

Nevertheless, important as this elementary contrast is, the formal remoteness of the transcendental approach from functional judgements about justice does not in itself indicate that the transcendental approach cannot be the right approach. There might well be some less obvious connection, some relationship between the transcendental and the comparative that could make the transcendental approach the right way of proceeding to comparative assessments. That investigation must be undertaken, but the temptation to believe that any transcendental theory must carry within its body some justificatory grounds that would also help to resolve all comparative issues is not well founded. As it happens, some transcendental theorists not only concede that there is a gap here, but do so proudly enough, asserting the folly of going into the comparative sidetrack (and it is indeed a sidetrack in the purely transcendental perspective). Robert Nozick, for example, is content to demand that all libertarian rights be fulfilled (this is *his* transcendental picture), but dismisses the issue of trade-offs between failures in the fulfilment of different types of rights (he has little use for what he calls 'utilitarianism of rights').[14] Similarly, it is not easy to see how the diagnosis of perfection in the frameworks of

Hobbes, or Locke or Rousseau would take us to decisive comparisons among imperfect alternatives.

The story is more complex with Kant or Rawls, since their elaborate reasoning about the identification of the transcendental solution does offer clues to some – though not all – comparative issues as well. For example, Rawls's formulation of the difference principle, a component of his second principle of justice, gives us ground enough to rank other alternatives in terms of the respective advantages of the worst-off.[15] And yet this cannot be said about the other part of Rawls's second principle, in which different violations of fair equality of opportunity would have to be assessed by criteria on which Rawls does not give us anything like a definitive guidance. The same can be said of the violations of liberties, which would negate the fulfilment of the first principle, since liberties are of different types (as Rawls himself discusses), and it is not at all clear how different violations of liberties would be comparatively assessed. There are different ways of doing this, and Rawls does not privilege any one way over others. Indeed, he says relatively little on this question altogether. And that is, of course, fine for Rawls's purpose, since a transcendental identification does not demand that this further comparative issue be addressed. A transcendental theory need not be what was called, in the Introduction, a 'conglomerate' theory (resolving transcendental and comparative issues simultaneously), and even though there is more articulation in Rawlsian reasoning about comparative questions than in many other transcendental theories, a big chasm still remains. A conglomerate theory is not needed by Rawls for his principles of justice (identifying perfectly just institutions), and he does not offer one.

But does not a transcendental identification in itself tell us something about comparative issues, even when those issues are not explicitly confronted? Are there not some *analytical* connections here? Are we being led astray by artificial separations that do not exist? These doubts demand serious investigation. There are two questions, in particular, to address. First, could it be the case that transcendental identification of the perfectly just social arrangement will automatically tell us how to rank the other alternatives as well? In particular, can the answers to transcendental queries also take us, indirectly, to comparative assessments of justice as a kind of 'by-product'? In particular, could comparisons of 'distance from transcendence' at which the different societal arrangements stand be the basis of such comparative assessment? Could the transcendental approach be 'sufficient' for yielding much more than what its formal content suggests?

Second, if there is a query about sufficiency here, there is also one about necessity. Could it be the case that the transcendental question ('what is a just society?') has to be answered first, as an essential requirement, for a cogent and well-founded theory of *comparative* justice, which would otherwise be foundationally disjunctive and frail? Is the transcendental approach, aimed at identifying a perfectly just state, *necessary* for comparative judgements of justice as well?

Implicit beliefs in the sufficiency or the necessity (or both) of a transcendental approach for comparative assessment clearly have had a powerful role in the widespread conviction that the transcendental approach is crucial for the entire theory of justice.[16] Without denying the practical relevance of, or intellectual interest in, comparative judgements, the transcendental approach has appeared to many theorists to be a central requirement of a well-grounded theory of justice. The hypotheses of sufficiency and of necessity would, therefore, need closer examination to determine the substantive place of transcendental theories in the political philosophy of justice.

## IS THE TRANSCENDENTAL APPROACH SUFFICIENT?

Does a transcendental approach produce, as a by-product, relational conclusions that are ready to be drawn out, so that transcendence may end up giving us a great deal more than its overt form articulates? In particular, is the specification of an entirely just society sufficient to give us rankings of departures from justness in terms of comparative distances from perfection, so that a transcendental identification might *inter alia* entail comparative gradings as well?

The distance-comparison approach, even though it has some apparent plausibility, does not actually work. The difficulty lies in the fact that there are different features involved in identifying distance, related, among other distinctions, to different fields of departure, varying dimensionalities of transgressions, and diverse ways of weighing separate infractions. The identification of transcendence does not yield any means of addressing these problems to arrive at a relational ranking of departures from transcendence. For example, in a Rawlsian analysis of the just society, departures may occur in many different areas, including the breaching of liberty, which, furthermore, can involve diverse violations of distinctive liberties (many of which figure in Rawls's capacious coverage of liberty and its priority). There can also be violations – again, possibly in disparate forms – of the demands of equity in the distribution of primary goods (there can be many different departures from the demands of the 'difference principle').

There are many different ways of assessing the extent of each such discrepancy and of appraising the comparative remoteness of actual distributions from what the principles of full justice would demand. We have to consider, further, departures in procedural equality (such as infringements of fair equality of public opportunities or facilities) which figure within the domain of Rawlsian demands of justice (in the first part of second principle). To weigh these procedural departures *against* infelicities of emergent patterns of interpersonal distribution (for example, distributions of primary goods), which also figure in the Rawlsian system, would require distinct specification – possibly in axiomatic terms – of relative importance or significance (or 'trade-offs' as they are sometimes called in the somewhat crude vocabulary of multidimensional assessment). But these valuations, helpful as they would be, lie beyond the specific exercise of the identification of transcendence and are indeed the basic ingredients of a 'comparative' rather than a 'transcendental' approach to justice. The characterization of spotless justice, even if such a characterization were to emerge clearly, would not entail any delineation whatever of how diverse departures from spotlessness would be compared and ranked.

The absence of such comparative implications is not, of course, an embarrassment for a transcendental theory itself, seen as a free-standing achievement. The relational silence is not, in any sense, an 'internal' difficulty; indeed, some pure transcendentalists would be utterly opposed even to flirting with gradings and comparative assessments, and may quite plausibly shun relational conclusions altogether. They may point in particular to their understanding that a 'right' social arrangement must not, in any way, be understood as a 'best' social arrangement, which could open the door to what is sometimes seen as the intellectually slippery world of graded evaluations in the form of 'better' or 'worse' (linked with the relationally superlative 'best'). The absoluteness of the transcendental 'right' – against the relativities of the 'better' and the 'best' – may or may not have a powerfully reasoned standing of its own (I refrain from going into that issue here).* But it does not, of course, help at all – and that is the central point here – in comparative assessments of justice and therefore in the choice between alternative policies.

To be sure, members of any polity can imagine how a gigantic and totally comprehensive reorganization might be brought about, moving them at one go to the ideal of a fully just society. A no-nonsense transcendental theory can serve, in this sense, as something like the grand revolutionary's 'one-shot handbook'. But that marvellously radical handbook would not be much invoked in the actual debates on justice in which we are ever engaged. Questions on how to reduce the manifold injustices that characterize the world tend to define the domain of application of the analysis of justice; the jump to transcendental perfection does not belong there. It is also worth noting here the general analytical point, already noted in the Introduction, that the diagnosis of injustice does not demand a unique identification of 'the just society', since a univocal diagnosis of the deficiency of a society with, say, large-scale hunger, or widespread illiteracy, or rampant medical neglect, can go with very different identifications of perfectly just social arrangements in other respects.

Even if we think of transcendence not in the gradeless terms of 'right' social arrangements, but in the graded terms of the 'best' social arrangements, the identification of the best does not, in itself, tell us much about the full grading, such as how to compare two non-best alternatives, nor does it specify a unique ranking with respect to which

* See, however, Will Kymlicka, 'Rawls on Teleology and Deontology', *Philosophy and Public Affairs*, 17 (Summer 1988).

the best stands at the pinnacle; indeed, the same best may go with a great many different rankings at the same pinnacle.

To consider an analogy used earlier, the fact that a person regards the *Mona Lisa* as the best picture in the world does not reveal how she would rank a Picasso against a Van Gogh. The search for transcendental justice can be an engaging intellectual exercise in itself, but – irrespective of whether we think of transcendence in terms of the gradeless 'right' or in the framework of the graded 'best' – it does not tell us much about the comparative merits of different societal arrangements.

## IS THE TRANSCENDENTAL APPROACH NECESSARY?

Consider now the hypothesis that the identification of the best, or the right, is necessary, even if not sufficient, to rank any two alternatives in terms of justice. In the usual sense of necessity, this would be a somewhat odd possibility. In the discipline of comparative judgements in any field, relative assessment of two alternatives tends in general to be a matter between them, without there being the necessity to beseech the help of a third – 'irrelevant' – alternative. Indeed, it is not at all obvious why in making the judgement that some social arrangement X is better than an alternative arrangement Y, we have to invoke the identification that some quite different alternative, say Z, is the very 'best' (or absolutely 'right') social arrangement. In arguing for a Van Gogh over a Picasso we do not need to get steamed up about identifying the most perfect picture in the world, which would beat the Van Goghs and the Picassos and all other paintings in the world.

It might, however, be thought that the analogy with aesthetics is problematic since a person might not even have any idea of a perfect picture, in a way that the idea of 'the just society' has appeared to many to be clearly identifiable, within transcendental theories of justice. (I will argue presently that the existence of a best – or inviolate – alternative is actually not guaranteed even by as complete a ranking of relative achievements of justice as possible, but I proceed, for the moment, on the presumption that such an identification can be made.)

The possibility of having an identifiably perfect alternative does not indicate that it is necessary, or indeed useful, to refer to it in judging the relative merits of two other alternatives; for example, we may indeed be willing to accept, with great certainty, that Mount Everest is the tallest mountain in the world, completely unbeatable in terms of stature by any other peak, but that understanding is neither needed, nor particularly helpful, in comparing the peak heights of, say, Mount Kilimanjaro and Mount McKinley. There would be something deeply odd in a general belief that a comparison of any two alternatives cannot be sensibly made without a prior identification of a supreme alternative. There is no analytical connection there at all.

## DO COMPARATIVES IDENTIFY TRANSCENDENCE?

A transcendental identification is thus neither necessary nor sufficient for arriving at comparative judgements of justice. We should, however, examine a third type of connection that might conceivably link the comparative with the transcendental. Could it be the case that the comparative rankings of the different alternatives must *inter alia* also be able to identify the transcendentally just social arrangement? Would the transcendental invariably follow from the full use of the comparative? If that were the case, we could plausibly argue that in a somewhat weak sense there is a necessity for the tractability of the transcendental alternative. It would not, of course, imply that there is any need to go via the transcendental approach to comparative assessments, but it would at least give transcendental identification a necessary presence in the theory of justice, in the sense that if the transcendental question cannot be answered, then we should conclude that we cannot fully answer the comparative question either.

Would a sequence of pairwise comparisons invariably lead us to the very best? That presumption has some appeal, since the superlative might indeed appear to be the natural end-point of a robust comparative. But this conclusion would, in general, be a non sequitur. In fact, it is only with a 'well-ordered' ranking (for example, a complete and transitive ordering over a finite set) that we can be sure that the set of pairwise comparisons must also always identify a 'best' alternative.

We must, therefore, ask: how complete should the assessment be for it to be a systematic discipline? In the 'totalist' approach that characterizes the standard theories of justice, including Rawls's, incompleteness tends to appear as a failure, or at least as a sign of the unfinished nature of the exercise. Indeed, the survival of incompleteness is sometimes seen as a defect of a theory of justice, which calls into question the positive assertions that such a theory makes. In fact, a theory of justice that makes systematic room for incompleteness can allow one to arrive at quite strong – and strongly relevant – judgements (for example, about the injustice of continuing famines in a world of prosperity, or of persistently grotesque subjugation of women, and so on), without having to find highly differentiated assessments of every political and social arrangement in comparison with every other arrangement (for example, addressing such questions as: exactly how much tax should be put on the sale of petrol in any particular country, for environmental reasons?)

I have discussed elsewhere why a systematic and disciplined theory of reasoned evaluation, including assessment of social justice, need not take a 'totalist' form.* Incompleteness may be of the lasting kind for several different reasons, including unbridgeable gaps in information, and judgemental unresolvability involving disparate considerations that cannot be entirely eliminated, even with full information. For example, it may be hard to resolve the conflicting claims of different equity considerations, of which a very special case is the one chosen by Rawls in the form of lexicographic maximin, which gives total priority to the minutest gain of the worst-off group even when this entails huge losses for groups that are not the worst-off but

---

* This was a central feature of the approach to social choice theory that I tried to develop in my book *Collective Choice and Social Welfare* (1970). The issue is revisited, with response to critical comments, in some of my recent essays, including: 'Maximization and the Act of Choice', *Econometrica*, 65 (1997); 'The Possibility of Social Choice', *American Economic Review*, 89 (1999); and 'Incompleteness and Reasoned Choice', *Synthese*, 140 (2004). See also Isaac Levi's response to the last, in 'Amartya Sen', in the same number of *Synthese*, and his important book, *Hard Choices* (Cambridge: Cambridge University Press, 1986).

are very badly off, on which quite different reasonable positions can be taken by impartial observers. There may also be varying reasonable compromises in balancing small gains in liberty, which is given priority in Rawls's first principle, against any reduction in economic inequality – no matter how large. The importance of recognizing the plurality of reasons of justice has already been discussed earlier in this book, and this issue will be further examined in later chapters.

And yet, despite such durable ambiguity, we may still be able to agree readily that there is a clear social failure involved in persistent famines or in widespread exclusion from medical access, which calls urgently for remedying (thereby yielding an advancement of justice), even after taking note of the costs involved. Similarly, we may acknowledge the possibility that the liberty of different individuals may, to some extent, conflict with each other (so that any fine-tuning of the demands of 'equal liberty' may be hard to work out), and yet strongly agree that government-arranged torture of prisoners, or arbitrary incarceration of accused people without access to court procedures, would be an unjust violation of liberty that calls for urgent rectification.

There is a further consideration that may work powerfully in the direction of making political room for incompleteness of judgements about social justice, even if it were the case that every person had a complete ordering over the possible social arrangements. Since a theory of justice, in the standard forms, invokes agreement between different parties (for example in the unanimous agreement that is sought in the 'original position' in the Rawlsian framework), incompleteness can also arise from the possibility that distinct persons may continue to have some differences in assessments (consistently with agreeing on a great many comparative judgements). Even after vested interests and personal priorities have been somehow 'taken out' of consideration through such devices as the 'veil of ignorance', there may remain possibly conflicting views on social priorities, for example in weighing the claims of needs over entitlement to the fruits of one's labour (as in the example of the three children quarrelling about the use of a flute).

Even when all the parties involved have their own complete orderings of justice that are not congruent, the 'intersection' between the rankings – that is the *shared* beliefs of the different parties –

will yield a partial ranking, with different extents of articulation (depending on the extent of similarity between the orderings).[17] The acceptability of evaluative incompleteness is indeed a central subject in social choice theory in general, and it is relevant to theories of justice as well, even though Rawlsian 'justice as fairness' and other such theories firmly assert (and it *is* an assertion rather than something that is actually established by the arguments presented) that a full agreement will definitely emerge in the 'original position' and in other such formats.

Thus, for reasons both of incomplete individual evaluations and of incomplete congruence between different individuals' assessments, persistent incompleteness may be a hardy feature of judgements of social justice. This can be problematic for the identification of a perfectly just society, and make transcendental conclusions difficult to derive.* And yet, such incompleteness would not prevent making comparative judgements about justice in a great many cases – where there might be fair agreement on particular pairwise rankings – about how to enhance justice and reduce injustice.

Thus the hiatus between the relational approach and the transcendental approach to justice seems to be quite comprehensive. Despite its own intellectual interest, the question 'what is a just society?' is not, I have argued, a good starting-point for a useful theory of justice. To that has to be added the further conclusion that it may not be a plausible end-point either. A systematic theory of comparative justice does not need, nor does it necessarily yield, an answer to the question 'what is a just society?'

---

* On a mathematical point, it must be acknowledged that a transitive but incomplete ordering over a finite set will invariably yield one or more 'maximal' elements, in the sense of there being one or more alternatives that are undominated by any other element. A maximal set must not, however, be confused with a set of 'best' elements, since maximality does not guarantee the existence of a best element (only one that is no worse than any other). On the far-reaching relevance of the distinction between maximality (needed for an acceptable choice) and optimality (needed for making a perfect choice), see my 'Internal Consistency of Choice', *Econometrica*, 61 (1993), and 'Maximization and the Act of Choice', *Econometrica*, 65 (1997). The foundational nature of the mathematical distinction involved can be seen in N. Bourbaki, *General Topology*, Parts I and II, English translation (Reading, MA: Addison-Wesley, 1966), and *Theory of Sets* (Reading, MA: Addison-Wesley, 1968).

## SOCIAL CHOICE AS A FRAMEWORK FOR REASONING

What, then, are the points of relevance of social choice theory for the theory of justice? There are many connections, but I will focus here on seven points of significant contribution, in addition to the focus on social realizations (already discussed).[18]

### (1) Focus on the comparative, not just the transcendental

Perhaps the most important contribution of the social choice approach to the theory of justice is its concern with comparative assessments. This relational, rather than transcendental, framework concentrates on the practical reason behind what is to be chosen and which decisions should be taken, rather than speculating on what a perfectly just society (on which there may or may not be any agreement) would look like. A theory of justice must have something to say about the choices that are actually on offer, and not just keep us engrossed in an imagined and implausible world of unbeatable magnificence. As I have already discussed this contrast fairly extensively, I shall not comment further on it here.

### (2) Recognition of the inescapable plurality of competing principles

Social choice theory has given considerable recognition to the plurality of reasons, all of which demand our attention when issues of social justice are considered, and they may sometimes conflict with each other. This inescapable plurality may or may not lead to an impossibility result, yielding an impasse, but the need to take note of the possibility of durable conflicts of non-eliminable principles can be quite important in the theory of justice. In the chapters to follow, this plurality will be more fully explored.

## (3) Allowing and facilitating re-examination

Another feature of some importance is the way social choice theory has persistently made room for reassessment and further scrutiny. Indeed, one of the main contributions of results like Arrow's impossibility theorem is to demonstrate that general principles about social decisions that initially look plausible could turn out to be quite problematic, since they may in fact conflict with other general principles which also look, at least initially, to be plausible.

We often think, if only implicitly, of the plausibility of principles in a number of specific cases which focus our attention on those ideas – the human mind cannot often enough grasp the immense reach of general principles. But once the principles are formulated in unconstrained terms, covering *inter alia* a great many cases other than those that motivated our interest in those principles, we can run into difficulties that were not foreseen earlier, when we signed up, as it were, on the dotted line. We then have to decide what has to give and why. Some may find social choice theory to be too permissive and indecisive (Condorcet saw his results as the beginning of a discussion, not the end of it), but the alternative, well illustrated by mainstream theories of justice, like Rawls's or Nozick's, of inflexible insistence on exacting and highly demanding rules does not give the idea of justice its due.

## (4) Permissibility of partial resolutions

Social choice theory allows the possibility that even a complete theory of justice can yield incomplete rankings of justice. Indeed, the incompleteness in many cases can be 'assertive', yielding statements such as x and y *cannot* be ranked in terms of justice. This contrasts with an incompleteness that is tentatively accepted, while awaiting – or working towards – completion, on the basis of more information, or more penetrating examination, or with the use of some supplementary criteria.

The theory of justice has to make room for both kinds of incompleteness, assertive and tentative. Tentative incompleteness may reflect operational difficulties, rather than any deeper conceptual or valuational deadlock. The operational problems may relate to limitation of knowledge, or complexity of calculation, or some other practical barriers in application (the kind of considerations that have been illuminatingly and powerfully explored by Herbert Simon, leading to his important notion of 'bounded rationality').[19] Even when incompleteness is in this sense tentative, it may still be hardy enough to demand incorporation in a functioning theory of justice, combined with room for re-examination and possible extension. In contrast, with assertive incompleteness the partial nature of the resolution is an integral part of the conclusions advanced by a theory of justice, even though that theory itself could remain open to further scrutiny and revision.

## (5) Diversity of interpretations and inputs

The formal structure of social choice theory, which often takes the form of exploring functional connections, guided by sets of axioms, between individual rankings and priorities on the one hand, and social conclusions on the other, is open to alternative interpretations. For example, there has been considerable interest within the discipline in the distinction between the aggregation of individual interests and that of individual judgements.[20]

A person's voice may count either because her interests are involved, or because her reasoning and judgement can enlighten a discussion. Also, a person's judgement may be seen as important either because she is one of the parties directly involved (this may be called 'membership entitlement'), or because the person's perspective and the reasons behind it bring important insights and discernment into an evaluation, and there is a case for listening to that assessment whether or not the person is a directly involved party (this can be called 'enlightenment relevance').[21] In the Rawlsian universe of justice as fairness, it is the membership entitlement that seems to get all the attention at the political level (though Rawls devises the original position with the aim of cutting out the influence of their vested interests in the choice of principles of justice), whereas in the approach advanced by Adam Smith, invoking 'impartial spectators', distant voices may be given a very important place for their enlightenment relevance, for example to avoid parochialism of local perspectives. This contrast will be more fully explored in Chapter 6.

Sometimes the so-called 'individual' rankings and priorities can be seen not as those of distinct persons, but of different approaches by the same person to the decisional issues involved, all of which could command some respect and attention. Another variation relates to the possibility that the individual rankings may not be those of individual preferences at all (in any of its various senses), as is usually presumed in mainstream social choice theory, but diverse rankings yielded by different types of reasoning. In general, social choice theory as a discipline is concerned with arriving at overall judgements for social choice based on a diversity of perspectives and priorities.

## (6) Emphasis on precise articulation and reasoning

There is some general merit in the explicitness of fully stated axioms and carefully established derivations, which make it easier to see what is being assumed and what exactly they entail. Since the demands that are linked to the pursuit of justice in public discussion, and sometimes even in theories of justice, often leave considerable room for clearer articulation and fuller defence, this explicitness can itself be something of a contribution.

Consider, for example, the Rawlsian claim that in the original position there would emerge a contract with the priorities that he specifies, including the overall priority of liberty under his first principle, and the conditional priority of the interests of the poorest group, judged by the holdings of primary goods, under his second principle.* But there are other alternative contracts that also have appeal, and there may or may not be any clear agreement on this even in the circumstances of the original position. Rawls's conviction that his two principles would unanimously emerge in the original position is not backed by any kind of definitive reasoning, and it is not even fully clear which normative premises would lead to that exact choice or

---

* Rawls presents several arguments in his *Theory of Justice* (1971) on why these principles may appeal in the original position, and backs them up with somewhat broader arguments in his later writings, particularly *Political Liberalism* (1993).

would be consistent with it. In fact, a number of fairly detailed investigations in social choice theory have actually identified the axiomatic basis of these Rawlsian presumptions,[22] and helped to clarify what the debates are about. Even though the axiomatic correspondences do not resolve the difficult issue of being sure about what should be chosen, they show on which lines the normative debates may fruitfully proceed.

Given the complex nature of human values and social reasoning, they may often be hard to capture in precise axiomatic terms, and yet the need for explicitness, to the extent that can be achieved, must have much dialogic merit. How far to go towards axiomatization cannot but be, to a considerable extent, a matter of judgement in dealing with the competing claims of precise characterization, on the one hand, and the need to take note, on the other, of the complexities that may be hard to axiomatize but which are nevertheless significant concerns that can be usefully discussed in more general – and somewhat looser – terms. Social choice theory can play an important clarificatory role in this interactive process.

## (7) Role of public reasoning in social choice

Even though social choice theory was initiated by a number of mathematicians, the subject has had close association with the championing of public reason. The mathematical results can be inputs into public discussion, as Condorcet, himself a mathematician of distinction, wanted them to be. The impossibility results, including the voting paradox identified by Condorcet and the much more sweeping impossibility theorem established by Arrow, are partly designed to be contributions to a public discussion on how these problems can be addressed and which variations have to be contemplated and scrutinized.*

* A big contribution has been made in clarifying the role and importance of public reasoning in the works of James Buchanan, and the school of 'Public Choice' pioneered by him. See James Buchanan, 'Social Choice, Democracy, and Free Markets', and 'Individual Choice in Voting and the Market', both published in the *Journal of Political Economy*, 62 (1954). See also his *Liberty, Market and the State* (Brighton: Wheatsheaf Books, 1986), and jointly with Gordon Tullock, *The Calculus of Consent* (Ann Arbor, MI: University of Michigan Press, 1962).

Consider another impossibility theorem in social choice theory ('the impossibility of the Paretian liberal'), which shows the incompatibility of even a minimal insistence on the liberty of individuals over their respective personal lives, along with respect for unanimous preferences of all over any other choice.[23] This result, which I presented in 1970, was followed by a large literature on the nature and causation of this impossibility result and of course on its implications.[24] It leads, in particular, to critical scrutiny of the relevance of preference (making it clear that the reasoning behind a preference, even when unanimously held, can make a difference) as well as the right way of capturing the value of liberty and liberalism in social choice. (These issues will be further discussed in Chapter 14, 'Equality and Liberty'.) It has also led to discussions about the need for people to respect each other's rights over their own personal lives, since the impossibility result draws also on a condition that is called 'universal domain', which makes any set of individual preferences equally admissible. If it turns out, for example, that in order to safeguard the liberties of all, we have to cultivate tolerance of each other in our respective values, then that is a public reasoning justification for cultivating tolerance.[25] What is, formally, a mere impossibility result can thus have implications for various kinds of public reasoning, including questioning the normative standing of preferences, the understanding of the demands of liberty, and the need for re-examination of the norms of reasoning and behaviour.[26]

## MUTUAL DEPENDENCE OF INSTITUTIONAL REFORM AND BEHAVIOURAL CHANGE

As discussed earlier, there is a two-way relationship between the encouragement given to rethinking behaviour on grounds of social justice and the institutional need to advance the pursuit of social justice, given the behavioural parameters in a society. For example, Condorcet's insistence on the importance of women's education was linked, among other things, to his recognition of the need for women's voices in public affairs as well as in family and social life. The role of women's voices can, in turn, take us to giving priority in public policy to women's education as a part of the promotion of justice in society, both for its direct benefits and for its indirect consequences.

The role of education and enlightenment is central to Condorcet's approach to society. Consider, for example, his nuanced views on the population problem, in contrast with Malthus's single-minded worry about the failure of human rationality in stemming the tide. Condorcet preceded Malthus in pointing out the possibility of serious overpopulation in the world if the growth rate did not slow down – an observation from which Robert Malthus himself drew, as he acknowledged, when he developed his own alarmist theory of population catastrophe.

However, Condorcet also decided that a more educated society, with social enlightenment, public discussion, and more widespread women's education, would reduce the population growth rate dramatically and could even halt or reverse it – a line of analysis that Malthus completely denied and about which he chastised Condorcet for his gullibility.* Today, as Europe struggles with the fear of population contraction rather than explosion, and all over the world evidence accumulates on the dramatic effects of education in general and women's education in particular in reducing the growth rate of population, Condorcet's appreciation of enlightenment and interactive understanding has received much more vindication than Malthus's dire cynicism, which denied the role of uncoerced human reasoning in reducing family size.[27] Condorcet's emphasis on the role of individual and public reasoning on family decisions and social processes is well reflected in the theoretical underpinning of social choice theory as a general approach.

Indeed, the basic connection between public reasoning, on the one hand, and the demands of participatory social decisions, on the other,

---

* See Marie-Jean-Antoine-Nicolas de Caritat, Marquis de Condorcet's *Esquisse d'un tableau historique des progrès de l'esprit humain* (for later reprints of that volume, see *Œuvres de Condorcet*, vol. 6 (Paris: Firmin Didot Frères, 1847); recently republished, Stuttgart: Friedrich Frommann Verlag, 1968); Thomas Robert Malthus, *Essay on the Principle of Population, As It Affects the Future Improvement of Society with Remarks on the Speculation of Mr. Godwin, M. Condorcet, and Other Writers* (London: J. Johnson, 1798; in the Penguin Classics edition, edited by Anthony Flew, *An Essay on the Principle of Population* (Harmondsworth: Penguin Books, 1982)).

is central not just to the practical challenge of making democracy more effective, but also to the conceptual problem of basing an adequately articulated idea of social justice on the demands of social choice and fairness. Both these exercises have an important place in the task in which this work is engaged.

# 5

# Impartiality and Objectivity

The great royal fortress and prison in Paris, the Bastille, was stormed on 14 July 1789. As the revolution gathered momentum, the French National Assembly adopted the 'Declaration of the Rights of Man' in August, and in November forbade any of its members to accept office under Louis XVI. Did Edmund Burke, who spoke with such sympathy for the oppressed Indians under the rule of the East India Company (as was discussed in the Introduction) and who spoke up for the subjugated Americans in their own revolution in 1776, immediately welcome the French Revolution? Was he sympathetic to the Revolutionary Society which, in their famous meeting in London in November 1789, congratulated the French National Assembly for its radical commitment? The answer is no. Burke was thoroughly opposed to the French Revolution and unequivocally denounced it in Parliament in London in a speech in February 1790.

Burke was a Whig, but his position on the French Revolution was clearly conservative. Indeed, his assessment of that revolution led to his formulation of one of the foundation statements of modern conservative philosophy, in his *Reflections on the Revolution in France*. There is, however, no conflict in this with Burke's radical position on India, which was, at a basic level, conservative as well, since Burke was lamenting, among other things, the destruction of the old Indian social order and functioning society. Consistently with his conservative inclination, Burke was against the upheaval caused by the new British rule in India, and also against the upheaval occurring in France. In today's classificatory thinking, the former (Burke on British rule in India) may appear to be on the 'left', while the latter (Burke on the French Revolution) would be placed on the 'right', but they fit together perfectly well in terms of Burke's own principles and cohere nicely.

But what about the American War of Independence? There Burke was surely not conservative, supporting the upheaval in America, and in favour of big change. How does that fit? It is, I think, a mistake to try to interpret the different decisions that a person takes on a variety of disparate subjects in terms of just one classificatory idea – in this case conservatism. This applies particularly to Burke who had a far-reaching intellect and was involved with many distinct concerns, and who could draw attention to a number of separate features. But it also applies to a cluster of different reasons for justice that bear on any individual event. It would be absurd to try to explain Burke's attitudes to different events across his eighteenth-century world in terms of *one* inclination – conservative, radical or whatever.

And yet even in the case of the American Revolution, there was a strongly conservative element in the vision for the United States that Burke supported. Mary Wollstonecraft, the British radical activist and early feminist thinker, put some searching questions to Burke, not long after his speech in Parliament denouncing the French Revolution. Her critique came in a book in the form of a long letter: it included a criticism of Burke's position, not just on the French Revolution, but also on the American Revolution, which he supported. In an apparently puzzling remark, Wollstonecraft wrote: 'on what principle Mr Burke could defend American independence, I cannot conceive'.* What could the radical Mary Wollstonecraft be talking about in criticizing Burke for his support for the American Revolution?

Wollstonecraft was talking, in fact, about the inadequacy of a defence of liberty when it separates out some people whose liberty and independence should be cherished and protected, leaving the

---

* This was in the first of Wollstonecraft's two books on what we would now call 'human rights': the first one was entitled *A Vindication of the Rights of Men, in a Letter to the Right Honourable Edmund Burke; occasioned by his Reflections on the Revolution in France*, completed in 1790, to be followed two years later by her second book, *A Vindication of the Rights of Woman*. Both the monographs are included in Mary Wollstonecraft, *A Vindication of the Rights of Men and A Vindication of the Rights of Woman*, edited by Sylvana Tomaselli (Cambridge: Cambridge University Press, 1995).

plight of the others unaddressed. Wollstonecraft's opposition was to Burke's silence on the rights of American slaves while defending the freedom of the *non-slave* people clamouring for independence. This is what she said:

the whole tenor of his [Burke's] plausible arguments settles slavery on an everlasting foundation. Allowing his servile reverence for antiquity, and prudent attention to self-interest, to have the force which he insists on, the slave trade ought never to be abolished; and because our ignorant forefathers, not understanding the native dignity of man, sanctioned a traffic that outrages every suggestion of reason and religion, we are to submit to the inhuman custom, and term an atrocious insult to humanity the love of our country, and a proper submission to the laws by which our property is secured.[1]

Slavery would be abolished in the USA much later than its abolition in the British Empire: that would happen only after the Civil War in the 1860s. Wollstonecraft's criticism of Burke's view on the American Revolution can be seen, in hindsight, as going well beyond issues of theoretical consistency. Indeed, the United States took its time in coming to terms with the anomaly that seriously compromised America's commitment to freedom for all, thanks to the treatment of slaves. Indeed, even President Abraham Lincoln had not initially demanded political and social rights for the slaves – only some minimal rights, concerning life, liberty and fruits of labour – and this was seventy years after Mary Wollstonecraft's unequivocal pointer to the contradictions in the rhetoric of liberty in the United States.

The principal point that Mary Wollstonecraft is making here, as she does elsewhere, is that it is unsustainable to have a defence of the freedom of human beings that separates some people whose liberties matter from others not to be included in that favoured category.* Two years after Wollstonecraft's letter to Burke, she published the second of her two treatises on human rights, *A Vindication of the Rights of Woman*.[2] One of the themes running through this second

---

* Wollstonecraft's argument has a huge reach, applying, for example, to the status of untouchables in India (untouchability was tolerated in imperial days and would be abolished only after Indian independence in 1947), to the position of non-whites in apartheid-based South Africa (changed only after the fall of that regime), and to less clear-cut cases of exclusion based on class, or religion, or ethnicity.

volume is that we cannot defend being in favour of the rights of men without taking a similar interest in the rights of women. One of her central points here, as elsewhere, is that justice, by its very nature, has to have a universal reach, rather than being applicable to the problems and predicaments of some people but not of others.

## IMPARTIALITY, UNDERSTANDING AND OBJECTIVITY

Can there be a satisfactory understanding of ethics in general and of justice in particular that confines its attention to some people and not others, presuming – if only implicitly – that some people are relevant while others simply are not? Contemporary moral and political philosophy has by and large gone in Mary Wollstonecraft's direction, in denying that possibility and demanding that everyone be seen as morally and politically relevant.* Even if, for one reason or another, we end up concentrating on the freedoms of a particular group of people – for example, members of a nation, or a community, or a family – there has to be some kind of pointer that locates such narrow exercises within a broader and capacious framework that can take everyone into account. Selective inclusion on an arbitrary basis in a favoured category – among those whose interests matter or voices count – would be an expression of bias. The universality of inclusion of the kind that Wollstonecraft demands is, in fact, an integral part of impartiality, the place of which in ethics in general and in the theory of justice in particular was discussed earlier (in Chapter 1 in particular).

No one perhaps did as much as Immanuel Kant to make that universalist demand understood, including principles of the kind that are captured in the often-repeated Kantian formulation: 'Act always on such a maxim as thou canst at the same time will to be a universal

---

* A good collection of essays by a number of leading philosophers on how this battle for inclusion has been engaged – and largely won at the level of theory – can be found in the volume dedicated to the memory of Susan Moller Okin, *Toward a Humanist Justice: The Political Philosophy of Susan Moller Okin*, edited by Debra Satz and Rob Reich (New York: Oxford University Press, 2009).

law.'[3] When Henry Sidgwick, the great utilitarian economist and philosopher, enunciated his own demand for universal coverage, he attributed his understanding to Kant, despite the distance between utilitarianism and Kantian philosophy. Sidgwick put it this way in the Preface to his classic book, *The Methods of Ethics*: 'That whatever is right for me must be right for all persons in similar circumstances – which was the form in which I accepted the Kantian maxim – seemed to me to be certainly fundamental, certainly true, and not without practical importance.'[4] In describing Kant's maxim to be 'certainly true', Sidgwick makes use of language that some like to confine only to issues of science and epistemology, rather than being applicable in ethics.

Earlier I discussed how the impartiality of evaluation can provide an understandable and plausible idea of objectivity in moral and political philosophy. What may, in terms of the conventional separation of science and values, appear to be just mistaken speech, can reflect a discipline that the language itself has come to absorb. Indeed, when Sidgwick describes Kant's claim to be 'certainly true', the point that Sidgwick is making is clear enough, without our having to enter into an extensive debate on the sense in which ethical claims can be objective or true. The language of justice and injustice reflects a good deal of shared understanding and communication of the content of statements and claims of this kind, even when the substantive nature of the claims may be disputed after it is understood.

There are really two different issues of non-subjectivity here: one of comprehension and communication on an objective basis (so that each person's beliefs and utterances are not inescapably confined to some personal subjectivity that others may not be able to penetrate), and the other of objective acceptability (so that people can engage in debates about the correctness of the claims made by different persons). Wollstonecraft's claim about the essential correctness of including all persons in moral and political accounting, or Sidgwick's assertion of the truth of universality and unbiasedness, involve issues both of interpersonal comprehension, and of general verity. Both relate to the idea of objectivity in distinct ways. The literature on ethical objectivity has gone into each of these questions, and while they are interrelated, they are not exactly the same.

## ENTANGLEMENTS, LANGUAGE AND COMMUNICATION

I begin with the first subject – that of communication and interpersonal comprehension, which are central to public reasoning. Our language reflects the variety of concerns on which our ethical assessments draw. There are vast entanglements of facts and values here but, as Vivian Walsh has perceptively observed, 'while the phrase "entanglement of fact and value" is a convenient shorthand, what we are typically dealing with (as [Hilary] Putnam makes clear) is a *triple* entanglement: of fact, convention and value'.[5] The role that an understanding of conventions plays in making sense of our social and ethical inquiries is particularly worth emphasizing here.

Indeed, as Antonio Gramsci, perhaps the most innovative Marxist philosopher of the twentieth century, put it, nearly eighty years ago, in his *Letters from Prison*, while incarcerated in a fascist jail in Turi: 'In acquiring one's conception of the world one always belongs to a particular grouping which is that of all the social elements which share the same mode of thinking and acting. We are all conformists of some conformism or other, always man-in-the-mass or collective man.'[6]

There is a case for what may look like a bit of a digression here, to wit, Gramsci's focus on entanglements and the use of rules of language, which has far-reaching relevance for the development of contemporary philosophy. Gramsci's line of thinking had, I have tried to argue elsewhere,[7] a distant but important role in the substantial transition of Ludwig Wittgenstein, significantly influenced by Piero Sraffa, away from his largely doomed search for a full account of what is sometimes called, a little deceptively, 'the picture theory of meaning', broadly reflected in the *Tractatus Logico-Philosophicus* (1921). That putative understanding sees a sentence as representing a state of affairs by being a kind of a picture of it, so that a proposition and what it describes are meant to have, in some sense, the same logical form.

Wittgenstein's doubts about the soundness of this approach developed and matured after his return to Cambridge in January 1929 (he had been a student there earlier, working with Bertrand Russell).

In this transformation a major part was played by Piero Sraffa, an economist in Cambridge (located also, like Wittgenstein, at Trinity College) who was much influenced by, and closely collaborated with, Antonio Gramsci (among other places, in the intellectually active world of *L'Ordine Nuovo*, a journal founded by Gramsci and later banned by the fascist government of Mussolini). Wittgenstein would later describe to Henrik von Wright, the distinguished Finnish philosopher, that these conversations made him feel 'like a tree from which all branches have been cut'. It is conventional to divide Wittgenstein's work between the 'early Wittgenstein' and the 'later Wittgenstein', and the year 1929 was clearly the dividing line that separated the two phases. In the Preface to his momentous book *Philosophical Investigations*, Wittgenstein noted his debt to the criticism that 'a teacher of this university, Mr P. Sraffa, for many years unceasingly practised on my thoughts', adding that he was 'indebted to *this* stimulus for the most consequential ideas of this book'.[8]

Wittgenstein also told a friend (Rush Rhees, another Cambridge philosopher) that the most important thing that Sraffa taught him was an 'anthropological way' of seeing philosophical problems.[9] While the *Tractatus* tries to see language in isolation from the social circumstances in which it is used, the *Philosophical Investigations* emphasizes the conventions and rules that give the utterances particular meaning. And this is, of course, a part of what Vivian Walsh calls the 'triple entanglement', which greatly interested both Gramsci and Sraffa. The connection of this perspective with what came to be known as 'ordinary language philosophy', which became such a big discipline in Anglo-American philosophy, to a great extent under the influence of the 'later Wittgenstein', is easy to see.*

* Perhaps I should comment briefly here, if only in the interest of gossip, on an often-repeated anecdote about what is supposed to have been a pivotal moment in moving Wittgenstein from the world of the *Tractatus* to that of *Philosophical Investigations*. According to this story, when Wittgenstein told Sraffa that the way to understand the meaning of a statement is to look at its logical form, Sraffa responded by brushing his chin with his fingertips, which apparently is readily understood as a Neapolitan gesture of scepticism, and then asked, 'What is the logical form of *this*?' Piero Sraffa (whom, later on, I had the privilege of knowing well, first as a student and then as a colleague, at Trinity College, Cambridge) insisted that this account, if not entirely apocryphal ('I can't remember such a specific occasion'), was more of a

Gramsci put much emphasis on bringing out the role of ordinary language in philosophy, and he linked the importance of this epistemological issue with his social and political concerns. In an essay on 'the study of philosophy', Gramsci discusses 'some preliminary points of reference', which include the bold claim that 'it is essential to destroy the widespread prejudice that philosophy is a strange and difficult thing just because it is the specific intellectual activity of a particular category of specialists or of professional and systematic philosophers'. Rather, argued Gramsci, 'it must first be shown that all men are "philosophers", by defining the limits and characteristics of the "spontaneous philosophy" which is proper to everybody'. And what is part of this 'spontaneous philosophy'? The first item that Gramsci lists under this heading is 'language itself, which is a totality of determined notions and concepts and not just of words grammatically devoid of content'. The relevance of this to seeing language and communication in 'the anthropological way', which Sraffa championed to Wittgenstein, would be hard to miss, and it is indeed one of the important preoccupations of Gramsci's *Prison Notebooks*.

## PUBLIC REASONING AND OBJECTIVITY

Conformism is clearly needed in some form to enable understanding in any field, including ethical pronouncements, but then there is the further issue of acceptance of, or disagreement with, a claim that has been understood. As a political radical, Gramsci wanted to change people's thinking and priorities, but this also required an engagement with the shared mode of thinking and acting, since for our communication we have to be, as Gramsci was quoted earlier as saying, 'conformists of some conformism or other, always man-in-the-mass or

---

tale with a moral than an actual event ('I argued with Wittgenstein so often and so much that my fingertips did not need to do much talking'). But the story does illustrate rather graphically that the scepticism that is conveyed by the Neapolitan brushing of chin with fingertips (even when done by a Tuscan boy from Pisa, born in Turin) can be interpreted in terms of – and *only* in terms of – established rules and conventions (indeed, the 'stream of life' as Gramsci's circle used to call it) in the Neapolitan world.

collective man'. This is a kind of a dual task, using language and imagery that communicate efficiently and well through the use of conformist rules, while trying to make this language express non-conformist proposals. The object was to formulate and discuss ideas that are significantly new but which would nevertheless be readily understood in terms of old rules of expression.

The relevance of this dual task is easy to see when pursuing established ideas of justice and at the same time proposing additional ideas that a theory of justice needs to take into account. Since public reasoning and debates are central to the pursuit of justice (for reasons already discussed), the role of this dual engagement is quite central to the project of this book. What is particularly under scrutiny here in examining the correctness of an ethical proposal is the reasoning on which that claim is based and the acceptability of that way of reasoning. As was argued earlier (in Chapter 1), the issue of objectivity is centrally involved in this exercise. The demands of ethical objectivity, it was argued, relate closely to the ability to stand up to open public reasoning, and this, in turn, has close connections with the impartial nature of the proposed positions and the arguments in their support.

Mary Wollstonecraft's critique of Burke involves, first, establishing that Burke is really supporting the settlement of slavery on, as it were, 'an everlasting foundation' through his defence of the American demand for independence without any qualification. That expository exercise, then, takes Wollstonecraft to the denunciation of Burke's general position because of its exclusionary character, which goes against impartiality and objectivity. It would fall foul, for example, of Rawls's requirement for 'a political conviction [to be] objective', that 'there are reasons, specified by a reasonable and mutually recognizable political conception (satisfying those essentials), sufficient to convince all reasonable persons that it is reasonable'.[10] The need of objectivity for communication and for the language of public reasoning is followed by the more specific requirements of objectivity in ethical evaluation, incorporating demands of impartiality. Objectivity in each sense has a role in this exercise in public reasoning, and the roles are interrelated but not exactly the same.

# DIFFERENT DOMAINS
# OF IMPARTIALITY

The place of impartiality in the evaluation of social justice and societal arrangements is central to the understanding of justice, seen from this perspective. There is, however, a basic distinction between two quite different ways of invoking impartiality, and that contrast needs more investigation. I shall call them respectively 'open' and 'closed' impartiality. With 'closed impartiality', the procedure of making impartial judgements invokes only the members of a given society or nation (or what John Rawls calls a given 'people') for whom the judgements are being made. Rawls's method of 'justice as fairness' uses the device of an original position, and a social contract based on that, among the citizens of a given political community. No outsider is involved in, or a party to, such a contractarian procedure.

In contrast, in the case of 'open impartiality', the procedure of making impartial assessments can (and in some cases, must) invoke judgements, among others, from outside the focal group, to avoid parochial bias. In Adam Smith's famous use of the device of the 'impartial spectator', the requirement of impartiality requires, as he explains in *The Theory of Moral Sentiments*, the invoking of disinterested judgements of 'any fair and impartial spectator', not necessarily (indeed sometimes ideally not) belonging to the focal group.[11] Impartial views may come from far or from within a community, or a nation, or a culture. Smith argued that there is room for – and need for – both.

This distinction, which is important for the theory of justice, is the subject matter of the next chapter.

# 6

# Closed and Open Impartiality

Adam Smith's thought-experiment on impartiality invokes the device of the 'impartial spectator', and this differs substantially from the closed impartiality of 'justice as fairness'. The basic idea is pithily put by Smith in *The Theory of Moral Sentiments*, as the requirement, when judging one's own conduct, to 'examine it as we imagine an impartial spectator would examine it', or as he elaborated in a later edition of the same book: 'to examine our own conduct as we imagine any other fair and impartial spectator would examine it'.[1]

The insistence on impartiality in contemporary moral and political philosophy reflects, to a great extent, a strong Kantian influence. Even though Smith's exposition of this idea is less remembered, there are substantial points of similarity between the Kantian and Smithian approaches. In fact, Smith's analysis of the 'impartial spectator' has some claim to being the pioneering idea in the enterprise of interpreting impartiality and formulating the demands of fairness which so engaged the world of the European Enlightenment. Smith's ideas were not only influential among Enlightenment thinkers such as Condorcet who wrote on Smith. Immanuel Kant too knew *The Theory of Moral Sentiments* (originally published in 1759), and commented on it in a letter to Markus Herz in 1771 (even though, alas, Herz referred to the proud Scotsman as 'the Englishman Smith').[2] This was somewhat earlier than Kant's classic works, *Groundwork* (1785) and *Critique of Practical Reason* (1788), and it seems quite likely that Kant was influenced by Smith.

There is something of a sharp dichotomy between the Smithian approach of the 'impartial spectator', and the contractarian approach, of which Rawlsian 'justice as fairness' is a pre-eminent application.

The need to invoke how things would look to 'any other fair and impartial spectator' is a requirement that can bring in judgements that would be made by disinterested people from other societies as well – far as well as near. In contrast, the institutionally constructive character of the Rawlsian system restricts the extent to which the perspectives of the 'outsiders' can be accommodated within the exercise of impartial assessment. Even though Smith often refers to the impartial spectator as 'the man within the breast', one of the main motivations of Smith's intellectual strategy was to broaden our understanding and to widen the reach of our ethical inquiry.* Smith puts the issue thus (*The Theory of Moral Sentiments*, III.3.38, pp. 153–4):

In solitude, we are apt to feel too strongly whatever relates to ourselves ... The conversation of a friend brings us to a better, that of a stranger to a still better temper. The man within the breast, the abstract and ideal spectator of our sentiments and conduct, requires often to be awakened and put in mind of his duty, by the presence of the real spectator: and it is always from that spectator, from whom we can expect the least sympathy and indulgence, that we are likely to learn the most complete lesson of self-command.

Smith invoked the reflective device of the impartial spectator to go beyond reasoning that may – perhaps imperceptibly – be constrained by local conventions of thought, and to examine deliberately, as a procedure, what the accepted conventions would look like from the perspective of a 'spectator' at a distance. Smith's justification of such a procedure of open impartiality is spelt out thus:

We can never survey our own sentiments and motives, we can never form any judgment concerning them; unless we remove ourselves, as it were, from our own natural station, and endeavour to view them as at a certain distance from us. But we can do this in no other way than by endeavouring to view them with the eyes of other people, or as other people are likely to view them.[3]

* In his fine exposition of the importance of 'the common point of view' in moral philosophy, Simon Blackburn interprets Smith's use of the impartial spectator in that perspective (*Ruling Passions: A Theory of Practical Reasoning* (Oxford: Clarendon Press, 1998)). There is certainly that particular use of the impartial spectator in Smith's work. But Smith also uses that thought-experiment as a dialectical device to question and dispute commonly agreed beliefs. This is certainly an important use even if no common point of view, the relevance of which Blackburn rightly stresses, were to emerge.

Smithian reasoning thus not only admits but requires consideration of the views of others who are far as well as near. This procedure of achieving impartiality is, in this sense, open rather than closed and confined to the perspectives and understandings of the local community only.

## THE ORIGINAL POSITION AND THE LIMITS OF CONTRACTARIANISM

Even as the Rawlsian 'veil of ignorance' addresses effectively the need to remove the influence of the vested interests and personal slants of the diverse individuals within the focal group, it abstains from invoking the scrutiny of (in Smith's language) 'the eyes of the rest of mankind'. Something more than an 'identity blackout' *within* the confines of the local focal group would be needed to address this problem. In this respect, the procedural device of closed impartiality in 'justice as fairness' can be seen as being 'parochial' in construction.

In order to avoid a misunderstanding, let me explain that in pointing to the limited reach of Rawls's way of arriving at his 'principles of justice' (and through that, the determination of 'just institutions'), I am not accusing Rawls of parochialism (that would, of course, be preposterous). The questioning relates only to the particular strategy that Rawls uses in getting to 'justice as fairness' through the original position, which is only one part of his large corpus of work on political philosophy; for example, Rawls's analysis of the need for 'reflective equilibrium' in the determination of our personal preferences, priorities and sense of justice does not have any such restriction. Many of the points that Adam Smith made about the need for openness in being interested in what would be seen by 'the eyes of the rest of mankind' would have been, it is quite clear, endorsed rather than rejected by Rawls. Rawls's generally ecumenical interest as a political philosopher in arguments coming from different quarters is not in any doubt.* In the part of Rawlsian analysis that relates to the importance

---

* In response to some points I raised with Rawls in 1991, based on my first reading of the manuscript of his initial paper on 'Law of Peoples', which was later extended

of a 'public framework of thought', and the need to 'look at our society and our place in it objectively',[4] there is, in fact, much in common with Smithian reasoning.*

And yet the procedure of segregated 'original positions', operating in devised isolation, is not conducive to guaranteeing an adequately objective scrutiny of social conventions and parochial sentiments, which may influence which rules are chosen in the original position. When Rawls says that 'our moral principles and convictions are objective to the extent that they have been arrived at and tested by assuming [a] general standpoint', he is attempting to unlock the door for an open scrutiny, and yet, later on in the same sentence, the door is partially bolted by the procedural form of requiring conformity with the territorially isolated original position: 'and by assessing the arguments for them by the restrictions expressed by the conception of the original position'.[5]

It is the contractarian framework of 'justice as fairness' that makes Rawls confine the deliberations in the original position to a politically segregated group whose members 'are born into the society in which they lead their lives'.† There is not only no procedural barricade here against susceptibility to local prejudices, there is no systematic way of opening up the reflections in the original position to the eyes of

---

into a book, I received a characteristically kind and reassuring reply, in a letter dated 16 April 1991: 'I have a kind of cosmopolitan view of world society, or the possibility of one, though there are surely many variations.'

* There is even more similarity, as will be discussed later, between the Smithian framework of public reasoning and Thomas Scanlon's 'contractualist' approach, which differs from Rawls's contractarian model but retains what Scanlon sees as 'a central element in the social contract tradition going back to Rousseau', that is, 'the idea of a shared willingness to modify our private demands in order to find a basis of justification that others also have reason to accept' (Scanlon, *What We Owe to Each Other* (1998), p. 5). In the present discussion on contractarian reasoning, based on Rawlsian formulation, I am not including Scanlon's 'contractualist' approach, but I will come back to it in Chapters 8, 'Rationality and Other People', and 9, 'Plurality of Impartial Reasons'.

† More fully: 'Justice as fairness recasts the doctrine of the social contract . . . the fair terms of social cooperation are conceived as agreed to by those engaged in it, that is, by free and equal citizens who are born into the society in which they lead their lives' (Rawls, *Political Liberalism*, p. 23).

mankind. What is a matter of concern here is the absence of some procedural insistence on forceful examination of local values that may, on further scrutiny, turn out to be preconceptions and biases that are common in a focal group.

Rawls does, in fact, go on to note a limitation of his regionally confined formulation of justice, fashioned for the 'people' of one particular country or polity: 'At some point a political conception of justice must address the just relations between peoples, or the law of peoples, as I shall say.' That issue is indeed addressed by Rawls's later work (*The Law of Peoples* (1999)). But the 'just relations between peoples' is an altogether different issue from the need for an open scrutiny of the values and practices of any given society or polity, through a non-parochial procedure. The closed formulation of the programme of the Rawlsian 'original position' extracts a heavy price in the absence of any procedural guarantee that local values will be subjected to an open scrutiny.

The Rawlsian 'veil of ignorance' in the 'original position' is a very effective device for making people see beyond their personal vested interests and goals. And yet it does little to ensure an open scrutiny of local and possibly parochial values. There is something to learn from Smith's scepticism about the possibility of going beyond local presuppositions – or even implicit bigotry – 'unless we remove ourselves, as it were, from our own natural station, and endeavour to view them as at a certain distance from us'. The Smithian procedure includes, as a result, the insistence that the exercise of impartiality must be open (rather than locally closed), since 'we can do this in no other way than by endeavouring to view them with the eyes of other people, or as other people are likely to view them'.[6]

## CITIZENS OF A STATE AND OTHERS BEYOND

What are the problems in confining the coverage of points of view and concerns to members of a sovereign state? Is that not the way actual politics proceeds in a world made up of sovereign states? Should the idea of justice go beyond what practical politics tends to accommodate? Should those broader concerns not be placed instead in the basket of humanitarianism, rather than being included in the idea of justice?

There are at least three distinct problems here. First, justice is partly a relation in which ideas of obligation to each other are important. Rawls gives plentiful recognition to what we ought to do for each other, and how we may arrive at a 'reflective equilibrium' about what we – at least minimally – really ought to do for other human beings. As Immanuel Kant argued, many of the obligations that we recognize take the form of what he calls 'imperfect obligations', which are not defined in any particularly precise way, and yet they are neither absent nor negligible (I shall come back to this question in Chapter 17 of this book, in the context of discussing human rights). To argue that we do not really owe anything to others who are not in our neighbourhood, even though it would be very virtuous if we were to be kind and charitable to them, would make the limits of our obligations very narrow indeed. If we do owe some concern to others – people far as well as near, and even if the characterization of that responsibility is rather vague – then a suitably capacious theory of justice has to include those people within the orbit of our thoughts on justice (not just in the sequestered sphere of benign humanitarianism).

A theory of impartiality that is confined exactly within the borders of a sovereign state proceeds along territorial lines that do, of course, have legal significance but may not have similar political or moral perspicuity.* This is not to deny that we often do think of our identities in terms of groups that include some and firmly exclude others. But our sense of identities – in fact we have many – is not confined only within the borders of the state. We identify with people of the same religion, same language group, same race, same gender, same political beliefs, or same profession.[7] These multiple identities cut across national boundaries, and people indeed do things that they feel they really 'must' do, rather than virtuously accept to do.

Second, the actions of one country can seriously influence lives elsewhere. This is not only through the deliberate use of forceful means (for example, the occupation of Iraq in 2003), but also through

* I shall return to this issue for further investigation in the next chapter.

less direct influences of trade and commerce. We do not live in secluded cocoons of our own. And if the institutions and policies of one country influence lives elsewhere, should not the voices of affected people elsewhere count in some way in determining what is just or unjust in the way a society is organized, typically with profound effects – direct or indirect – on people in other societies?

Third, in addition to these concerns, there is Smith's pointer to the possibility of parochialism in neglecting all voices from elsewhere. The point here is not that voices and views elsewhere have to be taken into account just because they exist – they may be there but entirely uncompelling and irrelevant – but that objectivity demands serious scrutiny and taking note of different viewpoints from elsewhere, reflecting the influence of other empirical experiences. A different viewpoint poses a question, and even if in many cases the question may merit dismissal after adequate consideration, that need not always be the case. If we live in a local world of fixed beliefs and specific practices, parochialism may be an unrecognized and unquestioned result (as Smith illustrated with the intellectual support that the ancient Athenians, even Plato and Aristotle, gave to their established practice of infanticide, being unfamiliar as they were with societies that functioned well without that alleged necessity). Considering the views of others and the reasoning behind them can be an effective way of determining what objectivity demands.

To conclude this discussion, assessment of justice demands engagement with the 'eyes of mankind', first, because we may variously identify with the others elsewhere and not just with our local community; second, because our choices and actions may affect the lives of others far as well as near; and third, because what they see from their respective perspectives of history and geography may help us to overcome our own parochialism.

## SMITH AND RAWLS

Adam Smith's use of the impartial spectator relates to contractarian reasoning in a somewhat similar way to that in which models of fair arbitration (views on which can be sought from anyone) relate to those of fair negotiation (in which participation is confined to the members of the group involved in the original contract for a given 'people' of a particular sovereign country). In Smithian analysis, the relevant judgements can come from outside the perspectives of the negotiating protagonists; indeed, they can come from, as Smith puts it, any 'fair and impartial spectator'. In invoking the impartial spectator, it is not, of course, Smith's intention to give over the decision-making to the final arbitration of some disinterested and uninvolved person, and in this sense the analogy with legal arbitration does not work here. But where the analogy does work is in making room to listen to voices not on grounds of their coming from the group of deciders, or even from interested parties, but because of the importance of hearing the point of view of others, which may help us to achieve a fuller – and fairer – understanding.

This would, of course, be a hopeless move if we wanted to reach one complete assessment of justice that resolves every decisional problem.* The admissibility of incompleteness discussed earlier (in the Introduction and in Chapter 1), in a tentative or an assertive form, is part of the methodology of a discipline that can allow and facilitate making use of views of impartial spectators from far as well as near. They come in not as arbitrators but as people whose reading and assessment help us to achieve a less partial understanding of the ethics and justice of a problem, compared with confining attention only to the voices of those who are directly involved (and telling all others to go mind their own business). A person's voice may be relevant because he or she is a member of the group that is involved in the negotiated contract for a particular polity, but it may also be relevant because of the enlightenment and the broadening of perspectives that such a voice coming from outside the contracting parties might provide. The contrast between what were respectively called 'membership

---

* John Gray has argued, persuasively I think, that 'if liberalism has a future, it is in giving up the search for a rational consensus on the best way of life' (*Two Faces of Liberalism* (Cambridge: Polity Press, 2000), p. 1). There are also reasons for scepticism about a rational consensus on complete assessment of justice. This does not rule out reasoned agreement on ways and means of enhancing justice, for example through the abolition of slavery, or the removal of some particularly counter-productive economic policies (as, indeed, Smith discussed).

entitlement' and 'enlightenment relevance' in Chapter 4 is indeed a significant distinction. The pertinence of the former does not eliminate the importance of the latter.

There are also significant similarities between parts of Rawls's own reasoning and the exercise of open impartiality with the help of impartial spectators. As was mentioned earlier, despite the 'contractarian' form of Rawlsian theory of justice as fairness, the social contract is not the only device that Rawls invokes in his general approach to political philosophy, and even in his particular understanding of justice.* There is a 'background' to the imagined events in the original position that is important to examine here. Indeed, much of the reflective exercise happens even before the representatives of people are imagined to be congregating at the original position. The 'veil of ignorance' can be seen as a procedural demand of impartiality that is meant to constrain any person's moral and political reflections whether or not a contract is ultimately invoked. Furthermore, while the form of that exercise of impartiality remains 'closed' in the sense already discussed, it is clear that Rawls's intentions include *inter alia* the elimination of the hold of arbitrary influences related to past history (as well as individual advantages).

In seeing the original position as 'a device of representation', Rawls attempts to address various types of arbitrariness that may influence our actual thinking, which have to be subjected to ethical discipline to arrive at an impartial point of view. Even in the first statement of the motivation behind the original position, Rawls clarified this aspect of the exercise:

* It is particularly important not to try to box Rawls's far-reaching contribution to political philosophy into some sealed compartment called 'Original Position' or even 'Justice as Fairness'. My own experience is that one gains some major insights by reading Rawls's writings together, despite the hugeness of the corpus. This is now easier than it used to be, because in addition to his *A Theory of Justice* (1971), *Political Liberalism* (1993), and *The Law of Peoples* (1999), we have access to John Rawls, *Collected Papers*, edited by Samuel Freeman (Cambridge, MA: Harvard University Press, 1999); *Lectures on the History of Moral Philosophy* (2000); *A Theory of Justice* (revised edition, 2000); and *Justice as Fairness: A Restatement*, edited by Erin Kelly (Cambridge, MA: Harvard University Press, 2001). All of us who are influenced by Rawls's ideas and reasoning owe a huge debt to Erin Kelly and Samuel Freeman for putting together the later volumes of Rawls's work, often from difficult manuscripts.

The original position, with the formal features I have called 'the veil of ignorance,' is this point of view . . . These contingent advantages and accidental influences from the past should not affect an agreement on the principles that are to regulate the institutions of the basic structure itself from the present into the future.[8]

Indeed, given the use of the discipline of the 'veil of ignorance', the parties (that is, individuals under this veil) would already agree with each other when the point comes to negotiate a contract. In fact, noting this, Rawls does ask whether a contract is needed at all, given the pre-contract agreement. He explains that despite the agreement that would precede the contract, the original contract does have a significant role because the act of contracting, even in its hypothetical form, is itself important, and because the contemplation of the act of contracting – with a 'binding vote' – may influence the pre-contractual deliberations that occur:

Why, then, the need for an agreement when there are no differences to negotiate? The answer is that reaching a unanimous agreement without a binding vote is not the same thing as everyone's arriving at the same choice, or forming the same intention. That it is an undertaking that people are giving may similarly affect everyone's deliberations so that the agreement that results is different from the choice everyone would have otherwise made.[9]

Thus the original contract remains important for Rawls, and yet a substantial part of Rawlsian reasoning concerns pre-contractarian reflections, and in some ways runs on parallel lines to Smith's procedure involving fair arbitration. What, however, distinguishes the Rawlsian method, even in this part, from the Smithian approach, is the 'closed' nature of the participatory exercise that Rawls invokes through restricting the 'veil of ignorance' to the members of a given focal group.\*

\* There is also a difference between Smith and Rawls on how much unanimity we would expect from impartiality and fairness. We can have distinct – and competing – lines of reasoning that could all pass the test of impartiality: for example, all of them may satisfy Scanlon's requirement of being 'not reasonably rejectable', presented in his *What We Owe to Each Other* (1998). This is entirely consistent with Smith's approval of specific comparative judgements but not with a unique social contract that 'justice as fairness' expects from the Rawlsian original position.

This is in line with Rawls's inclination to acknowledge, in this context, only 'membership entitlement', without giving enough recognition in this specific exercise to 'enlightenment relevance'. This, as I have been arguing, is a serious limitation, and yet before I move on to the Smithian alternative approach (in which enlightenment relevance is extremely important), I must reaffirm that, despite the limitation of the Rawlsian framework, we do learn something very foundational from it about the place of impartiality in the idea of justice. Rawls shows with powerful reasoning why judgements of justice cannot be an entirely private affair that is unfathomable to others, and the Rawlsian invoking of 'a public framework of thought', which does not in itself demand a 'contract', is a critically important move: 'we look at our society and our place in it objectively: we share a common standpoint along with others and do not make our judgments from a personal slant'.[10] That move is further consolidated by Rawls's argument, particularly in *Political Liberalism*, that the relevant standard of the objectivity of ethical principles is basically congruent with their defensibility within a public framework of thought.*

How does this Rawlsian theory differ from the approach to a theory of justice that may be derived from extending Adam Smith's idea of the impartial spectator? There are many points of difference, but the three most immediate ones are: first, Smith's insistence on what is being called here open impartiality, accepting the legitimacy and importance of the 'enlightenment relevance' (and not just 'membership entitlement') of views from others; secondly, the comparative (and not just transcendental) focus of Smith's investigation, going beyond the search for a perfectly just society; and thirdly, Smith's involvement with social realizations (going beyond the search only for just institutions). These differences are, in some ways, related to

---

* As discussed earlier (pp. 42–4), there can be an argument about whether the Rawlsian approach is normative and not at all procedural in the way Habermas's approach is. Such a distinction would be, I argued, rather overdrawn and would miss some central elements in Rawls's own priorities and his characterization of democratic deliberation aided by the 'two moral powers' that he attributes to all free and equal persons. See, however, Christian List, 'The Discursive Dilemma and Public Reason', *Ethics*, 116 (2006).

each other, since the broadening of admissible voices beyond the confines of the local territory or polity can allow more non-congruent principles to be brought into consideration in answering a wide variety of justice-related questions. There will, of course, be considerable divergence between different impartial views – from far as well as near – but for reasons already outlined in the Introduction, this would yield an incomplete social ranking, based on congruently ranked pairs, and this incomplete ranking could be seen as being shared by all. Consideration of this shared partial ordering as well as reflection on the differences involved (related to the incomplete parts of the ranking) can very substantially enrich public reasoning on justice and injustice.*

The Smithian 'impartial spectator' is, of course, a device for critical scrutiny and public discussion. It need not, therefore, seek unanimity or total agreement in the way that the institutional straitjacket of Rawlsian theory of justice demands.† Any concurrence that may emerge need not go beyond a partial ordering with limited articulation, which can nevertheless make firm and useful statements. And, correspondingly, the agreements arrived at need not demand that some proposal is uniquely just, but perhaps only that it is plausibly just, or at least not manifestly unjust. Indeed, the demands of reasoned practice can, in one way or another, live with a good deal of incompleteness or unresolved conflicts. The agreement to emerge from 'a public framework of thought' can be of a partial but useful kind.

---

* However, it would also make it very difficult to expect that a perfectly just society can be unanimously identified. Agreements on particular justice-enhancing moves are material enough for public action (what was described earlier as 'plural grounding'), and for that guidance, unanimity on the nature of the perfectly just society is not needed.

† However, as was discussed earlier, Rawls's general reasoning goes well beyond his formal modelling. Indeed, despite the main features of his transcendental theory, based on translating the deliberations in the original position into principles that firmly establish a particular institutional structure for a just society, Rawls does allow himself the thought: 'given the many obstacles to agreement in political judgment even among reasonable persons, we will not reach agreement all the time, or perhaps even much of the time' (*Political Liberalism*, p. 118). This seems eminently right, even though it is not absolutely clear how this recognition tallies with the Rawlsian programme of structuring the basic institutions of the society in line with unique social contracts reflecting complete agreements between the parties involved.

## ON RAWLS'S INTERPRETATION
## OF SMITH

There are substantial similarities as well as differences between the open impartiality of the impartial spectator and the closed impartiality of the social contract. The question can be asked: can the impartial spectator really be the basis of a viable approach to moral or political assessment without being, directly or indirectly, parasitic on some version of closed impartiality, such as contractarianism? In fact, this issue has been addressed by John Rawls himself in the *Theory of Justice*, when he comments on the general device of the impartial spectator (*A Theory of Justice*, section 30, pp. 183–92).

Rawls interprets the impartial spectator conception as one particular example of the 'ideal observer' approach (p. 184). Seen in this way, the idea allows some freedom, as Rawls rightly notes, about how we may proceed from there to make the conception more specific. He argues that interpreted in this way, 'there is no conflict so far between this definition and justice as fairness' (p. 184). Indeed, it 'may well be the case that an ideally rational and impartial spectator would approve of a social system if and only if it satisfies the principles of justice which would be adopted in the contract scheme' (pp. 184–5).

This is certainly a possible interpretation of an 'ideal observer', but it is definitely not, as we have seen, Smith's conception of the 'impartial spectator'. It is indeed the case that the spectator can take note of what may be expected had there been an attempt to get to a Rawlsian social contract, but Smith requires the impartial spectator to go beyond that and at least see what the issues would look like with 'the eyes of other people', from the perspective of 'real spectators' – from both far and near.

Rawls, too, goes on to note that 'while it is possible to supplement the impartial spectator definition with the contract point of view, there are other ways of giving it a deductive basis' (p. 185). However, Rawls then proceeds, oddly enough, by looking at David Hume's writings rather than Adam Smith's. This, not surprisingly, leads him to consider the alternative of making the impartial spectator rely on 'satisfactions' generated by sympathetic consideration of the experiences of others, interpreting that: 'the strength of his approval is determined by the balance of satisfactions to which he had sympathetically responded' (p. 186). This, in turn, takes Rawls to the interpretation that the impartial spectator may really be a 'classical utilitarian' in disguise. Once that extremely odd diagnosis is made, Rawls's response is, of course, quite predictable – and predictably forceful. He points out that even in the first chapter of the *Theory of Justice* he has dealt with that point of view, and found reason to dispense with that approach since 'there is a sense in which classical utilitarianism fails to take seriously the distinction between persons' (p. 187).

Adding to this confusion, in discussing the history of classical utilitarianism, Rawls lists Adam Smith among its early proponents, along with Hume.[11] This is a hugely incorrect diagnosis, since Smith had firmly rejected the utilitarian proposal of basing ideas of the good and the right on pleasure and pain, and had also spurned the view that the reasoning needed for complex moral judgements can be reduced simply to counting pleasure and pain, or more generally, to reducing different relevant considerations into 'one species of propriety'.[12]

Thus, the Rawlsian interpretation of Adam Smith and of his use of the 'impartial spectator' is altogether mistaken.* More importantly, the impartial spectator approach need not in fact be based either on Rawlsian contractarianism or on Benthamite classical utilitarianism – the only two options that Rawls considers. Rather, the kind of diverse moral and political concerns that Rawls himself discusses so illuminatingly are precisely the ones that the impartial spectator has to grapple with, but without the additional (and in the Smithian perspective, inescapably arbitrary) insistence on closed impartiality. In the

---

* Given Rawls's command over the history of ideas and his extraordinary generosity in presenting the views of others, it is uncharacteristic that he pays so little attention to the writings of Smith, especially to *The Theory of Moral Sentiments*. In Rawls's far-reaching *Lectures on the History of Moral Philosophy* edited by Barbara Herman (Cambridge, MA: Harvard University Press, 2000), Smith does get five mentions, but these passing references are confined to his being (1) a Protestant, (2) a friend of Hume, (3) an amusing user of words, (4) a successful economist, and (5) the author of the *Wealth of Nations* published in the same year (1776) in which David Hume died. In general, it is rather amazing how little attention the Professor of Moral Philosophy at Glasgow, so influential in philosophical thinking of his time (including Kant's), gets from moral philosophers of our time.

approach of the impartial spectator, the need for the discipline of ethical and political reasoning firmly remains, and the requirement of impartiality stays paramount: it is only the 'closing' of that impartiality that is absent. The impartial spectator can work and enlighten without being *either* a social contractor, *or* a utilitarian in camouflage.

## LIMITATIONS OF THE 'ORIGINAL POSITION'

The original position as a device for generating principles of justice through the use of a particular interpretation of fairness can be subjected to scrutiny from several distinct perspectives. There is a question of motivational adequacy, in particular the possibility that Rawlsian reasoning is too confined to reasons of 'extended prudence', and restricts the reflections of 'reasonable persons' to thinking ultimately about how they can benefit from 'cooperating with others'.* This can be seen as something of a general limitation on the reach of impartial thinking modelled within the specific approach of a 'social contract', since a contract of this kind, as Thomas Hobbes had noted, is basically a device for mutually gainful cooperation. Impartiality need not always take the form of being linked with mutually gainful cooperation, and can also accommodate unilateral obligations that we may acknowledge because of our power to achieve social results that we have reason to value (without necessarily benefiting from those results).†

In what follows, I shall concentrate on some specific issues that are firmly related to the closed form of the impartiality pursued through the original position.[13] The possible limitations can be placed under three rather general headings.

(1) *Exclusionary neglect*: Closed impartiality can exclude the voice of people who do not belong to the focal group, but whose lives are

---

* See Rawls, *Political Liberalism* (1993). An immediate contrast can be found in Thomas Scanlon's more general criterion that does not draw on extended prudence (*What We Owe to Each Other*, 1998).
† This issue will be examined in Chapters 8, 'Rationality and Other People', and 9, 'Plurality of Impartial Reasons'.

affected by the decisions of that group. The problem is not adequately resolved by multi-staged formulations of closed impartiality, as in Rawls's 'the law of peoples'.

This problem will not arise if decisions taken by the focal group (for example, in the original position) do not have any effect on anyone outside the focal group, though that would be quite extraordinary unless the people lived in a world of completely separated communities. This issue can be particularly problematic for 'justice as fairness' in dealing with justice across borders, since the basic social structure chosen for a society can have an influence on the lives not only of members of that society, but also those of others (who are not accommodated in the original position for that society). There can be much vexation without representation.

(2) *Inclusionary incoherence*: Inconsistencies can potentially arise in the exercise of 'closing' the group when the decisions to be taken by any focal group can influence the size or composition of the group itself.

For example, when the size or composition of the population of a country (or a polity) is itself influenced – directly or indirectly – by the decisions taken in the original position (in particular, the choice of the basic social structure), the membership of the focal group would vary with decisions that are meant to be taken by the focal group itself. Structural arrangements, such as the Rawlsian 'Difference Principle', cannot but influence the pattern of social – and biological – intercourse and thus generate populations of different size and composition.[14]

(3) *Procedural parochialism*: Closed impartiality is devised to eliminate partiality towards the vested interests or personal objectives of individuals in the focal group, but it is not designed to address the limitations of partiality towards the shared prejudices or biases of the focal group itself.

The last two problems (viz. 'procedural parochialism' and 'inclusionary incoherence') have not received any systematic attention at all in the general literature, and have hardly even been identified. The first problem, 'exclusionary neglect', in contrast, has received much attention already, in one way or another. I begin with an examination of this relatively better recognized problem of the Rawlsian model of fairness, namely exclusionary neglect.

## EXCLUSIONARY NEGLECT AND GLOBAL JUSTICE

There is clearly an important issue in the neglect of the interests and perspectives of those who are not parties to the social contract of a polity but who bear some of the consequences of decisions taken in that particular polity. I would also argue that, in this context, we have to see clearly why the demands of 'global justice' may differ substantially from those of 'international justice'.[15] Open impartiality, through such devices as the Smithian impartial spectator, has insights to offer on this difficult subject. Relations between different countries or polities are omnipresent in an interdependent world, and operate in interactive ways. John Rawls himself, among others, has addressed this question specifically in the context of justice across borders through his proposal of 'the law of peoples', which invokes a second original position between representatives of different polities (or 'peoples').[16] Others too, including Charles Beitz, Brian Barry, Thomas Pogge, have also investigated this problem and suggested ways and means of dealing with it.[17]

Rawls's way of addressing the problem involves invoking another 'original position', this time involving representatives of different 'peoples'. With some oversimplification – not central in the present context – the two 'original positions' can be seen as being respectively *intra*national (between individuals in a nation) and *inter*national (between representatives of different nations). Each exercise is one of closed impartiality, but the two together cover the entire world population.

This procedure does not, of course, eliminate the asymmetry between different groups of affected people, since the different polities are diversely endowed in assets and opportunities, and there would be a clear contrast between covering the world population through a sequence of prioritized impartialities (as in Rawls's method), and covering it through one comprehensive exercise of impartiality (as in the 'cosmopolitan' version of the Rawlsian original position, presented by Thomas Pogge and others). However, the idea of one global exercise of social contract for the entire world population would appear to be deeply unrealistic – now or in the foreseeable future. Certainly, there is an institutional lacuna here.\*

What has to be borne in mind, however, is that the recognition of this forceful practical point nevertheless need not rule out the possibility of invoking the insights and instructions generated by a cross-border 'public framework of thought', as Smith (among many others) have tried to do. The relevance and influence of global discussions are not conditional on the existence of a global state, or even of a well-organized planetary forum for gigantic institutional agreements.

More immediately, even in the politically divisive world in which we live, we have to give fuller recognition to the fact that different persons across borders need not operate only through international (or 'inter-people') relations. The world is certainly divisive, but it is diversely divisive, and the partitioning of the global population into distinct 'nations' or 'peoples' is not the only line of division.† Nor does the national partitioning have any pre-eminent priority over other categorizations (as implicitly presumed in 'the law of peoples').

Interpersonal relations across country borders go far beyond international interactions in many different ways. The 'original position' of nations or 'peoples' would be peculiarly restricted in dealing with many of the cross-border effects of human action. If the effects of

---

\* Thomas Nagel's scepticism of global justice, in 'The Problem of Global Justice' (*Philosophy and Public Affairs*, 33 (2005)), discussed in the Introduction, would seem to have much greater relevance to the search for a cosmopolitan social contract than for global justice through the less demanding Smithian route of open impartiality. The cosmopolitan social contract is more heavily dependent on global institutions than the 'looser' Smithian approach is.

† It is interesting that the priority of exactly one specific partitioning of the global population has been proposed in many different political discussions, giving the pride of place, respectively, to a variety of *disparate* single categorizations. The categorization underlying the so-called 'clash of civilizations' is an example of a rival partitioning (see Samuel P. Huntington, *The Clash of Civilizations and the Remaking of the World Order* (New York: Simon & Schuster, 1996)), since national or polity-based categories do not coincide with categories of culture or civilization. The coexistence of these rival claims in itself illustrates why none of these putatively foundational partitions – allegedly foundational for ethics and politics – can easily drown the competing relevance of other partitions, and related to that, the need to consider other identities of human beings across the world. This question is further discussed in my *Identity and Violence: The Illusion of Destiny* (New York: W. W. Norton & Co., and London and Delhi: Penguin, 2006).

the operation of transnational corporations are to be assessed or scrutinized, they have to be seen for what they are, namely corporations that operate without borders, that take business decisions about legal registration, tax homes and similar contingent matters according to the convenience of business. They can hardly be fitted into the model of one 'people' (or 'nation') impacting on another.

Similarly, the ties that bind human beings in relations of duty and concern across borders need not operate *through* the collectivities of the respective nations.* To illustrate, a feminist activist in America who wants to do something to remedy particular features of women's disadvantage in, say, Sudan would tend to draw on a sense of affinity that need not work through the sympathies of the American nation for the predicament of the Sudanese nation. Her identity as a fellow woman, or as a person (male or female) moved by feminist concerns, may be more important in a particular context than her citizenship, and the feminist perspective may well be introduced in an exercise of 'open impartiality' without its being 'subsequent' to national identities. Other identities, which may be particularly invoked in other exercises of 'open impartiality', may involve class, language, literature, profession, etc., and can provide different and competing perspectives on the priority of nation-based politics.

Even the identity of being human – perhaps our most basic identity – may have the effect, when fully seized, of broadening our viewpoint correspondingly. The imperatives that we may associate with our humanity may not be mediated by our membership of smaller collectivities such as specific 'peoples' or 'nations'. Indeed, the normative demands of being guided by 'humanity' or 'humaneness' can build on our membership of the wide category of human beings, irrespective of our particular nationalities, or sects, or tribal affiliations (traditional or modern).†

---

* The variety of channels through which people interact with each other across the globe today, and their ethical and political significance, are illuminatingly discussed by David Crocker, *Ethics of Global Development: Agency, Capability and Deliberative Democracy* (Cambridge: Cambridge University Press, 2008).
† The nature of identity-based reasoning, even of the most permissive kind, including the identity of belonging to the group of all human beings, must, however, be distinguished from those arguments for concern that make no use of any particular *shared*

Behavioural correlates of global commerce, global culture, global politics, global philanthropy, even global protests (like those recently on the streets of Seattle or Washington or Melbourne or Prague or Quebec or Genoa) draw on direct relations between human beings – with their own standards, and their respective inclusions and priorities related to a variety of classifications. These ethics can, of course, be supported or scrutinized or criticized in different ways, even by invoking other inter-group relations, but they need not be confined to – or even be led by – international relations (or by 'the law of peoples'). There is something of a tyranny of ideas in seeing the political divisions of states (primarily, national states) as being, in some way, fundamental, and in seeing them not only as practical constraints to be addressed, but as divisions of basic significance in ethics and political philosophy.* They may involve very many diverse groups, with identities that range from seeing oneself as a businessman or a worker, as a woman or a man, as a libertarian or a conservative or a socialist, as being poor or rich, or as a member of one professional group or another (of, say, doctors or lawyers).† Collectivities of many different types may be invoked. International justice is simply not adequate for global justice.

This issue has a bearing also on contemporary discussions on human rights. The notion of human rights builds on our shared humanity. These rights are not derived from the citizenship of any country, or the membership of any nation, but are presumed to be claims or entitlements of every human being. They differ, therefore, from

---

*membership*, but nevertheless invoke ethical norms (of, say, kindness, fairness or humaneness) that may be expected to guide the behaviour of any human being. I will not, however, pursue this distinction further here (but see my *Identity and Violence: The Illusion of Destiny* (New York: W. W. Norton & Co., and London: Penguin, 2006)).

* There is a related issue of the tyranny that is imposed by the privileging of an alleged 'cultural' or 'racial' identity over other identities and over non-identity-based concerns; on this see K. Anthony Appiah and Amy Gutmann, *Color Conscious: The Political Morality of Race* (Princeton, NJ: Princeton University Press, 1996), and Susan Moller Okin, with respondents, *Is Multiculturalism Bad for Women?* (Princeton, NJ: Princeton University Press, 1999).

† Similarly, dedicated activists working for global NGOs (such as OXFAM, Amnesty International, Médecins sans Frontières, Human Rights Watch, and others) explicitly focus on affiliations and associations that cut across national boundaries.

THE IDEA OF JUSTICE

constitutionally created rights guaranteed for specified people (such as American or French citizens); for example, the human right of a person not to be tortured or subjected to terrorist attacks is affirmed independently of the country of which this person is a citizen, and also is quite irrespective of what the government of that country – or any other – wants to provide or support.

In overcoming the limitations of 'exclusionary neglect', use can be made of the idea of open impartiality embedded in a universalist approach, of the kind that relates closely to Smith's concept of the impartial spectator. That broad framework of impartiality makes it particularly clear why considerations of basic human rights, including the importance of safeguarding elementary civil and political liberties, need not be contingent on citizenship and nationality, and may not be institutionally dependent on a nationally derived social contract. Further, there is no need to presume a world government, or even to invoke a hypothetical global social contract. The 'imperfect obligations' associated with the recognition of these human rights can be seen as falling broadly on anyone who is in a position to help.*

The liberating role of open impartiality allows different types of unprejudiced and unbiased perspectives to be brought into consideration, and encourages us to benefit from the insights that come from differently situated impartial spectators. In scrutinizing these insights together, there may well be some common understanding that emerges forcefully, but there is no need to presume that all the differences arising from distinct perspectives can be settled similarly. As was discussed earlier, systematic guidance to reasoned decisions can come from incomplete orderings that reflect unresolved conflicts. Indeed, the recent literature in 'social choice theory', which allows 'relaxed' forms of outcomes (such as partial orderings), has made clear, social judgements are not rendered useless or hopelessly problematic just because the evaluative process leaves many pairs unranked and many conflicts unsettled.[18]

For the emergence of a shared and useful understanding of many substantive issues of rights and duties (and also of rights and wrongs)

---

* These issues will be more fully discussed later, in Chapter 17, 'Human Rights and Global Imperatives'.

there is no need to insist that we must have agreed complete orderings or universally accepted full partitions of the just, strictly separated from the unjust; for example, a common resolve to fight for the abolition of famines, or genocide, or terrorism, or slavery, or untouchability, or illiteracy, or epidemics, etc. does not require that there be a similarly extensive agreement on the appropriate formulae for inheritance rights, or income tax schedules, or levels of minimum wages, or copyright laws. The basic relevance of the distinct perspectives – some congruent, some divergent – of the people of the world (diversely diverse as we human beings are) is part of the understanding that open impartiality tends to generate. There is nothing defeatist in this recognition.

## INCLUSIONARY INCOHERENCE AND FOCAL GROUP PLASTICITY

The fact that the members of the focal group have a status in the contractarian exercise that non-members do not enjoy creates problems even when we confine our attention to one society – or one 'people' – only. The size and composition of the population may alter with public policies (whether or not they are dedicated 'population policies') and the populations can vary even with the 'basic structure' of the society. Any rearrangement of economic, political or social institutions (including such rules as the 'difference principle') would tend to influence, as Derek Parfit has illuminatingly argued, the size and composition of the group that would be born, through changes in marriages, mating, cohabitation and other parameters of repro- duction.[19] The focal group that would be involved in the choice of the 'basic structure' would be influenced by that choice itself, and this makes the 'closing' of the group for closed impartiality a potentially incoherent exercise.

To illustrate this problem of group plasticity, suppose there are two institutional structures, A and B, that would yield, respectively, 5 million and 6 million people. They could, of course, be all different people, but to show how difficult the problem is even with the most favourable assumptions, let us assume that the 6 million we are talking about include all the same 5 million people and then another million more. Who, we can now ask, are included in the original position in which social decisions are made which would *inter alia* affect the choice between A and B and thus influence the size and composition of the respective population groups?

To avoid this difficulty, suppose we take instead the larger group of 6 million people as the focal group who are included in the original position, and suppose also that it turns out that the institutional structure chosen in the corresponding original position is A, leading to an actual population of 5 million people. But then the focal group was wrongly specified. We can also ask: how did the non-existent – indeed, *never* existent – extra one million people participate in the original position? If, on the other hand, the focal group is taken to be the smaller number of 5 million people, what if the institutional structure chosen in the corresponding original position is B, leading to an actual population of 6 million people? Again, the focal group would turn out to be wrongly specified. The additional one million people, then, did not participate in the original position, which would have decided the institutional structures that would extensively influence their lives (indeed not just whether they are to be born or not, but also other features of their actual lives). If the decisions taken in the original position influence the size and composition of the population, and if the population size and composition influence the nature of the original position or the decisions taken there, then there is no way of guaranteeing that the focal group associated with the original position is coherently characterized.

The foregoing difficulty applies even when we consider the so-called 'cosmopolitan' or 'global' version of the Rawlsian 'justice as fairness', including all the people in the world in one large contractual exercise (as proposed, for example, by Thomas Pogge and others). The population plasticity problem would apply no matter whether we consider one nation or the entire world population.

However, when the Rawlsian system is applied to one particular 'people' in a larger world, there are further problems. In fact, the dependence of births and deaths on the basic social structure has some parallel also in the influence of that structure on the movements of people from one country to another. This general concern has some similarity with one of David Hume's grounds for scepticism about the conceptual relevance as well as the historical force of 'the original contract', already proposed in his own time:

> The face of the earth is continually changing, by the increase of small kingdoms into great empires, by the dissolution of great empires into smaller kingdoms, by the planting of colonies, by the migration of tribes . . . Where is the mutual agreement or voluntary association so much talked of?[20]

However, the point at issue, in the present context, is not only – indeed, not primarily – that the size and composition of the population is continually changing (important though this problem is), but that these changes are not independent of the basic social structures that are meant to be arrived at, in contractual reasoning, through the original position itself.

We must, however, examine further whether the dependence of focal group on the basic social structure is really a problem for Rawlsian justice as fairness. Does the focal group actually have to determine the basic social structure through the corresponding original position? The answer, of course, is straightforwardly yes, if the parties to the original position are meant to be exactly the focal group (that is, *all* – and *only* – the members of the polity or society). But sometimes Rawls speaks of 'the original position' as 'simply a device of representation'.[21] It might, thus, be tempting to argue that we do not have to assume that everyone in the society or polity has to be a party to the original contract, and it could be argued that, therefore, the dependence of the focal groups on the decisions taken in the original position need not be a problem.

I do not think that this is an adequate rebuttal of the problem of inclusionary incoherence for at least two reasons. First, Rawls's use of the idea of 'representation' does not, in fact, amount to marshalling a wholly new set of people (or phantoms) as parties to the original position, different from the actual people in that polity. Rather, it is the *same* people under the 'veil of ignorance' who are seen as 'representing' themselves (but from behind 'the veil'). Rawls explains this by saying: 'This is expressed figuratively by saying that the parties are behind a veil of ignorance. In sum, the original position is simply a device of representation' (*Collected Papers*, p. 401). Indeed, Rawls's justification of the need for a contract, which invokes (as was noted earlier) 'an undertaking people are giving', indicates concrete participation (albeit under the veil of ignorance) of the very people involved in the original contract.[22]

Second, even if the representatives were to be different people (or imagined phantoms), they would have to represent the focal group of people (for example, through the veil of ignorance of possibly being any member of the focal group). So the variability of the focal group would now be reflected in – or transformed into – the variability of the people *whom the representatives represent* in the original position.*

This would not be much of a problem *if*, first, the size of the population did not make any difference to the way the basic structure of the society could be organized (complete scale invariance), and second, every group of individuals was exactly like every other in terms of its priorities and values (complete value invariance). Neither is easy to assume without further restrictions in the structure of any substantive theory of justice.† Group plasticity, therefore, does remain a problem for the exercise of closed impartiality, applied to a *given* focal group of individuals.

---

* To forestall a possible line of response, I should emphasize that this is not the same problem as the difficulty of representing members of the future generation (seen as a *fixed group*). There is, to be sure, a problem there too (for example, about how much can be assumed about the future generations' reasoning since they are not here yet), but it is nevertheless a different issue. There is a distinction between the problem of what can be presumed about the agreement of the future generations (seen as a fixed group) to be represented, and the impossibility of having a fixed group to be represented, in choosing the basic structure of the society when the set of actual persons itself varies depending on the choice of that structure.

† It is also important to avoid a misunderstanding, which I have already encountered in trying to present this argument (which was also contained in my paper, 'Open and Closed Impartiality', 2002), that takes the form of arguing that differing populations cannot make any difference to the Rawlsian original position, since every individual is exactly like any other under the 'veil of ignorance'. The point to note is that even though the 'veil of ignorance' makes *different individuals within a given group* ignorant of their respective interests and values (making everyone much the same in the *as if* deliberative exercise for a given group), it does not, by itself, have any implication whatever in making *different groups of individuals* have exactly the same cluster of interests and values. More generally, to make the exercise of closed impartiality fully independent of the size and composition of the focal group, the substantive reach of that exercise has to be severely impoverished.

We must, however, also ask whether the Smithian approach of the impartial spectator is not similarly troubled by incongruity arising from group plasticity, and if not, why not. It is not, in fact, similarly troubled precisely for the reason that the impartial spectator need not come from the given focal group. Indeed, Smith's 'abstract and ideal spectator' is a 'spectator' and not a 'participant' in any exercise like a group-based contract. There is no contracting group, and there is no insistence even that the evaluators must be congruent with the affected group. Even though there remains the very difficult problem of how an impartial spectator would go about deciding on such issues as variable population size (an ethical issue of profound complexity),* the problem of incoherence and incongruity in 'inclusionary closure' in the contractarian exercise does not have an immediate analogue in the case of the impartial spectator.

## CLOSED IMPARTIALITY AND PAROCHIALISM

That closed impartiality in the form of the original position can incarcerate the basic idea – and the principles – of justice within the narrow confines of local perspectives and prejudices of a group or a country was discussed earlier. To that discussion I want to add three particular points here.

First, we must give some recognition to the fact that procedural parochialism is not universally taken to be a problem at all. In some approaches to social judgements there is no particular interest in avoiding group leanings – indeed, sometimes quite the contrary. To illustrate, some versions of communitarianism may even celebrate the 'local' nature of such priorities. The same may apply to other forms of local justice.

To consider an extreme case, when the Taliban rulers of Afghani-

---

* The complexity would have been even greater if it were necessary that these judgements must take the form of *complete* orderings, but, as has been already discussed, this is not needed for a useful public framework of thought, nor for the making of public choices based on 'maximality' (on which see also my 'Maximization and the Act of Choice', *Econometrica*, 65, 1997).

stan insisted, before the military intervention, that Osama bin Laden should be tried only by a group of Islamic clerics, all committed to the Shariah, the need for some kind of impartiality (against offering personal favours or partial treatment to bin Laden) was not denied, at least not in principle.* Rather, what was being proposed was that the impartial judgements should come from a closed group of people who all accepted a particular religious and ethical code. There is therefore no internal tension in such cases between closed impartiality and the underlying affiliative norms. The broader tensions, related to the acceptability of confining attention only to locally sequestered reasoning, do of course remain. And those difficulties and limitations are the ones that came under Smith's scrutiny.

Indeed, when we leave the world of locally confined ethics, and try to combine a procedure of closed impartiality with otherwise universalist intentions, procedural parochialism must be seen as a serious difficulty. This is certainly the case with Rawlsian 'justice as fairness'. Despite the thoroughly non-parochial intentions of the general Rawlsian approach, the use of closed impartiality involved in the 'original position' (with its programme of impartial assessment confined only to members of the focal group under a 'veil of ignorance' regarding individual interests and goals) does not, in fact, include any procedural guarantee against being swayed only by local group prejudices.

Second, we have to pay particular attention to the *procedure* of the original position, and not only to the intentions that may try to prevail over the recommended procedures. Despite his general universalist inclinations, the formal procedure of the original position proposed by Rawls seems to be geared to allowing little exposure to fresh wind from outside. Indeed, Rawls insists that the closed nature of the original position must be, at least in principle, strongly fortified (*Political Liberalism*, p. 12):

I assume that the basic structure is that of a closed society: that is, we are to regard it as self-contained and as having no relations with other societies . . . That a society is closed is a considerable abstraction, justified only because it enables us to focus on certain main questions free from distracting details.

* The reference here is, of course, only to the principles of justice that the Taliban rulers were invoking, not to their practice.

The question that is begged here is whether considering ideas and experiences from elsewhere are matters of 'distracting details' that are somehow to be shunned for the purity of the exercise of fairness.

Third, despite these strong grounds for open impartiality, it might be thought that a serious difficulty can arise from the limitation of the human mind and our ability to go beyond our local world. Can comprehension and normative reflection cross geographical borders? While some are evidently tempted by the belief that we cannot follow each other beyond the borders of a given community or a particular country, or beyond the limits of a specific culture (a temptation that has been fuelled particularly by the popularity of some versions of communitarian separatism), there is no particular reason to presume that interactive communication and public engagement can be sought only within such boundaries (or within the confines of those who can be seen as 'one people').

Adam Smith argued strongly for the possibility that the impartial spectator could draw on the understanding of people who are far as well as those who are near. This was indeed a significant theme in the intellectual concerns of Enlightenment writers. The possibility of communication and cognizance across the borders should be no more absurd today than it was in Smith's eighteenth-century world. Even though we do not have a global state or a global democracy, Smith's emphasis on the use of the impartial spectator has immediate implications for the role of global public discussion in the contemporary world.

In today's world, global dialogue, which is vitally important for global justice, comes not only through institutions like the United Nations or the WTO, but much more broadly through the media, through political agitation, through the committed work of citizens' organizations and many NGOs, and through social work that draws not only on national identities but also on other commonalities, like trade union movements, cooperative operations, human rights campaigns or feminist activities. The cause of open impartiality is not entirely neglected in the contemporary world.

Moreover, just at this time when the world is engaged in discussions of ways and means of stopping terrorism across borders (and in debates about the roots of global terrorism), and also about how the global economic crises that are plaguing the lives of billions of people across the world can be overcome, it is hard to accept that we simply cannot understand each other across the borders of our polity.* Rather, it is the firmly 'open' outlook, which Smith's 'impartial spectator' invokes, that may be in some need of reassertion today. It can make a substantial difference to our understanding of the demands of impartiality in moral and political philosophy in the interconnected world in which we live.

---

* In the literature on the difficulties of cross-cultural communication, lack of agreement is sometimes confused with the absence of understanding. They are, of course, quite distinct phenomena. A genuine disagreement presupposes an understanding of what is being disputed. On the constructive role of understanding in confronting violence in the contemporary world, see the report of the Commonwealth Commission for Respect and Understanding, which I was privileged to chair: *Civil Paths to Peace* (London: Commonwealth Secretariat, 2007).

# PART II

# Forms of Reasoning

# 7

# Position, Relevance and Illusion

When King Lear told the blind Gloucester, 'A man may see how this world goes with no eyes,' he also told Gloucester how to 'look with thine ears'.

> see how yond justice rails upon yond simple thief. Hark, in thine ear: change places; and, handy-dandy, which is the justice, which is the thief? Thou has seen a farmer's dog bark at a beggar?[1]

Changing places has been one way to 'see' hidden things in the world, which is the general point that Lear makes here, in addition of course to drawing Gloucester's attention, in a politically subversive statement, to the remarkable fact that in the farmer's dog he 'mightst behold the great image of authority'.

The need to transcend the limitations of our positional perspectives is important in moral and political philosophy, and in jurisprudence. Liberation from positional sequestering may not always be easy, but it is a challenge that ethical, political and legal thinking has to take on board. We have to go beyond 'yond justice' that freely rails upon 'yond simple thief'.

## POSITIONALITY OF OBSERVATION
## AND KNOWLEDGE

Trying to go beyond positional confinement is also central to epistemology. There is, however, a problem with observability and often a barrier to comprehension of what is going on from the limited perspective of what we observe. What we can see is not independent of where we stand in relation to what we are trying to see. And this in turn can influence our beliefs, understanding and decisions. Positionally dependent observations, beliefs and choices can be important for the enterprise of knowledge as well as for practical reason. Indeed, epistemology, decision theory and ethics all have to take note of the dependence of observations and inferences on the position of the observer. Not all objectivity is, of course, about objects, as was discussed earlier,* but to the extent that observations and observational understandings are involved in the nature of the objectivity being sought, the positionality of observations has to be taken into account.

The point about positional variation of observations is elementary enough. It can be illustrated with a very straightforward physical example. Consider the claim: *'The sun and the moon look similar in size.'* The observation made is, obviously, not position independent, and the two bodies could look very dissimilar in size from elsewhere, say from the moon. But that is no reason for taking the cited claim as non-objective, or purely as a mental phenomenon special to a particular person. Another person observing the sun and the moon from the same place (the earth), should be able to confirm the claim that they look to be of the same size.

Even though the positional reference is not explicitly invoked in the statement, it is clearly a positional claim, which can be spelled out as: *'From here on earth, the sun and the moon look similar in size.'* Observers can, of course, also make a claim about how things would appear from a position different from the one they currently occupy, which would not be in any necessary tension with the second statement. Standing on the earth, we can still say: *'From the moon, the sun and the moon would not look similar in size.'*

Positional objectivity requires interpersonal invariance when the observational position is fixed, and that requirement is entirely compatible with variations of what is seen from different positions.†

---

* See Chapter 5, 'Impartiality and Objectivity'. The possibility of 'objectivity without objects', for example in mathematics and in ethics, is illuminatingly discussed by Hilary Putnam, *Ethics without Ontology* (Cambridge, MA: Harvard University Press, 2004).
† I tried to explore the idea of positional objectivity first in my Storrs Lectures (1990) at the Yale Law School, and later in my Lindley Lecture, *Objectivity and Position* (Kansas City: University of Kansas, 1992). See 'Positional Objectivity', *Philosophy*

Different persons can occupy the same position and confirm the same observation; and the same person can occupy different positions and make dissimilar observations.

## THE ILLUMINATION AND ILLUSION OF POSITIONALITY

Positional dependence of observational results can both illuminate (in this case, answering the question: how large does an object look from here?) and possibly mislead (in answering other questions standardly associated with size, such as how large in fact is this object in terms of body mass?). The two aspects of positional variability answer very different questions, but neither is entirely subjective. This point may call for a little elaboration, especially since the characterization of objectivity as a position-dependent phenomenon is not the typical understanding of the idea of objectivity.

In his far-reaching book *The View from Nowhere*, Thomas Nagel characterizes objectivity in the following way: 'A view or form of thought is more objective than another if it relies less on the specifics of the individual's makeup and position in the world, or on the character of the particular type of creature he is.'[2] This way of seeing objectivity has some clear merit: it focuses on an important aspect of the classical conception of objectivity – position independence. To come to the conclusion that the sun and the moon are equally large in terms of, say, mass, on grounds that they look to be of the same size from here on earth would be a gross violation of position-independent objectivity. Positional observations can, in this sense, mislead if we do not take adequate note of positional variability of observations and try to make appropriate corrections.

In contrast, what can be called 'positional objectivity' is about the objectivity of what can be observed from a specified position. We are concerned here with person-invariant but position-relative observations and observability, illustrated by what we are able to see from a

---

*and Public Affairs*, 22 (1993); reprinted in *Rationality and Freedom* (Cambridge, MA: Harvard University Press, 2002).

given position. The subject matter of an objective assessment in the positional sense is something that can be ascertained by any normal person occupying a given observational position. As exemplified by the statements about the relative sizes of the sun and the moon, what is observed can vary from position to position, but different people can conduct their respective observations from the same position and make much the same observations.

The subject matter in this case is the way an object looks from a specified position of observation, and it would so look to anyone with the same positional features.* The positional variations in observations can hardly be attributed to 'subjectivity', as some might be tempted to do. In terms of two standard criteria of subjectivity, there is no particular reason here to see the statement 'the sun and the moon look similar in size' as 'having its source in the mind', or as 'pertaining or peculiar to an individual subject or his mental operations' (to go by definitions of subjectivity in the *Oxford English Dictionary*).

An observational statement is not necessarily a statement about the special working of a person's mind. It identifies a phenomenon that has physical qualities as well, independently of anyone's mind; for example, it is precisely because the sun and the moon have the same visible size from the earth that a complete solar eclipse can occur, with the small mass of the moon obscuring the large mass of the sun in the special perspective of the earth, and a solar eclipse can hardly be seen as having 'its source in the mind'. If predicting eclipses is the job in which we are involved, then what is particularly relevant in talking about the relative sizes of the sun and the moon is the congruence of their positional projections from the earth, and not – that is, not directly – their respective body masses.

Aryabhata, the mathematician and astronomer in early fifth-century India, had gone into the size of projections in explaining the eclipses:

---

* The positional features need not, of course, be only locational (or related only to spatial placing), and can include any general, particularly non-mental, condition that may both influence observation, and that can systematically apply to different observers and observations. The positional features may sometimes be linked to a person's special non-mental characteristics, for example being blind. Different persons can share the same type of blindness and have the same observational correspondences.

this was one of his many astronomical contributions.* Aryabhata was, not unexpectedly, attacked for departing so radically from religious orthodoxy, and the critics included his brilliant disciple Brahmagupta, another great mathematician, who made pro-orthodoxy statements, but used Aryabhata's innovations, and indeed extended them. Several hundred years later, in the early eleventh century, when the distinguished Iranian mathematician and astronomer, Alberuni, came to Aryabhata's defence, he emphasized the fact that the practical predictions of eclipses, including those by Brahmagupta, followed Aryabhata's method of projections, rather than reflecting Brahmagupta's own compromise with Hindu orthodoxy. In a remarkable intellectual defence a thousand years ago, Alberuni addressed the following critique to Brahmagupta:

we shall not argue with him [Brahmagupta], but only whisper into his ear: . . . Why do you, after having spoken such [harsh] words [against Aryabhata and his followers], then begin to calculate the diameter of the moon in order to explain the eclipsing of the sun, and the diameter of the shadow of the earth in order to explain its eclipsing the moon? Why do you compute both eclipses in agreement with the theory of those heretics, and not according to the views of those with whom you think it is proper to agree?[3]

Positional objectivity can indeed be the appropriate understanding of objectivity, depending on the exercise in which we are involved.

Different types of examples of positional parameters that arc not quirks of mental attitudes or psychology, and which can be shared by different individuals, include: knowing or not knowing a specific language; being able or not being able to count; or being colour blind rather than having normal eyesight (among a great many similar parametric variations). It does not violate positional objectivity to make a statement on how the world would look to a person with certain specified 'positional' attributes.

The claim here, it is important to note, is not that anything that can be 'explained' in causal terms is positionally objective. Much would

---

* Aryabhata's original contributions included his disputation of an orbiting sun around the earth, and his pointer to the existence of a gravitational force in explaining why objects are not thrown away from the earth despite its diurnal rotating motion.

depend on the nature of the variability involved. To take a classic example much discussed in early Indian epistemology, to mistake a rope for a snake because of one's special nervousness, or one's morbid fear of snakes, does not make that clearly subjective diagnosis positionally objective. The idea of positional objectivity may, however, be legitimately invoked in a case in which a rope is taken to be a snake because that is exactly the way that piece of rope looks to everyone, for example the way the prominent snake-like features of a rope may appear to those observing it in a dim light.

There is a similar distinction within ethical and political evaluation, comparable to the contrast between the illuminating and diverting roles of positionality, respectively. In pursuing theories of relation-based personal responsibilities that demand a special role, for example, of parents in looking after their own children, giving special prominence to the interests of one's own children may be plausibly seen to be ethically appropriate. To take an asymmetric interest in the lives of one's own children may not be, in that context, a subjective folly – rather the reflection of an ethical perspective that is objectively sought (which is linked, in this case, with the positional relevance of parenthood).*

In that framework, there would therefore be something of a lacuna in thinking of ethical objectivity only in terms of 'the view from nowhere', rather than 'from a delineated somewhere'. There can be special relevance in positional features that a capacious ethics must adequately acknowledge and appropriately take into account. Indeed, one's duty to one's children, to consider the same example again, does not have its source just 'in the mind', and real significance may be attached to it in specific approaches to ethics.

When questions of agent-relative – more generally, position-relative

---

* The relevance of personal connections and relationships is a subject of considerable importance and complexity in the discipline of moral evaluation. Bernard Williams has discussed many of the underlying issues with force and clarity, particularly – but not exclusively – in his critique of utilitarianism; see his 'A Critique of Utilitarianism', in J. J. C. Smart and B. Williams, *Utilitarianism: For and Against* (Cambridge: Cambridge University Press, 1973), and *Moral Luck: Philosophical Papers, 1973–1980* (Cambridge: Cambridge University Press, 1981), especially the essay entitled 'Persons, Character and Morality'.

– assessments and responsibilities are examined, as they will be in Chapter 10, the illuminating aspects of positional objectivity will be of relevance. And yet in other contexts, giving such a special prominence to the interests of one's own children must be seen, from the perspective of a non-relational ethics, as a clear mistake. For example, if a public official in pursuit of his civil duties gives greater importance to the interests of his own children, that could be seen as a political or ethical failure, notwithstanding the fact that his children's interests would be more prominent to him, thanks to their positional closeness.

What may be needed in this exercise is a 'positionally unbiased' approach. The demand in this case would be for an adequate recognition of the fact that other children may have similarly large and important interests at stake as one's own children, and the view from 'a delineated somewhere' (linked for example with parental relations) would be, in that context, a mistake.

The search for some kind of position-independent understanding of the world is central to the ethical illumination that may be sought in a non-relational approach. When Mary Wollstonecraft pilloried Edmund Burke for his support of the American Revolution without taking any interest in the status of the slaves, as if the freedom that he supported for white American people need not apply to its black slaves (as was discussed in Chapter 5), Wollstonecraft was arguing for a universalist perspective that would overcome positional prejudice and sectional favouritism. The point there is not positional comprehension, but some kind of a transpositional understanding. Taking a 'view from nowhere' would obviously be the appropriate idea in that context.

## OBJECTIVE ILLUSIONS AND POSITIONAL OBJECTIVITY

Even when a position-independent view is appropriate for an epistemological, ethical or political assessment, the reality of position dependence of observations may have to be taken into account in explaining the difficulty of achieving a positionally unbiased comprehension. The hold of positional perspectives can have an important role in making it hard for people to transcend their positionally limited visions. For example, in a society that has a long-established tradition of relegating women to a subordinate position, the cultural norm of focusing on some alleged features of women's supposed inferiority may be so strong that it may require considerable independence of mind to interpret those features differently. If there are, for instance, very few women scientists in a society that does not encourage women to study science, the observed feature of paucity of successful women scientists may itself serve as a barrier to understanding that women may be really just as good at science, and that even with the same native talents and aptitudes to pursue the subject, women may rarely excel in science precisely because of a lack of opportunity or encouragement to undertake the appropriate education.

The observation that there are few women scientists in a particular society may not be at all mistaken, even when the conclusion that women are no good at science – when drawn from that positional observation – would be entirely erroneous. The need for going beyond the positionality of local observations within societies with entrenched discrimination can be very strong here. Observations from other societies where women have more opportunities could confirm that women have the ability to do just as well as men in the pursuit of science, given the necessary opportunities and facilities. The argument relates here to the case for 'open impartiality', invoking such ideas as Adam Smith's methodological device of the impartial spectator, seeking perspectives from far as well as near.*

When the confines of local beliefs are strong and difficult to overcome, there can be a steadfast refusal to see that a real inequity is involved in the way women are treated in their own society, and many women are themselves led to a belief about women's alleged intellectual inferiority based on the supposed 'evidence of the eyes', drawing on a faulty reading of local observations within a stratified society. In explaining the protest-free tolerance of social asymmetry and discrimination that can be seen in many traditionalist societies, the idea of positional objectivity has something of a scientific contribution to make, in giving us an insight into the genesis of an illegiti-

---

* See the discussion in Chapter 6, 'Closed and Open Impartiality'.

mate application of positional comprehension (when the need is for a transpositional understanding).

The important notion of 'objective illusion', used in Marxian philosophy, can also be helpfully interpreted in terms of positional objectivity.* An objective illusion, thus interpreted, is a positionally objective belief that is, in fact, mistaken in terms of transpositional scrutiny. The concept of an objective illusion invokes both the idea of positionally objective belief, *and* the transpositional diagnosis that this belief is, in fact, mistaken. In the example involving the relative sizes of the sun and the moon, the similarity of their appearances (positionally objective as this is from here on earth) can lead – in the absence of other information and ideas and the opportunity for critical scrutiny – to a positional 'understanding' of the similarity of their 'actual sizes' (for example in terms of the time that would be taken to go around them respectively). The falsity of that belief would, then, be an illustration of an objective illusion.

There is an interesting discussion by G. A. Cohen in his book, *Karl Marx's Theory of History: A Defence*, about the idea of objective illusion in Marxian theory:

For Marx the senses mislead us with respect to the constitution of the air and the movements of heavenly bodies. Yet a person who managed through breathing to detect different components in the air would have a nose that did not function as healthy human noses do. And a person who sincerely claimed to perceive a stationary sun and a rotating earth would be suffering from some disorder of vision, or motor control. Perceiving the air as elementary and the sun as in motion are experiences more akin to seeing mirages than to having hallucinations. For if a man does not see a mirage under the appropriate conditions, there is something wrong with his vision. His eyes have failed to register the play of lights in the distance.[4]

* The concept of objective illusion figures in Marx's economic writings (not just in the more philosophical ones), including *Capital*, Volume I, and *Theories of Surplus Value*. Marx was particularly concerned with showing that the common belief about the fairness of exchange in the labour market is, in fact, illusory, and yet that claim to fairness is 'objectively' accepted by people who see how things exchange in terms of equal values at market prices. Even the exploited workers who, in Marxian analysis, are robbed of part of the value of their products, might find it hard to see that there was anything other than exchange of 'equal values' in the labour market.

Here the observations, which are taken to be objective, relate to the positional features of breathing the air with a normal nose, seeing the sun with normal eyes, observing the play of light in the distance with a normal vision and so on. And these observed features are indeed positionally objective, though misleading or mistaken in terms of other – contextually more compelling – criteria of truth that can be invoked once we go beyond positional perspectives.

## HEALTH, MORBIDITY AND POSITIONAL VARIATIONS

Marx's own use of the idea of objective illusion was primarily in the context of class analysis and it led him to his investigation of what he called 'false consciousness'. A very different type of example concerns the self-perception of morbidity, and this can be particularly important in analysing the health situation in developing economies. For example, among the Indian states, Kerala has by a big margin the longest life expectancy at birth (higher than China and closer to Europe), and professional medical assessment gives much evidence of Kerala's successful health transition. And yet in the surveys of self-perceived morbidity rates, Kerala also reports by far the highest rates of self-perceived morbidity (both on the average and in terms of age-specific rates). At the other end are states like Bihar and Uttar Pradesh with very low life expectancy and exceptionally high age-specific mortality rates (and little evidence of any health transition), and yet astonishingly low rates of self-assessed morbidity. If the medical evidence and the testimony of mortality rates are accepted (and there are no particular reasons to rule them out), then the picture of relative morbidity rates as given by self-assessment must be taken to be erroneous – or at least highly problematic.

Nevertheless, it would be odd to dismiss these self-assessed morbidity rates as simply accidental errors, or as results of individual subjectivism. Why is there such a systematic pattern of dissonance between mortality rates and self-perceived morbidity rates? The concept of objective illusion is helpful here. The population of Kerala has a remarkably higher rate of literacy (including female literacy) than the rest of India, and also has much more extensive public health services. Thus in Kerala there is a much greater awareness of possible illnesses and of the need to seek medical remedies and to undertake preventive measures. The very ideas and actions that help to reduce actual morbidity and mortality in Kerala also have the effect of heightening the awareness of ailments. At the other end, the populations of Uttar Pradesh or Bihar, with less literacy and education, and severely undersupplied with public health facilities, have less discernment of possible illnesses. This makes the health conditions and life expectancy much worse in these states, but it also makes the awareness of morbidity more limited there than in Kerala.

The illusion of low morbidity in the socially backward states in India does indeed have an objective – a positionally objective – basis, for a population with limited school education and medical experience.* The positional objectivity of these parochially mistaken diagnoses commands attention, and social scientists can hardly dismiss them as simply subjective and capricious. But nor can these self-perceptions be taken to be accurate reflections of health and illness in an appropriate transpositional understanding.

The possibility and frequency of this type of objective illusion have some far-reaching implications for the way comparative medical and health statistics are currently presented by national and international organizations. The comparative data on self-reporting of illness and

---

* The empirical work on this has been based substantially on Indian data and their interpretation; see the discussion, and the extensive literature cited, in my joint books with Jean Drèze, *India: Economic Development and Social Opportunity* (Delhi and Oxford: Oxford University Press, 1995), and *India: Development and Participation* (Delhi and Oxford: Oxford University Press, 2002). However, there is empirical information from elsewhere in the developing world that fits broadly into this reading; see my *Development as Freedom* (New York: Knopf, and Oxford: Oxford University Press, 1999), Chapter 4. This line of explanation is reinforced by comparisons of self-assessed morbidity rates in the USA with those in India (including Kerala). In disease by disease comparison, it turns out that while Kerala has much higher self-assessed rates for most illnesses than the rest of India, the United States has even higher rates for the same illnesses. On this, see Lincoln Chen and Christopher Murray, 'Understanding Morbidity Change', *Population and Development Review*, 18 (September 1992).

the seeking of medical attention call for critical scrutiny, taking serious note of positional perspectives.*

## GENDER DISCRIMINATION AND POSITIONAL ILLUSIONS

Another interesting case relates to the dissonance between the ranking of perceived morbidity and that of observed mortality of men and women. Women have, on the whole, tended to have survival disadvantages compared to men in India (as in many other countries in Asia and North Africa, such as China, Pakistan, Iran or Egypt). The mortality rates have typically been, until very recently, higher for women of all age groups (after a short neo-natal period of some months) up to the ages of thirty-five to forty years, contrary to what one would expect biologically, given the medical evidence for lower age-specific mortality rates for women than for men, when they receive symmetric care.†

Despite the relative disadvantage in mortality rates, the self-perceived morbidity rates of women in India are often no higher – sometimes much lower – than those of men. This seems to relate to women's deprivation in education, and also to the social tendency to see gender disparity as a 'normal' phenomenon.‡ Happily (I use the expression here in a way that utilitarians might not approve of),

---

* I shall not pursue further this important practical issue; see, however, my book, *Development as Freedom* (New York: Knopf, and Oxford: Clarendon Press, 1999), Chapter 4.

† The life expectancy of women in India has recently overtaken that of men, but the ratio of women's to men's longevity in India is still considerably below what can be expected under symmetric care. Kerala is an exception in this respect too, with female life expectancy substantially higher than men's (with a ratio similar to that in Europe and America).

‡ On an earlier occasion, I have discussed the remarkable fact that in a study of post-famine Bengal in 1944, widows had hardly reported any incidence of being in 'indifferent health', whereas widowers complained massively about just that (see my *Commodities and Capabilities* (Amsterdam: North-Holland, 1985), Appendix B). On related issues, see my *Resources, Values and Development* (Cambridge, MA: Harvard University Press, 1984), and also, jointly with Jocelyn Kynch, 'Indian Women: Well-being and Survival', *Cambridge Journal of Economics*, 7 (1983).

women's unhappiness about their health has systematically increased across the country, which indicates a declining hold of positionally confined perception of good and bad health. It is interesting to see that as the subject of women's deprivation has become politicized (including by women's organizations), the biases in the perception of the deprivation of women has become less common. A better understanding of the nature of the problem and illusions about women's health has, in fact, substantially contributed to the reduction (and in many regions of India, elimination) of sex bias in mortality.*

The idea of positional objectivity is particularly crucial in understanding gender inequality in general. The working of families involves some conflict as well as some congruence of interest in the division of benefits and chores (a feature of group relations that can be called 'cooperative conflict'), but the demands of harmonious family living require that the conflicting aspects be resolved implicitly, rather than through explicit bargaining. Dwelling on such conflicts would generally be seen as abnormal behaviour. As a result, customary patterns of conduct are simply taken as legitimate and even reasonable, and in most parts of the world there is a shared tendency not to notice the systematic deprivation of females vis-à-vis males in one field or another.

## POSITIONALITY AND THE THEORY OF JUSTICE

This issue is quite important for the formulation of a theory of justice and, more specifically, for exploring a theory that gives a special role to public reasoning in the understanding of the demands of justice.

* The phenomenon of 'missing women' in India, China and many other countries in the world, reflecting the number of women who are 'not there', compared with what could be expected in the absence of any gender bias, should have gone down sharply as a result of fairly widespread progress in the world in the reduction of sex bias in mortality. Unfortunately, the relatively new phenomenon of gender bias in natality (through sex-selective abortion of female foetuses) has worked in the opposite direction. The changing picture is discussed in two articles of mine: 'Missing Women', *The British Medical Journal*, 304 (March 1992), and 'Missing Women Revisited', *British Medical Journal*, 327 (December 2003).

The reach of public reasoning may be limited in practice by the way people read the world in which they live. And if the powerful influence of positionality has an obscuring role in that social understanding, then that is indeed a subject that calls for special attention in appreciating the challenging difficulties that have to be faced in the assessment of justice and injustice.

While positionality of observation and construction plays an important part in the process of advancing scientific knowledge, it is more broadly significant in belief formation in general: in social comprehension as well as in the pursuit of the natural sciences. Indeed, the role of positionality may be particularly crucial in interpreting systematic and persistent illusions that can significantly influence – and distort – social understanding and the assessment of public affairs.

Let me return to the simple example involving the relative size of the sun vis-à-vis the moon, as seen from the earth. Consider a person who belongs to a community that does not have familiarity with distance-dependent projections, nor with any other source of information about the sun and the moon. Lacking the relevant conceptual frameworks and ancillary knowledge, that person may decide, on the basis of positional observations, that the sun and the moon are indeed of the same size, even in the sense that it would take much the same time to go around them respectively (moving at the same speed). This would, of course, be a very peculiar judgement *if* the person knew about distances, projections and such, but not if he knew none of those things. His belief that the sun and the moon are really of the same size (in particular, that it would take the same time to go around each) is, of course, a mistake (an illusion), but his belief cannot, under the circumstances, be seen as purely subjective, given the totality of his positional features. Indeed, anyone in exactly his position (in particular sharing the same ignorance of relevant concepts and related information) can understandably take much the same view, prior to critical scrutiny, for much the same reasons.*

---

* Philosophers of the *Nyaya* school in India, which achieved prominence in the first few centuries AD, had argued that not only knowledge but also illusions depend on pre-existing concepts. When a person mistakes a rope for a snake in dark light (a classic example that was discussed earlier), this illusion occurs precisely because of the prior understanding – the *genuine* understanding – of the 'snake-concept'. A person

Illusions that are associated with some positional objectivity can be very hard to dislodge, even when the positionality involved misleads and misinforms rather than illuminates.* Given the misperceptions, it may be a difficult task to overcome received gender inequalities, and indeed even to identify them clearly as inequalities that demand attention.[5] Since gender inequalities within the family tend to survive by making allies out of the deprived, the opaqueness of the positional perspectives plays a major part in the prevalence and persistence of these inequalities.

## OVERCOMING POSITIONAL LIMITATIONS

In the pursuit of justice, positional illusions can impose serious barriers that have to be overcome through broadening the informational basis of evaluations, which is one of the reasons why Adam Smith demanded that perspectives from elsewhere, including from far away, have to be systematically invoked (see Chapter 6). Though much can be done through the deliberate use of open impartiality, the hope of proceeding smoothly from positional views to an ultimate 'view from nowhere' cannot hope to succeed fully.

Our entire understanding of the world, it can be argued, is thoroughly dependent on the perceptions we can have and the

who has no idea of what a snake looks like and who cannot tell between the 'snake-concept' and, say, the 'pig-concept', would not be inclined to mistake a rope for a snake. On the implications of this (and related) connections between concepts and reality, as explored in the *Nyaya* and rival schools in that period, see Bimal Matilal, *Perception: An Essay on Classical Indian Theories of Knowledge* (Oxford: Clarendon Press, 1986), Chapter 6.

* As was mentioned earlier, a theory of justice may also make room for relational concerns, in which positional perspectives may be important and have to be taken into account. This applies to such issues as agent-relative duties and priorities (in which an agent responsible for an action may be seen as having special accountability) as well as to particular obligations associated with specific human relations, such as parental responsibilities. The real relevance of positional perspectives (when that can be justified) is quite different from what is being considered here in the context of non-relational ethics and politics. The former will be taken up in Chapter 10, 'Realizations, Consequences and Agency'.

thoughts we can generate, given the kind of creatures we are. Our thoughts as well as our perceptions are integrally dependent on our sense organs, and our brains, and other human bodily capacities. Even the very idea of what we call a 'view' – no matter from where – is parasitic on our understanding of vision with our own eyes, which is a bodily activity in the physical form in which human beings have evolved.

In our speculative thoughts we can, of course, consider going beyond the anchors that seem to fix us to the world in which we live and the bodily activities that govern our discernment and cogitation. We can even try to think about a world in which we are able to accommodate perceptions other than those of light, sound, heat, smell, taste, touch and other signals that we do receive (as we are in fact constituted), but it is hard going to make any concrete sense of what the world would 'look' like in that different sensory universe. The same limitation applies to the range of our thinking process and to the broadening of our capacity to contemplate. Our very understanding of the external world is so moored in our experiences and thinking that the possibility of going entirely beyond them may be rather limited.

All this does not, however, indicate that positionality cannot be partly or wholly overcome in ways that take us to a less confined view. Here too (as in choosing the focus of a theory of justice), we may reasonably search for comparatives, and not for the utopian objective of transcendence. Comparative broadening is part of the persistent interest in innovative epistemological, ethical and political work, and it has yielded a great many rewards in the intellectual history of the world. The 'nirvana' of complete independence from personal features is not the only issue in which we have reason to take an interest.

## WHO IS OUR NEIGHBOUR?

There is a long history of attempts to go beyond the positional confinement of our moral concerns to the proximate 'neighbourhood', resisting the relational vision that something is owed to one's neighbours that is not, in any way, owed to people outside the neighbourhood. The question of one's duty to one's neighbours has a huge place in the history of ethical ideas in the world. Indeed, the Anglican Book of Common Prayer includes the following unambiguous answer to the question, 'What dost thou chiefly learn by these Commandments?': 'I learn two things: my duty towards God, and my duty to my Neighbour.'

If this understanding of our obligations is right and the claims of our neighbours are incomparably stronger than those of others, is it not possible to think that this would do something to smooth the roughness of 'justice in one country' (an approach that I have been arguing against)? But the ethical basis for giving such a hugely unharmonious priority to thinking only about our neighbours is itself in need of some justification. No less importantly, there is a deep fragility in the intellectual basis of thinking of people in terms of fixed communities of neighbours.

The last point is made with compelling clarity by Jesus of Nazareth in his recounting of the story of 'the good Samaritan' in the Gospel of Luke.* Jesus's questioning of fixed neighbourhoods has sometimes been ignored in seeing the good Samaritan story as a moral for universal concern, which is also fair enough, but the main point of the story as told by Jesus is a reasoned rejection of the idea of a fixed neighbourhood.

At this point in Luke, Jesus is arguing with a local lawyer about his limited conception of those to whom we owe some duty (only our physical neighbours). Jesus tells the lawyer the story of the wounded man lying on one side of the street who was helped eventually by the good Samaritan, an event that was preceded by the refusal of a priest and a Levite to do anything for him. Indeed, instead of helping, the priest and the Levite just crossed and walked on the other side of the street, without facing the wounded man.†

---

* On this, see also Jeremy Waldron's excellent analysis, with a slightly different focus, in 'Who Is My Neighbor? Humanity and Proximity', *The Monist*, 86 (July 2003).
† My late colleague, the redoubtable John Sparrow, the former head of All Souls College at Oxford, enjoyed arguing that we owe nothing to others if we had not harmed them, and he liked posing the question whether the priest and the Levite who crossed to the other side of the street rather than helping 'acted wrongly', as is commonly supposed. To this, John Sparrow's own emphatic answer was, 'Of course,

Jesus does not, on this occasion, directly discuss the duty to help others – *all* others – in need, neighbours or not, but rather raises a classificatory question regarding the definition of one's neighbour. He asks the lawyer with whom he is arguing: 'Who was the wounded man's neighbour?' The lawyer cannot avoid answering, 'The man who helped him'. And that was, of course, Jesus's point exactly. The duty to neighbours is not confined only to those who live next door. In order to understand the force of Jesus's argument, we have to remember that Samaritans did not only live some distance away, but also were typically disliked or despised by the Israelites.*

The Samaritan is linked to the wounded Israelite through the event itself: he found the stricken man, saw the need to help, provided that help and was now in a relationship with the injured person. It does not matter whether the Samaritan was moved by charity, or by a 'sense of justice', or by some deeper 'sense of fairness in treating others as equals'. Once he finds himself in this situation, he is in a new 'neighbourhood'.

The neighbourhood that is constructed by our relations with distant people is something that has pervasive relevance to the understanding of justice in general, particularly so in the contemporary world. We are linked with each other through trade, commerce, literature, language, music, arts, entertainment, religion, medicine, healthcare, politics,

---

yes.' He greatly relished spelling out, to a largely shocked audience (that was, of course, the point), that the Levite and the priest behaved wrongly, not because they should have helped (not at all), but because they should not have had to cross the street with an evident sense of guilt, rather than face the wounded man. They should have had the moral courage to go right past the wounded man on the same side of the street, walking straight on, without helping, and without any sense of needless shame or unnecessary embarrassment. To get some insight into this no-nonsense view of 'what we owe to each other' (more specifically, 'what we *do not* owe to each other'), see John Sparrow, *Too Much of a Good Thing* (Chicago, IL: University of Chicago Press, 1977).

* When recollecting this story from the Gospels and its remarkable reach and effectiveness, I remember being reminded of what Ludwig Wittgenstein said about the Gospels, in contrast with the more formidable Epistles of St Paul: 'In the Gospels – as it seems to me – everything is *less pretentious*, humbler, simpler. There you find huts; in Paul a church. There all men are equal and God himself is a man; in Paul there is already something of a hierarchy; honours and official positions' (Ludwig Wittgenstein, *Culture and Value*, edited by G. H. von Wright (Oxford: Blackwell, 1980), p. 30).

news reports, media communication and other ties. While commenting on the importance of increased contact in expanding the reach of our sense of justice, David Hume noted, nearly a quarter of a millennium ago:

again suppose that several distinct societies maintain a kind of intercourse for mutual convenience and advantage, the boundaries of justice still grow larger, in proportion to the largeness of men's views, and the force of their mutual connexions.[6]

It is 'the largeness of men's views' on which the pursuit of open impartiality draws. And it is the growing 'force of their mutual connexions' that make 'the boundaries of justice still grow larger'.*

We may debate the extent to which our concerns should extend in a theory of justice that can have any plausibility today, and we may not expect any unanimity on the appropriate domain of our coverage. But no theory of justice today can ignore the whole world except our own country, and fail to take into account our pervasive neighbourhood in the world today, even if there are attempts to persuade us that it is only to our local neighbours we owe any help to overcome injustice.† We are increasingly linked not only by our mutual economic, social and political relations, but also by vaguely shared but far-reaching concerns about injustice and inhumanity that challenge our world, and the violence and terrorism that threaten it. Even our shared frustrations and shared thoughts on global helplessness can unite rather than divide. There are few non-neighbours left in the world today.

---

* The recent transformation of the world into a much smaller place, thanks to innovations in communication and transport, and the ongoing development of global media and transnational organizations, have made it hard not to take note of our extensive connections across the world, which have profound implications not only for the form and contents of a theory of justice (with which I am primarily concerned here), but also for global politics – and indeed survival. On related subjects, see also Chris Patten, *What Next? Surviving the Twenty-first Century* (London: Allen Lane, 2008).

† Our broader global concerns sometimes find organized outlets in demonstrations and loud protests, and at other times seek quieter expression in political commentary, media articulation or just in personal conversations. I will return to this issue in Chapters 15–17.

# 8

# Rationality and Other People

In 1638 Pierre de Fermat, the great mathematician, sent to René Descartes a communication dealing with maximization and minimization. The manuscript had been circulating in Paris for a few years before it was sent to Descartes, who was not particularly impressed when it eventually reached him. And yet what Fermat said was momentous in firmly establishing the mathematical discipline of maximization and minimization.* The discipline is important for mathematics and philosophy, but it is also extensively used in the sciences, including in the social sciences and in particular in economics.

Maximization is mainly invoked in economics and in the social sciences as a behavioural characteristic (on which more presently), but it is interesting to note that Fermat's 'principle of least time' in optics (dealing with the quickest way for light to go from one spot to another), which was a fine minimization exercise, was not at all a case of conscious behaviour, since no volition is involved in the light's 'choice' of a minimum time path from one point to another. Indeed, in physics and the natural sciences, maximization typically occurs without a deliberate 'maximizer'. The absence of decisional choice also applies generally to the early analytical uses of maximization and minimization, including those in geometry, going back all the way to the search for 'the shortest arc' by Greek mathematicians, and other such exercises considered by the 'great geometers' in the ancient world, such as Apollonius of Perga.

---

* The analytical features of maximization and minimization are not essentially different from each other, since both seek 'extremal' values. Indeed, a maximization exercise can be readily turned into one of minimization simply by reversing the sign of the variable in question (and vice versa).

In contrast, the maximization process in economics is seen mainly as the result of conscious choice (even though '*habitual* maximizing behaviour' is sometimes given a role), and the exercise of rational choice is typically interpreted as the deliberate maximization of what a person has the best reason to promote. As Jon Elster puts it in his short, concise and elegant book, *Reason and Rationality*, 'The rational actor is one who acts for sufficient reasons.'[1] It is indeed difficult to avoid the thought that rationality of choice must have a strong connection with reasoning. And it is because of the belief, often implicit rather than explicit, that reasoning is likely to favour the maximization of what we want to advance or pursue (not by any means an outrageous idea) that maximization is taken to be central to rational behaviour. The discipline of economics uses the approach of 'extremal' search very extensively to predict what choices can be expected to emerge, including utility maximization by consumers, cost minimization by producers, profit maximization by firms, and so on.

This way of thinking about the rationality of choice can take us, in turn, to the common presumption in contemporary economics that people's actual choices can be best interpreted as being based on some appropriate kind of maximization. The nature of what would be reasonable for people to maximize must, therefore, occupy a central position in the present inquiry into the nature of rational choice and the determination of actual choice.

There is, however, a fairly basic methodological question about the use of maximization in economics that demands some attention first. This concerns the double use of maximizing behaviour in economics *both* as a predictive device (trying to guess what is likely to happen), and as a criterion of rationality (assessing what norms must be followed for choice to be seen as rational). The identification of two rather different issues (namely, rational choice and actual choice), which is now a fairly standard practice in a large part of contemporary economics, raises a major question about whether rational choice (no matter how it might be properly characterized) would, in fact, be a good predictor of what is actually chosen. There is obviously something to discuss and scrutinize here.

## RATIONAL DECISIONS AND
## ACTUAL CHOICE

Are people invariably, or even typically, guided by reason, rather than, say, by passion or impulse? If the norms of rational behaviour are not followed by people in their *actual* behaviour, how can we seek the same answer to two rather different questions: what would be *rational* for a person to do? and what would the person *actually* do? How can we hope, as a general rule, to tackle two quite different questions with exactly the same answer? Shouldn't the economists who make such double use of maximization – whether through explicit reasoning or by implicit presumption – be invited to apply their minds to this?

A number of economists have indeed paid attention to systematic departures from rationality in actual choices made by people. One argument that has been invoked, in a line of reasoning proposed by Herbert Simon, goes by the name of bounded rationality.[2] It concerns the possibility that people may not, in all cases, look for fully rational choices because of their inability to be sufficiently focused, or adequately steadfast or alert enough in seeking and using information that would be needed for the complete pursuit of rationality. Various empirical works have added to the evidence that the actual behaviour of people may depart from complete maximization of their goals and objectives. There is considerable evidence, powerfully presented, for example, by Kahneman, Slovik and Tversky, that people may fail to understand adequately the nature of the uncertainty that may be involved in deciding on what to expect in any specific case based on the evidence available.[3]

There can also be what is sometimes called the 'weakness of will', a subject that has received attention from many philosophers for a very long time – the ancient Greeks called it *akrasia*. One may know fairly well what one should do rationally, and yet fail to act in that way. People may over-eat or over-drink in a way that they themselves may think is foolish or irrational, and yet they might still fail to resist the temptations. In the economic literature, this is sometimes called 'bounded willpower' or 'insufficient self-command',

and this problem too has received far-reaching attention from a number of economists – from Adam Smith in the eighteenth century to Thomas Schelling in our time.[4] It is important to note that this problem is concerned with the failure of people to act in a fully rational way, but these departures in actual behaviour do not, in themselves, suggest that the idea of rationality or its demands should themselves be modified.[5]

The relation between rational choice and actual behaviour connects, in fact, with a long-standing divide in the discipline of economics, with some authors tending to think that it is by and large correct to assume that people's actual behaviour would follow the dictates of rationality, while others remain deeply sceptical of that presumption. This difference in foundational assumptions about human behaviour, and in particular the scepticism about taking actual behaviour to be identifiably rational, has not, however, prevented modern economics from using rational choice quite extensively as a predictive device. The assumption is used often enough without any particular defence, but when some defence is given, it tends to take the form of either arguing that as a general rule this is close enough to the truth (despite some well-known divergence), or that the assumed behaviour is useful enough for the purpose at hand, which may differ from seeking the most truthful description.

Arguments for allowing certain departures from truthful description for some purpose to be distinguished from the accuracy of description, for example for their usefulness in making predictions using simple models with good track record, have been presented with much enthusiasm by Milton Friedman in particular.[6] Friedman has gone on to claim that even what we regard as 'realistic' description should not be based on the truthfulness of the depiction, but 'by seeing whether the theory works, which means whether it yields sufficiently accurate predictions'. This is, in fact, a very special view of descriptive realism and, not surprisingly, it has been powerfully criticized, particularly by Paul Samuelson (Samuelson has called it 'the F-twist'). I shall not go into this debate or the issue underlying it, since they are not central to the subject matter of this book, but I have assessed the debate (and the underlying methodological issues) elsewhere.[7]

In scrutinizing the rationality of actual behaviour, there are also some important interpretational issues that sometimes make the immediate diagnosis of irrational behaviour too rapid.[8] It is, for example, possible that what appears to others as hugely irrational and even downright stupid might not actually be so inane. The diagnosis of imprudent behaviour might sometimes be based on failing to see the underlying reasons behind particular choices even when these reasons exist and are cogent enough.

Making room for irrational action is indeed important, but the diagnosis of irrationality may be a far more complex exercise than it might at first appear.[9] What is important for the present work is not any presumption that people invariably act in a rational way, but rather the idea that people are not altogether alienated from the demands of rationality (even if they get things wrong from time to time, or fail to follow the dictates of reason in each and every case). The *nature* of the reasoning to which people may respond is more central to this work than the exactness of people's ability to do what reason dictates in every case without exception. People can respond to reasoning not merely in their day-to-day behaviour, but also in thinking about bigger questions, such as the nature of justice and the characteristics of an acceptable society. People's ability to consider and respond to different types of reasoning (some of which may be well known while others not so) is often invoked in this work. The relevance of that exercise would not vanish merely because people's actual behaviour might fail to coincide with rational choice in every case. What is more important for the purpose of the present exploration is the fact that people are, by and large, able to reason and scrutinize their own decisions and those of others. There is no unbridgeable breach there.

## RATIONAL CHOICE VERSUS SO-CALLED 'RATIONAL CHOICE THEORY'

Even when we accept, with or without reservations, the understanding that actual behaviour would not be unrelated to, or uninfluenced by, the demands of rationality, the big question of the characterization of rational choice remains. What exactly are the demands of rational choice?

One answer that has gained popularity in economics, and more recently in politics and law, is that people choose rationally if and only if they intelligently pursue their self-interest, and nothing else. This exceedingly narrow approach to rational choice goes under the ambitious – and oddly non-denominational – name of the 'Rational Choice Theory' (it is called just that, somewhat amazingly, with no further qualification). Indeed, the brand-named 'rational choice theory', or RCT for short, characterizes rationality of choice simply as smart maximization of self-interest. It is somehow taken for granted in this approach that people would fail to be rational if they did not intelligently pursue only their own self-interest, without taking note of anything else (except to the extent that 'the something else' might – directly or indirectly – facilitate the promotion of their self-interest). Since human beings can easily have good reason also to pay some attention to objectives other than the single-minded pursuit of self-interest, and can see arguments in favour of taking cognizance of broader values or of normative rules of decent behaviour, RCT does reflect an extremely limited understanding of reason and rationality.

Not unexpectedly, there is a large literature on this subject, including various attempts at sophisticated defence of the understanding of rationality as self-interest promotion. One of the important issues concerns the interpretation of altruistic acts based on one's reasoning: does the existence of such a reason seen by a person indicate that he or she would actually benefit personally from acting according to that reason ('his own reason')? The answer must depend on the nature of the reason that is involved. If a person finds it painful to live in a society with large inequalities, and that is the reason for his trying to do something to reduce those inequalities, then his self-interest is clearly mixed up with the social goal of reducing inequality. If, on the other hand, a person wants to lessen inequality, not for diminishing one's pain at seeing it, but because it is judged by him to be a bad thing for society (whether or not he is also pained at the sight of inequality), then the social argument must be distinguished from the personal pursuit of private gain. The different arguments involved in this large – and hugely researched – subject are examined in my *Rationality and Freedom* (2002).[10]

The remarkably miniaturized view of human rationality exclusively in terms of the pursuit of self-interest will be scrutinized presently but before that I would like to consider a proposal, which I have presented elsewhere, about how rationality of choice may be – less restrictively and more cogently – characterized. Rationality of choice, in this view, is primarily a matter of basing our choices – explicitly or by implication – on reasoning that we can reflectively *sustain* if we subject them to critical scrutiny.* The discipline of rational choice, in this view, is foundationally connected with bringing our choices into conformity with critical investigation of the reasons for that choice. The essential demands of rational choice relate to subjecting one's choices – of actions as well as objectives, values and priorities – to reasoned scrutiny.

This approach is based on the idea of a link between what would be rational for us to choose and what we have reason to choose. Having reason to do something is not just a matter of an unscrutinized conviction – a strong 'gut feeling' – that we have 'excellent grounds' for doing what we choose to do. Rather, it demands that we investigate the reasons underlying the choice and consider whether the alleged reasons survive searching and critical examination, which one can undertake if and when the importance of such self-scrutiny is understood. The grounds of choice have to survive investigation based on close reasoning (with adequate reflection and, when necessary, dialogue with others), taking note of more information if and when it is relevant and accessible. We can not only assess our decisions, given our objectives and values; we can also scrutinize the critical sustainability of these objectives and values themselves.[11]

---

* While some technical issues, including some mathematical ones, are involved in developing this point of view, the main argument can be fairly easily understood in terms of seeing rationality as conformity with reasons that one can sustain, even after scrutiny, and not just at first sight. For a general presentation and defence of this approach, see my essay 'Introduction: Rationality and Freedom' in *Rationality and Freedom* (2002). The more technical questions are addressed in essays 3–7 in the same volume. See also Richard Tuck, *Free Riding* (Cambridge, MA: Harvard University Press, 2008).

This is not, of course, the same thing as demanding that every time we choose something, we must undertake an extensive critical scrutiny – life would be intolerable if rational behaviour were to demand that. But it can be argued that a choice would count as rational only if it would be sustainable *had* a reasoned critical scrutiny been undertaken. When the reasons for a particular choice are established in our mind through experience or habit formation, we may often choose reasonably enough without sweating over the rationality of every decision. There is nothing particularly contrary in such norms of sensible behaviour (even though we may sometimes get deceived by old fixed habits to which we are wedded when new circumstances demand a departure). A person whose habitual choice of after-dinner coffee tends to be decaffeinated, even though she enjoys decaffeinated coffee less than regular coffee, may not be acting irrationally, despite not undertaking a reasoned scrutiny on each occasion. Her habit may be based on her implicit reasoning because of her general understanding that coffee at that hour would keep her awake, as shown by her past experience. She does not have to recollect on every occasion the tossing and turning in the bed that would result from her drinking regular coffee at that hour. Sustainable reasoning can exist without undertaking explicit scrutiny on every occasion.

This general approach to rational choice – seeing rational choice as choice based on sustainable reasons – has appeared to some to be so general that there has been an evident temptation to think that it could not possibly amount to saying anything much at all. In fact, however, the understanding of rational choice as choice based on sustainable reasoning makes quite strong claims of its own, while rejecting a variety of other claims about the nature of 'rational choice'. Indeed, seeing rational choice as critically scrutinized choice is both exacting and permissive.

It is exacting in that no simple formula (such as the maximization of self-interest) is automatically taken to be rational without subjecting that formula to a searching scrutiny, including critical examination of both the objects to pursue and the constraints of sensible behaviour that one may have reason to follow. For example, the narrow view of rationality reflected in the so-called rational choice theory would not have any immediate claim to being taken to be appropriate.

It is worth noting here that the general framework of maximization which provides a mathematical structure to disciplined choice is itself much broader than maximization of self-interest in particular.* If one's goals go beyond one's own specific interest and bring in broader values that one has reason to advance or appreciate, then the maximization of goal fulfilment can depart from the specific demands of self-interest maximization. Further, if one has reason to accept certain self-imposed constraints of 'decent behaviour' (varying from following safety rules of orderly exit without jostling one's way to the exit door as the fire alarm sounds, to more mundane practices like not racing to take the most comfortable chair in a social gathering, leaving others far behind), then goal maximization subject to those self-imposed constraints can conform to the broad demands of rationality.†

If the approach of rational choice as 'critically scrutinized choice' is, in this sense, more exacting than following the simple formula of self-interest maximization, it is also more permissive in that it does not rule out the possibility that more than one particular identification

* The ability of the mathematics of maximization to take on board different types of constraints and varieties of goals (including menu-dependent preferences) is discussed in my 'Maximization and the Act of Choice', *Econometrica*, 65 (1997). See also *Rationality and Freedom* (2002). I should, however, note here that the analytical characterization of maximization does not quite capture the way in which that term is often used in loose speech. If I am told that I should be aware of the fact that 'Paul is a ferocious maximizer', I would not be tempted to think that Paul relentlessly pursues the maximization of the social good in a selfless way. The common and distinctly unflattering use of the term 'maximizer' is perfectly fine within its own linguistic context, but it has to be distinguished from the analytical characterization of maximization.

† Sometimes these rules of decent behaviour are also in one's self-interest in the long run, but the justification for it need not be based only on the pursuit of self-interest. The point to ascertain is not so much whether a practice serves one's self-interest (that can be one important reason among others to follow a rule), but whether one has reason enough to follow that rule (whether based on self-interest or on some other reasoned ground). The distinction is analysed in my 'Maximization and the Act of Choice', *Econometrica*, 65 (1997). See also Walter Bossert and Kotaro Suzumura, 'Rational Choice on General Domains', in Kaushik Basu and Ravi Kanbur (eds), *Arguments for a Better World: Essays in Honor of Amartya Sen*, Vol. 1 (Oxford: Oxford University Press, 2009), and Shatakshee Dhongde and Prasanta K. Pattanaik, 'Preference, Choice and Rationality: Amartya Sen's Critique of the Theory of Rational Choice in Economics', in Christopher W. Morris (ed.), *Amartya Sen*, Contemporary Philosophy in Focus series (Cambridge: Cambridge University Press, 2009).

of what can be chosen with reason could survive a person's critical scrutiny. One person could be rather more altruistic than another without either of them violating the norms of rationality. We might also find one person more reasonable than another, invoking – perhaps implicitly – what our idea of being 'reasonable' is in a social context (as John Rawls has done), but that would not make the latter person necessarily irrational. Though the demands of critical self-scrutiny are exacting, it can still allow a variety of competing reasons to receive contending attention.*

There is, however, a rather straightforward implication of this permissibility that is worth commenting on. Since the demands of rational choice might not invariably yield the identification of a unique alternative that must be chosen, the use of rational choice for predictive purposes cannot but be problematic. How can rational choice point to what would be actually chosen if there is more than one alternative that could count as rational? It is one thing to accept the need to understand the nature of rational choice because of its own importance and also for its relevance in analysing actual choice, but it is quite another to expect that an understanding of rationality of choice could be immediately translated into the prediction of actual choice based on the set of choices that all count as rational, even when human beings are assumed to stick invariably to choices that are rational.

The possibility of plurality of sustainable reasons is not only important in giving rationality its due, it also distances the idea of rational choice from its putative role as a simple predictor of actual choice, as it has been widely used in mainstream economics. Even if every actual choice happens to be invariably rational in the sense of being sustainable by critical scrutiny, the plurality of rational choice makes it hard to obtain a unique prediction about a person's actual choice from the idea of rationality alone.

* See also George Akerlof, 'Economics and Identity', *Quarterly Journal of Economics*, 115 (2000); John Davis, *Theory of the Individual in Economics: Identity and Value* (London: Routledge, 2003); Richard H. Thaler and Cass R. Sunstein, *Nudge: Improving Decisions about Health, Wealth and Happiness* (New Haven, Conn.: Yale University Press, 2008).

# THE NARROWING OF
# MAINSTREAM ECONOMICS

In his classic book on economic theory, *Mathematical Psychics*, the remarkable economist Francis Edgeworth, perhaps the leading economic theorist at the end of the nineteenth century, talked about an interesting dichotomy between the assumption of human behaviour on which his economic analysis was based (in common with the tradition of ongoing economics), and his own belief about the actual nature of individual behaviour.[12] Edgeworth noted that 'the first principle of economics is that every agent is actuated only by self-interest'. He was not going to depart from that, at least in his formal theory, even though he did believe that the contemporary human being is 'for the most part an impure egoist, a mixed utilitarian'. If we are a little bothered by the fact that so great an economist would spend so much of his life and analytical power in developing a line inquiry 'the first principle' of which he believed to be false, the experience of economic theory in the century to follow has made us rather more used to this particular dissonance between belief and assumption. The assumption of the completely egoistic human being has come to dominate much of mainstream economic theory, while many of the great practitioners of the discipline have also expressed their serious doubts about the veracity of that assumption.

This dichotomy has not, however, always been present in economics. The early authors on economic matters, such as Aristotle, as well as medieval practitioners (including Aquinas, Ockham, Maimonides and others), took ethics as an important part of understanding human behaviour; they gave ethical principles important roles in behavioural relations in society.* This applied also to the economists

---

* I am referring here to the Western traditions, but similar analysis can be made of other traditions; for example, Kautilya, the Indian political economist of 4th century BC (a contemporary of Aristotle), had discussed the role of ethical behaviour in economic and political success, even though he was fairly sceptical about the actual reach of moral sentiments (see Kautilya, *The Arthasastra*, translated and edited by L. N. Rangarajan (Harmondsworth: Penguin Books, 1992)). See also Chapter 3, 'Institutions and Persons'.

of the early modern age (such as William Petty, Gregory King, François Quesnay and others), who were all much concerned, in various ways, with ethical analysis.

The same holds – and in a much more articulate way – for the line of thinking on these issues by Adam Smith, the father of modern economics. Smith is often wrongly thought to be a proponent of the assumption of the exclusive pursuit of self-interest, in the form of the so-called 'economic man'. In fact, Smith discussed fairly elaborately the limitations of the assumption of a universal pursuit of self-interest. He pointed to the fact that 'self-love', as he called the underlying impulse behind narrowly self-interested behaviour, might be just one of many motivations that human beings have. He distinguished clearly between different reasons for going against the dictates of self-love, including *inter alia* the following:

*sympathy* ('the most humane actions require no self-denial, no self-command, no great exertion of the sense of priority', and 'consist only in doing what this exquisite sympathy would of its own accord prompt us to do');
*generosity* ('it is otherwise with generosity', when 'we sacrifice some great and important interest of our own to an equal interest of a friend or of a superior');
*public spirit* ('when he compares those two objects with one another, he does not view them in the light in which they naturally appear to himself, but in that in which they appear to the nation he fights for').[13]

A person's basic 'sympathy' can, in many cases, make him or her do spontaneously things that are good for others, with 'no self-denial' involved, since the person enjoys helping others. In other cases, he may invoke the 'impartial spectator' (an idea that I have already discussed) to guide 'the principles of his conduct'.[14] This would permit consideration of 'public spirit' as well as 'generosity'. Smith discussed extensively the need for non-self-interested behaviour, and went on to argue that while 'prudence' was 'of all virtues that which is most helpful to the individual', we have to recognize that 'humanity, justice, generosity, and public spirit, are the qualities most useful to others'.[15]

The interpretation of Smith has been a veritable battleground. Despite Smith's frequent discussion of the importance of motivations other than self-interest, he has somehow developed the reputation for being a champion of the unique pursuit of self-interest by all human beings. For example, in two well-known and forcefully argued papers, the famous Chicago economist George Stigler has presented his 'self-interest theory' (including the belief that 'self-interest dominates the majority of men') as being 'on Smithian lines'.[16] Stigler was not being idiosyncratic in that diagnosis: this is indeed the standard view of Smith that has been powerfully promoted by many writers who constantly invoke Smith to support their view of society.[17] This bit of misinterpretation of Smith has even found a place in English literature through a limerick of Stephen Leacock (who was both a literary writer and an economist):

> Adam, Adam, Adam Smith
> Listen what I charge you with!
> Didn't you say
> In a class one day
> That selfishness was bound to pay?
> Of all doctrines that was the Pith.
> Wasn't it, wasn't it, wasn't it, Smith?[18]

While some men are born small and some achieve smallness, it is clear that Adam Smith has had much smallness thrust upon him.[19]

One reason for this confusion is the tendency of many economists to concentrate on a different issue, that is, Smith's elaboration of the point that to explain the motivation for economic exchange in the market we do not have to invoke any objective other than the pursuit of self-interest. In his most famous and widely quoted passage from the *Wealth of Nations*, Smith wrote: 'It is not from the benevolence of the butcher, the brewer, or the baker that we expect our dinner, but from their regard to their own interest. We address ourselves, not to their humanity but to their self-love . . .'.[20] The butcher, the brewer and the baker want to get our money by giving us the meat, the beer and the bread they make, and we – the consumers – want their meat, beer and bread and are ready to pay for them with our money. The exchange benefits us all, and we do not have to be raving altruists for such exchanges to go through.

In some schools of economics, the readers of Smith do not seem to go beyond those few lines, even though that discussion is addressed only to one very specific issue, namely *exchange* (rather than distribution or production), and in particular, the *motivation* underlying exchange (rather than what makes normal exchanges sustainable, such as trust). In the rest of Smith's writings there are extensive discussions of the role of other motivations that influence human action and behaviour.

Smith also made the point that sometimes our moral behaviour tends to take the form of simply following established conventions. While he noted that 'men of reflection and speculation' can see the force of some of these moral arguments more easily than 'the bulk of mankind',[21] there is no suggestion in Smith's writings that people in general systematically fail to be influenced by moral considerations in choosing their behaviour. What is important to note, however, is Smith's recognition that even when we are moved by the implications of moral arguments, we may not see them in that explicit form and may perceive our choices in terms of acting according to well-established practice in our society. As he put in *The Theory of Moral Sentiments*: 'Many men behave very decently, and through the whole of their lives avoid any considerable degree of blame, who yet, perhaps, never felt the sentiment upon the propriety of which we found our approbation of their conduct, but acted merely from a regard to what they saw were the established rules of behaviour.'[22] This focus on the power of 'established rules of behaviour' plays a very important part in the Smithian analysis of human behaviour and its social implications. The established rules are not confined to following the dictates of self-love.

However, while Smith was perfectly clear on the importance of a variety of motivations that, directly or indirectly, move human beings (as was noted at the beginning of this chapter), a very large part of modern economics has increasingly fallen for the simplicity of ignoring all motivations other than the pursuit of self-interest, and brand-named 'rational choice theory' has even elevated this falsely alleged uniformity in human behaviour into the basic principle of rationality. To that connection I now turn.

## SELF-INTEREST, SYMPATHY AND COMMITMENT

Even though so-called 'rational choice theory' takes the rationality of choice to be characterized by intelligent pursuit of self-interest, it need not rule out the possibility that a person may have sympathy or antipathy towards others. In a more restricted version of RCT (increasingly out of fashion now), it has sometimes been assumed that rational persons must not only be self-seeking, but they must also be detached from others, so that they are completely unaffected by the well-being or achievements of others. But taking an interest in others need not make people any less self-seeking (or involve 'no self-denial', as Smith put it), if they end up promoting their own welfare, taking note of their own enjoyment – or suffering – from the welfare of others. There is a significant difference between, first, taking note of how one's own welfare is affected by the circumstances of others and then exclusively pursuing one's own welfare (including what comes from reaction to the lives of other people), and second, departing from the single-minded pursuit of one's own welfare altogether. The former is still a part of the broader story of self-interested behaviour and can be accommodated within the approach of RCT.

More than thirty years ago, I tried in a paper entitled 'Rational Fools' (it was my Herbert Spencer Lecture at Oxford) to explore the distinction between 'sympathy' and 'commitment' as possible foundations for other-regarding behaviour.* Sympathy (including antipathy when it is negative) refers to 'one person's welfare being affected by the position of others' (for example, a person can feel depressed at the sight of misery of others), whereas 'commitment' is 'concerned

* Amartya Sen, 'Rational Fools: A Critique of the Behavioural Foundations of Economic Theory', *Philosophy and Public Affairs*, 6 (1977), reprinted in *Choice, Welfare and Measurement* (Oxford: Blackwell, 1982; Cambridge, MA: Harvard University Press, 1997), and also in Jane J. Mansbridge (ed.), *Beyond Self-Interest* (Chicago, IL: University of Chicago Press, 1990). This two-fold distinction between sympathy and commitment, while much less articulate than Adam Smith's multi-category differentiation between a variety of distinct motivations, which go against the dominance of a narrow pursuit of self-interest, is, as should be obvious, much inspired by Smith's analysis.

with breaking the tight link between individual welfare (with or without sympathy) and the choice of action (for example, being committed to help remove some misery even though one personally does not suffer from it)'.[23] Sympathy is combinable with self-interested behaviour, and is indeed compatible even with what Adam Smith called self-love. If one tries to remove the misery of others only because – and only to the extent that – it affects one's own welfare, this does not signify a departure from self-love as the only accepted reason for action.* But if one is committed, say, to doing what can be done to remove the misery of others – whether or not one's own welfare is affected by it, and not merely to the extent to which one's own welfare is so influenced – then that *is* a clear departure from self-interested behaviour.

One of the leading architects of contemporary rational choice theory, Professor Gary Becker, has provided an illuminating exposition of RCT in its broader form, by making systematic room for sympathy for others as part of human sentiment, while still sticking to the exclusive pursuit of self-interest. Indeed, people need not be self-centred to be self-interested, and may take note of others' interests *within* their own utility. But Becker's new analysis in *Accounting for Tastes* (1996), while breaking much fresh ground, does not depart fundamentally at all from the basic beliefs presented earlier by him in his classic and much-cited work, *Economic Approaches to Human Behavior* (1976): 'All human behavior can be viewed as involving participants who (1) maximize their utility (2) form a stable set of preferences and (3) accumulate an optimal amount of information and other inputs in a variety of markets.'[24]

What is really central to the approach of RCT, without any unnecessary restriction, is that the maximand for one's choice of

---

* Thomas Nagel also made another important distinction in his pioneering critique of the exclusive reliance on self-interested behaviour (*The Possibility of Altruism* (Oxford: Clarendon Press, 1970)), between a case in which a person may benefit from altruistic action but does not undertake altruistic action for that reason, and a person who undertakes that action precisely *because* he expects to benefit personally from it. Even though in terms only of observed choices, without any motivational scrutiny, the two cases may look much the same, it is nevertheless important to note that the latter fits into the general approach of self-interest-based RCT in a way that the former case would not.

behaviour is nothing other than one's own interest or well-being, and this central assumption is compatible with recognizing that various influences on one's own interest and well-being may come from the lives and well-being of other people. Thus the Beckerian 'utility function' that the person is seen as maximizing stands for *both* the person's maximand in reasoned choice, and as a representation of the person's own self-interest. That congruence is extremely important for many of the economic and social analyses that Becker undertakes.

For RCT, then, with its focus on the pursuit of self-interest as the only rational basis of choice, we can easily accommodate sympathy, but must avoid commitment: thus far and no further. Becker's is certainly a welcome broadening of RCT from the unnecessarily restrictive version championed earlier, but we must also note what RCT in this Beckerian form still leaves out. It does not, in particular, make room for any reason that may lead one to pursue a different goal from one's own welfare (for example, 'no matter what happens to me, I must help her', or 'I am ready to sacrifice a lot for fighting for the independence of my country'), or – going further – even depart from the exclusive pursuit of one's own goal (for example, 'this is indeed my goal, but I must not promote my own goal single-mindedly since I should be fair to others as well'). Perhaps the most important issue to clarify here, in the context of the present discussion of reason and rationality, is that not only does RCT, even in its broader form, presume that people do not actually have different goals from the pursuit of their own welfare, but it also assumes that they would be violating the demands of rationality if they were to accommodate any goal or any motivation other than the single-minded pursuit of their own welfare, after taking note of whatever external factors influence it.*

---

\* See also the important paper of Christine Jolls, Cass Sunstein and Richard Thaler, 'A Behavioral Approach to Law and Economics', *Stanford Law Review*, 50 (May 1998). Jolls, Sunstein and Thaler go much further along the path of reducing the self-centred characterization of self-interest, and the extensions they suggest have empirical plausibility and explanatory value. But they are not any more hostile, in this paper, to the basic congruence of (1) one's own welfare (with all sympathies and antipathies taken into account), and (2) the maximand one uses for reasoned choice. The critique that these authors present is thus an important contribution to the debate 'within' the basic conception of rationality as formulated in rational choice theory

## COMMITMENTS AND GOALS

It is easy to see that there is nothing particularly unusual, or especially contrary to reason, for a person to choose to pursue a goal that is not exclusively confined to his or her own self-interest. As Adam Smith noted, we do have many different motivations, taking us well beyond the single-minded pursuit of our interest. There is nothing contrary to reason in our willingness to do things that are not entirely self-serving. Some of these motivations, like 'humanity, justice, generosity and public spirit', may even be very productive for society, as Smith noted.*

There tends to be, however, more resistance to accepting the possibility that people may have good reasons even to go beyond the pursuit of their own goals (whether or not the goals themselves are based only on self-interest). The argument runs: if you are consciously not pursuing what you think are your goals, then clearly those cannot actually be your goals. Indeed, many authors have taken the view that the claim that one can have reason not to be confined to the pursuit of one's goals is 'nonsensical since even strongly heterogeneous or altruistic agents cannot pursue other people's goals without making them their own'.†

The point to note here is that in denying that rationality demands

---

(RCT) in its broadest form. I have discussed the reach and the limits of the critique presented by Jolls, Sunstein and Thaler in the introductory essay to *Rationality and Freedom*: 'Introduction: Rationality and Freedom' (Cambridge, MA: Harvard University Press, 2002), pp. 26–37.

* *The Theory of Moral Sentiments*, p. 189. Smith considers various reasons for giving room to a variety of such motivations, including moral appeal and behavioural grace as well as their social usefulness.

† This is how Fabienne Peter and Hans Bernhard Schmid summarize a line of critique of departing from 'self-goal choice' in their introductory essay to a very interesting collection of papers on this and related themes: 'Symposium on Rationality and Commitment: Introduction', *Economics and Philosophy*, 21 (2005), p. 1. My treatment of this objection draws on my response to a larger collection of essays put together by Peter and Schmid (with their own important contributions on this subject) included in that volume: 'Rational Choice: Discipline, Brand Name and Substance', in Fabienne Peter and Hans Bernhard Schmid (eds), *Rationality and Commitment* (Oxford: Clarendon Press, 2007).

that you must act single-mindedly according to your own goals (subject only to constraints that are *not* self-imposed), you do not necessarily dedicate yourself to the promotion of the goals of others. We can reason our way towards following decent rules of behaviour that we see as being fair to others as well, which can restrain the unique dominance of single-minded pursuit of our own goals. There is nothing particularly mysterious about our respect for sensible rules of conduct, which can qualify the pursuit of what we rightly – and reasonably – see as goals that we would in general like to advance.

Consider an example of such restraint that does not force us to take on other people's goals as our 'real goals'. You happen to be occupying a window seat in a plane journey, with the window shade up on a sunny day. That is when you hear the occupant of the aisle seat next to you requesting you to pull down the shade ('if you would, please') so that he can see his computer screen better, to be able to devote himself fully to playing some computer game. You know that game and it is in your view a 'plainly silly' game ('a great waste of time'). You are, in general, frustrated that there is so much ignorance around, with so many people playing inane games rather than reading the news – boning up on what is actually happening in Iraq, or Afghanistan, or for that matter in your home town. You decide, nevertheless, to behave well and comply with the game-enthusiast's request, and you oblige him by pulling the shutter down.

What can we say about your choice? There is no difficulty in understanding that you are not averse to helping your neighbour – or anyone else – pursue his or her well-being, but it so happens that you do not think that your neighbour's well-being is, in fact, best advanced by his wasting his time – and by your helping him to waste his time – on a very silly game. You remain, in fact, entirely willing to lend him your copy of the *New York Times*, reading which would be, you are convinced, much better for your neighbour's edification and well-being. Your action is not a corollary of any general pursuit of well-being.

The main issue here may rather be whether you should impose – or refuse to dismantle – barriers to the pursuit of other people's goals, when these goals are not in any sense evil, even if – as in this case – you do think that they are not conducive to promoting their own well-being. Perhaps you are reluctant, as a general rule, to be unhelpful to your neighbour (no matter what you think of their goals). Or maybe you judge that, while having a window seat gives you control over the proximate shutter, this incidental advantage should not be used by you without taking into account what others want to do and how that would be affected by your choice regarding the window shade (even though you yourself were rather enjoying the sun which would now be shut out and even though you think very little of the goal that the other guy wants to pursue).

These arguments may be explicitly invoked or implicitly considered in your decision, but is it right to think that your socially influenced behaviour shows that your objective is to help others to pursue their own goals, no matter what you think of their goals? Thanks to your acceptance of social norms of behaviour, you have certainly ended up helping the guy next to you to pursue his own goal. But it is surely too much to say either that your objective is to maximally help others to pursue their respective goals, or that their goals have somehow become yours as well ('Thank God, no,' you heave a sigh of relief). Rather, you are just following a norm of good behaviour you happen to approve of (let others do what they really want), which is a self-imposed behavioural restraint you accept in your choice of what to do.

There is nothing very peculiar, or silly, or irrational about your decision to 'let others be'. We live in a world in which there are a lot of other people, and we can give them room for their own way of living even without adopting their way as something that we must see as a good thing to promote. Commitment may take the form not only of wanting to pursue goals that are not entirely parasitic on self-interest; it can also take the form of following rules of passable, even perhaps generous, behaviour, that restrain our inclination to be guided exclusively by the promotion of our own goals, irrespective of its impact on others. Being considerate of the desires and pursuits of others need not be seen as a violation of rationality.

# 9

# Plurality of Impartial Reasons

It was argued in the last chapter that there is nothing extraordinary or irrational in making choices and decisions that cross the narrow boundaries of exclusive pursuit of personal self-interest. People's goals can go well beyond the single-minded promotion of self-interest only, and their choices may even go beyond the single-minded pursuit of their personal goals, perhaps moved by some concern for decency of behaviour, allowing others to pursue their goals as well. The insistence of so-called rational choice theory on defining rationality simply as intelligent promotion of personal self-interest sells human reasoning extremely short.

The connection between rationality of choice and the sustainability of the reasons behind the choice was discussed in the last chapter. In this understanding, rationality is primarily a matter of basing – explicitly or by implication – our choices on reasoning that we can reflectively *sustain*, and it demands that our choices, as well as our actions and objectives, values and priorities, can survive our own seriously undertaken critical scrutiny. It was also discussed why there is no particular ground for imagining that every motivation other than the pursuit of self-interest must somehow be guillotined by such a critical scrutiny.

However, while rationality of choice can easily allow non-self-interested motivations, rationality does not on its own demand this. While there is nothing odd or irrational about someone being moved by concern for others, it would be harder to argue that there is some necessity or obligation to have such concern on grounds of rationality alone. We can have sustainable reasons for action that reflect our inclinations and our own individual lines of self-scrutiny. Rationality as a characteristic of choice behaviour rules out neither the dedicated altruist, nor the reasoned seeker of personal gain.

If Mary decides, in a cogent and intelligent way, to pursue her idea of the social good, even at great sacrifice to herself, it would be hard to see her, for that reason, as being 'irrational'. And yet the charge of irrationality may be difficult to sustain against Paul even if he were a no-nonsense maximizer of self-interest, provided his values, priorities and choices would survive his own serious scrutiny.* Commitment to the concerns of others might simply be less important for Paul than for Mary.† We may well think that Paul is a less 'reasonable' person than Mary, but as John Rawls has discussed, this is a different issue from irrationality as such.[1] Rationality is in fact a rather permissive discipline, which demands the test of reasoning, but allows reasoned self-scrutiny to take quite different forms, without necessarily imposing any great uniformity of criteria. If rationality were a church, it would be a rather broad church. Indeed, the demands of reasonableness, as characterized by Rawls, tends to be more exacting than the requirements of mere rationality.‡

---

* Paul would have to take note, among other considerations, of the fact that a no-nonsense pursuit of self-love may adversely affect his relations with others, which could be a loss even for self-interested reasons.

† The term 'rational' allows a further distinction that has been illuminatingly pursued by Thomas Scanlon: (1) what a person has most reason to do, and (2) what a person must do to avoid being irrational (see Scanlon, *What We Owe to Each Other* (Cambridge, MA: Harvard University Press, 1998), pp. 25–30). Mary and Paul could be seen as being rational in *both* senses. There remains, however, the further issue of sustainability of the reasons invoked, which is central to the idea of rationality as seen in this work (see Chapter 8), and is more fully discussed in my book *Rationality and Freedom* (2002).

‡ However, in illustrating the 'familiar distinction between reasonableness and rationality', Thomas Scanlon gives an example that seems to go the other way (*What We Owe to Each Other*, pp. 192–3). A person, Scanlon points out, may find a possible objection to a powerful person's behaviour to be entirely 'reasonable', and yet may decide that it would be 'irrational' to express that indictment because of the likely anger of that person: so a reasonable statement need not, rationally, be expressed in some circumstances. There are, it seems to me, two distinct issues placed together here. First, the respective demands of rationality and reasonableness are different and need not coincide (and I would tend to argue, in general, that reasonableness would typically demand something *more* than just rationality). Second, the rationality of an understanding or a decision has to be distinguished from the rationality of publicly

The demands of scrutiny would have to be sharpened and tightened when we move from the idea of rationality to that of reasonableness, if we broadly follow John Rawls in interpreting that distinction. As was discussed in Chapter 5 ('Impartiality and Objectivity'), the idea of objectivity in practical reason and behaviour can be systematically linked to demands of impartiality. Drawing on this, we can take the relevant standard of objectivity of ethical principles to be linked to their defensibility in an open and free framework of public reasoning.* Other people's perspectives and assessments as well as interests would have a role here in a way that rationality alone need not demand.†

We must, however, investigate more closely the idea of defensibility in reasoning with others. What does defensibility demand and why?

## WHAT OTHERS CANNOT REASONABLY REJECT

In the play *King John* by William Shakespeare, Philip the Bastard remarks that our general evaluation of the world is often influenced by our own special interests:

> Well, whiles I am a beggar, I will rail
> And say there is no sin but to be rich;

---

expressing that understanding or decision. The distinction between 'a good statement' and 'a good statement to make' can often be quite momentous in the dual discipline of thought and communication. I have tried to analyse the distinction in my essay 'Description as Choice', in *Choice, Welfare and Measurement* (Oxford: Blackwell, 1982, and Cambridge, MA: Harvard University Press, 1997).

* Rawls's own wording seems to concentrate on open dialogue, not with all, but only with 'reasonable people', and the distinction between this approach with some clearly stated normative elements (reflected in the diagnosis of 'reasonable persons' and what they would find to be 'reasonable') and the more fully procedural view of Habermas was discussed in Chapter 5. I argued there that the distinction may not be as sharp as it might at first appear.

† It is possible to define in different ways the reach of 'an open and free framework of public reasoning', and the differences in formulation may be quite significant in seeing the precise – and sometimes subtle – distinctions between Rawls's use of this approach and the uses made by others, including Kant and Habermas. I shall not, however, go further into these issues of differentiation here, since they are not central to the approach of this book.

And being rich, my virtue then shall be
To say there is no vice but beggary.*

It is hard to deny that our positions and predicaments can influence our general attitudes and political beliefs about social differences and asymmetries. If we take self-scrutiny very seriously, it is possible that we may be hard-minded enough to seek more consistency in our general evaluative judgements (so that, for example, our judgements on the rich do not radically vary depending on whether we are ourselves rich or poor). But there is nothing to guarantee that this type of exacting scrutiny will always occur, since we are capable of much self-indulgence in our views and opinions of things in which we are directly involved, and this may restrain the reach of our self-scrutiny.

In the social context, involving fairness to other people, there would be some necessity to go beyond the requirements of rationality in terms of permissive self-scrutiny, and to consider the demands of 'reasonable conduct' towards others. In that more demanding context, we must pay serious attention to the perspectives and concerns of others, as they would have a role in the scrutiny to which our decisions and choices can be sensibly subjected. In this sense, our understanding of right and wrong in society has to go beyond what Adam Smith called the dictates of 'self-love'.

Indeed, as Thomas Scanlon has persuasively argued, 'thinking about right and wrong is, at the most basic level, thinking about what could be justified to others on grounds that they, if appropriately motivated, could not reasonably reject'.[2] While survival under one's own engaged scrutiny is central to the idea of rationality, taking serious note of critical scrutiny from the perspectives of others must have a significant role in taking us beyond rationality into reasonable behaviour in relation to other people. There is clearly room here for the demands of political and social ethics.

Is Scanlon's criterion different from the demands of Rawlsian fairness, through the device of the 'original position', which was examined earlier? Certainly, there is a strong connection between the two. Indeed, the Rawlsian 'veil of ignorance' in the 'original position' (whereby no one knows who he or she is going to be in the real world)

* William Shakespeare, *King John*, II. 1. 593-6.

197

was devised by Rawls to make people see beyond their personal vested interests and goals. And yet there are substantial differences between Rawls's firmly 'contractarian' approach, focusing ultimately on mutual benefits through agreement, and Scanlon's broader analysis of reasoning (even though Scanlon rather muddies the water by insisting on calling his own approach 'contractualist').

In Rawlsian analysis, when the representatives of the people congregate and determine what principles must be seen as 'just' for guiding the basic institutional structure of the society, the interests of the different persons all count (in an anonymous way, since no one knows, thanks to 'the veil of ignorance', who exactly anyone is actually going to be). As Rawls characterized the original position in his *Theory of Justice*, the parties or their representatives do not unleash any specific moral views or cultural values of their own in the deliberations of the original position; their task is merely to best advance their own interests and the interests of those whom they represent. Even though all the parties pursue their respective interests, the contract on which a unanimity is meant to emerge can be seen, in the Rawlsian perspective, as the best for the interests of all, taken together, under the 'veil of ignorance' (since the veil prevents anyone from knowing who exactly he or she is going to be).* Impartial aggregation through the use of 'the veil of ignorance', it must be emphasized, need not be an unproblematic search, since it is not at all clear what would be chosen in that kind of devised uncertainty. The absence of a unique solution, unanimously chosen by all the parties, corresponds to the absence of a unique social aggregation of the conflicting interests of different people. For example, the Rawlsian distributional formula of prioritiz-

---

* See John Harsanyi, 'Cardinal Welfare, Individualistic Ethics, and Interpersonal Comparisons of Utility', *Journal of Political Economy*, 63 (1955). There are other claimants to a solution, for example maximizing an equity-adjusted sum-total of utilities, as proposed by James Mirrlees ('An Exploration of the Theory of Optimal Income Taxation', *Review of Economic Studies*, 38, 1971). See also John Broome, *Weighing Lives* (Oxford: Clarendon Press, 2004). I shall not go further into this question here, but it is addressed in my *Collective Choice and Social Welfare* (San Francisco, CA: Holden-Day, 1970, and Amsterdam: North-Holland, 1979); *On Economic Inequality* (Oxford: Clarendon Press, 1973, expanded edition, jointly with James E. Foster, 1997); and 'Social Choice Theory', in Kenneth Arrow and Michael Intriligator (eds), *Handbook of Mathematical Economics* (Amsterdam: North-Holland, 1986).

ing the interests of the worst-off has to compete with the utilitarian formula of maximizing the sum of the utilities of all: indeed, John Harsanyi arrives at this utilitarian solution precisely on the basis of a similar use of imagined uncertainty about who is going to be which person.

In contrast, in Scanlon's formulation, even though it is the interests of the parties that serve as the basis of the public discussion, the arguments can come from anyone in that society or elsewhere who can give specific grounds for thinking that the decisions to be made could or could not be 'reasonably rejected'. While the involved parties have standing precisely because their interests are affected, arguments about what can or cannot be reasonably rejected on their behalf can bring in different moral perspectives if they are judged to be reasonable, rather than confining attention to the lines of thinking of the involved parties themselves. In this sense, Scanlon's approach allows a move in the direction explored by Adam Smith in his idea of the 'impartial spectator' (see Chapter 8), even though the mooring of all the arguments remains confined, even in Scanlon's analysis, to the concerns and interests of the affected parties themselves.

There is also an inclusional broadening in the Scanlonian approach since the persons whose interests are affected need not all come from only one given society or nation or polity, as in the Rawlsian 'people by people' pursuit of justice. Scanlon's formulation allows broadening of the collectivity of people whose *interests* are seen as relevant: they need not all be citizens of a particular sovereign state, as in the Rawlsian model. Also, since the search is for generic reasons that people in various positions have, the assessments of the local people are not the only views that matter. I have already commented, in Chapter 6 in particular, on the restrictive nature of the Rawlsian 'contractarian' approach in limiting the range of the perspectives that are allowed to count in public deliberations and, to the extent that Scanlon's so-called 'contractualist' approach removes some of these restrictions, we have good reason to build on Scanlon's formulation rather than on Rawls's.

Scanlon's reason for calling his approach 'contractualist' (which does not, I think, help to bring out his differences with the contractarian mode of thinking) is, as he explains, his use of 'the idea of a shared willingness to modify our private demands in order to find a basis of justification that others also have reason to accept'. While this does not presuppose any contract, Scanlon is not wrong in seeing this idea 'as a central element in the social contract tradition going back to Rousseau' (p. 5). But in this general form this is also a basic idea that is shared by many other traditions as well, from Christian (I discussed, in Chapter 7, Jesus's arguments with the local lawyer on how to reason about the story of 'the good Samaritan') to the Smithian and even utilitarian (particularly in the Millian version). Scanlon's approach is a great deal more general than would appear from his own attempt to incarcerate it strictly within the confines of the 'social contract tradition'.

## THE PLURALITY OF NON-REJECTABILITY

I turn now to a different issue. It is important to see that Scanlon's way of identifying principles that can be seen as reasonable need not yield, in any way, a unique set of principles. Scanlon does not himself say much on the multiplicity of competing principles each of which may pass his test of non-rejectability. If he had done that, then the contrast between his so-called 'contractualist' approach and a proper 'contractarian' approach would have become even more transparent. A contractarian approach – whether that of Hobbes or Rousseau or Rawls – has to lead to one specific contract; in Rawls's case, it specifies a unique set of 'principles of justice' under 'justice as fairness'. Indeed, it is very important to see how crucial that uniqueness is for the institutional basis of Rawlsian thinking, since it is that unique set of demands that determines, as Rawls tells the story, the basic institutional structure of a society. The unfolding of the Rawlsian account of a just society proceeds from that first institutional step based on agreement on a unique set of principles, before going on to other features (for example, the working of 'the legislative phase'). Had there been competing principles, with different institutional demands that all plurally emerge from the original position, then the Rawlsian story could not be told in the form in which he tells the story.

I have discussed this question earlier, in Chapter 2 ('Rawls and Beyond'), with a related but different focus – the implausibility of assuming that some unique set of principles would be unanimously chosen in the Rawlsian original position. If there were many alternatives that all remained ready to be chosen at the end of the exercise of fairness, then there would be no unique social contract that could be identified and which could serve as the basis of the institutional account that Rawls gives.

Something rather important is involved in understanding the possible plurality of robust and impartial reasons that can emerge from searching scrutiny. As was discussed earlier (in the Introduction), we have different types of competing reasons of justice, and it may be impossible to reject them all with the exception of just one set of complementary principles that cohere nicely and entirely with each other. Even when a person does have a clearly favourite priority, such priorities may vary from person to person, and it may be difficult for someone to reject altogether possibly well-defended reasons to which others give priority.

For example, in the case of the three children quarrelling about a flute which was discussed in the Introduction, it can be argued that all of the three alternative courses of action have justificatory arguments in support that cannot be reasonably rejected, even after much deliberation and scrutiny. The justificatory arguments on which the claims of the three children were respectively based can all take 'impartial' forms, even though differing in the focus on the impersonal grounds on which the three cases were built. One claim was based on the importance of fulfilment and happiness, another on the significance of economic equity, and the third on the recognition of the case for being entitled to enjoy the products of one's own labour. We may, of course, end up taking up one side or another in dealing with these competing grounds, but it would be very hard to claim that all the proposed grounds presented, except one, must be rejected as being 'non-impartial'. Indeed, even entirely impartial judges, who are not moved by vested interest or by personal eccentricity, may see the force of several disparate reasons of justice in a case like this, and they may well end up differing from each other on what decisions should be taken, since the competing arguments all have some claim to impartial support.

# THE MUTUAL BENEFITS
# OF COOPERATION

It is not hard to see why the contractarian approach appeals to some alleged 'realists' who want decent behaviour to emerge from some ultimate consideration of personal advantage. Rawls's desire to see 'society as a fair system of cooperation'* fits well into this general outlook. As Rawls puts it, the idea of cooperation 'includes the idea of each participant's rational advantage, or good', and 'the idea of rational advantage specifies what it is that those engaged in co-operation are seeking to advance from the standpoint of their own good'. There is something in common here with the self-interested perspective of rational choice theory except that it is used under the conditions of the original position, with a veil of ignorance about personal identities. Also, all the people involved clearly recognize that they cannot achieve what they would like without the cooperation of others. So cooperative behaviour is chosen as a group norm for the benefit of all, and it involves the joint choice of 'terms each participant may reasonably accept, and sometimes should accept, provided that everyone else likewise accepts them'.[3]

This may well be social morality, but it is ultimately a *prudential* social morality. Since the idea of mutually beneficial cooperation is so central to the conception of the Rawlsian original position, and since Rawls's invoking of the foundational idea of fairness is mainly through the device of the original position, there is a quintessentially advantage-based underpinning to the Rawlsian approach to 'justice as fairness'.

The advantage-based perspective is indeed important for social rules and behaviour, since there are many situations in which the joint interests of a group of people are much better served by everyone following rules of behaviour that restrain each person from trying to snatch a little gain at the cost of making things worse for the others. The real world is full of a great many problems of this kind, varying from environmental sustainability and the preservation of shared

---

* Significantly, this is the title of the second section of Part I of Rawls's *Justice as Fairness: A Restatement* (Cambridge, MA: Harvard University Press, 2001), pp. 5–8.

natural resources ('the commons') to work ethics in production processes and civic sense in urban living.[4]

In dealing with such situations, there are two grand ways of bringing
about the attainment of mutual benefits through cooperation, namely
agreed contracts that can be enforced, and social norms that may
work voluntarily in that direction. While both these routes have been
discussed, in one way or another, in the contractarian literature in
political philosophy, which goes back at least to Hobbes, it is the
contract-based enforceable route that has had the pride of place. In
contrast, the route of the evolution of social norms has been the
subject of much exploration in the sociological and anthropological
literature. The advantages of cooperative behaviour and the vindication of that behaviour through voluntary restraint of members of a
group have been very illuminatingly investigated by visionary social
analysts, such as Elinor Ostrom, to discuss the emergence and survival
of collective action through social norms of behaviour.[5]

## CONTRACTARIAN REASONING
## AND ITS REACH

There can be little doubt that the prudential argument, based ultimately on mutual benefit, for social cooperation and through that for
social morality and politics, has extensive relevance for the understanding of societies and their successes and failures. The contractarian line of reasoning has done much to explicate and develop
the perspective of social cooperation through ethical departures as
well as institutional arrangements. Political philosophy as well as
explanatory anthropology has been greatly strengthened by the discernment generated by contractarian reasoning.

In Rawls's hands, and those of Kant before him, that perspective
has also been much enriched from the more primitive – though
enlightening – analysis of social cooperation presented originally by
Thomas Hobbes in terms of directly prudential reasoning. Indeed,
Rawls's use of the 'mutual benefit' perspective has several distinctive
features of great importance, particularly for the use of impartial
reasoning, despite the fact that the driving force of 'cooperation for

mutual benefit' cannot but be ultimately prudential, in one way or another.

First, even though the idea of contract is used by Rawls to determine the nature of just social institutions and corresponding behavioural demands, Rawls's analysis relies not so much on strong-armed enforcement of the agreement (as in many contractarian theories), but on people's willingness to follow how they have, as it were, 'agreed' to behave. This way of seeing the issue has tended to distance Rawls from the need for punitive enforcement, which can be entirely avoided, at least in theory. Behavioural norms, then, take a post-contract recon-structed form – an issue that was also discussed earlier, particularly in Chapters 2 ('Rawls and Beyond') and 3 ('Institutions and Persons'). The demonstration of mutual advantage as a prelude to the contract in the original position yields the contract, and that in turn – at least the imagination of it (since it is a purely hypothetical contract) – shapes the behaviour of human beings in societies with just institutions set up through the principles embedded in the contract.*

Second, another feature that takes Rawlsian analysis well beyond the usual arguments for decent behaviour for the sake of mutual advantage is Rawls's way of ensuring that in the original position no one can argue or bargain from the knowledge of his or her actual position in society, but has to do so from behind the veil of ignorance. This moves the exercise from the pursuit of actual advantage for oneself to the promotion of advantage for the community as a whole, without knowing what one's own personal advantage would be in that overall picture. There is surely impartiality enough in this respect in the Rawlsian story, and yet the tie with advantage-seeking justifica-tion of cooperation, in this case in an impartial form (thanks to the veil of ignorance), is not transcended through this extension.

Through Rawls's analysis of 'justice as fairness', contractarian reasoning develops a reach that takes it well beyond the old territory

---

* Rawls's political account goes in a somewhat different line from the sociological account of gradual evolution of social norms developed by Elinor Ostrom and others, even though there are similarities in the behavioural implications of the two lines of reasoning. In Rawls's case, what begins in the recognition of the possibility of mutually advantageous contracts produces in turn a restraining influence on actual behaviour in society, on the basis of the political morality of agreement on a social contract.

of the contractarian literature. And yet the focus on individual advantage in general and on mutual advantage in particular is central to Rawls's line of reasoning as well (though in a sophisticated form), in common with the entire contractarian approach. Despite what contractarian reasoning achieves in this extended form, a question that awaits examination is whether advantage-seeking, in either a direct or an indirect form, provides the only robust basis of reasonable behaviour in society. A related question is whether mutual benefit and reciprocity must be the foundations of all political reasonableness.

## POWER AND ITS OBLIGATIONS

As a contrast let me consider another line of reasoning that takes the general form of arguing that if someone has the power to make a change that he or she can see will reduce injustice in the world, then there is a strong social argument for doing just that (without his or her reasoning having to intermediate the case for action through invoking the benefits of some imagined cooperation). This obligation of effective power contrasts with the mutual obligation for cooperation, at the basic plane of motivational justification.

The perspective of obligations of power was presented powerfully by Gautama Buddha in *Sutta-Nipata*.[6] Buddha argues there that we have responsibility to animals precisely because of the asymmetry between us, not because of any symmetry that takes us to the need for cooperation. He argues instead that since we are enormously more powerful than other species, we have some responsibility towards other species that connects exactly with this asymmetry of power.

Buddha goes on to illustrate the point by an analogy with the responsibility of the mother towards her child, not because she has given birth to the child (that connection is not invoked in this particular argument – there is room for it elsewhere), but because she can do things to influence the child's life that the child itself cannot do. The mother's reason for helping the child, in this line of thinking, is not guided by the rewards of cooperation, but precisely from her recognition that she can, asymmetrically, do things for the child that will make a huge difference to the child's life and which the child itself

THE IDEA OF JUSTICE

cannot do. The mother does not have to seek any mutual benefit – real or imagined – nor seek any 'as if' contract to understand her obligation to the child. That is the point that Gautama was making.

The justification here takes the form of arguing that if some action that can be freely undertaken is open to a person (thereby making it feasible), and if the person assesses that the undertaking of that action will create a more just situation in the world (thereby making it justice-enhancing), then that is argument enough for the person to consider seriously what he or she should do in view of these recognitions. There can, of course, be many actions that individually satisfy these dual conditions, which one may not be able to undertake. The reasoning here is, therefore, not a demand for full compliance whenever the two conditions are met, but an argument for acknowledging the obligation to consider the case for action. While it is possible to bring in some contractarian reasoning in an extended form – given its ingenuity – to work out a case for the mother to consider helping her child, it would be a much more roundabout way of getting to a conclusion that reasoning from the obligation of power can directly yield.

The basic point to recognize here is the existence of different approaches to the pursuit of reasonable behaviour, not all of which need be parasitic on the advantage-based reasoning of mutually beneficial cooperation. The seeking of mutual benefits, in a directly Hobbesian or anonymously Rawlsian form, does have enormous social relevance, but it is not the only kind of argument that is relevant to discussing what would be reasonable behaviour.

I end this discussion of the plurality of impartial reasons by making one final observation. The understanding of obligations related to what is now called the human rights approach, but which has been pursued for a long time under different names (going back at least to Tom Paine and Mary Wollstonecraft in the eighteenth century), has always had a strong element of social reasoning, linked with the responsibility of effective power, as will be discussed in Chapter 17 ('Human Rights and Global Imperatives').[7] Arguments that do not draw on the perspective of mutual benefit but concentrate instead on unilateral obligations because of asymmetry of power are not only plentifully used in contemporary human rights activism, but they can also be seen in the early attempts to recognize the implications of valuing the freedoms – and correspondingly human rights – of all. For example, both Tom Paine's and Mary Wollstonecraft's writings on what Wollstonecraft called 'vindication' of the rights of women and men drew a great deal on this type of motivation, derived from reasoning about the obligation of effective power to help advance the freedoms of all. That line of thinking does, of course, receive strong support, as was mentioned earlier, from Adam Smith's analysis of 'moral reasons', including the invoking of the device of the impartial spectator in enlightening people about moral concerns and obligations.

Mutual benefit, based on symmetry and reciprocity, is not the only foundation for thinking about reasonable behaviour towards others. Having effective power and the obligations that can follow unidirectionally from it can also be an important basis for impartial reasoning, going well beyond the motivation of mutual benefits.

# 10

# Realizations, Consequences and Agency

An interesting conversation that occurs in the ancient Sanskrit epic *Mahabharata* was discussed in the Introduction. The dialogue is between Arjuna, the great warrior hero of the epic, and Krishna, his friend and adviser, on the eve of the massive battle at Kurukshetra, a place not far from the city of Delhi. The conversation is about the duties of human beings in general and of Arjuna in particular, and Arjuna and Krishna bring radically divergent perspectives to the debate. I begin this chapter with a fuller examination of the issues involved in the argument between Arjuna and Krishna.

The battle in Kurukshetra is between the Pandavas, the virtuous royal family presided over by Yudhisthira (Arjuna's eldest brother and the legitimate heir to the throne), on one side, and the Kauravas, their cousins, on the other, who have wrongly usurped the kingdom. Most of the royal families in different kingdoms in the north, west and east of India have joined one side or the other in this epic battle, and the two confronting armies include a considerable proportion of the able-bodied men in the land. Arjuna is the great and invincible warrior on the just side, the Pandavas. Krishna is Arjuna's charioteer, but he is also meant to be an incarnation of God in human form.

The force of the Arjuna–Krishna debate enriches the tale of the epic, but over the centuries it has also generated much moral and political deliberation. The part of the epic in which this conversation occurs is called the *Bhagavadgita*, or *Gita* for short, and it has attracted extraordinary religious and philosophical attention in addition to captivating lay readers by the exciting nature of the argument itself.

Arjuna and Krishna see the armies on the two sides and reflect on the gigantic battle that is about to begin. Arjuna then expresses his profound doubts about whether fighting is the right thing for him to do. He does not doubt that theirs is the right cause, and that this is a just war, and also that his side will definitely win the battle, given its strength (not least because of Arjuna's own remarkable skills as a warrior and as an extraordinary general). But there would be so much death, Arjuna observes, in the battle. He is also bothered by the fact that he will have to kill a great many people himself, and that most of the people who will be fighting and may well be killed have done nothing that is particularly reprehensible other than agreeing (often out of kinship loyalties or other ties) to back one side or the other. If part of Arjuna's anxiety comes from the tragedy that is about to overwhelm much of the land, which can be evaluated as a disaster without taking any particular note of his own role in the carnage to come, another part certainly comes from his own responsibility for the killing that he will be doing, including the killing of those with close ties to him, towards many of whom he has affection. There are, thus, both positional and transpositional features in Arjuna's argument for not wanting to fight.*

Arjuna tells Krishna that he really should not fight and kill, and perhaps they should simply let the unjust Kauravas rule the kingdom they have usurped, as this may be the lesser of the two evils. Krishna speaks against this, and his response concentrates on the priority of doing one's duty irrespective of consequences, which has been invoked again and again in Indian discussions in religious and moral philosophy. Indeed, with Krishna's gradual transformation from a noble but partisan patron of the Pandavas to an incarnation of God, the *Gita* has also become a document of great theological importance.

Krishna argues that Arjuna must do his duty, come what may, and in this case he has a duty to fight, no matter what results from it. It is a just cause, and as a warrior and a general on whom his side must rely, he cannot waver from his obligations. Krishna's high deontology, including his duty-centred and consequence-independent reasoning, has been deeply influential in moral debates in subsequent millennia.

* The distinction connected with positionality was discussed in Chapter 7, 'Position, Relevance and Illusion'.

It is, I suppose, a tribute to the power of pure theory that even the great apostle of non-violence, Mohandas Gandhi, felt deeply inspired by Krishna's words on doing one's duty irrespective of consequences (and quoted Krishna from the *Gita* quite frequently), even though the duty in this case was for Arjuna to fight a violent war and not to shrink from killing others, a cause to which Gandhi would not normally be expected to warm.

Krishna's moral position has also received eloquent endorsement from many philosophical and literary commentators across the world; and admiration for the *Gita*, and for Krishna's arguments in particular, has been a lasting phenomenon in parts of European intellectual culture.* Christopher Isherwood translated the *Bhagavadgita* into English,[1] and T. S. Eliot explicated Krishna's reasoning and encapsulated his main message in poetry in the form of an admonishment: 'And do not think of the fruit of action./ Fare forward. Not fare well,/ But fare forward, voyagers.'[2]

## ARJUNA'S ARGUMENTS

As the debate proceeds, both Arjuna and Krishna present reasonings on their respective sides, which can be seen as a classic debate between consequence-independent deontology and consequence-sensitive assessment. Arjuna ultimately concedes defeat, but not before Krishna backs up the intellectual force of his argument with some supernatural demonstration of his divinity.

But was Arjuna really mistaken? Why should we want only to 'fare forward' and not also 'fare well'? Can a belief in a consequence-independent duty to fight for a just cause convincingly override one's reasons for not wanting to kill people, including those for whom one has affection? The point here is not so much to argue that Arjuna

* *Gita* was spectacularly praised already in early nineteenth century by Wilhelm von Humboldt as 'the most beautiful, perhaps the only true philosophical song existing in any known tongue'. Jawaharlal Nehru, who quotes Humboldt, does however point out that 'every school of thought and philosophy . . . interprets [the *Gita*] in its own way' (*The Discovery of India* (Calcutta: The Signet Press, 1946; republished, Delhi: Oxford University Press, 1981), pp. 108–9).

would have been definitely right to refuse to fight (there were many arguments against Arjuna's withdrawal from battle other than the ones on which Krishna concentrated), but that there is much to weigh and balance and that Arjuna's human-life-centred perspective is not dismissable by the mere invoking of some apparent duty to fight, irrespective of consequences.

Indeed, this is a dichotomy with two substantial positions, each of which can be defended in different ways. The battle of Kurukshetra would change the lives of people in the land, as we see in the epic itself, and decisions about what should be done must call for a capacious and critical evaluation rather than a simple answer based on the dismissal of all concerns other than the identification of Arjuna's supposed duty to fight – come what may – arrived at in a consequence-independent way. Even though as a religious document, *Gita* is interpreted to be firmly on Krishna's side, the epic *Mahabharata* in which the conversation occurs as a part of a much larger story gives both sides much room to develop their respective arguments. Indeed, the epic *Mahabharata* ends largely as a tragedy, with a lamentation about death and carnage, and there is anguish and grief accompanying the victory and triumph of the 'just' cause. It is hard not to see in this something of a vindication of Arjuna's profound doubts.

J. Robert Oppenheimer, who led the American team that developed the atom bomb during the Second World War, was moved to quote Krishna's words from *Gita* ('I am become death, the destroyer of worlds') as he watched, on 16 July 1945, the amazing force of the first nuclear explosion devised by man.[3] Just like the advice that Arjuna, the 'warrior', had received from Krishna about his duty to fight for a just cause, Oppenheimer, the 'physicist', found justification, at that time, in his technical commitment to develop a bomb for what was clearly the right side. Later on, deeply questioning his own contribution to the development of the bomb, Oppenheimer would reconsider the situation with hindsight: 'When you see something that is technically sweet, you go ahead and do it and you argue about what to do about it only after you have had your technical success.'*

* See *In the Matter of J. Robert Oppenheimer: USAEC Transcript of the Hearing before Personnel Security Board* (Washington, DC: Government Publishing Office,

Despite that compulsion to 'fare forward', there was reason enough for Oppenheimer also to reflect on Arjuna's concerns (not just to be thrilled by Krishna's words): how can good come from killing so many people? And why should I only do my duty as a physicist, ignoring all other results including the miseries and deaths that would follow from my own actions?*

As we proceed from here to the relevance of all this to the understanding of the demands of justice, it is useful to distinguish between three rather different, though interlinked, elements in Arjuna's reasoning. They are often merged together in the large literature that has been generated by the *Gita*, but they are distinct points, each of which demands attention.

First, central to Arjuna's reasoning is his general belief that what happens to the world must matter and be significant in our moral and political thinking. One cannot close one's eyes to what actually happens, and stick to one's consequence-independent *niti*, ignoring altogether the state of affairs that will emerge. This part of Arjuna's claim, which can be called 'the relevance of the actual world', is complemented by the identification of a specific part of the actual world that particularly engages him: the life and death of the people

---

1954). See also the play, based on these hearings, by Heinar Kipphardt, *In the Matter of J. Robert Oppenheimer*, translated by Ruth Speirs (London: Methuen, 1967). I should emphasize here that even though Oppenheimer quotes Krishna, and even though his belief in the justness of the cause for which he was working is similar to Krishna's view of Arjuna's cause, the positions taken by Krishna and Oppenheimer are not exactly the same. Krishna invokes Arjuna's 'duty' to fight as a warrior in pursuit of a just cause, whereas Oppenheimer uses the more ambiguous justification of doing something 'technically sweet'. It is possible that the technical sweetness is connected with success in doing one's duty as a scientist, but there are ambiguities here compared with Krishna's more straightforward admonition to Arjuna. I am grateful to Eric Kelly for an illuminating discussion on this.

* As I have mentioned in an earlier book, *The Argumentative Indian* (London and Delhi: Penguin, 2005), as a high school student I had asked my Sanskrit teacher whether it would be permissible to say that the divine Krishna got away with an incomplete and unconvincing argument against Arjuna. My teacher said in reply: 'Maybe you could say that, but you must say it with adequate respect.' Many years later, I took the liberty of defending Arjuna's original position, arguing – I hope with adequate respect – why consequence-independent deontology in the form championed by Krishna was really quite unconvincing: 'Consequential Evaluation and Practical Reason', *Journal of Philosophy*, 97 (September 2000).

involved. There is a general argument here on the importance of our lives, no matter how our attention might be diverted by other types of advocacy, based, for example, on strictures on correct conduct, or the promotion of the glory of a dynasty or a kingdom (or, as it might have appeared in Europe during the blood-soaked First World War, the victory of 'the nation').

In terms of the classical distinction between *nyaya* and *niti*, discussed in the Introduction, Arjuna's arguments definitely lean towards the side of *nyaya*, rather than merely the *niti* of fighting a just war by giving priority to one's duty as a military leader. What we have been calling 'social realization' is critically important in this argument.* And within that general framework, one particular argument that is extensively present in Arjuna's reasoning is that we cannot ignore what happens to human lives in particular in an ethical or political evaluation of this kind. This part of Arjuna's understanding I shall call 'the significance of human lives'.

The second issue concerns personal responsibility. Arjuna argues that a person whose decisions bring about some serious consequences must take personal responsibility for what results from his own choices. The issue of responsibility is central to the debate between Arjuna and Krishna, though the two present quite different interpretations of how Arjuna's responsibilities should be seen. Arjuna argues that the results of one's choices and actions must matter in deciding what one should do, whereas Krishna insists that one must do one's duty no matter what happens, and that the nature of one's duty can be determined, as in this case, without having to examine the consequences of the chosen actions.

There is an extensive literature in political and moral philosophy on the respective claims of consequential evaluation and duty-based

---

* In the debate in the *Gita*, Krishna's focus is primarily on the basic *niti* of doing one's duty, whereas Arjuna both questions the *niti* (why should I kill so many people even if that appears to be my duty?) and asks about the *nyaya* of the society that would result from the war (can a just world be built through extensive killing?). The point I want to emphasize here is that aside from the discussion about duties and consequences (and related to them, the debate between deontology and consequentialism), which is the issue on which most attention is typically devoted in pursuing the arguments in the *Gita*, there are also other important issues that figure, directly or indirectly, in that rich intellectual debate, which must not be ignored.

reasoning, and this is certainly one point of difference between Krishna's extreme form of deontology and Arjuna's consequence-sensitive reasoning. A point to note here, which is sometimes missed, is that Arjuna is not denying that the idea of personal responsibility is important – he is concerned not only about good consequences but also about who does what and in particular what he will himself have to do, which in this case involves killing people. So his own agency and his consequent responsibilities are momentous in Arjuna's argument, in addition to the concern he has for the significance of human lives. Arjuna is not arguing, it is important to note, for a kind of agent-independent consequentialism.

Third, Arjuna also identifies the people who would be killed, and he is particularly bothered by having to kill people for whom he has affection, including his own relatives. Even though killing in general greatly bothers him, especially given the scale of that war, he still separates out the feature of having to kill people who are particularly important to him in one way or another. Underlying this concern is Arjuna's inclination to take note of personal relations with others involved in a particular act. This is a distinctly positional concern, and belongs broadly to the kind of idea that makes a person acknowledge a special responsibility towards others, such as one's children, or children one has brought up. (This issue was considered in Chapter 7, 'Position, Relevance and Illusion'.) Relational obligations linked with family connections and personal affection as well as agency-related concerns may be rightly excluded in some ethical contexts, for example in the making of social policy by public officials, but they call for accommodation within the broader reach of moral and political philosophy, including that of the theory of justice, when personal responsibilities are considered and given their rightful place.

Arjuna is not, of course, portrayed in the epic as a philosopher, and it would be wrong to expect any kind of elaborate defence of his particular concerns in the argument he presents in the *Gita*. But what is striking, nevertheless, is the way these distinct concerns all find clear articulation in Arjuna's elaboration of his conclusion, defending his view that it might be right for him to withdraw from the battle. In pursuing the content of the *nyaya* in this case, all these three points, in addition to Arjuna's basic human sympathies, have clear relevance.

# CULMINATION AND COMPREHENSIVE OUTCOMES

Since consequence-based arguments are often seen as being concerned with outcomes (and in some cases interpreted to be concerned *only* with outcomes), it would be useful, in understanding Arjuna's arguments, to examine the notion of 'the outcome' more closely and critically than the way it is usually treated. The outcome is meant to be the state of affairs that results from whatever decision variable we are concerned with, such as action or rule or disposition. Even though the possibility of describing any state of affairs 'in its entirety' is not credible (we can always add some more detail, if necessary by using a magnifying glass aimed at events and actions), the basic idea of a state of affairs can be informationally rich, and take note of all the features that we see as important.

There is no particular reason to insist on an impoverished account of a state of affairs in evaluating it. In particular, the state of affairs, or the outcome in the context of the choice under examination, can incorporate *processes* of choice, and not merely the narrowly defined ultimate result. The content of outcomes can also be seen as including all the agency information that may be relevant and all the personal and impersonal relations that may be seen as important in the decisional problem at hand.

In my earlier work on decision theory and rational choice, I have argued for the importance of paying particular attention to 'comprehensive outcomes' that include actions undertaken, agencies involved, processes used, etc. *along with* the simple outcomes seen in a way that is detached from processes, agencies and relations – what I have been calling 'culmination outcomes'.* This distinction can be central to

---

* The distinction between culmination outcomes and comprehensive outcomes was discussed in the Introduction, and is quite important for the approach to justice in this work, in which comprehensive outcomes have a role that cannot be played by culmination outcomes. Indeed, part of the problem with what are taken to be 'consequentialist' theories of practical reason lies in the tendency to focus on culmination outcomes only. On the broad reach of the distinction, see my essays 'Maximization and the Act of Choice', *Econometrica*, 65 (1997); 'Consequential Evaluation and Practical Reason', *Journal of Philosophy*, 97 (2000); and my book *Rationality and Freedom* (Cambridge, MA: Harvard University Press, 2002).

THE IDEA OF JUSTICE

certain problems in economics, politics, sociology, and in the general theory of rational decisions and games.* As it happens, the distinction is also crucial in assessing the reach of consequence-based reasoning, since a consequence is more than just the aftermath. The appraisal of comprehensive outcomes can be an integral part of the assessment of states of affairs, and thus a crucial building block in consequential evaluation.

How is this distinction relevant for understanding Arjuna's arguments? In philosophical discussions on the content of the *Gita*, it is common to see, as was mentioned earlier, Krishna as the quintessential deontologist, focusing relentlessly on duty, and Arjuna as the typical consequentialist, basing assessment of actions entirely on the goodness (or badness) of the consequences that follow from those actions. In fact, both these interpretations are significantly misleading. There is nothing to prevent a general deontological approach from taking considerable note of consequences, even if the approach begins with the importance of independently identified duties; so it would be a mistake to see Krishna's somewhat emaciated morality as archetypal deontology. We cannot, for example, understand Immanuel Kant's deontology on the basis of Krishna's extremism.† Krishna's deontology is of a particularly purist form, which goes beyond seeing the importance of duty-based reasoning, and denies the relevance of any concern, particularly any consequential concern, in determining whether some action should be undertaken or not.

Similarly, Arjuna is not a typical no-nonsense consequentialist, insisting on ignoring everything other than the culmination outcomes, which is indeed the way the typically narrow version of consequentialism is defined. In contrast, Arjuna's moral and political reasoning

---

* To illustrate one of the issues in a decisional context with a very simple example of the relevance of processes and agencies in the evaluation of a state of affairs, a person may quite like being assigned to a very comfortable chair at a long-lasting party, but not be particularly inclined to run to the most comfortable chair before others get to it. The structures of many decisions and games change when such process-based considerations are accommodated.

† The extent to which Kant is concerned with consequences in the exposition of his basic deontological position is, in fact, quite striking; see, for example, *Critique of Practical Reason* (1788; translated by L. W. Beck (New York: Bobbs-Merrill, 1956)). It is hard to think of these arguments as not being part of his overall ethical position.

is deeply concerned with outcomes in their comprehensive form. The idea of social realizations, as has been explained earlier, demands that outcomes be seen in these broader terms, taking note of actions, relations and agencies. It has already been discussed that Arjuna does make substantial room for his idea of duty, taking into account his responsibility for his own agency, and also acknowledging his special relationship with many of the potential victims of the war (in addition to his general grief at the prospect of massive human death and deliberate killing). That is certainly much broader than consequentialism based on culmination outcomes.

It is part of the approach of the work presented in this book that a comprehensive understanding of states of affairs can be integrated with an overall evaluation of social realizations. While consequences – even culmination outcomes – are taken seriously among other concerns, there is no defence here of the standard version of consequentialism as it has emerged from two centuries of work led by the utilitarian school. It is, however, useful to ask in what sense, if any, Arjuna's position is consequentialist, even if not an archetypal one.

## CONSEQUENCES AND REALIZATIONS

It is not easy to identify any definition of consequentialism that would satisfy all those who have invoked that idea, either in defence or in criticism. As it happens, the term 'consequentialism' was devised by enemies rather than by proponents of consequential evaluation, and it has been invoked mainly to be refuted, often with colourful counter-examples that have added a good deal of spice – and some intellectual fun – to moral philosophy. To admit to being a 'consequentialist' is almost like introducing oneself by saying, 'I am a wog from London' (or a 'frog' or a 'limey' from wherever). Indeed, the term 'consequentialism' is unattractive enough to be sensibly bequeathed to anyone who wants to take it away.*

* While I have no great interest in proposing any definition of what consequentialism really is, I should note here that Arjuna's approach is certainly compatible with Philip Pettit's definition of consequentialism, as presented in the introduction to the distinguished collection of essays on the subject edited by him: 'Roughly speaking,'

It is, however, important to see that consequence-sensitive reasoning is necessary for an adequately broad understanding of the idea of responsibility. This has to be a part of the discipline of responsible choice, based on the chooser's evaluation of states of affairs, including consideration of all the relevant consequences viewed in the light of the choices made and the comprehensive outcomes associated with what happens as a result.[4] This substantive issue is not, of course, directly concerned with the use of the term 'consequentialism'. Whether the ideas of responsibility and social realizations, as explored here, should be placed in some wide enough basket called 'consequentialism' is not a question of much substantial interest (in the way that the ideas themselves are).*

It is true that the importance of personal responsibility has not always been adequately recognized within what has been called consequentialist ethics. The standard versions of utilitarian ethics have been especially short in this, in particular by ignoring all consequences other than utilities, even when they are part and parcel of the state of affairs (for example, the actions of particular agents that have actually occurred). This has followed from the utilitarian programme of combining consequentialism with additional demands, particularly 'welfarism', which insists that states of affairs must be judged exclusively

---

Pettit says, 'consequentialism is the theory that the way to tell whether a particular choice is the right choice for an agent to have made is to look at the relevant consequences of the decision; to look at the relevant effects of the decision on the world' (*Consequentialism* (Aldershot: Dartmouth, 1993), p. xiii). Since there is no insistence here that the accounting of consequences be confined to culmination outcomes only, ignoring the relevance of agencies, processes or relations, capturable in the picture of a comprehensive outcome, there is no tension in seeing Arjuna as a consequentialist in Philip Pettit's sense.

* There is, in fact, also a 'signalling' issue that makes consequentialism an oddly unsuitable name for an approach that begins with – and focuses on – the evaluation of states of affairs. To see the states of affairs as 'consequences' raises the immediate question: consequence of *what*? So even though philosophers who see themselves as consequentialists seem inclined to start with the evaluation of states of affairs (and then proceed to the evaluation of other things such as acts or rules), the term consequentialism points in the opposite direction – to the prior relevance of something else (an action or a rule or whatever) of which a state of affairs is a consequence. It is like, first, defining a country merely as a colony, and then striving hard to show not only that the colony is important independently of the metropolis, but also that the metropolis itself should be assessed entirely in the light of the colony.

by the utility information (such as happiness or desire-fulfilment) related to them – no matter what the other features of the consequent states of affairs may be, such as the performance of particular acts, however nasty, or the violation of other people's liberties, however personal.*

## REALIZATIONS AND AGENCIES

Here endeth my discussion of consequentialism. But the substantial issues do, of course, remain, and there will be plenty of engagement with them in the rest of the book. But I do want to make a couple of further points before closing this chapter. I have emphasized the importance of recognizing that the perspective of social realizations is a great deal more inclusive than the narrow characterization of states of affairs seen as culmination outcomes. A person not only has good reason to note the consequences that would follow from a particular choice, but also to take an adequately broad view of the realizations that would result, including the nature of the agencies involved, the processes used and the relationships of people. Some of the deontological dilemmas that are presented, with evident relevance, to discredit narrowly consequentialist reasoning, need not arise, at least in those forms, in dealing with responsible choice based on assessment of social realizations that would follow from one choice or another.

Given the importance of states of affairs in social realizations, a question that would occur to many critics of consequential reasoning is this: if we want to take note of agencies, processes and personal relations, is there is any real hope of getting a *consistent* system of

---

* Indeed, utilitarian reasoning is an amalgam of three distinct axioms: (1) consequentialism, (2) welfarism, and (3) sum-ranking (the last stands for the requirement that utilities of different people must simply be added up to assess the state of affairs, paying no attention to, say, inequalities). On the factorization of utilitarianism, see my 'Utilitarianism and Welfarism', *Journal of Philosophy*, 76 (September 1979), pp. 463–89, and Amartya Sen and Bernard Williams (eds.) *Utilitarianism and Beyond* (Cambridge: Cambridge University Press, 1982); see particularly our joint Introduction.

evaluation of social realizations on which reasoned and responsible decisions can be based? Given the demands of consistency, how can two persons value the same state of affairs differently, depending on their respective actions and responsibilities? The perceived problem here clearly arises from the temptation to see the evaluation of social realizations in strictly impersonal terms. The insistence that you and I, if we follow the same system of ethics, must value a comprehensive outcome in exactly the same way does correspond to the demands of utilitarian ethics, which is of course a classic case of consequential reasoning, but informationally a highly restrictive one. To insist on the same requirement in the evaluation of comprehensive outcomes, even when we are concerned with agencies and relations and processes, would seem to be entirely arbitrary, and indeed motivationally contradictory.[5]

In fact, if the roles of different persons in the development of a state of affairs are totally different, it would be rather absurd to make the odd demand that the two must value that state of affairs in exactly the same way. This would make a nonsense of taking note of agencies that are integral parts of social realizations. When, for example, Othello explains to Lodovico that he has killed Desdemona by saying, 'That's he that was Othello; here I am', it would indeed be ridiculous to insist that Othello must see what has happened in exactly the same way as Lodovico would. The understanding of the nature of the deed and of his own agency in it that makes Othello take his own life would also demand that he cannot view what has happened without considering his own role in the murder, which would make his perspective altogether different from that of others. Othello's positionality is central to the evaluation – not a detail that can be lost in his own evaluation of the event.*

It is not surprising that Arjuna's consequence-sensitive reasoning attached particular importance to the fact that he himself would have

---

* As was discussed in Chapter 7, 'Position, Relevance and Illusion', whether a positional connection is an important concern for a person's assessment of a state of affairs, or merely a distorting influence that should be overcome, is a matter for reasoned evaluation. In this case it would be hard to argue that Othello's role in Desdemona's murder is a distracting detail that should be overlooked as Othello evaluates what exactly has happened.

to do a good deal of the killing, and that some of the people killed would be those related to him for whom he has affection. Sensitivity to consequence does not demand insensitivity to agencies and relations in evaluating what is happening in the world. There can be good reasons to take note of both agent-relative and agent-independent concerns in the appraisal of what happens in the world, and thus in assessing justice in the sense of *nyaya*.* There is, however, no exemption from personal scrutiny, or indeed public argument, in the evaluation of their respective relevance and importance. The demand for reason in the assessment of reasonableness applies to both.

---

* The idea of responsibility can have very different bearings depending on the context and the purpose of the investigation. For some important distinctions, which I have not addressed here, see Jonathan Glover, *Responsibility* (London: Routledge, 1970); Hilary Bok, *Freedom and Responsibility* (Princeton, NJ: Princeton University Press, 1998); and Ted Honderich, *On Determinism and Freedom* (Edinburgh: Edinburgh University Press, 2005), among a number of other relevant studies. See also Samuel Scheffler, 'Responsibility, Reactive Attitudes, and Liberalism in Philosophy and Politics', *Philosophy and Public Affairs*, 21 (Autumn 1992).

# PART III

# The Materials of Justice

# 11

# Lives, Freedoms and Capabilities

Twenty-five hundred years ago, when young Gautama, later known as Buddha, left his princely home in the foothills of the Himalayas in search of enlightenment, he was moved specifically by the sight of mortality, morbidity and disability around him, and it agitated him greatly. He was also distressed by the ignorance he encountered. It is easy to understand the sources of Gautama Buddha's agony, particularly the deprivations and insecurities of human life, even if we may have to ponder more about his subsequent analysis of the ultimate nature of the universe. It is not difficult to appreciate the centrality of human lives in reasoned assessments of the world in which we live. That, as has already been discussed in the Introduction and later, is a central feature of the perspective of *nyaya* in contrast with the rule-bound *niti*, even though the idea of *nyaya* is not at all alone in pointing to the relevance of human lives for assessing how a society is doing.

Indeed, the nature of the lives people can lead has been the object of attention of social analysts over the ages. Even though the much-used economic criteria of advancement, reflected in a mass of readily produced statistics, have tended to focus specifically on the enhancement of inanimate objects of convenience (for example, in the gross national product (GNP), and the gross domestic product (GDP), which have been the focus of a myriad of economic studies of progress), that concentration could be ultimately justified – to the extent it could be – only through what these objects do to the human lives they can directly or indirectly influence. The case for using instead direct indicators of the quality of life and of the well-being and freedoms that human lives can bring has been increasingly recognized.[1]

Even the originators of quantitative national income estimation, which receives such attention and adherence, did try to explain that their ultimate interest lay in the richness of human lives, even though it is their measures, rather than their motivational justifications, that have received wide attention. For example, William Petty, the seventeenth-century pioneer of national income estimation (he proposed ways and means of assessing national income through the use of both 'the income method' and 'the expenditure method', as they are now called), spoke about his interest in examining whether 'the King's subjects' were in 'so bad a condition, as discontented Men would make them'. He went on to explain the various determinants of the condition of people, including 'the Common Safety' and 'each Man's particular Happiness'.[2] That motivating connection has often been ignored in economic analysis that concentrates on the means of living as the endpoint of investigation. There are excellent reasons for not confusing means with ends, and for not seeing incomes and opulence as important in themselves, rather than valuing them conditionally for what they help people to achieve, including good and worthwhile lives.*

It is important to note that economic opulence and substantive freedom, while not unconnected, can frequently diverge. Even in terms of being free to live reasonably long lives (free of preventable ailments and other causes of premature mortality), it is remarkable that the extent of deprivation of particular socially disadvantaged groups, even in very rich countries, can be comparable to that in the developing economies. For example, in the United States, inner-city African-Americans as a group frequently have no higher – indeed, often a substantially lower – chance of reaching an advanced age than do people born in the many poorer regions, such as Costa Rica, Jamaica, Sri Lanka or large parts of China and India.[3] Freedom from premature mortality is, of course, by and large helped by having a higher income (that is not in dispute), but it also depends on many other features,

* The motivation behind the 'human development approach', pioneered by Mahbub ul Haq, a visionary economist from Pakistan who died in 1998 (whom I had the privilege to have as a close friend from our students days), is to move from the means-based perspective of the gross national product (GNP) to concentrating, to the extent that the available international data would allow, on aspects of human lives themselves. The United Nations has regularly published *Human Development Reports* from 1990 onwards.

particularly of social organization, including public healthcare, the assurance of medical care, the nature of schooling and education, the extent of social cohesion and harmony, and so on.* It does make a difference whether we look merely at the means of living rather than directly at the lives that people manage to have.[4]

In assessing our lives, we have reason to be interested not only in the kind of lives we manage to lead, but also in the freedom that we actually have to choose between different styles and ways of living. Indeed, the freedom to determine the nature of our lives is one of the valued aspects of living that we have reason to treasure. The recognition that freedom is important can also broaden the concerns and commitments we have. We could choose to use our freedom to enhance many objectives that are not part of our own lives in a narrow sense (for example, the preservation of animal species that are threatened with extinction). This is an important issue in addressing such questions as the demands of environmental responsibility and of 'sustainable development'. I shall return to that important question later, after a general examination of the perspective of freedom in assessing human lives.

## VALUING FREEDOM

The valuing of freedom has been a battleground for centuries, indeed millennia and there have been supporters and enthusiasts as well as critics and severe detractors. The divisions are not, however, primarily geographical, as is sometimes suggested. It is not as if 'Asian values', to invoke a term frequently used in contemporary debates, have all been authoritarian – and sceptical of the importance of freedom – while traditional 'European values' are all pro-freedom and

---

* Going beyond well-discussed applications of the capability approach, the reach of capability-based reasoning may extend to less traversed territory as well, for example the importance of taking note in urban design and architecture of the freedom associated with the capability to function. This is well illustrated by the pioneering work of great importance by Romi Khosla and his colleagues; see Romi Khosla and Jane Samuels, *Removing Unfreedoms: Citizens as Agents of Change in Urban Development* (London: ITDG Publishing, 2004).

anti-authoritarian. It is true that many contemporary 'categorizers' see belief in individual liberty as a significant classificatory device separating the 'West' from the 'East'. Indeed, the advocacy of that line of classification has come from both the jealous guardians of the uniqueness of 'Western culture' and from resonant Eastern champions of what are called 'Asian values', allegedly giving priority to discipline over liberty. There is, however, very little empirical basis for dividing the history of ideas in this way.[5]

Freedom has had its supporters as well as detractors in classical Western writings (contrast, for example, Aristotle with Augustine), and it has received similarly mixed support in non-Western writings as well (contrast Ashoka with Kautilya, discussed in Chapter 3). We can, of course, try to make statistical comparisons of the relative frequency with which the idea of freedom is invoked in different regions in the world in diverse periods of history, and there might indeed emerge some interesting numerical findings, but there is little hope of capturing the ideological distinction between being 'for' or 'against' freedom in some large geographical dichotomy.

## FREEDOM: OPPORTUNITIES AND PROCESSES

Freedom is valuable for at least two different reasons. First, more freedom gives us more *opportunity* to pursue our objectives – those things that we value. It helps, for example, in our ability to decide to live as we would like and to promote the ends that we may want to advance. This aspect of freedom is concerned with our ability to achieve what we value, no matter what the process is through which that achievement comes about. Second, we may attach importance to the *process* of choice itself. We may, for example, want to make sure that we are not being forced into some state because of constraints imposed by others. The distinction between the 'opportunity aspect' and the 'process aspect' of freedom can be both significant and quite far-reaching.*

* It is very important to appreciate that freedom as an idea has these two quite distinct aspects, and that some approaches to evaluation may capture one aspect better than

Let me first consider a simple illustration of the distinction between the opportunity aspect and the process aspect of freedom. Kim decides one Sunday that he would prefer to stay at home rather than go out and do anything active. If he manages to do exactly what he wants, we can call it 'scenario A'. Alternatively, some strong-armed thugs arrive to interrupt Kim's life and drag him out and dump him in a large gutter. This terrible, indeed repulsive, situation may be called 'scenario B'. In a third instance, 'scenario C', the thugs restrain Kim by commanding that he must not go out of his house, with the threat of severe punishment if he violates this restriction.

It is easy to see that in scenario B the freedom of Kim is badly affected: he cannot do what he would like to do (to stay at home), and his freedom to decide for himself is also gone. So there are violations of both the opportunity aspect of Kim's freedom (his opportunities are severely curtailed) and the process aspect (he cannot decide for himself what to do).

What about scenario C? Clearly the process aspect of Kim's freedom is affected (even if he does under duress what he would have done anyway, the choice is no longer his): he could not have done anything else without being badly punished for it. The interesting question concerns the opportunity aspect of Kim's freedom. Since he does the same thing in both cases, with or without duress, could it be said that therefore his opportunity aspect is the same in both cases?

If the opportunity that people enjoy is to be judged only by whether they end up doing what they would respectively choose to do if unrestrained, then it must be said that there is no difference between scenarios A and C. The opportunity aspect of Kim's freedom is unaltered in this narrow view of opportunity, since he can stay at home in either case, exactly as he planned.

But does this give adequate recognition to what we understand by opportunity? Can we judge opportunities we have only by whether or not we end up in the state that we would choose to be in, irrespective of whether or not there are other significant alternatives that we could

---

the other. The nature and implications of the distinction were investigated in my Kenneth Arrow Lectures, 'Freedom and Social Choice', included in my book, *Rationality and Freedom* (Cambridge, MA: Harvard University Press, 2002), Chapters 20–22.

have chosen if we wanted? What about choosing to go for a nice walk – not Kim's preferred alternative that Sunday but perhaps an interesting enough possibility – certainly preferable to being dumped in the gutter? Or, what about the opportunity to change one's mind and, perhaps more immediately, what about the opportunity *to choose freely* to stay at home rather than the *opportunity* just to stay at home (and nothing else)? There are distinctions here between scenario C and scenario A even in terms of opportunities. If these concerns are serious, then it seems plausible to argue that in scenario C the opportunity aspect of Kim's freedom is also affected, though obviously not as radically as in scenario B.

The distinction between 'culmination outcome' and 'comprehensive outcome', discussed earlier, is relevant here. The opportunity aspect of freedom can be seen in different ways in light of that distinction. It can be defined only in terms of the opportunity for 'culmination outcomes' (what a person ends up with), if we see opportunity in that particularly narrow way and regard the existence of options and the freedom of choice to be somehow unimportant.[6] Alternatively, we can define opportunity more broadly – and I believe with greater plausibility – in terms of the achievement of 'comprehensive outcomes', taking note also of *the way* the person reaches the culmination situation (for example, whether through his own choice or through the dictates of others). In the broader view, the opportunity aspect of Kim's freedom is clearly undermined in scenario C, by his being ordered to stay at home (he cannot choose anything else). In scenario A, in contrast, Kim does have the opportunity to consider the various alternatives that are feasible and then choose to stay at home if he is that way inclined, whereas in scenario C he definitely does not have that freedom.

The distinction between the narrow and broad views of opportunity will turn out to be quite central when we move from the basic idea of freedom to more specific concepts, such as the capabilities that a person has. We must examine in that context whether a person's capability to lead the kind of life she values should be assessed only by the culmination alternative that she would actually end up with, or by using a broader approach that takes note of the process of choice involved, in particular the other alternatives that she could also choose, within her actual ability to do so.

## THE CAPABILITY APPROACH

Any substantive theory of ethics and political philosophy, particularly any theory of justice, has to choose an informational focus, that is, it has to decide which features of the world we should concentrate on in judging a society and in assessing justice and injustice.[7] It is particularly important, in this context, to have a view as to how an individual's overall advantage is to be assessed; for example, utilitarianism, pioneered by Jeremy Bentham, concentrates on individual happiness or pleasure (or some other interpretation of individual 'utility') as the best way of assessing how advantaged a person is and how that compares with the advantages of others. Another approach, which can be found in many practical exercises in economics, assesses a person's advantage in terms of his or her income, wealth or resources. These alternatives illustrate the contrast between utility-based and resource-based approaches in contrast with the freedom-based capability approach.*

In contrast with the utility-based or resource-based lines of thinking, individual advantage is judged in the capability approach by a person's capability to do things he or she has reason to value. A person's advantage in terms of opportunities is judged to be lower than that of another if she has less capability – less real opportunity – to achieve those things that she has reason to value. The focus here is on the freedom that a person actually has to do this or be that – things that

---

* My work on the capability approach was initiated by my search for a better perspective on individual advantages than can be found in the Rawlsian focus on primary goods: see 'Equality of What?' in S. McMurrin (ed.), *Tanner Lectures on Human Values*, vol. 1 (Cambridge: Cambridge University Press, and Salt Lake City, UT: University of Utah Press, 1980). But it was soon clear that the approach can have a much wider relevance: see *Commodities and Capabilities* (1985); 'Well-being, Agency and Freedom: The Dewey Lectures 1984', *Journal of Philosophy*, 82 (1985); *The Standard of Living* (Cambridge: Cambridge University Press, 1987); *Inequality Reexamined* (Oxford: Oxford University Press, and Cambridge, MA: Harvard University Press, 1992). The connection of this approach with Aristotelian ideas was pointed out to me by Martha Nussbaum, who has gone on to make pioneering contributions to this growing field of investigation and has strongly influenced the way the approach has developed. See also our jointly edited book, *The Quality of Life* (Oxford: Clarendon Press, 1993).

he or she may value doing or being. Obviously, the things we value most are particularly important for us to be able to achieve. But the idea of freedom also respects our being free to determine what we want, what we value and ultimately what we decide to choose. The concept of capability is thus linked closely with the opportunity aspect of freedom, seen in terms of 'comprehensive' opportunities, and not just focusing on what happens at 'culmination'.

It is important to emphasize certain specific features of this approach that should be clarified at the outset, since they have some-times been misunderstood or misinterpreted. First, the capability approach points to an *informational focus* in judging and comparing overall individual advantages, and does not, on its own, propose any specific formula about how that information may be used. Indeed, different uses may emerge depending on the nature of the questions that are being addressed (for example, policies dealing respectively with poverty, or disability, or cultural freedom) and, more practically, on the availability of data and of informative material that can be used. The capability approach is a general approach, focusing on information on individual advantages, judged in terms of opportunity rather than a specific 'design' for how a society should be organized. A number of very distinguished contributions have been made by Martha Nussbaum and others in recent years on matters of social assessment and policy through powerful use of the capability approach. The fullness and the definitive achievements of these contri-butions have to be distinguished from the informational perspective on which they are based.[8]

The capability perspective does point to the central relevance of the inequality of capabilities in the assessment of social disparities, but it does not, on its own, propose any specific formula for policy decisions. For example, contrary to an often-articulated interpretation, the use of the capability approach for evaluation does not demand that we sign up to social policies aimed entirely at equating everyone's capa-bilities, no matter what the other consequences of such policies might be. Similarly, in judging the aggregate progress of a society, the capa-bility approach would certainly draw attention to the huge significance of the expansion of human capabilities of all members of the society, but it does not lay down any blueprint for how to deal with conflicts between, say, aggregative and distributive considerations (even though each is judged in terms of capabilities). And yet the choice of an informational focus – a concentration on capabilities – can be quite momentous in drawing attention to the decisions that would have to be made and the policy analysis that must take account of the right kind of information. The assessment of societies and social institutions can be deeply influenced by the information on which the approach focuses, and that is exactly where the capability approach makes its main contribution.[9]

A second issue to emphasize is that the capability perspective is inescapably concerned with a plurality of different features of our lives and concerns. The various attainments in human functioning that we may value are very diverse, varying from being well nourished or avoiding premature mortality to taking part in the life of the community and developing the skill to pursue one's work-related plans and ambitions. The capability that we are concerned with is our ability to achieve various combinations of functionings that we can compare and judge against each other in terms of what we have reason to value.[*]

The capability approach focuses on human life, and not just on some detached objects of convenience, such as incomes or commodities that a person may possess, which are often taken, especially in economic analysis, to be the main criteria of human success. Indeed, it proposes a serious departure from concentrating on the *means* of living to the *actual opportunities* of living. This also helps to bring about a change from means-oriented evaluative approaches, most notably focusing on what John Rawls calls 'primary goods', which are all-purpose means such as income and wealth, powers and prerogatives of offices, the social bases of self-respect, and so on.

---

[*] Even though it is often convenient to talk about individual capabilities (seen in terms of the ability to achieve the corresponding individual functionings), it is important to bear in mind that the capability approach is ultimately concerned with the ability to achieve *combinations* of valued functionings. There may be, for example, a trade-off between a person's capability to be well nourished and her capability to be well sheltered (poverty may make such difficult choices inescapable), and we have to see the person's overall capability in terms of combined achievements that are open to her. And yet it is often convenient to talk about *individual* capabilities (with some implicit assumption about the fulfilment of other demands), and I shall do that from time to time, for the simplicity of presentation, in what follows.

While primary goods are, at best, means to the valued ends of human life, in the Rawlsian formulation of principles of justice they become the central issues in judging distributional equity. This, I have argued, is a mistake, for primary goods are merely means to other things, in particular freedom (as was briefly discussed in Chapter 2). But it was also briefly mentioned in that discussion that the motivation behind Rawlsian reasoning, in particular his focus on advancing human freedom, is quite compatible with – and may be better served by – a direct concentration on the assessment of freedom, rather than counting the means towards achieving it (so that I see the contrast as being less foundational than it might first appear). These issues will be more fully considered in the next chapter. The capability approach is particularly concerned with correcting this focus on means rather than on the opportunity to fulfil ends and the substantive freedom to achieve those reasoned ends.*

It is not hard to see that the reasoning underlying this departure in favour of capability can make a significant, and constructive, difference; for example, if a person has a high income but is also very prone to persistent illness, or is handicapped by some serious physical disability, then the person need not necessarily be seen as being very advantaged, on the mere ground that her income is high. She certainly has more of one of the means of living well (that is, a lot of income), but she faces difficulty in translating that into good living (that is, living in a way that she has reason to celebrate) because of the adversities of illness and physical handicap. We have to look instead at the extent to which she can actually achieve, if she so chooses, a state of good health and wellness, and being fit enough to do what she has reason to value. To understand that the *means* of satisfactory human living are not themselves the *ends* of good living helps to bring about a significant extension of the reach of the evaluative exercise. And the use of the capability perspective begins right there. Various aspects of the contribution that the capability perspective makes have been

---

* The relevance of 'human capability formation' for freedom suggests the need for new lines of investigation dealing with the development of cognitive and constructive powers. An important departure can be seen in James J. Heckman, 'The Economics, Technology, and Neuroscience of Human Capability Formation', *Proceedings of the National Academy of Sciences*, 106 (2007).

brought out by the contributions of a number of researchers in this field, including Sabina Alkire, Enrica Chiappero-Martinetti, Flavio Comim, David A. Crocker, Reiko Gotoh, Mozaffar Qizilbash, Jennifer Prah Ruger, Ingrid Robeyns, Tania Burchardt and Polly Vizard.[10]

There are other features of the capability approach that may also be worth commenting on here (if only to prevent misinterpretations), dealing respectively with (1) the contrast between capability and achievement; (2) the plural composition of capabilities and role of reasoning (including public reasoning) in the use of the capability approach; and (3) the place of individuals and communities and their interrelations in the conception of capabilities. I take these up in turn.

## WHY GO BEYOND ACHIEVEMENT TO OPPORTUNITY?

The focus of the capability approach is thus not just on what a person actually ends up doing, but also on what she is in fact able to do, whether or not she chooses to make use of that opportunity. This aspect of the capability approach has been questioned by a number of critics (such as Richard Arneson and G. A. Cohen), who have presented arguments, with at least some apparent plausibility, in favour of paying attention to the actual *achievement* of functionings (emphasized also by Paul Streeten and Frances Stewart), rather than to the *capability* to choose between different achievements.[11]

That line of reasoning is often driven by the view that life consists of what really happens, not of what could have happened had the persons involved been differently inclined. There is a bit of an oversimplification here, since our freedom and choices are parts of our actual lives. Kim's life *is* affected, in the example considered earlier, if he is forced to stay at home, rather than choosing to stay at home when he has other alternatives. Yet the achievement-based critique of the capability approach deserves serious consideration since it resonates with many people, and it is important to ask whether it would be more appropriate to base social judgements of the advantages or disadvantages of people on their actual achievements rather than on their respective capabilities to achieve.*

In response to this critique, I start first with a small and rather technical point, which is methodologically quite important but which many critics might find too formal to be really interesting. Capabilities are defined derivatively on functionings, and include *inter alia* all the information on the functioning combinations that a person can choose. The cluster of functionings actually chosen is obviously among the feasible combinations. And, if we were really keen on concentrating only on achieved functionings, there is nothing to prevent us from basing the evaluation of a capability set on the assessment of the chosen combination of functionings from that set.[12] If freedom had only *instrumental* importance for a person's well-being, and choice had no intrinsic relevance, then this could indeed be the appropriate informational focus for the analysis of capability.

Identifying the value of the capability set with the value of the chosen functioning combination permits the capability approach to put as much weight – including possibly *all* the weight – on actual achievements. In terms of versatility, the capability perspective is more general – and more informationally inclusive – than focusing only on achieved functionings. There is, in this sense at least, no loss in looking at the broader informational base of capabilities, which permits the possibility of simply relying on the valuation of achieved functionings (should we wish to go that way), but also allows the use of other priorities in evaluation, attaching importance to opportunities and choices. This preliminary point is obviously a minimalist argument, and there is much more to be said, positively and affirmatively, for the importance of the perspective of capabilities and freedom.

First, even an exact 'tie' between two persons in achieved functionings may still hide significant differences between the advantages of

---

* There is also a pragmatic argument for paying special attention to actual achievements when there is some doubt about the reality of some capability that particular persons are supposed to have. This can be an important issue in the assessment of gender equity, in which seeking some actual evidence of critically important achievements may be reassuring in a way that a belief in the existence of the corresponding capability may not be. On this and related concerns, see Anne Philips, *Engendering Democracy* (London: Polity Press, 1991).

the respective persons which could make us understand that one person may be really much more 'disadvantaged' than the other. For example, in terms of being hungry and undernourished, a person who voluntarily fasts, for political or religious reasons, may be just as deprived of food and nourishment as a famine-stricken victim. Their manifest under-nutrition – their achieved functioning – may be much the same, and yet the capability of the well-off person who *chooses* to fast may be much larger than that of the person who starves involuntarily because of poverty and destitution. The idea of capability can accommodate this important distinction, since it is oriented towards freedom and opportunities, that is, the actual ability of people to choose to live different kinds of lives within their reach, rather than confining attention only to what may be described as the culmination – or aftermath – of choice.

Second, the capability to choose between different affiliations in cultural life can have both personal and political importance. Consider the freedom of immigrants from non-Western countries to retain parts of the ancestral cultural traditions and lifestyles they value even after they have resettled in a European country or in America. This complex subject cannot be adequately assessed without distinguishing between *doing* something and being *free* to do that thing. A significant argument can be constructed in favour of immigrants having the freedom to retain at least some parts of their ancestral culture (such as their mode of religious worship, or loyalty to their native poetry and literature), if they value those things after comparing them with the prevalent behaviour patterns in the country in which they are now settled, and often after taking serious note of the prevalent reasoning in the country in favour of different practices.*

---

* The point is often made that tyrannical and nasty ancestral practices, such as the genital mutilation of young women, or punitive treatment of adulterous women, should not be practised in the country to which the persons have emigrated, since they are offensive to other citizens of that country. But surely the decisive argument against these practices is their terrible nature no matter where they occur, and the need to eliminate those practices is extremely strong, on the grounds of the loss of freedom of the victims, irrespective of whether the potential immigrants migrate or not. The argument is basically about the importance of freedom in general, including the freedom of the women involved. Whether these practices are offensive to others – the older residents – is hardly the strongest argument against them, which should be concerned with the victims rather than their neighbours.

However, the importance of this cultural freedom cannot be seen as an argument in favour of someone pursuing her ancestral lifestyle *whether or not* she find reasons to choose to do this. The central issue, in this argument, is the freedom to *choose* how to live – including the opportunity to pursue parts of her ancestral cultural preferences if so desired – and it cannot be turned into an argument in favour of her invariably pursuing those behaviour patterns, irrespective of whether she would like to do those things, or have reasons to retain those practices. The importance of capability, reflecting opportunity and choice, rather than the celebration of some particular lifestyle, irrespective of preference or choice, is central to the point at issue.

Third, there is also a policy-related question that makes the distinction between capabilities and achievements important for a different reason. This concerns the responsibilities and obligations of societies and of other people generally to help the deprived, which can be important for both public provisions within states and for the general pursuit of human rights. In considering the respective advantages of responsible adults, it may be appropriate to think that the claims of individuals on the society may be best seen in terms of freedom to achieve (given by the set of real opportunities) rather than actual achievements. For example, the importance of having some kind of a guarantee of basic healthcare is primarily concerned with giving people the capability to enhance their state of health. If a person has the opportunity for socially supported healthcare but still decides, with full knowledge, not to make use of that opportunity, then it could be argued that the deprivation is not as much of a burning social concern as would be the failure to provide the person with the opportunity for healthcare.

So there are many affirmative reasons for which it would make sense to use the broader informational perspective of capabilities rather than concentrating only on the informationally narrower viewpoint of achieved functionings.

# FEAR OF NON-COMMENSURABILITY

Functionings and capabilities are diverse, as indeed they must be since they deal with different features of our life and our freedom. This is, of course, a most unremarkable fact, but there is such a long tradition in parts of economics and political philosophy of treating one allegedly homogeneous feature (such as income or utility) as the sole 'good thing' that could be effortlessly maximized (the more the merrier), that there is some nervousness in facing a problem of valuation involving heterogeneous objects, such as the evaluation of capabilities – and functionings.

The utilitarian tradition, which works towards beating every valuable thing down to some kind of an allegedly homogeneous magnitude of 'utility', has contributed most to this sense of security in 'counting' exactly one thing ('is there more here or less?'), and has also helped to generate the suspicion of the tractability of 'judging' combinations of many distinct good things ('is this combination more valuable or less?'). And yet any serious problem of social judgement can hardly escape accommodating pluralities of values, as has been discussed, particularly by Isaiah Berlin and Bernard Williams.[13] We cannot reduce all the things we have reason to value into one homogeneous magnitude. Indeed, there is much diversity within utility itself (as Aristotle and John Stuart Mill noted), even if it is decided to overlook everything other than utility in social evaluation.*

If the long tradition of utilitarianism with the assumption of homogeneous utility has contributed to this sense of security in commensurable homogeneity, the massive use of gross national product (GNP) as the indicator of the economic condition of a nation has also made its contribution in that direction. Proposals for weaning economic evaluators away from exclusive reliance on the GNP have tended to generate the worry that with diverse objects to judge we shall not have the sense of ease that goes with just checking whether the GNP is higher or lower. But serious exercises of social evaluation cannot

---

* On this question, including a discussion of Aristotle's and Mill's pluralism, see my 'Plural Utility', *Proceedings of the Aristotelian Society*, 81 (1980–81).

avoid dealing, in one way or another, with the valuation of diverse objects which may compete for attention (in addition to complementing each other in many cases). While T. S. Eliot was insightful in noting (this occurs in 'Burnt Norton') that: 'Human kind/ Cannot bear very much reality',[14] humankind should be able to face a bit more reality than a picture of a world in which there is only one good thing.

The question has sometimes been linked with that of 'non-commensurability' – a much-used philosophical concept that seems to arouse anxiety and panic among some valuational experts. Capabilities are clearly non-commensurable since they are irreducibly diverse, but that does not tell us much at all about how difficult – or easy – it would be to judge and compare different capability combinations.[15]

What exactly is commensurability? Two distinct objects can be taken to be commensurable if they are measurable in common units (like two glasses of milk). Non-commensurability is present when several dimensions of value are irreducible to one another. In the context of evaluating a choice, commensurability requires that, in assessing its results, we can see the values of all the relevant results in exactly one dimension – measuring the significance of all the distinct outcomes in a common scale – so that in deciding what would be best, we need not go beyond 'counting' the overall value in that one homogeneous metric. Since the results are all reduced to one dimension, we need do no more than check how much of that 'one good thing', to which every value is reduced, is provided by each respective option.

We are certainly not likely to have much problem in choosing between two alternative options, each of which offers just the same good thing, but one offers more than the other. This is an agreeably trivial case, but the belief that whenever the choice problem is not so trivial, we must have 'great difficulty' in deciding what we should sensibly do seems peculiarly feeble (it is tempting to ask, how 'spoilt' can you get?). Indeed, if counting one set of real numbers is all we could do for reasoning about what to choose, then there would not be many choices that we could sensibly and intelligently make.

Whether we are deciding between buying different commodity baskets, or making choices about what to do on a holiday, or deciding whom to vote for in an election, we are inescapably involved in evaluating alternatives with non-commensurable aspects. Anyone who has ever gone to shop would know that one has to choose between non-commensurable objects – mangoes cannot be measured in units of apples, nor can sugar be reduced to units of soap (though I have heard some parents tell me that the world would have been much better if that were the case). Non-commensurability can hardly be a remarkable discovery in the world in which we live. And it need not, by itself, make it very hard to choose sensibly.

For example, having a medical intervention and enjoying a visit to a foreign country are two quite non-commensurate achievements, but a person may not have much problem in deciding which would be more valuable in her condition, and that judgement may of course vary with what she knows about her state of health and what her other concerns are. The choice and the weighting may sometimes be difficult, but there is no general impossibility here of making reasoned choices over combinations of diverse objects.

Making choices with non-commensurable rewards is like speaking prose. It is, in general, not particularly hard to speak in prose (even if M. Jourdain in Molière's *Le Bourgeois Gentilhomme* may have marvelled at our ability to perform so exacting a feat). But this does not negate the recognition that speaking can sometimes be very difficult, not because expressing oneself in prose is in itself arduous, but, for example, when one is overwhelmed by emotions. The presence of non-commensurable results only indicates that the choice-decisions will not be trivial (reducible just to counting what is 'more' and what is 'less'), but it does not at all indicate that it is impossible – or even that it must always be particularly difficult.

## VALUATION AND PUBLIC REASONING

Reflected evaluation demands reasoning regarding relative importance, not just counting. This is an exercise in which we are constantly engaged. To that general understanding has to be added the possible importance of public reasoning as a way of extending the reach and reliability of valuations and of making them more robust. The necessity of scrutiny and critical assessment is not just a demand for self-centred evaluation by secluded individuals, but a pointer to the fruitfulness of public discussion and of interactive public reasoning: social evaluations may be starved of useful information and good arguments if they are entirely based on separated and sequestered cogitation. Public discussion and deliberation can lead to a better understanding of the role, reach and significance of particular functionings and their combinations.

To illustrate, public discussion of gender-based inequalities in India has helped to bring out, in recent years, the importance of certain freedoms that did not receive adequate acknowledgement earlier.* Examples include the freedom to depart from fixed and time-honoured family roles that limit the social and economic opportunities of women, and also from a social value system that is more geared to recognizing men's deprivation than women's. These traditional antecedents of gender inequality in well-established, male-dominated societies demand not only individual concern but also informative public discussion and, often enough, agitation.

The connection between public reasoning and the choice and weighting of capabilities in social assessment is important to emphasize. It also points to the absurdity of the argument that is sometimes presented, which claims that the capability approach would be usable – and 'operational' – only if it comes with a set of 'given' weights on the distinct functionings in some fixed list of relevant capabilities. The search for given, pre-determined weights is not only conceptually ungrounded, but it also overlooks the fact that the valuations and weights to be used may reasonably be influenced by our own continued scrutiny and by the reach of public discussion.† It would be

---

* This will be discussed in Chapter 16, 'The Practice of Democracy'.
† Aside from general variations depending on social circumstances and political priorities, there is a good case for keeping open the possibility of raising new and interesting questions about inclusions and weights. For example, there have been very interesting and important arguments raised recently on placing a special emphasis on such values as 'civility' in developing the application of human capabilities to understand the reach of freedom and universality; on this, see Drucilla Cornell's insightful analysis in 'Developing Human Capabilities: Freedom, Universality, and Civility', in *Defending Ideals: War, Democracy, and Political Struggles* (New York: Routledge, 2004).

hard to accommodate this understanding with inflexible use of some pre-determined weights in a non-contingent form.*

It can, of course, be the case that the agreement that emerges on the weights to be used may be far from total, and we shall then have good reason to use ranges of weights on which we may find some agreement. This need not fatally disrupt evaluation of injustice or the making of public policy, for reasons that have already been discussed earlier on in this book (beginning in the Introduction). For example, to show that slavery severely reduces the freedom of the slaves, or that the absence of any guarantee of medical attention curtails our substantive opportunities of living, or that severe undernourishment of children, which causes immediate agony as well as underdevelopment of cognitive capabilities, including reduction of the ability to reason, is detrimental to justice, we do not need a unique set of weights on the different dimensions involved in such judgements. A broad range of not fully congruent weights could yield rather similar principal guidelines.†

The approach of capability is entirely consistent with a reliance on partial rankings and on limited agreements, the importance of which has been emphasized throughout this work. The main task is to get things right on the comparative judgements that can be reached through personal and public reasoning, rather than to feel compelled to opine on every possible comparison that could be considered.

* Also, the choice of weights may depend on the nature of the exercise (for example, whether we are using the capability perspective to assess poverty or to guide health policy, or using it to assess the inequality of overall advantages of different persons). Different questions can be addressed using the capability information, and the diversity of the exercises involved can, sensibly enough, lead to rather different choices of weights.

† The analytical and mathematical issues underlying the use of *ranges* of weights (rather than one unique set of weights) for generating regular partial orderings, are investigated in my 'Interpersonal Aggregation and Partial Comparability', *Econometrica*, 38 (1970); *On Economic Inequality* (Oxford: Oxford University Press, 1973, expanded edition, with James Foster, 1997). See also Enrica Chiappero-Martinetti, 'A New Approach to the Evaluation of Well-being and Poverty by Fuzzy Set Theory', *Giornale degli Economisti*, 53 (1994).

# CAPABILITIES, INDIVIDUALS AND COMMUNITIES

I turn now to the third of the complications identified earlier. Capabilities are seen primarily as attributes of people, not of collectivities, such as communities. There is, of course, no great difficulty in thinking about capabilities of groups. For example, if we consider the ability of Australia to subdue all other cricket-playing countries in test matches (as things looked when I started writing this book, but perhaps not any more), the object of discussion is the capability of the Australian cricket team, not of any particular Australian cricket player. Should considerations of justice not take note of such group capabilities, in addition to individual capabilities?

Indeed, some critics of the capability approach have seen, in the concentration on capabilities of persons, the evil influence of what is called – it is not a term of praise – 'methodological individualism'. Let me begin by discussing, first, why identifying the capability approach as methodological individualism would be a significant mistake. Even though what is called methodological individualism has been defined in many different ways,* Frances Stewart and Séverine Deneulin focus on the belief that 'all social phenomena must be accounted for in terms of what individuals think, choose and do'.[16] There have certainly been schools of thought based on individual thought, choice and action, detached from the society in which they exist. But the capability approach not only does not assume such detachment, its concern with people's ability to live the kind of lives they have reason to value brings in social influences both in terms of what they value (for example, 'taking part in the life of the community') and what influences operate on their values (for example, the relevance of public reasoning in individual assessment).

It is hard, then, to envision cogently how persons in society can think, choose or act without being influenced in one way or another

* On the complexities involved in the diagnosis of methodological individualism, see Steven Lukes, *Individualism* (Oxford: Blackwell, 1973), and also his 'Methodological Individualism Reconsidered', *British Journal of Sociology*, 19 (1968), along with the references cited by Lukes.

by the nature and working of the world around them. If, for example, women in traditionally sexist societies come to accept that women's position has to be standardly inferior to men, then that view – shared by individual women under social influence – is not, in any sense, independent of social conditions.* In pursuing a reasoned rejection of that presumption, the capability perspective demands more public engagement on such a subject. Indeed, the entire approach of the 'impartial spectator', on which the view developed in this work draws, focuses on the relevance of the society – and people far and near – in the valuational exercise of individuals. Uses of the capability approach (for example, in my book *Development as Freedom* (1999)) have been quite unequivocal in not assuming any kind of a detached view of individuals from the society around them.

Perhaps the misconstruction in this critique arises from its unwillingness to distinguish adequately between the individual characteristics that are used in the capability approach and the social influences that operate on them. The critique stops, in this sense, much too early. To note the role of 'thinking, choosing and doing' by individuals is just the beginning of recognizing what actually does happen (we do, of course, as individuals, think about issues and choose and perform actions), but we cannot end there without an appreciation of the deep and pervasive influence of society on our 'thinking, choosing and doing'. When someone thinks and chooses and does something, it is, for sure, that person – and not someone else – who is doing these things. But it would be hard to understand why and how he or she undertakes these activities without some comprehension of his or her societal relations.

The basic issue was put with admirably clarity and reach by Karl Marx more than a century and a half ago: 'What is to be avoided above all is the re-establishing of "Society" as an abstraction vis-à-vis the individual.'[17] The presence of individuals who think, choose and act – a manifest reality in the world – does not make an approach methodologically individualist. It is the illegitimate invoking of any presumption of independence of the thoughts and actions of persons from the society around them that would bring the feared beast into the living room.

* This issue was discussed in Chapter 7, 'Position, Relevance and Illusion'.

While the charge of methodological individualism would be hard to sustain, it can of course be asked: why restrict the relevant capabilities that are considered valuable, only to those of the individuals, and not of groups? There is indeed no particular analytical reason why group capabilities – the military strength of the American nation or game-playing ability of the Chinese – must be excluded *a priori* from the discourse on justice or injustice in their respective societies, or in the world. The case for not going that way lies in the nature of the reasoning that would be involved.

Since groups do not think in the obvious sense in which individuals do, the importance of capabilities that groups have would tend to be understood, for reasons that are clear enough, in terms of the value that members of the group (or for that matter, other people) place on the proficiency of that group. Ultimately, it is individual valuation on which we would have to draw, while recognizing the profound interdependence of the valuations of individuals who interact with each other. The valuation involved would tend to be based on the importance that people attach to being able to do certain things in collaboration with others.* In valuing a person's ability to take part in the life of the society, there is an implicit valuation of the life of the society itself, and that is an important enough aspect of the capability perspective.†

There is also a second issue that is relevant here. A person belongs to many different groups (related to gender, class, language group, profession, nationality, community, race, religion and so on), and to see them merely as a member of just one particular group would be a major denial of the freedom of each person to decide how exactly to

---

* There is also scope for distinguishing between 'collective guilt' and the guilt of individuals who constitute the collectivity. 'Collective guilt feelings' can also be distinguished from feelings of guilt of the individuals in that group; on this, see Margaret Gilbert, 'Collective Guilt and Collective Guilt Feelings', *Journal of Ethics*, 6 (2002).
† There is obviously no prohibition against taking note of such interrelated capabilities, indeed the argument for taking note can be quite strong. James E. Foster and Christopher Handy have investigated the role and operation of interdependent capabilities in their insightful paper, 'External Capabilities', mimeographed (Vanderbilt University, January 2008). See also James E. Foster, 'Freedom, Opportunity and Well-being', mimeographed (Vanderbilt University, 2008), and also Sabina Alkire and James E. Foster, 'Counting and Multidimensional Poverty Measurement', OPHI Working Paper 7 (Oxford University, 2007).

see himself or herself. The increasing tendency towards seeing people in terms of one dominant 'identity' ('this is your duty as an American', 'you must commit these acts as a Muslim', or 'as a Chinese you should give priority to this national engagement') is not only an imposition of an external and arbitrary priority, but also the denial of an important liberty of a person who can decide on their respective loyalties to different groups (to all of which he or she belongs).

As it happens, one of the early warnings against ignoring the multiple membership of individuals to different groups came from Karl Marx. Marx pointed, in *The Critique of the Gotha Programme*, to the need to go beyond class analysis even as one appreciates its social relevance (a subject on which he had, of course, made major contributions):

unequal individuals (and they would not be different individuals if they were not unequal) are measurable only by an equal standard in so far as they are brought under an equal point of view, are taken from one *definite* side only, for instance, in the present case, are regarded *only* as *workers*, and nothing more is seen in them, everything else being ignored.[18]

I believe the warning here, against seeing someone merely as a member of a group to which he or she belongs (Marx was protesting here against the Gotha Programme of the United Workers' Party of Germany which considered workers 'only as workers'), is particularly important in the present intellectual climate in which individuals tend to be identified as belonging to one social category to the exclusion of all others ('nothing more is seen in them'), such as being a Muslim or a Christian or a Hindu, an Arab or a Jew, a Hutu or a Tutsi, or a member of Western civilization (whether or not it is seen as clashing inevitably with other civilizations). Individual human beings with their various plural identities, multiple affiliations and diverse associations are quintessentially social creatures with different types of societal interactions. Proposals to see a person merely as a member of one social group tend to be based on an inadequate understanding of the breadth and complexity of any society in the world.*

* On this, see Kwame Anthony Appiah, *The Ethics of Identity* (Princeton, NJ: Princeton University Press, 2005), and Amartya Sen, *Identity and Violence: The Illusion of Destiny* (New York: W. W. Norton & Co., and London: Allen Lane, 2006).

# SUSTAINABLE DEVELOPMENT AND THE ENVIRONMENT

I end this discussion of the relevance of freedom and capabilities with a practical illustration that deals with sustainable development. The threat that the environment faces today has rightly been emphasized in recent discussions, but there is a need for clarity in deciding how to think about environmental challenges in the contemporary world. Focusing on the quality of life can help in this understanding, and throw light not only on the demands of sustainable development, but also on the content and relevance of what we can identify as 'environmental issues'.

The environment is sometimes seen (I believe oversimply) as the 'state of nature', including such measures as the extent of forest cover, the depth of the groundwater table, the number of living species and so on. To the extent that it is assumed that this pre-existing nature will stay intact unless we add impurities and pollutants to it, it might, therefore, appear superficially plausible that the environment is best protected if we interfere with it as little as possible. This understanding is, however, deeply defective for two important reasons.

First, the value of the environment cannot be just a matter of what there is, but must also consist of the opportunities it offers to people. The impact of the environment on human lives must be among the principal considerations in assessing the value of the environment. To take an extreme example, in understanding why the eradication of smallpox is not viewed as an impoverishment of nature (we do not tend to lament: 'the environment is poorer since the smallpox virus has disappeared'), in the way, say, the destruction of ecologically important forests would seem to be, the connection with lives in general and human lives in particular has to be taken into consideration.

It is, therefore, not surprising that environmental sustainability has typically been defined in terms of the preservation and enhancement of the quality of human life. The rightly celebrated Brundtland Report, published in 1987, defined 'sustainable development' as 'development that meets the needs of the present without compromising the ability of future generations to meet their own needs'.[19] It is open to argument

248

whether the Brundtland Committee's view of what to sustain is exactly right, and presently I will have more to say on Brundtland's particular formula. But I must say first how indebted we all are to Gro Brundtland and the committee she led for the understanding they have generated that the value of the environment cannot be divorced from the lives of living creatures.

Second, the environment is not only a matter of passive preservation, but also one of active pursuit. Even though many human activities that accompany the process of development may have destructive consequences, it is also within human power to enhance and improve the environment in which we live. In thinking about the steps that may be taken to halt environmental destruction, we have to include constructive human intervention. Our power to intervene with effectiveness and reasoning can be substantially enhanced by the process of development itself. For example, greater female education and women's employment can help to reduce fertility rates, which in the long run can reduce the pressure on global warming and the increasing destruction of natural habitats. Similarly, the spread of school education and improvements in its quality can make us more environmentally conscious; better communication and a more active and better informed media can make us more aware of the need for environment-oriented thinking. It is easy to find many other examples of positive involvement. In general, seeing development in terms of increasing the effective freedom of human beings brings the constructive agency of people engaged in environment-friendly activities directly within the domain of developmental achievements.

Development is fundamentally an empowering process, and this power can be used to preserve and enrich the environment, and not only to decimate it. We must not, therefore, think of the environment exclusively in terms of conserving pre-existing natural conditions, since the environment can also include the results of human creation. For example, purification of water is a part of improving the environment in which we live. The elimination of epidemics contributes both to development and to environmental enhancement.

There is, however, scope for argument on how exactly we should think about the demands of sustainable development. The Brundtland Report defined sustainable development as meeting 'the needs of the

THE IDEA OF JUSTICE

present without compromising the ability of future generations to meet their own needs'. This initiative in addressing the issue of sustainability has done much good already. But we still have to ask whether the conception of human beings implicit in this understanding of sustainability takes an adequately capacious view of humanity. Certainly, people do have needs, but they also have values and, in particular, cherish their ability to reason, appraise, choose, participate and act. Seeing people only in terms of their needs may give us a rather meagre view of humanity.

Brundtland's concept of sustainability has been further refined and elegantly extended by one of the foremost economists of our time, Robert Solow, in a monograph called *An Almost Practical Step toward Sustainability*.[20] Solow's formulation sees sustainability as the requirement that the next generation must be left with 'whatever it takes to achieve a standard of living at least as good as our own and to look after their next generation similarly'. His formulation has several attractive features. First, by focusing on sustaining living standards, which provides the motivation for environmental preservation, Solow extends the reach of Brundtland's concentration on the fulfilment of needs. Second, in Solow's neatly recursive formulation, the interests of all future generations receive attention through provisions to be made by each generation for its successor. There is an admirable comprehensiveness in the generational coverage for which Solow makes room.

But does even the Solow reformulation of sustainable development incorporate an adequately broad view of humanity? While the concentration on maintaining living standards has some clear merits (there is something deeply appealing in Solow's formula about trying to make sure that future generations can 'achieve a standard of living at least as good as our own'), it can still be asked whether the coverage of living standards is sufficiently inclusive. In particular, sustaining living standards is not the same thing as sustaining people's freedom and capability to have – and safeguard – what they value and have reason to attach importance to. Our reason for valuing particular opportunities need not always lie in their contribution to our living standards, or more generally to our own interests.*

---

* See the discussion on this in Chapter 8, 'Rationality and Other People'.

To illustrate, consider our sense of responsibility towards the future of other species that are threatened with destruction. We may attach importance to the preservation of species not merely because – nor only to the extent that – the presence of these species enhances our own living standards. For example, a person may judge that we ought to do what we can to ensure the preservation of some threatened animal species, say, spotted owls. There would be no contradiction if the person were to say: 'My living standards would be largely, indeed completely, unaffected by the presence or absence of spotted owls – I have in fact never even seen one – but I do strongly believe that we should not let those owls become extinct, for reasons that have nothing much to do with human living standards.'*

This is where Gautama Buddha's argument, presented in *Sutta-Nipata* (discussed in Chapter 9, 'Plurality of Impartial Reasons'), becomes directly and immediately relevant. Since we are enormously more powerful than other species, we have some responsibility towards them that links with this asymmetry of power. We can have many reasons for our conservational efforts – not all of which are parasitic on our own living standards (or need fulfilment) and some of which turn precisely on our sense of values and on our acknowledgement of our fiduciary responsibility.

If the importance of human lives lies not merely in our living standard and need-fulfilment, but also in the freedom that we enjoy, then the idea of sustainable development has to be correspondingly reformulated. There is cogency in thinking not just about sustaining the fulfilment of our needs, but more broadly about sustaining – or extending – our freedom (including the freedom to meet our needs). Thus recharacterized, sustainable freedom can be broadened from the formulations proposed by Brundtland and Solow to encompass the preservation, and when possible expansion, of the substantive freedoms and capabilities of people today 'without compromising the

---

* There is also a need for going beyond self-concerned motivations in understanding the commitment of many people to help protect vulnerable populations from environmental adversities that may not directly affect the lives of the individuals who make this commitment. The dangers of flooding in, say, the Maldives or Bangladesh from a rising sea level may influence the thoughts and actions of many people who would not themselves be affected by the threats facing the precariously placed populations.

capability of future generations' to have similar – or more – freedom.

To use a medieval distinction, we are not only 'patients' whose needs deserve consideration, but also 'agents' whose freedom to decide what to value and how to pursue what we value can extend far beyond our own interests and needs. The significance of our lives cannot be put into the little box of our own living standards, or our need-fulfilment. The manifest needs of the patient, important as they are, cannot eclipse the momentous relevance of the agent's reasoned values.

# 12

# Capabilities and Resources

That income or wealth is an inadequate way of judging advantage was discussed with great clarity by Aristotle in *Nicomachean Ethics*: 'wealth is evidently not the good we are seeking; for it is merely useful and for the sake of something else'.[1] Wealth is not something we value for its own sake. Nor is it invariably a good indicator of what kind of lives we can achieve on the basis of our wealth. A person with severe disability cannot be judged to be more advantaged merely because she has a larger income or wealth than her able-bodied neighbour. Indeed, a richer person with disability may be subject to many restraints that the poorer person without the physical disadvantage may not have. In judging the advantages that the different people have compared with each other, we have to look at the overall capabilities they manage to enjoy. This is certainly one important argument for using the capability approach over the resource-centred concentration on income and wealth as the basis of evaluation.

Since the idea of capability is linked with substantive freedom, it gives a central role to a person's *actual* ability to do the different things that she values doing. The capability approach focuses on human lives, and not just on the resources people have, in the form of owning – or having use of – objects of convenience that a person may possess. Income and wealth are often taken to be the main criteria of human success. By proposing a fundamental shift in the focus of attention from the *means* of living to the *actual opportunities* a person has, the capability approach aims at a fairly radical change in the standard evaluative approaches widely used in economics and social studies.

It also initiates a very substantial departure from the means-orientation in some of the standard approaches in political philosophy, for example John Rawls's focus on 'primary goods' (incorporated in his 'Difference Principle') in assessing distributional issues in his theory of justice. Primary goods are all-purpose means such as income and wealth, powers and prerogatives of office, the social bases of self-respect and so on. They are not valuable in themselves, but they can, to varying extents, help the pursuit of what we really value. Nevertheless, even though primary goods are, at best, means to the valued ends of human life, they themselves have been seen as the primary indicator of judging distributional equity in the Rawlsian principles of justice. Through the explicit recognition that the *means* of satisfactory human living are not themselves the *ends* of good living (the point that Aristotle was making), the capability approach helps to bring about a significant extension of the reach of the evaluative exercise.*

## POVERTY AS CAPABILITY DEPRIVATION

One of the central issues in this context is the criterion of poverty. The identification of poverty with low income is well established, but there is, by now, quite a substantial literature on its inadequacies. Rawls's focus on primary goods is more inclusive than income (indeed, income is only one of its constituents), but the identification of primary goods is still guided, in Rawlsian analysis, by his search for general all-purpose means, of which income and wealth are particular – and particularly important – examples. However, different people can have quite different opportunities for converting income and other primary goods into characteristics of good living and into the kind of freedom valued in human life. Thus, the relationship between resources and poverty is both variable and deeply contingent on the characteristics of the respective people and the environment in which they live – both natural and social.†

---

* I have presented arguments for this change of focus in 'Well-being, Agency and Freedom: The Dewey Lectures 1984', *Journal of Philosophy*, 82 (April 1985), and 'Justice: Means versus Freedoms', *Philosophy and Public Affairs*, 19 (Spring 1990).
† In an early contribution in 1901, Rowntree noted an aspect of the problem by referring to 'secondary poverty', in contrast with 'primary poverty', defined in terms

There are, in fact, various types of contingencies which result in variations in the conversion of income into the kinds of lives that people can lead. There are at least four important sources of variation.

(1) *Personal heterogeneities*: People have disparate physical character-istics in relation to age, gender, disability, proneness to illness and so on, making their needs extremely diverse; for example, a dis-abled or an ill person may need more income to do the same elementary things that a less afflicted person can do with a given level of income. Indeed, some disadvantages, for example severe disabilities, may not be entirely correctable even with huge expen-diture on treatment or prosthesis.

(2) *Diversities in the physical environment*: How far a given income will go will depend also on environmental conditions, including climatic circumstances, such as temperature ranges, or flooding. The environmental conditions need not be unalterable – they could be improved with communal efforts, or worsened by pollution or depletion. But an isolated individual may have to take much of the environmental conditions as given in converting incomes and personal resources into functionings and quality of life.

(3) *Variations in social climate*: The conversion of personal resources into functionings is influenced also by social conditions, including public healthcare and epidemiology, public educational arrange-ments and the prevalence or absence of crime and violence in the particular location. Aside from public facilities, the nature of community relationships can be very important, as the recent literature on 'social capital' has tended to emphasize.[2]

(4) *Differences in relational perspectives*: Established patterns of behaviour in a community may also substantially vary the need for income to achieve the same elementary functionings; for example, to be able to 'appear in public without shame' may require higher standards of clothing and other visible consumption

_____

of low income (B. Seebohm Rowntree, *Poverty. A Study of Town Life* (London: Macmillan, 1901)). In pursuing the phenomenon of secondary poverty, Rowntree focused specifically on influences of habits and behaviour patterns that affect the commodity composition of a family's consumption. That issue remains important even today, but the distance between low income and actual deprivation can arise for other reasons as well.

in a richer society than in a poorer one (as Adam Smith noted more than two centuries ago in the *Wealth of Nations*).* The same applies to the personal resources needed for taking part in the life of the community, and in many contexts, even to fulfil the elementary requirements of self-respect. This is primarily an inter-societal variation, but it influences the relative advantages of two persons located in different countries.†

There can also be some 'coupling' of disadvantages between different sources of deprivation, and this can be a critically important consideration in understanding poverty and in making public policy to tackle it.[3] Handicaps, such as age or disability or illness, reduce one's ability to earn an income. But they also make it harder to convert income into capability, since an older, or more disabled or more seriously ill person may need more income (for assistance, for prosthetics, for treatment) to achieve the same functionings (even if that achievement were, in fact, at all possible).‡ Thus real poverty (in terms of capability deprivation) can easily be much more intense than we can deduce from income data. This can be a crucial concern in assessing public action to assist the elderly and other groups with

* See Adam Smith, *An Inquiry into the Nature and Causes of the Wealth of Nations* (1776; republished, R. H. Campbell and A. S. Skinner (eds) (Oxford: Clarendon Press, 1976)), pp. 351–2. On the relation between relative disadvantage and poverty, see the more recent works of W. G. Runciman, *Relative Deprivation and Social Justice: A Study of Attitudes to Social Inequality in Twentieth-Century England* (London: Routledge, 1966), and Peter Townsend, *Poverty in the United Kingdom* (Harmondsworth: Penguin, 1979).

† In fact, relative deprivation in terms of incomes can yield absolute deprivation in terms of capabilities. Being relatively poor in a rich country can be a great capability handicap, even when one's absolute income is high by world standards. In a generally opulent country, more income is needed to buy enough commodities to achieve the same social functioning. On this, see my 'Poor, Relatively Speaking', *Oxford Economic Papers*, 35 (1983), reprinted in *Resources, Values and Development* (Cambridge, MA: Harvard University Press, 1984).

‡ There is also a problem of coupling in (1) under-nutrition generated by income poverty, and (2) income poverty resulting from work deprivation due to under-nutrition. On these connections, see Partha Dasgupta and Debraj Ray, 'Inequality as a Determinant of Malnutrition and Unemployment: Theory', *Economic Journal*, 96 (1986), and 'Inequality as a Determinant of Malnutrition and Unemployment: Policy', *Economic Journal*, 97 (1987).

conversion difficulties in addition to their low income-earning ability.*

Distribution of facilities and opportunities within the family raises further complications for the income approach to poverty. Income accrues to the family through its earning members, and not to all the individuals within it irrespective of age, gender and working ability. If the family income is disproportionately used to advance the interests of some family members and not others (for example, if there is a systematic preference for boys over girls in the family allocation of resources), then the extent of the deprivation of the neglected members (girls, in the example considered) may not be adequately reflected by the aggregate value of the family income.[4] This is a substantial issue in many contexts; sex bias does appear to be a major factor in the family allocation in many countries in Asia and north Africa. The deprivation of girls is more readily – and more reliably – assessed by looking at capability deprivation reflected, for example, in greater mortality, morbidity, undernourishment or medical neglect, than can be found on the basis of comparing incomes of different families.†

---

* The contribution of such handicaps to the prevalence of income poverty in Britain was brought out sharply by a pioneering empirical study by A. B. Atkinson, *Poverty in Britain and the Reform of Social Security* (Cambridge: Cambridge University Press, 1969). In his later works, Atkinson has further pursued the connection between income handicap and deprivation of other kinds; see his 'On the Measurement of Poverty', *Econometrica*, 55 (1987), and *Poverty and Social Security* (New York: Harvester Wheatsheaf, 1989). For a powerful examination of the general idea of disadvantage and its far-reaching relevance both for social evaulation and for public policy, see Jonathan Wolff, with Avner De-Shalit, *Disadvantage* (Oxford: Oxford University Press, 2007).

† Gender bias is, clearly, not as central a concern in assessing inequality and poverty in Europe or North America, but the presumption – often implicitly made – that the issue of gender inequality does not apply to 'Western' countries can be quite misleading. For example, Italy had one of the highest ratios of 'unrecognized' labour by women (mostly unglamorous family work) among all the countries of the world included in the standard national accounts in the mid-1990s, according to UNDP's *Human Development Report 1995* (New York: United Nations, 1995). The accounting of effort and time expended, and its implications for the personal freedom of women, have some bearing for Europe and North America as well. There is also in many cases considerable gender bias in the richest countries in terms of opportunities for advanced education, or for the prospects of being selected for top levels of employment.

## DISABILITY, RESOURCES
## AND CAPABILITY

The relevance of disability in the understanding of deprivation in the world is often underestimated, and this can be one of the most important arguments for paying attention to the capability perspective. People with physical or mental disability are not only among the most deprived human beings in the world, they are also, frequently enough, the most neglected.

The magnitude of the global problem of disability in the world is truly gigantic. More than 600 million people – about one in ten of all human beings – live with some form of significant disability.[5] More than 400 million of them live in developing countries. Furthermore, in the developing world, the disabled are quite often the poorest of the poor in terms of income, but in addition their *need* for income is greater than that of able-bodied people, since they require money and assistance to try to live normal lives and to attempt to alleviate their handicaps. The impairment of income-earning ability, which can be called 'the earning handicap', tends to be reinforced and much magnified in its effect by 'the conversion handicap': the difficulty in converting incomes and resources into good living, precisely because of disability.

The importance of the 'conversion handicap' from disability can be illustrated with some empirical results from a pioneering study of poverty in the United Kingdom undertaken by Wiebke Kuklys, in a remarkable thesis completed at Cambridge University shortly before her untimely death from cancer: the work was later published as a book.[6] Kuklys found that 17.9 per cent of individuals lived in families with income below the poverty line. If attention is shifted to individuals in families with a disabled member, the percentage of such individuals living below the poverty line is 23.1. This gap of about 5 percentage point largely reflects the income handicap associated with disability and the care of the disabled. If the conversion handicap is now introduced, and note is taken of the need for more income to ameliorate the disadvantages of disability, the proportion of individuals in families with disabled members jumps up to 47.4 per cent, a gap of nearly 20 percentage points over the share of individuals below the poverty line (17.9 per cent) for the population as a whole. To look at the comparative picture in another way, of the 20 extra percentage points for poverty disadvantage for individuals living in families with a disabled member, about a quarter can be attributed to income handicap and three-quarters to conversion handicap (the central issue that distinguishes the capability perspective from the perspective of incomes and resources).

An understanding of the moral and political demands of disability is important not only because it is such a widespread and impairing feature of humanity, but also because many of the tragic consequences of disability can actually be substantially overcome with determined societal help and imaginative intervention. Policies to deal with disability can have a large domain, including the amelioration of the effects of handicap, on the one hand, and programmes to prevent the development of disabilities, on the other. It is extremely important to understand that many disabilities are preventable, and much can be done not only to diminish the *penalty* of disability but also to reduce its *incidence*.

Indeed, only a fairly moderate proportion of the 600 million people living with disabilities were doomed to these conditions at conception, or even at birth. For example, maternal malnutrition and childhood undernourishment can make children prone to illnesses and handicaps of health. Blindness can result from diseases linked to infection and lack of clean water. Other disabilities can originate through the effects of polio, measles or AIDS, as well as road accidents and injuries at work. A further issue is that of landmines which are scattered across the troubled territories of the world, and maim as well as kill people, especially children. Social intervention against disability has to include prevention as well as management and alleviation. If the demands of justice have to give priority to the removal of manifest injustice (as I have been arguing throughout this work), rather than concentrating on the long-distance search for the perfectly just society, then the prevention and alleviation of disability cannot but be fairly central in the enterprise of advancing justice.

Given what can be achieved through intelligent and humane intervention, it is amazing how inactive and smug most societies are about the prevalence of the unshared burden of disability. In feeding this inaction, conceptual conservatism plays a significant role. In particular, the concentration on income distribution as the principal guide to distributional fairness prevents an understanding of the predicament of disability and its moral and political implications for social analysis. Even the constant use of income-based views of poverty (such as the repeated invoking of the numbers of people who live below $1 or $2 of income per day – a popular activity by international organizations) can distract attention from the full rigour of social deprivation, which combines conversion handicap with earning handicap. The 600 million handicapped people in the world are not plagued just by low income. Their freedom to lead a good life is blighted in many different ways, which act individually and together, to place these people in jeopardy.

## RAWLS'S USE OF PRIMARY GOODS

Given the importance of the distance between capabilities and resources, for reasons already discussed, it is hard not to be sceptical of John Rawls's difference principle which concentrates entirely on primary goods in judging distributional issues in his 'principles of justice' for the institutional basis of society. This divergence, important as it is, does not of course reflect Rawls's lack of concern about the importance of substantive freedom – a point I have already made earlier on in this work. Even though Rawls's principles of justice concentrate on primary goods, he pays attention elsewhere to the need for correcting this resource focus in order to have a better grip on people's real freedom. Rawls's pervasive sympathy for the disadvantaged is plentifully reflected in his writings.

In fact, Rawls does recommend special correctives for 'special needs', such as disability and handicap, even though this is not a part of his principles of justice. These corrections come not in setting up 'the basic institutional structure' of the society at the 'constitutional stage', but as something that should emerge later on in the *use* of the institutions thus set up, particularly in the 'legislative stage'. This makes the reach of Rawls's motivation clear enough, and the question to be asked is whether this is adequate as a way of rectifying the partial blindness of the perspective of resources and primary goods in Rawlsian principles of justice.

In the exalted place that Rawls gives to the metric of primary goods, there is some general downplaying of the fact that different people, for reasons of personal characteristics, or the influences of physical and social environments, or through relative deprivation (when a person's absolute advantages depend on her relative standing compared with others), can have widely varying opportunities to convert general resources (like income and wealth) into capabilities – what they can or cannot actually do. The variations in conversion opportunities are not just matters of what can be seen as 'special needs', but reflect pervasive variations – large, small and medium – in the human condition and in relevant social circumstances.

Rawls does indeed talk about the eventual emergence of special provisions for 'special needs' (for example, for the blind or for those who are otherwise clearly disabled), at a later phase in the unfolding of his multi-stage story of justice. The move indicates Rawls's deep concern about disadvantage, but the way he deals with this pervasive problem has quite a limited reach. First, these corrections occur, to the extent they do, only after the basic institutional structure has been set up through the Rawlsian 'principles of justice' – the nature of these basic institutions are not at all influenced by such 'special needs' (primary goods such as incomes and wealth rule supreme in setting up the institutional base dealing with distributional issues, through the role of the difference principle).

Second, even at a later stage, when particular note is taken of 'special needs', there is no attempt to come to terms with the ubiquitous variations in conversion opportunities between different people. The prominent and easily identifiable handicaps (such as blindness) are, of course, important to pay attention to, but the variations in many different ways (linked, for example, with greater proneness to illness, more adverse epidemiological surroundings, various levels and types of physical and mental disabilities, etc.) make the informational focus on functionings and capabilities essential for thinking about social arrangements and social realizations, both in setting up the institutional structure and in making sure that they function well and with adequate use of humane and sympathetic reasoning.

I believe Rawls is also motivated by his concern for fairness in the distribution of freedom and capabilities, but by founding his principles of justice on the informational perspective of primary goods in the difference principle, he leaves the determination of 'just institutions' for distributional fairness exclusively on the slender shoulders of primary goods to provide the basic institutional guidance. This does not give his underlying concern for capabilities enough room for influence at the institutional phase with which his principles of justice are directly concerned.

## DEPARTURES FROM RAWLSIAN THEORY

Unlike in Rawls's focus on transcendental institutionalism, the approach to justice explored in this work does not pursue a sequential and prioritized scenario of the unfolding of a perfectly just society. In focusing on the enhancement of justice through institutional and other changes, the approach here does not, therefore, relegate the issue of conversion and capabilities into something of second-category status, to be brought up and considered later. Understanding the nature and sources of capability deprivation and inequity is indeed central to removing manifest injustices that can be identified by public reasoning, with a good deal of partial accord.*

The Rawlsian approach has also had extensive influences outside its own domain as specified by Rawls, since it has been such a dominant mode of reasoning on justice in contemporary moral and political

---

* In investigating the limitations of focusing on the index of primary goods in the formulation of the principles of justice in the Rawlsian general approach, it is not, of course, my intention to suggest that all would be well in his transcendental institutionalist approach if concentration on primary goods were to be replaced by direct engagement with capabilities. The serious difficulties arising from Rawls's transcendental rather than comparative orientation and from the purely institutional focus of his principles of justice, discussed earlier, would remain no matter what informational focus is used to assess distributional concerns. I am arguing here that in addition to the general problems of relying on a transcendental institutionalist approach, the Rawlsian theory is *further* impaired by its concentration on primary goods to deal with distributional issues in its principles of justice.

philosophy. For example, those who have tried to retain the Rawlsian contractarian foundation in a new – and more ambitious – theory of justice encompassing the whole world (such a 'cosmopolitan theory of justice' has a much larger domain than Rawls's country-by-country approach) have continued to look for a complete ordering for distributional judgements, needed for transcendental institutional justice for the entire globe.[7] Not surprisingly, these theorists are not placated by the partially incomplete ordering based on capabilities and, as Thomas Pogge puts it, there is a demand for much more than 'merely a partial ordinal ranking' needed to work out 'how an institutional order ought to be designed'.[8] I would like to wish good luck to the builders of a transcendentally just set of institutions for the whole world, but for those who are ready to concentrate, at least for the moment, on reducing manifest injustices that so severely plague the world, the relevance of a 'merely' partial ranking for a theory of justice can actually be rather momentous.*

The central issue, I would submit, is not whether a certain approach has a total reach in being able to compare any two alternatives, but whether the comparisons it can make are appropriately directed and reasoned. Comparisons of freedoms and capabilities place us in the right territory, and we should not be moved to relocate ourselves to a different territory through being tempted by the attractions of a complete ordering (seen independently of *what* it completely orders).

The advantage of the capability perspective over the resource perspective lies in its relevance and substantive importance, and not in any promise of yielding a total ordering. Indeed, as Elizabeth Anderson has persuasively discussed, the capability metric is 'superior to a resource metric because it focuses on ends rather than on means, can better handle discrimination against the disabled, is properly sensitive to individual variations in functioning that have democratic import, and is well suited to guide the just delivery of public services, especially in health and education'.[9]

---

* This issue was discussed in the Introduction and in Chapters 1–4.

THE IDEA OF JUSTICE

THE IDEA OF JUSTICE

## DWORKIN'S EQUALITY OF RESOURCES

While Rawls uses the perspective of resources in his principles of justice through the index of primary goods, effectively ignoring the conversion variations between resources and capabilities, Ronald Dworkin's use of the resource perspective is to make room explicitly for taking note of these variations through artful market-oriented thinking, in particular by the use of an imagined primordial market for insurance against conversion handicaps. In this thought-experiment it is assumed that people, under a Rawls-like veil of ignorance of an original position, enter this hypothetical market, which sells insurance against having these respective handicaps. While no one, in this imagined situation, knows who is going to have which handicap, if any, they all buy this insurance against possible adversities, and ('later on', as it were) the ones that actually end up having the handicaps can claim their compensation as determined by the insurance markets, thereby obtaining more resources of other kinds in compensation. That is, argues Dworkin, as fair as you can get, based on what he sees as effective 'equality of resources'.

This is certainly an interesting and highly ingenious proposal (having taught a class jointly with Ronald Dworkin for ten years at Oxford and knowing the astonishing reach of his mind, I could not, of course, have expected anything less). But after that brilliantly imagined contribution about a possible hypothetical market, Dworkin seems to go straight into something of a 'beat that!' programme, addressed particularly to those afflicted by the capability-based approach.* He claims *either* that equality of capability amounts really to equality of welfare, in which case (Dworkin argues) it is a mistaken view of equity, *or* that it amounts actually to the same solution as his own equality of resources, in which case there is no real difference between us (and no advantage in pursuing the capability approach).

* I suppose I should feel honoured to be taken seriously enough to be identified as the main protagonist of what he sees as the less than satisfactory approach of capabilities. See Dworkin's *Sovereign Virtue: The Theory and Practice of Equality* (Cambridge, MA: Harvard University Press, 2000), pp. 65–119. See also his 'Sovereign Virtue Revisited', *Ethics*, 113 (2002).

Despite my immense admiration for Ronald Dworkin's work, I have to say I am somewhat at a loss in deciding where to begin in analysing what is wrong with this argument against a capability-based approach. First (to begin with a very minor point, only to get it out of the way), even if equality of capability were to amount to equality of the capability for welfare, that would not be the same thing as equality of welfare.* (The distinction between capability and achievement was discussed in the last chapter.) However, more importantly, it should have been clear from what I had said about the capability perspective from its first presentation that I am arguing neither for equality of welfare nor for equality of capability to achieve welfare.†

Second, if equality of resources were no different from equality of capability and substantive freedom, why is it more interesting normatively to think about the former rather than the latter, since resources are only instrumentally important as means to other ends? Since resources are 'merely useful and for the sake of something else' (as Aristotle put it), and since the case for equality of resources rests ultimately on that 'something else', why not put equality of resources in its place as a way of getting to equality of the capability to achieve – if the congruence between the two does actually hold?

There is, of course, no great mathematical difficulty in thinking of one object that can be seen as an end (such as utility or capability) in terms of 'equivalent' amounts of something else (such as income or resource) that serves as a means to achieve the corresponding end, so long as the latter is instrumentally powerful enough to allow us to get

---

* For example, the *actual* pursuit of expensive modes of living by some, which Dworkin does not want to subsidize, should not be confused with the *capability* to indulge in expensive modes – a capacity that many people may share without actually using it.
† My 1979 Tanner Lecture on the use of capability, which was published as 'Equality of What?' in S. McMurrin (ed.), *Tanner Lectures on Human Values*, vol. I (Cambridge: Cambridge University Press, 1980), presented the capability perspective not merely as a contrast with the Rawlsian focus on primary goods but also as a rival to – and critique of – any welfare-based approach. Dworkin does not comment on it in his first paper on equality of resources: 'What Is Equality?: Part 1: Equality of Welfare', and 'What Is Equality? Part 2: Equality of Resources', *Philosophy and Public Affairs*, 10 (1981), and the attribution first occurs, as far as I can see (unless I have missed something), in Dworkin's *Sovereign Virtue: The Theory and Practice of Equality* (Cambridge, MA: Harvard University Press, 2000).

to any particular level of the former. This analytical technique has been much used in economic theory, dealing particularly with utility analysis, in thinking of utility not directly but in terms of equivalent incomes (often called 'indirect utility'). Capability equality and Dworkinian resource equality, which can be seen in this sense as 'indirect capability', could be congruent if and only if insurance markets were to work in such a way that under Dworkin's formula for equality of resources everyone would have much the same capability. But then why thrill merely at the instrumental achievement ('all have the same resources – hurrah!'), rather than about what really matters (all have the same substantive freedom or capability)?

Third, the congruence may not actually hold, since insurance markets can deal more easily with some objects than with others. Some of the sources of capability disadvantage arise not from personal features (like disability), but from relational and environmental features (like being relatively deprived, originally discussed by Adam Smith in the *Wealth of Nations*). It is easily checked why the market for insurance against such non-personal characteristics is much harder to accommodate in insurance markets with individual clients.*

Another reason for the possibility of non-congruence is that whereas the assessment of interpersonal differences in deprivation is the subject matter of public reasoning in my approach, that assessment is left to the atomistic operators in Dworkin's insurance markets. In Dworkin's system, it is the interplay of the different individuals' respective assessments that determines the market prices and compensation levels of different types of insurance. The market in the Dworkin system is charged to do the valuation exercise which may actually demand engaging public reasoning and interactive discussion.

Fourth, Dworkin's focus, in common with other transcendental institutionalist approaches, is on getting to perfectly just institutions (in one step). But in dealing with the task of advancing justice through the removal of radical cases of injustice, even when there is no hope of achieving perfectly just institutions (or even any agreement on

---

* Some of the reasons for the divergence of resource equality and capability equality have been analysed by, among others, Andrew William, 'Dworkin on Capability', *Ethics*, 113 (2002), and Roland Pierik and Ingrid Robeyns, 'Resources versus Capabilities: Social Endowments in Egalitarian Theory', *Political Studies*, 55 (2007).

what they would be like), we can have much use for what has been dismissively called 'merely a partial order ranking'. The *as if* market for insurance against disability in the Dworkinian form does not even claim to take us to ways and means of identifying advancements of justice, because of its exclusive concentration on the make-believe exercise of transcendental justice.

Fifth, Dworkin takes the existence, uniqueness and efficiency of perfectly competitive market equilibria, which he needs for his institutional story, to be entirely unproblematic. And this is all assumed, without much defence, despite what we know about the huge difficulties that exist in these presumptions, as shown by half a century of economic research on 'general equilibrium' theory. Indeed, many of the problematic features, related to informational limitations (especially asymmetric information), the role of public goods, economies of scale and other impediments apply particularly strongly to the markets for insurance.[10]

There is, I am afraid, some institutional fundamentalism in Dworkin's approach, and some innocence in his presumption that once we have agreed on some rules for insurance-based resource redistribution, we would be able to forget about the actual outcomes and the actual capabilities that different people enjoy. It is assumed that the actual freedoms and outcomes can be left in the secure hands of institutional choice through *as if* markets, without ever having to second-guess the correspondence between what people expected and what actually happened. The insurance markets are supposed to work as one-shot affairs – with no surprises, no repeats and no discussions about what was hoped for and what actually emerged.

If there is usefulness in Dworkin's ingenious device of imagined insurance markets, that use lies elsewhere than in its claim as a new and viable theory of distributional justice. Resource equality in Dworkin's way is hardly a substitute for the capability approach, but it can serve as one way – one of several ways* – of understanding

---

* An important alternative to giving extra private income to the handicapped is, of course, the much-used practice of providing free or subsidized social services – a procedure that is central to the 'welfare state' of Europe. That is how, for example, a national health service runs, rather than giving ill people more income to pay for their medical needs.

how compensation for handicaps can be thought of in terms of income transfers. In this difficult field, we can do with any help that thought-experiments can provide, so long as they do not pretend to have imperial powers as institution-based arbitrators.

As was discussed earlier (particularly in Chapter 3), advancement of justice and the removal of injustice demand joint engagement with institutional choice (dealing among other things with private incomes and public goods), behavioural adjustment and procedures for the correction of social arrangements based on public discussion of what is promised, how the institutions actually work out and how things can be improved. There is no leave to shut off interactive public reasoning, resting on the promised virtue of a once-and-for-all market-based institutional choice. The social role of institutions, including imaginary ones, is more complex than that.

# 13

# Happiness, Well-being and Capabilities

Since economics is meant to be my profession, no matter what I make of my love affair with philosophy, I might as well begin by acknowledging that my profession has had something of a troubled relation with the perspective of happiness. It is frequently described, following Thomas Carlyle, as 'the dismal science'. Economists are often seen as terrible kill-joys who want to drown the natural cheerfulness of human beings and their friendliness towards each other in some kind of a formulaic concoction of economic discipline. Indeed, Edmund Clerihew Bentley placed the economic writings of that great utilitarian, John Stuart Mill, in that cheerless box of political economy – with little joy and no friendliness:

> John Stuart Mill,
> By a mighty effort of will,
> Overcame his natural bonhomie,
> And wrote the 'Principles of Political Economy'.

Is economics really so hostile to happiness and congeniality that bonhomie must be ruthlessly overcome before we are able to consider political economy?

Of course, it cannot be doubted that the subject matter of economics is often rather grave and sometimes quite depressing, and it may well be quite hard to retain one's natural cheerfulness in studying, say, hunger or poverty, or in trying to understand the causes and effects of devastating unemployment or dreadful destitution. But that is as it should be: cheerfulness per se is not a major help in the analysis of, say, unemployment, poverty or famine.

But what about economics in general, which covers so many

269

different issues not all of which are terribly disturbing? Does it get anywhere in accommodating the perspective of happiness and in acknowledging its importance for human life and therefore for good economic policy? That is the first question I address in this chapter.

The second is, how adequate is the perspective of happiness in judging a person's well-being or advantage? We could err either through not being fair to the importance of happiness, or through overestimating its importance in judging the well-being of people, or being blind to the limitations of making happiness the main – or only – basis of assessment of social justice or social welfare. In addition to examining the connections between happiness and well-being, it is relevant to ask how happiness relates to the perspective of freedom and capability. Since I have been discussing the significance of capability, it is important to examine the extent of the divergence between the two perspectives of happiness and capability.

Third, how does capability link with the well-being of a person? Is an expansion of capability always a welfare-enhancing change? If not, in what sense is capability an indicator of a person's 'advantage'?

These questions will be examined presently, but before that I want to discuss the fact that the relevance of capability is not confined only to its role in telling us about the advantages of a person (it is in that role that capability may compete with happiness), since it also carries implications regarding a person's duties and obligations, at least in one perspective. As was noted earlier, capability is also a kind of power, in a way that happiness clearly is not. How significant are the implications of this contrast for moral and political philosophy in general and for the theory of justice in particular?

## HAPPINESS, CAPABILITY AND OBLIGATIONS

The question here relates to the responsibility of effective power, which was discussed earlier, in Chapter 9 ('Plurality of Impartial Reasons'). Unlike the contractarian argument, the case for duty or obligation of effective power to make a difference does not arise, in that line of reasoning, from the mutuality of joint benefits through cooperation, or from the commitment made in some social contract. It is based, rather, on the argument that if someone has the power to make a difference that he or she can see will reduce injustice in the world, then there is a strong and reasoned argument for doing just that (without having to dress all this up in terms of some imagined prudential advantage in a hypothetical exercise of cooperation). It is a line of reasoning that I traced to Gautama Buddha's analysis of obligations that go with effectiveness of one's ability and power (the cited argument is presented by Buddha in *Sutta-Nipata*), but it has emerged in different forms in moral and political philosophy in many different countries, in many different eras.

Freedom in general and agency freedom in particular are parts of an effective power that a person has, and it would be a mistake to see capability, linked with these ideas of freedom, only as a notion of human advantage: it is also a central concern in understanding our obligations. This consideration yields a major contrast between happiness and capability as basic informational ingredients in a theory of justice, since happiness does not generate obligations in the way that capability inescapably must do, if the argument on the responsibility of effective power is recognized. There is, in this respect, a significant difference between well-being and happiness, on one side, and freedom and capability, on the other.

Capability has a role in social ethics and political philosophy that goes well beyond its place as a rival to happiness and well-being as a guide to human advantage. I will not pursue this distinction further here – at least directly, even though it will figure in explaining why an enhancement of a person's freedom may not necessarily increase his or her well-being. I will concentrate instead on the relevance of capability in the assessment of personal states and advantages, in contrast with the perspective of happiness emphasized in traditional welfare economics. The issue of obligation related to capability is an important part of the overall approach to justice presented in this work.

## ECONOMICS AND HAPPINESS

The discipline of welfare economics, which is the part of economics that is concerned with the assessment of the goodness of states of affairs and the appraisal of policies, has had a long history in placing happiness at the very centre of the discipline of evaluation, seeing it as a sole guide to human well-being and to the advantages enjoyed by different people. Indeed, for a long time – for well over a century – welfare economics was dominated by one particular approach, namely utilitarianism, initiated in its modern form by Jeremy Bentham, and championed by such economists as John Stuart Mill, Francis Edgeworth, Henry Sidgwick, Alfred Marshall and A. C. Pigou, among many other leaders of economic thought. It gave happiness the status of being uniquely important in assessing human well-being and advantage, and thus serving as the basis for social evaluation and the making of public policy. Utilitarianism was for a very long time something like 'the official theory' of welfare economics, though (as John Roemer has illuminatingly analysed) there are many compelling theories now.[1]

Indeed, even a substantial part of contemporary welfare economics is still largely utilitarian, at least in form. And yet the importance of happiness in human life has frequently been treated with some neglect in the dominant discourse of contemporary economic issues. There is considerable empirical evidence that even as people in many parts of the world have become richer, with much more income to spend in real terms than ever before, they have not felt particularly happier than before. Cogently reasoned and empirically backed doubts have been raised about the implicit premise of no-nonsense advocates of economic growth as an all-purpose remedy of all economic ailments, including misery and unhappiness, by asking the question, to quote from the title of a justly famous essay by Richard Easterlin, 'Will raising the income of all raise the happiness of all?'[2] The nature and causes of 'joylessness' in the lives of people in prosperous economies have also received attention from a number of economists who have been ready to step beyond the simple functional presumption that the utility level will always increase with income and wealth. Tibor

Scitovsky's analysis – part economic, part sociological – of 'the joyless economy' (to quote the title of his famous book) has been a landmark in this neglected area of research.[3]

There is little reason to doubt the importance of happiness in human life, and it is good that the tension between the income perspective and the happiness perspective is, at long last, receiving more mainstream attention. Even though I have had many occasions to argue with my long-standing friend, Richard Layard (and will go into some of these arguments presently), I cannot over-emphasize the importance I attach to his extensive investigation of a paradox that motivates his engaging and combative book, *Happiness: Lessons from a New Science*: 'There is a paradox at the heart of our lives. Most people want more income and strive for it. Yet as Western societies have got richer, their people have become no happier.'[4] The questions that do arise come only after the importance of happiness for human life has been fully acknowledged, with its far-reaching implications for styles of living and with the consequent recognition of the fact that the relation between income and happiness is far more complex than income-oriented theorists have tended to presume.

Those questions concern the status of other ways of judging the goodness of human lives, and the importance of freedom in the way we live, and whether all these other concerns should be seen as unimportant, or subsidiary to utility, or perhaps seen only in terms of their role as determinants of – or instruments for – enhancing happiness. The central issue is not the significance of happiness, but the alleged insignificance of everything else, on which many advocates of the happiness perspective seem to insist.

## THE REACH AND LIMITS
## OF HAPPINESS

It is hard to deny that happiness is extremely important and we have very good reason to try to advance people's happiness, including our own. Richard Layard, in his forcefully argued and enjoyably spirited (I should say, happiness-creating) advocacy for the perspective of happiness, may have underestimated a little our ability to discuss awkward questions, but it is easy to see what he means when he claims: 'If we are asked why happiness matters, we can give no further, external reason. It just obviously does matter.'[5] Certainly, happiness is a momentous achievement, the importance of which is apparent enough.

Where problems arise is in the claim that: 'Happiness is that ultimate goal because, unlike all other goals, it is self-evidently good.' Layard points to the fact that 'the American Declaration of Independence says, it is a "self-evident" objective'.[6] (In fact, what the American Declaration of Independence did say was that it was 'self-evident' that everyone is 'endowed by their Creator with certain inalienable rights', and it is in the elaboration of those diverse rights that the right to happiness figured – among several other objectives – not entirely 'unlike all other goals'). It is the claim that nothing else ultimately matters – liberty, equality, fraternity or whatever – that may not resonate so easily with the way people have thought and continue to think about what looks self-evidently good. This is so whether we examine what moved people in the French Revolution more than two centuries ago, or what people champion today, whether in political practice, or in philosophical analysis (the latter includes, for example, Robert Nozick's overarching emphasis on the self-evident nature of the importance of liberty, and Ronald Dworkin's singular focus on equality as the sovereign virtue).[7] Something more would be needed in the form of reasoning to give happiness the unique position that Layard wants to offer to it, rather than pointing just to its being 'self-evidently good'.

Despite Layard's strongly stated belief that in defending the criterion of happiness, 'we can give no further, external reason', he actually does go on to give such a reason – indeed, one with some plausibility. In disputing the claim of capabilities, Layard presents the critical argument: 'But unless we can justify our goals by how people feel, there is a real danger of paternalism' (p. 113). The avoidance of paternalism is surely an external reason, different from the allegedly undiscussable self-evident goodness of happiness. Layard invokes the charge of paternalism – that of playing 'God and deciding what is good for others' – against any social observer who notes that the hopelessly deprived often adapt to their deprivation to make life more bearable, without making that deprivation go away.

Layard's operative assumption lies in the tail of his remark, asking us to refrain from doing what we think is 'good for others, even if they will never feel it to be so' (*Happiness*, pp. 120–21). Is this fair to those whose views Layard wants to refute? What the critics of unreasoning acceptance of persistent deprivation want is more reasoning about what ails the perennial underdogs, with the expectation that, with more scrutiny, the 'well-adapted' deprived would see – and 'feel' – reason enough to grumble. It was noted earlier, in Chapter 7 ('Position, Relevance and Illusion'), that the obedient and unagonized acceptance by women of their subjugation in traditionalist India has been giving way over the decades to some 'creative discontent', demanding social change, and that in this change a large role is played by questioning women's inactive acceptance of a subjugated role without complaint or disquiet.* The role of interactive public discussion on the toleration of chronic deprivation plays a big part, often led by women's movements, but also more generally through radical political re-examination of diverse sources of inequality in India.

We can – and often do – reason with ourselves in our own reflections, and with each other in public discussions, about the reliability of our convictions and mental reactions in order to check that our immediate feelings are not misleading us. From King Lear's insistence that we have to place ourselves in the position of others to be able to assess our own inclinations (for example, the inclination to accept uncritically when 'yond justice' rails over 'yond simple thief'), to Adam Smith's argument about how culturally sequestered people, even in the intellectual glory of classical Athens, may have reason to scrutinize their positive feelings about the common practice of infanticide in that society, the need for reasoning about our unscrutinized feelings can be cogently defended.†

This applies also to the role of public education today, for example on healthcare, food habits or smoking, and it is relevant for understanding the need for open debate on issues of immigration, racial intolerance, lack of medical entitlements or women's position in

* I wish I could move my friend Richard Layard from all Bentham to a little Mill.
† For an excellent analysis of the case for persistent re-examination of one's lives, beliefs and practices, see Robert Nozick, *The Examined Life: Philosophical Meditations* (New York: Simon & Schuster, 1989).

society, without unleashing alleged paternalism. There is a lot of reasoning that can – and in many societies does – challenge the unquestioned hegemony of 'feelings' and unexamined sentiments over all else.

## THE EVIDENTIAL INTEREST
## OF HAPPINESS

Happiness, important as it is, can hardly be the only thing that we have reason to value, nor the only metric for measuring other things that we value. But when being happy is not given such an imperialist role, it can, with good reason, be seen as a very important human functioning, among others. The capability to be happy is, similarly, a major aspect of the freedom that we have good reason to value. The perspective of happiness illuminates a critically important part of human life.

In addition to its own importance, happiness can also be seen to have some evidential interest and pertinence. We have to take note of the fact that the achievement of other things that we do value (and have reason to value) very often influences our sense of happiness – generated by that fulfilment. It is natural to take pleasure in our success in achieving what we are trying to achieve. Similarly, on the negative side, our failure to get what we value can be a source of disappointment. So happiness and frustration relate, respectively, to our successes and failures to achieve the fulfilment of our objectives – no matter what these objectives are. This can be of great circumstantial relevance in checking whether people are succeeding or failing to get what they value and have reason to value.

This recognition need not, however, lead us to the belief that we value the things that we do value just for the reason that not getting them would lead to frustration. Rather, the reasons that we have for the valuation of our objectives (no matter how remote these objectives are from merely seeking happiness) actually help to explain why we may sensibly feel happy about achieving what we are trying to achieve, and frustrated when we do not succeed. Happiness can thus have indicative merit in being, typically, related to our successes and failures in life. This is so even though happiness is not the only thing we seek, or have reason to seek.

## UTILITARIANISM AND
## WELFARE ECONOMICS

I return now to the treatment of happiness in economics in general and what is called welfare economics in particular (dealing with the well-being of people both as a subject of interest and as a guide to policy-making). Utilitarians, such as Bentham, or Edgeworth, or Marshall, or Pigou, saw no great difficulty in asserting that the ranking of social goodness and the selection of what is to be chosen must be done simply on the basis of the sum total of individual welfares. And they took individual welfare as being represented by individual 'utility', and typically identified utility with individual happiness. They also tended to ignore the problems of distributional inequality of welfares and utilities among different people. Thus all alternative states were judged by the sum total of happiness that can be found in the respective states, and alternative policies were assessed by the 'total happiness' that resulted from these policies, respectively.

The subject of welfare economics suffered a major blow in the 1930s when economists came to be persuaded by arguments presented by Lionel Robbins and others (influenced by 'logical positivist' philosophy) that interpersonal comparisons of utility have no scientific basis and cannot be sensibly made. One person's happiness, it was argued, could not be compared, in any way, with the happiness of another. 'Every mind is inscrutable to every other mind,' Robbins argued, quoting W. S. Jevons, 'and no common denominator of feeling is possible.'[8]

This dismissal is deeply problematic since there are plausible rules of comparative assessment of the joys and pains of human life and, even when there remain areas of doubt and dispute, it is not difficult to see why agreements emerge easily enough on some interpersonal comparisons, thereby generating a partial ordering (an issue I have discussed elsewhere).* These agreements are also reflected in the language we use to describe the happiness of distinct persons, which does not place different human beings on disparate islands that are all isolated from each other.† It would be hard to follow, say, the tragedy of *King Lear*, if interpersonal comparisons communicated nothing.

However, since economists came, by and large, to be convinced – far too rapidly – that there was indeed something methodologically wrong in using interpersonal comparison of utilities, the fuller version of the utilitarian tradition soon gave way, in the 1940s and the 1950s, to an informationally impoverished version of relying on utility or happiness. It came to be known as 'the new welfare economics'. This took the form of continuing to rely on utilities *only* (this is often called 'welfarism'), but of dispensing with interpersonal comparisons altogether. The 'informational basis' of welfare economics remained narrowly confined to utilities, but the permitted ways of using the utility information were further restricted by the ban on interpersonal comparisons of utilities. Welfarism without interpersonal comparisons is, in fact, a very restrictive informational basis for social judgements. We could discuss whether the same person is happier in one state than in another, but could not compare, we were told, the happiness of one person with that of another.

---

* See *Collective Choice and Social Welfare* (San Francisco, CA: Holden-Day, 1970; republished, Amsterdam: North-Holland, 1979), which argued for the systematic use of interpersonal comparisons of welfare in the form of partial orderings in social choice theory. See also my essay 'Interpersonal Comparisons of Welfare', in *Choice, Welfare and Measurement* (Oxford: Blackwell, 1982; republished, Cambridge, MA: Harvard University Press, 1997). See also Donald Davidson, 'Judging Interpersonal Interests', in Jon Elster and Aanund Hylland (eds), *Foundations of Social Choice Theory* (Cambridge: Cambridge University Press, 1986) and Allan Gibbard, 'Interpersonal Comparisons: Preference, Good, and the Intrinsic Reward of a Life', in Elster and Hylland (eds), *Foundations of Social Choice Theory* (1986). On related matters, see Hilary Putnam, *The Collapse of the Fact/Value Dichotomy and Other Essays* (Cambridge, MA: Harvard University Press, 2002).

† The discipline of language in reflecting an aspect of objectivity was discussed in Chapter 1, 'Reason and Objectivity' and 5, 'Impartiality and Objectivity'.

# INFORMATIONAL LIMITATIONS
# AND IMPOSSIBILITIES

It was in the context of the ongoing search for acceptable formulations of social welfare that Kenneth Arrow presented his well-known 'impossibility theorem'. His book *Social Choice and Individual Values* (published in 1951) launched the new subject of social choice theory.[9] As discussed in Chapter 4 ('Voice and Social Choice'), Arrow considered a set of very mild-looking conditions relating social choices or judgements to the set of individual preferences, and took them to be something like a minimal set of requirements that any decent procedure for social assessment must satisfy. Arrow showed that it is impossible to satisfy those apparently undemanding conditions simultaneously. The 'impossibility theorem' precipitated a major crisis in welfare economics, and it is, in fact, a landmark in the history of social and political study as well as economics.

In formulating the problem of social choice based on individual preferences, Arrow took the viewpoint (following what was by then the dominant tradition) that 'interpersonal comparison of utilities has no meaning'.[10] The combination of relying only on individual utilities and denying any use of interpersonal comparison of utilities had a decisive role in precipitating the impossibility theorem.

Let me illustrate an aspect of this difficulty. Consider, for example, the problem of choosing between different distributions of a cake between two or more persons. It turns out that in terms of informational availability in Arrow's 1951 framework, we cannot, in effect, be guided by any equity consideration that would require the identification of the rich vis-à-vis the poor. If 'being rich' or 'being poor' is defined in terms of income or commodity holdings, then that is a non-utility characteristic of which we cannot take any direct note in the Arrow system, because of the requirement to rely exclusively on utilities only. But nor can we identify a person's 'being rich' or 'being poor' with having a high or a low level of happiness, since that would involve interpersonal comparison of happiness or utilities, which is also ruled out. Equity considerations basically lose their applicability in this framework. The extent of happiness as an indicator of a person's situation is applied to each individual *separately* – without any comparison between the levels of happiness of two different people – and no use can be made of the happiness metric to assess inequality and to take note of the demands of equity.

All this informational restriction leaves us with a class of decision procedures that are really some variant or other of *voting* methods (like majority decision). Since they do not need any interpersonal comparison, these voting procedures remain available in Arrow's informational framework. But these procedures have consistency problems (discussed in Chapter 4), as had been noted more than two hundred years ago by French mathematicians such as Condorcet and Borda. For example, an alternative A can defeat B in a majority vote, while B defeats C, and C defeats A, all in majority voting. We are left, then, with the unattractive possibility of having a dictatorial method of social judgement (i.e. handing it over to one person, the 'dictator', whose preferences could then determine the social rankings). Dictatorial decision-making may, of course, be ferociously consistent, but that would be clearly a politically unacceptable method of decision-making, and it is in fact ruled out explicitly by one of Arrow's conditions (that of 'non-dictatorship'). This is how Arrow's impossibility result emerges. A number of other impossibility results were identified soon after, largely under the shadow of Arrow's theorem, with different axioms but yielding similarly discouraging conclusions.

The ways and means of resolving such impossibilities have been fairly extensively explored since those pessimistic days and, among other things, it has clearly emerged that enriching the informational basis of social choice is an important necessity for overcoming the negative implications of an information-starved decisional system (as voting systems inescapably are, especially when applied to economic and social issues). For one thing, interpersonal comparisons of the advantages and disadvantages of individuals have to be given a central role in such social judgements. If utility is the chosen indicator of individual advantage, then it is interpersonal comparison of utilities that become a crucial necessity for a viable system of social assessment.

This is, however, not to deny that it is possible to have social choice mechanisms that do without any interpersonal comparisons of advantages or utilities, but the claims of such mechanisms in fulfilling the demands of justice are weakened by their not being able to compare the well-being and relative advantages of different people in congruent scales.* Alternatively, as was discussed earlier, the informational inputs in a social choice exercise in the form of individual rankings can also be interpreted in ways other than as utility rankings or happiness orderings. Indeed, Arrow himself noted that, and the nature of the debate on the consistency of social choice systems can be – and has been – moved to a broader arena through reinterpreting the variables incorporated in the mathematical model underlying social choice systems. This issue was discussed in Chapter 4 ('Voice and Social Choice'), and indeed 'voice' is a very different – and in many ways a more versatile – idea than the concept of happiness.[11]

Questions have been raised powerfully in this context about the wisdom of relying only on utility – interpreted as happiness or desire-fulfilment – as the basis of social evaluation, that is, the acceptability of welfarism. As it happens, welfarism in general is in itself a very special approach to social ethics. One of the major limitations of this approach lies in the fact that the same collection of individual welfares may go with a very different overall social picture, with different societal arrangements, opportunities, freedoms and personal liberties.

Welfarism demands that the evaluation pays no direct attention to any of those different (non-utility) features – only to utility or happiness associated with them. But the same set of utility numbers may go, in one case, with serious violations of very basic human freedoms, but not in another. Or it may involve the denial of some recognized individual rights in one case but not in another. No matter what happens in these other respects, welfarism would still demand that those differences be ignored in the evaluative exercises, with each alternative being judged only by the utility totals generated. There is

---

* Fine examples of such social choice exercise include the classic model of 'the bargaining problem' by John Nash ('The Bargaining Problem', *Econometrica*, 18 (1950)) as well as innovative recent departures, such as Marc Fleurbaey's institutional exploration ('Social Choice and Just Institutions', *Economics and Philosophy*, 23 (2007), and *Fairness, Responsibility, and Welfare* (Oxford: Clarendon Press, 2008)) that look for symmetry of processes but do not explicitly invoke interpersonal comparisons of well-being.

something quite peculiar in the insistence that no intrinsic importance at all is given to anything other than utility or happiness in the assessment of alternative states or policies.

The neglect applies strongly to freedoms, including substantive opportunities – what are sometimes called 'positive' freedoms (for example, the freedom to have free or affordable school education, or the freedom to have basic healthcare). But the neglect applies also to 'negative' freedoms which demand the absence of intrusive interference by others, including the state (e.g. the right to personal liberties).* Welfarism demands a very limited view of normative evaluation and welfare economics. It is one thing to see utility as important, which it must be, but it is quite another to insist that nothing else matters. In particular, we may have much reason to want that substantive note be taken of considerations of freedom in assessing social arrangements.

Second, the informational limitation is made even stronger by the particular utilitarian interpretation of individual welfare, seeing it entirely either in terms of happiness or as the fulfilment of desires and longings. This narrow view of individual well-being can be particularly restrictive when making *interpersonal* comparisons of deprivation. The issue calls for some discussion here.

## HAPPINESS, WELL-BEING AND ADVANTAGE

The utilitarian calculus based on happiness or desire-fulfilment can be deeply unfair to those who are persistently deprived, since our mental make-up and desires tend to adjust to circumstances, particularly to make life bearable in adverse situations. It is through 'coming to terms' with one's hopeless predicament that life is made somewhat bearable

---

* I should note here that the use of the distinction between 'positive' and 'negative' freedoms in welfare economics tends to be rather different from the philosophical contrast outlined by Isaiah Berlin in his classic 1969 lecture at Oxford on 'The Two Concepts of Liberty', the focus of which was on the difference between *internal* and *external* constraints on a person's ability to do things he or she may have reason to value; see Berlin, *Four Essays on Liberty* (London: Oxford University Press, 1969).

by the traditional underdogs, such as oppressed minorities in intolerant communities, sweated workers in exploitative industrial arrangements, precarious share-croppers living in a world of uncertainty, or subdued housewives in deeply sexist cultures. The hopelessly deprived people may lack the courage to desire any radical change and typically tend to adjust their desires and expectations to what little they see as feasible. They train themselves to take pleasure in small mercies.

The practical merit of such adjustments for people in chronically adverse positions is easy to understand: this is one way of being able to live peacefully with persistent deprivation. But the adjustments also have the consequential effect of distorting the scale of utilities in the form of happiness or desire-fulfilment. In terms of pleasure or desire-fulfilment, the disadvantages of the hopeless underdog may thus appear to be much smaller than what would emerge on the basis of a more objective analysis of the extent of their deprivation and unfreedom. Adaptation of expectations and perceptions tends to play a particularly major part in the perpetuation of social inequalities, including the relative deprivation of women.*

The perspective of happiness has received some strong advocacy recently, and not only from Richard Layard.[12] It is important to be clear about the distinct issues involved in this renewed championing of the utilitarian perspective of happiness – the attempted revival of the philosophy of the eighteenth-century Enlightenment, as articulated by Jeremy Bentham.[13] We have to examine in particular whether – and to what extent – these claims can be accepted without having to deny what has just been said about adaptive scales of happiness, related to persistent deprivation.

A particular distinction of great importance in this context is that between interpersonal comparisons of well-being, and interstate comparisons for the same person. The adaptive phenomenon particularly

---

* I have discussed the far-reaching effects of the adaptive adjustment of utility scales to deprivation in my 'Equality of What?' in S. McMurrin (ed.), *Tanner Lectures on Human Values*, vol. I (Cambridge: Cambridge University Press, 1980); *Resources, Values and Development* (Cambridge, MA: Harvard University Press, 1984); *Commodities and Capabilities* (Amsterdam: North-Holland, 1985; Delhi: Oxford University Press, 1987). See also Martha Nussbaum, *Women and Human Development: The Capability Approach* (Cambridge: Cambridge University Press, 2000).

affects the reliability of interpersonal comparisons of utilities, by tending to downplay the assessment of the hardship of the chronically deprived, because the small breaks in which they try to take pleasure tend to reduce their mental distress without removing – or even substantially reducing – the actual deprivations that characterize their impoverished lives. To overlook the intensity of their disadvantage merely because of their ability to build a little joy in their lives is hardly a good way of achieving an adequate understanding of the demands of social justice.

This is perhaps a less serious problem for making comparisons for the same person. Since happiness is not irrelevant to the quality of life, even though it is not a good guide to all other features that may also have considerable relevance, the building of some joy through adaptive expectations and through making desires more 'realistic' may be seen as a clear gain for the persons who achieve that. This can be seen as a point in the direction of attaching some importance to the happiness and desire-fulfilment even when generated by the adaptation to persistent deprivation. There is some obvious sense in that recognition. However, even for the same person, the use of the happiness scale can be quite misleading if it leads to ignoring the significance of other deprivations that may not be at all well judged in the scale of happiness.

Indeed, the relation between social circumstances and perceptions also yields other problems for the mental metric of utilities, since our perceptions may tend to blind us to the deprivations that we do actually have, which a clearer and more informed understanding can bring out. Let me illustrate the issue with an example involving health and happiness.

## HEALTH: PERCEPTION AND MEASUREMENT

One of the complications in evaluating states of health arises from the fact that the person's own understanding of their health may be limited by lack of medical knowledge and by inadequate familiarity with comparative information. More generally, there is a conceptual contrast between the 'internal' views of health based on the patient's own perception, and 'external' views based on observations and examinations by trained doctors or pathologists. While the two perspectives can often be fruitfully combined (a good medical practitioner would be interested in both), there can also be considerable tension between evaluations based on the two different outlooks.[14]

The external view has come under considerable criticism recently, particularly in powerful anthropological analyses by Arthur Kleinman and others, for taking a distanced and less sensitive view of illness and health.[15] These works bring out the importance of seeing suffering as a central feature of illness. No mechanically observed medical statistics can provide an adequate understanding of this dimension of bad health, since pain, as Wittgenstein had noted, is a matter of self-perception. If you *feel* pain, then you *have* pain, and if you *do not feel* pain, then no external observer can sensibly reject the view that you *do not have* pain. In dealing with this aspect of illness, the empirical material on which health planners, economic allocators – and cost-benefit analysts frequently rely may therefore be fundamentally deficient. There is a need to draw on the rich discernment provided by anthropological investigation of these matters.

It is in fact sensible to argue that public health decisions are quite often inadequately responsive to the patient's actual suffering and the experience of healing. On the other hand, in assessing this debate, which has figured in past discussions as well as contemporary ones, the extensive limitations of the internal perspective must also be considered.* Even though for sensory assessment the priority of the internal view can hardly be disputed, medical practice is not concerned only with the sensory dimension of ill-health (important as it undoubtedly is). One problem with relying on the patient's own view on medical matters lies in the fact that the internal view of the patient may be seriously limited by his or her knowledge and social experience. A person reared in a community with a great many diseases and little

* Self-reported morbidity is in fact already widely used as a part of social statistics, and the scrutiny of these statistics brings out difficulties that can thoroughly mislead public policy on healthcare and medical strategy. I have discussed some of the problems involved in 'Health: Perception versus Observation', *British Medical Journal*, 324 (April 2002).

medical facilities may be inclined to take certain symptoms as 'normal' when they are clinically preventable. Like adaptive desires and pleasures, there is also an issue here of adaptation to social circumstances, with rather obscuring consequences. This issue was discussed earlier, in Chapter 7 ('Position, Relevance and Illusion').

While the 'internal' view is privileged with respect to some information (that of a sensory nature), it can be deeply deficient in others. There is a strong need for socially situating the statistics of self-perception of illness, taking note of levels of education, availability of health facilities and public information on illness and remedy. While the 'internal' view of health deserves attention, relying on it in assessing healthcare or in evaluating medical strategy can be extremely misleading.

That recognition has relevance for health policy, and more generally for policy for good health which is influenced by a great many variables other than narrowly defined 'health policies' (such as general education and social inequalities).* However, for the subject of the present discussion, what the lacuna between health perceptions and actual health conditions bring out is the limitations of the perspective of subjective evaluation in assessing the well-being of people. Happiness, pleasure and pain have an importance of their own, but to treat them as general-purpose guides to all aspects of well-being would be, at least partly, a leap in the dark.

## WELL-BEING AND FREEDOM

I turn now to the third question that was identified earlier: how does capability link with the well-being of a person? Related to that we also must address the question whether an expansion of capability must invariably be a welfare-enhancing change.

* The important contrast between health policies per se and policies that yield health advancement has been extensively investigated by Jennifer Prah Ruger, 'Aristotelian Justice and Health Policy: Capability and Incompletely Theorized Agreements', Ph.D. dissertation, Harvard University, 1998 (to be published by Clarendon Press as *Health and Social Justice*). See also her 'Ethics of the Social Determinants of Health', *Lancet*, 364 (2004) and 'Health, Capability and Justice: Toward a New Paradigm of Health

Capability, as already discussed, is an aspect of freedom, concentrating in particular on substantive opportunities. Any claim that an assessment of capability must be a good guide to the well-being of a person must be restrained by the understanding of two important distinctions: (1) the contrast between agency and well-being; and (2) the distinction between freedom and achievement. Both these differences have come up, in other contexts, earlier in this work; but there is a case for a more direct discussion of these contrasts to assess the relation between capability and well-being.

The first distinction is between the promotion of the person's well-being, and the pursuit of the person's overall agency goals. Agency encompasses all the goals that a person has reasons to adopt, which can *inter alia* include goals other than the advancement of his or her own well-being. Agency can thus generate orderings different from those of well-being. A person's agency objectives will standardly include, *inter alia*, his or her own well-being, and thus agency and well-being will typically have something in common (e.g. an increase in well-being, given other things, would tend to involve a higher agency achievement). Also, a failure to achieve one's *non*-well-being objectives may also cause frustration, thereby reducing one's well-being. These and other connections exist between well-being and agency, but they do not make the two concepts congruent.

The second distinction is between achievement and the freedom to achieve, which was discussed earlier, in Chapter 11 in particular. This contrast can be applied both to the perspective of well-being and that of agency. The two distinctions together yield four different concepts of advantage, related to a person: (1) 'well-being achievement'; (2) 'agency achievement'; (3) 'well-being freedom'; and (4) 'agency freedom'. We can have a four-fold classification of points of evaluative interest in assessing human advantage, based on these two different distinctions.[16]

---

Ethics, Policy and Law', *Cornell Journal of Law and Public Policy*, 15 (2006), and the doctoral thesis of Sridhar Venkatapuram, 'Health and Justice: The Capability to Be Healthy', Ph.D. dissertation, Cambridge University, 2008. The WHO Commission on Social Determinants of Health, chaired by Michael Marmot, examines the policy implications of a broader understanding of health determination (World Health Organization, *Closing the Gap in a Generation: Health Equity through Action on the*

The assessment of each of these four types of benefit involves an evaluative exercise, but they are not the *same* evaluative exercise. They can also have very disparate bearings on matters for which the evaluation and comparison of individual advantages are relevant. For example, in determining the extent to which a person is deprived in a way that calls for assistance from others or from the state, a person's well-being may be, arguably, more relevant than his or her agency success (e.g. the state may have better grounds for offering support to a person for overcoming hunger or illness than for helping him to build a monument to the person's hero, even if the loyal guy were to attach more importance to the monument than to avoiding hunger or illness).

Furthermore, in the making of state policy for adult citizens, well-being freedom may be of greater interest, in this context, than well-being achievement. For example, the state may have reasons to offer the person adequate opportunities to overcome hunger, but not to insist that the person must take up that offer, without fail.* Offering the opportunity to all to lead a minimally decent life need not be combined with an insistence that everyone makes use of all the opportunities that the state offers; for instance, making everyone entitled to an adequate amount of food does not have to be combined with a state ban on fasting.

Taking note of agency achievements or agency freedom shifts the focus away from seeing a person as just a vehicle of well-being, ignoring the importance of the person's own judgements and priorities, with which the agency concerns are linked. Corresponding to this distinction, the content of capability analysis can also take different forms. A person's capability can be characterized as well-being freedom (reflecting the freedom to advance one's own well-being), and

---

*Social Determinants of Health* (Geneva: WHO, 2008).

* There is a serious complication for social policy when the capability of the family to avoid hunger for all its members is not translated into that achievement, because of the differing priorities of the dominant members of the family (for example, when the male 'head' is keener on goals other than the interests of each member of his family). The distance between capability and achievement arising from such multi-person decisions tends to strengthen the relevance of the perspective of achievement in assessing the advantage of all the persons involved.

agency freedom (concerned with the freedom to advance whatever goals and values a person has reason to advance). While the former may be of more general interest to public policy (such as poverty removal, in the form of eradicating major deprivation in well-being freedom), it is the latter that can, arguably, be seen as being of primary interest to the person's own sense of values. If a person attaches more importance to some goal, or some rule of behaviour, than to personal well-being, it is a decision that could be seen to be for him or her to make (except for special cases, such as mental dysfunction that may prevent the person from thinking clearly enough about their priorities).

The distinctions discussed here also answer the question about whether a person's capability can go against his or her well-being. Indeed, agency freedom – and that particular version of capability – can, for reasons already discussed, be contrary to the single-minded pursuit of personal well-being, or for that matter, the cultivation of well-being freedom. There is no mystery in that divergence. If agency objectives differ from the maximization of personal well-being, then it follows that capability seen as agency freedom can diverge from both the perspective of well-being achievement and that of well-being freedom. As was discussed in Chapter 9, ('Plurality of Impartial Reasons') and also earlier in this chapter, when more capability includes more power in ways that can influence other people's lives, a person may have good reason to use the enhanced capability – the larger agency freedom – to uplift the lives of others, especially if they are relatively worse off, rather than concentrating only on their own well-being.

And, for the same reason, there is no mystery in understanding that a person's advantage as an agent may, quite possibly, go against the same person's advantage from the line of vision of well-being. When, for example, Mohandas Gandhi was released by the authorities in British India from being restrained at home and from not being allowed to take part in political activities, his agency freedom (and typically his agency achievements as well) expanded, but at the same time the hardship he chose to undergo and the pains that he accepted as a part of his non-violent agitation for India's independence clearly had some negative effects on his own personal well-being, which he was ready to accept for his cause. Indeed, even Gandhi's decision to fast for long periods for political reasons was clearly a reflection of his broad priority for agency over his own well-being.

Having more capability in terms of agency freedom is an advantage, but only in that specific perspective, and particularly not – at least not necessarily – in the perspective of well-being. Those who are unable to find any meaning in the idea of advantage, except in line with self-interest (there are schools of thought that go in that direction, as discussed in Chapter 8, 'Rationality and Other People'), would have difficulty in seeing why agency freedom can be seen as an advantage to the person involved. But one does not have to be a Gandhi (or a Martin Luther King, or a Nelson Mandela, or Aung San Suu Kyi) to understand that one's objectives and priorities could stretch well beyond the narrow limits of one's own personal well-being.

# 14

# Equality and Liberty

Equality was not only among the foremost revolutionary demands in eighteenth-century Europe and America, there has also been an extraordinary consensus on its importance in the post-Enlightenment world. In an earlier book, *Inequality Reexamined*, I commented on the fact that every normative theory of social justice that has received support and advocacy in recent times seems to demand equality of *something* – something that is regarded as particularly important in that theory.[1] The theories can be entirely diverse (focusing on, say, equal liberty or equal income or equal treatment of everyone's rights or utilities), and they may be in combat with each other, but they still have the common characteristic of wanting equality of something (some feature of significance in the respective approach).

It is not surprising that equality figures prominently in the contributions of political philosophers who would usually be seen as 'egalitarian', and in American usage as 'liberal', for example, John Rawls, James Meade, Ronald Dworkin, Thomas Nagel or Thomas Scanlon, to name a few. What is perhaps more significant is that equality is demanded in some basic form even by those who are typically seen as having disputed the 'case for equality' and expressed scepticism about the central importance of 'distributive justice'. For example, Robert Nozick may not lean towards equality of utility (as James Meade does), or towards equality of holdings of primary goods (as John Rawls does), and yet Nozick does demand equality of libertarian rights – that no one person should have any more right to liberty than anyone else. James Buchanan, the pioneering founder of 'public choice theory' (in some ways a conservative rival to social choice theory), which appears to be quite sceptical of the claims of equality, does, in fact, build equal legal and political treatment of people (and equal respect to the objection of anyone opposed to any proposed change) into his view of a good society.[2] In each theory, equality *is* sought in some 'space' (that is, in terms of some variables related to respective persons), a space that is seen as having a central role in that theory.*

Does this generalization apply to utilitarianism? That suggestion would be readily resisted, since utilitarians do not, in general, want the equality of the utilities enjoyed by different people – only the maximization of the *sum-total* of utilities, irrespective of distribution, which may not look particularly egalitarian. And yet there is an equality that utilitarians seek, to wit, equal treatment of human beings in attaching equal importance to the gains and losses of utilities by everyone, without exception. In the insistence on equal weights on everyone's utility gains, the utilitarian objective does make use of a particular kind of egalitarianism incorporated in its accounting. Indeed, it is precisely this egalitarian feature that relates, it has been argued, to the foundational principle of utilitarianism of 'giving equal weight to the equal interests of all the parties' (to quote one great utilitarian of our time, Richard Hare), and to the utilitarian requirement for always assigning 'the same weight to all individuals' interests' (to quote another contemporary leader of utilitarian thought, John Harsanyi).[3]

Is there any particular significance to be attached to this formal similarity in wanting equality of something – indeed, something that the particular normative theory takes to be very important? It is tempting to think that this must be a coincidence, since the similarities are entirely formal and not about the substance of 'equality of what?'

---

* G. A. Cohen's criticism of John Rawls in *Rescuing Justice and Equality* (Cambridge, MA: Harvard University Press, 2008) for allowing inequalities needed on grounds of incentives within his principles of justice, on which I commented earlier (in Chapter 2), can be seen as a critique of Rawls for not taking sufficiently seriously his own reasoning on the importance of equalizing primary goods in defining perfect justice. The relevance of behavioural and other constraints in practical policy-making is not denied by Cohen, and Cohen's reproach to Rawls concerns only the transcendental characterization of the perfectly just society. As was discussed earlier, Rawls clearly has non-transcendental elements in his thoughts about justice, and this could be present here in his choice not to extend the behavioural demands in a post-contract world to assume incentive-free just behaviour.

And yet the need for some egalitarian formula in defending a theory indicates the significance widely attached to non-discrimination, which can be seen as being motivated by the idea that in the absence of such a requirement a normative theory would be arbitrary and biased. There seems to be a recognition here of the need for impartiality in some form for the viability of a theory.* In terms of Thomas Scanlon's criterion of the need for principles that no one involved can 'reasonably reject', there may well be a strong connection between general acceptability and non-discrimination, demanding that, at some basic level, people must be seen as equal, whose rejections would respectively matter.†

## EQUALITY, IMPARTIALITY AND SUBSTANCE

The capability approach, with which a number of the previous chapters have been concerned, draws on the understanding, discussed above, that the really critical question is 'equality of what?' rather than whether we need equality at all in any space whatsoever.‡ To say this is not to claim that the latter question is a negligible one. Nor does the fact that there is so much agreement in demanding equality in some space or other establish that this presumption is right. It is certainly possible to take the position that all those theories are mistaken. What gives the shared characteristic such plausibility? This is a grand question to which we can hardly do justice here, but it is worth considering the direction to which we must look to seek a plausible answer.

The demand for seeing people as equals (in some important perspective) relates, I would argue, to the normative demand for impartiality,

---

* This recognition can be linked to the arguments examined in Chapter 5, 'Impartiality and Objectivity'.

† Scanlon's criterion has been discussed earlier, particularly in Chapters 5–9.

‡ The importance of that question and the place of capability in answering it was presented in my 1979 Tanner Lecture at Stanford University, 'Equality of What?', published under that title in S. McMurrin (ed.), *Tanner Lectures in Human Values*, vol. I (Cambridge: Cambridge University Press, 1980).

and the related claims of objectivity. This cannot, of course, be seen as a freestanding answer, complete in itself, since acceptable justifications for impartiality and objectivity also have to be scrutinized (some ideas in that direction were considered in Chapter 5). But that is the kind of scrutiny that would be ultimately involved in understanding why each of the pre-eminent theories of justice tends to involve some way of treating persons as equal at some basic level (basic, that is, for the respective theory).

Being an egalitarian is not, in any obvious sense, a 'uniting' feature, given the disagreements on ways of answering the question: 'equality of what?'. Indeed, it is precisely because there are such substantive differences between the endorsement of different spaces in which equality is recommended by various authors that the fact that there is a basic egalitarian similarity in the respective approaches of these very diverse authors has tended to escape widespread attention. The similarity, however, is of some importance.

To illustrate this point, let me refer to the collection of interesting and important essays edited by William Letwin, called *Against Equality*.[4] In one of the powerfully argued articles in Letwin's collection, Harry Frankfurt argues against 'equality as a moral ideal' by cogently disputing the claims of what he calls economic egalitarianism in the form of 'the doctrine that it is desirable for everyone to have the same amounts of income and wealth (for short, "money")'.[5] Although in the language chosen to express this rejection Frankfurt interprets his disputation as an argument against 'equality as a moral ideal', this is primarily because he uses that general term to refer specifically to a particular version of 'economic egalitarianism': 'This version of economic egalitarianism (for short, simply "egalitarianism") might also be formulated as the doctrine that there should be no inequalities in the *distribution* of money.' Frankfurt's arguments can be seen as disputing the specific demand for a common interpretation of economic egalitarianism by (1) disputing that such an equality is of any intrinsic interest, *and* (2) showing that it leads to the violation of intrinsically important values – values that link closely to the need for paying equal attention to all in *some other*, more relevant, way. The choice of space for equality is thus critically important in the development of Frankfurt's well-argued thesis.[6]

All this fits into the general pattern of arguing against equality in some space, on the grounds that it violates the more important requirement of equality in some other space. Seen in this way, the battles on distributional issues tend to be not about 'why equality?', but about 'equality of what?'. Since some areas of concentration (identifying corresponding spaces on which equality is sought) are traditionally associated with claims of equality in political or economic or social philosophy, it is equality in those spaces (for example, income, wealth, utilities) that tends to go under the heading of 'egalitarianism', whereas equality in other spaces (for example, rights, liberties or what are seen as just deserts of people) looks like anti-egalitarian claims. But we should not be too trapped by the conventions of characterization, and must also note the basic similarity among all these theories in arguing for equality in *some* space, and insisting on egalitarian priority there, while disputing – explicitly or by implication – the conflicting demands of equality in other (in their view, less relevant) spaces.

## CAPABILITY, EQUALITY AND OTHER CONCERNS

If equality is important, and capability is indeed a central feature of human life (as I have tried to argue earlier on in this book), would it not be right to presume that we should demand equality *of* capability? I have to argue that the answer is, no. This is so for several distinct reasons. We may, of course, attach significance to equality of capability, but that does not imply that we must demand equality of capability even if it conflicts with other important considerations. Significant as it is, equality of capability does not necessarily 'trump' all other weighty considerations (including other significant aspects of equality), with which it might be in conflict.

First, capability is, as I have tried to emphasize, only one aspect of freedom, related to substantive opportunities, and it cannot pay adequate attention to fairness and equity involved in procedures that have relevance to the idea of justice. While the idea of capability has considerable merit in the assessment of the opportunity aspect of freedom, it cannot possibly deal adequately with the process aspect of freedom. Capabilities are characteristics of individual advantages, and while they may incorporate some features of the processes involved (as was discussed in Chapter 11), they fall short of telling us enough about the fairness or equity of the processes involved, or about the freedom of citizens to invoke and utilize procedures that are equitable.

Let me illustrate the point with what may appear to be a fairly harsh example. It is now fairly well established that, given symmetric care, women tend to live longer than men, with lower mortality rates in each age group. If one were concerned exclusively with capabilities (and nothing else), and in particular with equality of the capability to live long, it would be possible to construct an argument for giving men relatively more medical attention than women to counteract the natural masculine handicap. But giving women less medical attention than men for the same health problems would flagrantly violate a significant requirement of process equity (in particular, treating different persons similarly in matters of life and death), and it is not unreasonable to claim that, in cases of this kind, demands of equity in the process aspect of freedom could sensibly override any single-minded concentration on the opportunity aspect of freedom, including prioritizing equality in life expectancy.

While the capability perspective may be very important in judging people's substantive opportunities (and may do better, as I have claimed, in assessing equity in the distribution of opportunities than the alternative approaches that focus on incomes, primary goods or resources), that point does not in any way go against the need to pay fuller attention to the process aspect of freedom in the assessment of justice.* A theory of justice – or more generally an adequate theory of normative social choice – has to be alive to both the fairness of the processes involved and to the equity and efficiency of the substantive opportunities that people can enjoy.

Capability is, in fact, no more than a perspective in terms of which

---

* A similar point can be made about the content of human rights, as the idea is generally understood, and will be discussed in Chapter 17, 'Human Rights and Global Imperatives'.

the advantages and disadvantages of a person can be reasonably assessed. That perspective is of significance on its own, and it is also critically important for theories of justice and of moral and political evaluation. But neither justice, nor political or moral evaluation, can be concerned only with the overall opportunities and advantages of individuals in a society.* The subject of fair process and a fair deal goes beyond individuals' overall advantages into other – especially procedural – concerns, and these concerns cannot be adequately addressed through concentrating only on capabilities.

The central issue here concerns the multiple dimensions in which equality matters, which is not reducible to equality in one space only, be that economic advantage, resources, utilities, achieved quality of life or capabilities. My scepticism about a unifocal understanding of the demands of equality (in this case, applied to the capability perspective) is part of a larger critique of a unifocal view of equality.

Second, even though I have argued for the importance of freedom in judging personal advantages, and thus in assessing equality, there can be *other* demands on distributional judgements, which may not be best seen as demands for equal overall freedom for different people, in any clear sense. Indeed, as the example about the dispute among the three children quarrelling over a flute, discussed in the Introduction, brings out, the argument of one of the children to have just recognition of the fact that he has made the flute on his own, could not be readily dismissed. The line of reasoning that gives an important status to efforts and the rewards that should be associated with labour, which also yields such normative ideas as exploitation, can suggest grounds for pausing before going single-mindedly for equality of capability.[7] The literature on the exploitation of sweated labour and the unjust rewards received by those who do the 'real work' has a strong connection with this perspective.

Third, capability does not speak in one voice, since it can be defined in different ways, which include the distinction between well-being freedom and agency freedom (discussed in Chapter 13, 'Happiness,

* Indeed, even in terms of the Rawlsian characterization of distinct problems of justice, capability is a rival only to the use of primary goods in judging relative advantages in the Difference Principle, and that leaves out other issues, including the place of personal liberties and the need for fair procedures.

Well-being and Capabilities'). Further, as has already been discussed, the ranking of capabilities, even with a specific focus (such as agency or well-being) need not generate a complete ordering, particularly because of the reasonable variations (or inescapable ambiguities) in the choice of relative weights to be attached to different types of capabilities, or different types of functionings. While a partial ordering may be adequate enough to judge inequalities in some cases, especially in identifying some situations of blatant inequality, it need not yield clear inequality judgements in other instances. All this does not indicate that it is useless to pay attention to reducing inequality of capabilities. That surely is a big concern, but it is important to see the limits of the reach of capability equality as one part of the demands of justice.

Fourth, equality is itself not the only value with which a theory of justice need be concerned, and it is not even the only subject for which the idea of capability is useful. If we make the simple distinction between aggregative and distributive considerations in social justice, the capability perspective with its pointer to an important way of assessing advantages and disadvantages has implications for *both* aggregative and distributive concerns. For example, an institution or a policy may well be defended not on the grounds that it enhances capability equality, but for the reason that it expands the capabilities of all (even if there is no distributional gain). Equality of capability, or more realistically reduction of capability inequality, certainly has claims on our attention, but so has the general advancement of the capabilities of all.

Through denying the case for single-minded concentration on capability equality, or for that matter on capability-based considerations in general, we do not denigrate the critically significant role of capabilities in the idea of justice (discussed earlier, particularly Chapters 11–13). The reasoned pursuit of a very important element in social justice, which does not crowd out everything else, can still have a crucial role in the enterprise of enhancing justice.

## CAPABILITY AND
## PERSONAL LIBERTIES

As discussed in Chapter 2, in departing from John Rawls's focus on primary goods in the Difference Principle in addressing distributional issues, and in bringing in the far-reaching role of capabilities in that exercise, there is no hidden intention of disputing Rawls's reasoning on other issues. Those issues include the priority of liberty, which forms the subject matter of the first principle in Rawls's theory of justice.

Indeed, as I have already argued (in Chapter 2, 'Rawls and Beyond'), there are good grounds for giving personal liberty some kind of a real priority (though not necessarily in the extremist lexicographic form chosen by Rawls). Giving a special place – a general pre-eminence – to liberty goes well beyond taking note of the importance of liberty as one of many influences on a person's overall advantage. Liberty is indeed useful, like income and other primary goods, but that is not all that is involved in the importance of liberty, since it touches our lives at a very basic level and it demands that others should respect these deeply personal concerns that everyone tends to have.

This distinction is crucial to bear in mind when we compare the competing claims of primary goods and capabilities for one limited purpose in the assessment of justice, to wit, how to evaluate general distributive concerns, based on comparisons of overall individual advantages. That is, of course, the subject matter of Rawls's difference principle, but it is just one part of a larger theory of Rawlsian justice. When it is claimed, as I have, that capabilities can do the job of judging the overall advantages of different people better than primary goods, then that is precisely what is being affirmed – and not anything more. There is no claim here that the capability perspective can take over the work that other parts of Rawlsian theory demand, particularly the special status of liberty and the demands of procedural fairness. Capabilities cannot do that work any more than primary goods can. The contest between primary goods and capabilities is in a limited arena, in a specified domain, concerned with the assessment of overall advantages that the individuals respectively have.

Since I am broadly in agreement with the Rawlsian reasoning underlying the first principle, that is, the importance of the priority of
personal liberty shared equally by all, it is perhaps useful to consider
whether this priority must be as absolute as Rawls makes it out to be.
Why must any violation of liberty, significant as it is, invariably be
judged to be more crucial for a person – or for a society – than suffering
from intense hunger, starvation, epidemics and other calamities? As
was discussed in Chapter 2 ('Rawls and Beyond'), we have to distinguish between giving some priority to liberty (not treating it merely
as one of the components in the large bag of 'primary goods', since
liberty is so central to our personal lives), *and* the 'extremist' demand
of placing a *lexicographic* priority on liberty, treating the slightest
gain of liberty – no matter how small – as enough reason to make
huge sacrifices in other amenities of a good life – no matter how large.

Rawls argues persuasively for the former, and yet chooses, in the
formulation of the difference principle, the latter. But as was discussed
in Chapter 2, the mathematics of differential weighting allows many
intermediate possibilities between no extra weight on liberty and
complete priority of liberty over all else. We can be 'Rawlsian' in the
former sense, as far as the 'priority of liberty' is concerned, without
signing up for the latter.

The exact extent of priority that may be given, in a particular
case, to personal liberty would certainly be a good subject for public
reasoning, but Rawls's main success here seems to me to lie in showing
why personal liberty has to be given a pre-eminent place in public
reasoning in general. His work has helped to generate the understanding that justice in the world in which we live demands a very special
concern with liberties that all can share.* The important point to note
here is that liberty has a place in a just social arrangement that goes
well beyond recognizing liberty to be a part of personal advantage, in
the way income or wealth is. Even as the role of substantive freedoms
in the form of capabilities is emphasized in the present work (departing

---

* Sharing is very important here, rather than liberty being demanded for some but not
for others. Mary Wollstonecraft's criticism of Edmund Burke's support for American
independence, without raising the question of the liberty of slaves, was discussed
earlier (in Chapter 5, 'Impartiality and Objectivity').

from Rawls), there is no necessity there to deny the special role of liberty.*

## THE PLURAL FEATURES OF FREEDOM

Given the importance of freedom in different forms in theories of justice, I must now go into a closer examination of the *contents* of liberty and freedom, which has been a veritable battleground in the literature. The terms 'freedom' and 'liberty' are used in many different ways, and something more must be said on their respective domains.

One distinction in particular, between the opportunity aspect and the process aspect, was explored in Chapter 11 ('Lives, Freedoms and Capabilities'). The plurality of aspects of freedom can be approached and identified in other ways as well, besides the already discussed distinction between the opportunity and process aspects. Freedom to achieve what one reasonably wants to achieve relates to a variety of factors, and they can have varying relevance to different concepts of freedom.

The question whether a person can bring about the objects of her reasoned choice is crucial to the idea of freedom that is being pursued here, of which the notion of capability is a part.† But the effectiveness of preference can occur in different ways. First, a person can bring about the chosen result through her own actions, yielding that particular outcome – this is the case of *direct control*. But direct control is not necessary for effectiveness. Second, there is the broader

---

* The priority of liberty plays an important part in the social choice result presented in my 'The Impossibility of a Paretian Liberal', *Journal of Political Economy*, 78 (1970). John Rawls comments illuminatingly on this connection in his essay, 'Social Unity and Primary Goods', in Amartya Sen and Bernard Williams (eds), *Utilitarianism and Beyond* (Cambridge: Cambridge University Press, 1982). I shall return to this issue later on in the chapter.
† In seeing freedom in terms of the power to bring about the outcome one wants with reasoned assessment, there is, of course, the underlying question whether the person has had an adequate opportunity to reason about what she really wants. Indeed, the opportunity of *reasoned assessment* cannot but be an important part of any substantive understanding of freedom. As was discussed in Chapter 8, 'Rationality and Other People', this is a central question in assessing the rationality of preference and choice.

consideration of whether a person's preferences can be effective – whether through direct control or through the help of others. Illustrations of the 'indirect power' to bring about the preferred results vary from such simple cases of acting through an attorney or loyal friends or relations, to more complex ones in which a doctor takes decisions for a person to bring about a result that the patient would actually choose, given enough knowledge and understanding: the issue of *effective power*. The importance of effective power through indirect control calls for some discussion here, particularly since it is so common to see freedom as being nothing other than control, and being given the choice to do certain things oneself.

Many of the freedoms that we exercise in society work through some process other than direct control.[8] For example, a wounded and unconscious victim of an accident may not take the decisions about what is to be done to him, but in so far as the doctor chooses a course which the doctor knows the patient would have preferred had he been conscious, there is no violation of the patient's freedom – indeed, there is an affirmation of that freedom in the sense of 'effective power', if the doctor's choice is guided by what the patient would have wanted.[9] This is a distinct issue from the welfare of the patient as she – the doctor – reads it, which could also guide the doctor. Even though respecting the freedom of the patient may often have the same requirements as the advancement of the well-being of the patient, the two need not coincide. For example, a doctor may respect the unconscious patient's well-known rejection of medicines derived from cruel experiments on animals, even though in the doctor's view the well-being of the patient would have been enhanced by the use of precisely that medicine. The guidance of well-being can differ – possibly quite sharply – from the demands of the effective freedom of the patient.

The idea of effective freedom can be extended to more complex cases of societal arrangements, for example where the civic authorities looking after regional epidemiology arrange to eliminate local epidemics (what the people, it is known, want). The idea of effectiveness would apply to the group and its members, and effective freedom here takes a social – or a collaborative – form, but it is still a case of effectiveness without any individual having any specific control over the societal decision. The distinction is between the local authorities undertaking some policy on the grounds that this is what the people want and would, given the option, choose, and the authorities undertaking that policy on the grounds that this would enhance, in the view of the administrators, the welfare of the people in the locality. The second is, of course, a worthy enough reason, but it is not quite the same reason as the first (even though the two arguments have causal connections since consideration of well-being may plausibly influence the choice – or would-be choice – of the people involved).

A different kind of distinction would be that between being able to get some result precisely because of having that preference, perhaps in conformity with the preferences of the others involved (for example, a person wanting the elimination of epidemics in unison with others in that region – a preference that, ultimately, may guide public policy), and a person being able to get what one wants due to good luck. It may just turn out, for one reason or another, that precisely what this person wants actually does occur. There is fulfilment here, but not necessarily any effectiveness of one's preferences since there may be no influence of one's priorities on what occurs (it may not at all be the person's wanting the result, individually or jointly, that brings the result about). There is not only no control here (direct or indirect), but not even any exercise of power, through whatever means, to produce a result in line with one's preferences. One succeeds with one set of preferences but does not necessarily do so with another.

For example, a person's religious practice may happen to be in conformity with what the state wants to enforce, and the person may thus see his religious preferences fulfilled, without those preferences having any particular role in the state decisions. It may look as if there is nothing substantial that can be called 'freedom' in the person's piece of good luck, and in terms of bringing about a particular result – whether through direct or indirect control – this scepticism about the presence of freedom is well justified, since the person here is just in a favourable situation, rather than being effective in getting whatever he wants.* And yet the person's freedom to live as he would like can

---

* Philip Pettit takes this view and sees freedom only in 'content-independent' terms (so that one's effectiveness must be independent of what exactly the person wants).

contrast sharply with the predicament of someone else who subscribes to some heterodox beliefs and may face obstacles to his practice (in another age, he could have been unlucky enough to face the Inquisition). There is a freedom of some importance in being able to follow one's preferred lifestyle, despite there being no real freedom of choice here (that is, irrespective of the content of one's preference). When, for example, Akbar pronounced and legalized his freedom-favouring decision that no one 'should be interfered with on account of religion, and anyone is to be allowed to go over to a religion that pleases him', he guaranteed the effective freedom of a great many people – indeed, a majority of his subjects who earlier faced discrimination on grounds of not being Muslim – and yet those subjects would have had no power to stop him had Akbar chosen differently.

This distinction relates to one to be discussed presently, involving the contrast between capability in general and capability without dependence, emphasized in a specific approach to freedom (to be discussed presently), called the 'republican' view, developed particularly by Philip Pettit. But I hope the preceding discussion has done something to establish the need to see freedom in plural terms, rather than seeing it as having only one feature.

## CAPABILITY, DEPENDENCE
## AND INTERFERENCE

Some people use the terms liberty and freedom quite interchangeably, and treat the two as if they were much the same. In Rawls's arguments for priority of liberty there is, however, a special concern with freedom in personal lives, and especially freedom from intrusive interference by others, including the state. Going beyond what people can – taking everything into account – actually do, Rawls also investigates the importance of people being at liberty to lead their own lives as they would like, and in particular the liberty not to be messed around by

---

See his *Republicanism: A Theory of Freedom and Government* (Oxford: Clarendon Press, 1997), and 'Capability and Freedom: A Defence of Sen', *Economics and Philosophy*, 17 (2001).

the interference of others. And that, of course, is the classic territory of John Stuart Mill's pioneering work, *On Liberty*.[10]

In some theories of freedom, for example what is called 'republican' or 'neo-Roman' theory, liberty is defined not just in terms of what a person is able to do in a certain sphere, but also includes the demand that others could not have eliminated that ability of this person even if they wanted to do so. In this view, a person's liberty may be compromised even in the absence of any interference, simply by the existence of the arbitrary power of another which *could* hinder the freedom of the person to act as they like, even if that intervening power is not actually exercised.[11]

Philip Pettit has argued against the view of freedom as capability on 'republican' grounds, since a person may have the capability to do many things that are dependent on the 'favour of others', arguing that to the extent the person's actual choices (or achievements) are dependent in this way, he is not really free. As Pettit explains: 'Imagine that you have a disposition to choose between A and B that is content-independently decisive but that your enjoyment of such decisive preference depends on the goodwill of those around you . . . You may be said to have decisive preferences but their decisiveness is favour-dependent.'* Certainly being free to do something independently of others (so that it does not matter what they want) gives one's substantive freedom a robustness that is absent when the freedom to do that thing is conditional either on the help – or on the tolerance – of others, or dependent on a coincidence ('it so happens') between what the person wants to do and what the other people who could have stopped it happen to want. To take an extreme case, it can certainly be argued

---

* Philip Pettit, 'Capability and Freedom: A Defence of Sen', *Economics and Philosophy*, 17 (2001), p. 6. I am commenting here not on the 'defence' part of Pettit's arguments, but on his critique of my focus on capability, suggesting that it should be extended in the direction of the 'republican' view, so that capabilities that are favour-dependent do not count as real freedoms. Pettit sees this as a natural extension of the idea of capability and its defence (as presented by me): 'Under my reading, Sen's theory of freedom coincides with the republican approach in this emphasis on the connection between freedom and non-dependency' (p. 18). I see the relevance of that connection, but have to argue that both concepts – the republican and the capability-based views of freedom – have value since they reflect distinct aspects of the inescapably plural idea of freedom.

that enslaved people remain slaves even if their choices never conflict with the will of their master.

There can be little doubt that the republican concept of freedom is important and captures one aspect of our intuitions about the claims of freedom. Where I would disagree is in the claim that the republican idea of freedom can *replace* the perspective of freedom as capability. There is room for both ideas, which need not be a source of tension at all, unless we insist on a single-focus idea of freedom, against which I have already argued.

Consider three alternative cases related to a disabled person A who cannot do certain things by herself, without help.*

*Case 1*: Person A is not helped by others, and she is thus unable to go out of her house.

*Case 2*: Person A is always helped by helpers arranged either by a social security system in operation in her locality (or, alternatively, by volunteers with goodwill), and she is, as a result, fully able to go out of her house whenever she wants and to move around freely.

*Case 3*: Person A has well-remunerated servants who obey – and have to obey – her command, and she is fully able to go out of her house whenever she wants and to move around freely.

In terms of 'capability', as defined in the capability approach, Cases 2 and 3 are largely similar as far as the disabled person is concerned (this refers to the freedom of the disabled person only, and not to that of the servants, which would raise other issues), and they both contrast in the same way with Case 1, in which she does lack the capability in question. There is clearly something of substance in this contrast between being able to do something and not being able to do it, since it does matter what a person is actually capable of doing.

The republican approach would, however, see the disabled person as being unfree in both Cases 1 and 2: in Case 1 because she cannot do what she wants to do (that is, come out of the house), and in

---

* This illustration is adapted from my 'Reply' to Pettit's essay, along with two other interesting and important contributions respectively from Elizabeth Anderson and Thomas Scanlon in *Economics and Philosophy*, 17 (2001).

Case 2 because her ability to do what she wants to do (in this case, to go out of the house) is 'context-dependent', depending as it does on the existence of a particular social security system, and it may even be 'favour-dependent' on the goodwill and generosity of others (to invoke distinctions invoked by Pettit). It can certainly be said that A is free in a way in Case 3 that she is not in Case 2. The republican approach captures this difference, and has a particular discriminating power that the capability approach lacks.

However, all this does not remove the importance of the distinction on which the capability approach focuses: *can the person actually do these things or not?* There is an extremely important contrast between Case 1, on the one hand, and Cases 2 and 3, on the other. In the former case, A lacks the capability to come out of her house and is unfree in this respect, whereas in Cases 2 and 3 she has the capability and freedom to go out of her house whenever she wants. It is this distinction that the capability approach tries to capture, and it is a momentous distinction to acknowledge in general and to be recognized in the making of public policy in particular. Placing Cases 1 and 2 in the same box of non-freedom, without further distinction, would steer us towards the view that instituting social security provisions, or having a supportive society, cannot make any difference to anyone's freedom, when dealing with disabilities or handicaps. For a theory of justice that would be a huge lacuna.

Indeed, there are many exercises in which it is particularly important to know whether a person is really able to do the things that she would choose to do and has reason to choose to do. For example, individual parents may not be able to set up their own school for their children, and may be dependent on public policy, which may be determined by a variety of influences, such as national or local politics. And yet the establishment of a school in that region can be sensibly seen as increasing the freedom of the children to be educated. To deny this would seem to miss out an important way of thinking about freedom that has both reason and practice behind it. This case contrasts sharply with a case in which there are no schools in the region and no freedom to receive school education. The distinction between the two cases is important enough and on this the capability approach concentrates, even though in neither case can the person bring about her own schooling independently of the support of the state or support from others. We live in a world in which being completely independent of the help and goodwill of others may be particularly difficult to achieve, and sometimes may not even be the most important thing to achieve.

The tension between capability and republicanism as approaches to freedom arises if and only if we have room for 'at most one idea'. It arises when looking for a single-focus understanding of freedom, despite the fact that freedom as an idea has irreducibly multiple elements.* The republican view of freedom, I would argue, *adds* to the capability-based perspective, rather than demolishing the relevance of that perspective as an approach to freedom.

The plurality does not, however, end there. There is also a distinction that concentrates on whether a person's failure of capability is due to the interference of others – an issue that was already raised. We concentrate here not on the power to intervene effectively whether or not that power is exercised – that would be a republican concern – but the actual use of such interference. The distinction between potential and actual interference is significant, and one that evidently did engage that pioneer of modern political thought – Thomas Hobbes. Even though Hobbes might have had some sympathy for the 'republican' or 'neo-Roman' point of view in his early thought (an approach that was quite current in the political thinking in Britain at that time), Quentin Skinner shows convincingly that Hobbes's understanding of freedom crystallized on a non-republican view, focusing on whether there is actual interference or not.† The focus on

---

* Philip Pettit is clearly tempted by the unifocal view – what he sees as a comprehensive understanding of freedom: 'the position defended here will help to bear out the case for thinking about freedom comprehensively, not just in a compartmentalized way' (*A Theory of Freedom*, 2001, p. 179). Pettit is talking here about a different kind of duality, involving such issues as free will, but his motivational remark would seem to apply also to the particular internal contrast – what he may see as 'compartmentaliz-ation' – under discussion, involving the republican and the capability-based approaches to freedom.

† See Quentin Skinner, *Hobbes and Republican Liberty* (Cambridge: Cambridge University Press, 2008). Even in his early work, *Elements of Law* (1640), Hobbes showed some hostility to the thesis that there would be some violation of liberty even in the absence of actual interference, but he did not develop an alternative theory in that

the interference of others as the central feature of the negation of liberty is, thus, a Hobbesian idea.

There is no embarrassment in accommodating several distinct features within the idea of freedom, focusing respectively on capability, lack of dependence and lack of interference.[12] Those who want one canonical understanding of the 'true' nature of freedom may underestimate the very different ways in which ideas of freedom and nonfreedom can enter our perception, assessment and evaluation. As William Cowper puts it, 'Freedom has a thousand charms to show/ That slaves, howe'er contented, never know.' When it comes to distinct concepts, a thousand may be difficult to manage, but there should be no great difficulty in being able to see several different aspects of freedom as being complementary rather than competitive. A theory of justice can pay attention to each. Indeed, the approach to justice presented in this work makes room for pervasive plurality as a constituent feature of the assessment of justice. The plurality of aspects of freedom fits right into that capacious framework.

## THE IMPOSSIBILITY OF THE PARETIAN LIBERAL

The capability to influence an outcome in the direction one wants can be, as has already been argued, an important part of freedom. The understanding of an outcome can, when relevant, take substantive note of the process through which a final state – a culmination outcome – comes about (the process-inclusive view of an outcome is called a 'comprehensive' outcome). In social choice theory, which is concerned with social states (as discussed in Chapter 4), the result-oriented view of freedom has particularly received attention. And

---

particular book. But his rejection of that republican perspective came through loud and clear by the time he wrote *Leviathan* (1651), which is armed with an alternative approach as well, in which actual interference is the central issue. Indeed, as Skinner argues, 'Hobbes is the most formidable enemy of the republican theory of liberty, and his attempts to discredit it constitute an epoch-making moment in the history of Anglophone political thought' (*Hobbes and Republican Liberty*, p. xiv).

many of the issues of liberty and freedom that have been discussed in social choice theory have been within this framework.

A result that has generated something of a literature of its own is a rather simple theorem called 'the impossibility of the Paretian liberal'. This takes the form of showing that if people can have any preferences they like, then the formal demands of Pareto optimality may conflict with some minimal demands of personal liberty.[13] I shall not try to show how this impossibility theorem works, but illustrate it instead with an example that has been much discussed. There is an allegedly pornographic book and two possible readers.* The person called Prude hates the book, will not like to read it, but would suffer even more from its being read by the other person – called Lewd – who loves the book (Prude is particularly bothered that Lewd may be chuckling over the book). Lewd, on the other hand, would love to read the book, but would prefer even more that Prude reads it (agonizingly, Lewd hopes).

So, 'what to do?' as we say in the subcontinent. There is here no liberty-supported case for no one reading the book, since Lewd clearly wants to read it, and it is none of Prude's business to interfere in that decision. Nor is there a liberty-based case for Prude reading the book, since he clearly does not want to read the book, and it is none of Lewd's business to weigh in in that choice in which he is not directly involved. The only remaining alternative is for Lewd to read the book, which would of course be exactly what would happen if each person were to decide what to read (or not read). However, in their preferences, as described, both Prude and Lewd prefer Prude's reading the book over Lewd's reading it, so that self-chosen alternative seems to go against the Pareto principle judged in terms of what the two individuals like, since both like Lewd's reading it less than Prude's reading it. But the other two alternatives violated minimal demands of liberty, so nothing can be chosen that satisfies the specified demands of social choice, since each available alternative is worse than some

---

* In the early, innocent days of the 1960s I fear I was naive enough to choose as an example D. H. Lawrence's *Lady Chatterley's Lover*. I was influenced by the fact that Penguin Books had just before that time fought and won a case in the British courts to be allowed to publish precisely this book.

other alternative. Hence the impossibility of simultaneously satisfying both the principles.

This impossibility result, like other impossibility theorems in social choice theory, is meant to be the *beginning* of a discussion about how the choice problem is to be tackled – not the *end* of any possible argument. And it certainly has served that purpose. Some have used the impossibility result to argue that, for liberty to be effective, people should respect other people's liberty to make their own choices rather than paying more attention to the choices of other people in their personal lives than they do to their own personal lives (as is the case with both Prude and Lewd here).[14] Others have used the mathematical result to argue that even the Pareto principle, allegedly sacred in traditional welfare economics, may have to be violated sometimes.[15] The case for this lies in the fact that the individual preferences here are narrowly other-regarding, and their status is compromised by the recognition that, as John Stuart Mill put it, 'there is no parity between the feeling of a person for his opinion, and the feeling of another who is offended at his holding it'.* Still others have argued for making the right to liberty to be conditional on the person respecting the liberty of others in his own personal preferences.[16]

There have been other proposed solutions as well. One that has been much discussed can be called 'solution by collusion'. This is the suggestion that the problem is resolved if the parties involved have a Pareto-improving contract, whereby Prude reads the book to prevent Lewd from reading it.† How much of a solution is this?[17]

There is, first, a very general methodological point. A Pareto-improving contract is always a possibility in any Pareto-*inefficient* situation. To say that does nothing to undermine the problem faced in a world in which individual choices take one to a Pareto-inefficient outcome. Note also a general problem with this way of seeking a

* Questioning the unconditional acceptance of the priority of the Pareto principle was, I must confess, my principal motivation in presenting this result. See also Jonathan Barnes, 'Freedom, Rationality and Paradox', *Canadian Journal of Philosophy*, 10 (1980); Peter Bernholz, 'A General Social Dilemma: Profitable Exchange and Intransitive Group Preferences', *Zeitschrift für Nationalökonomie*, 40 (1980).
† A great many commentators have sought this way 'out'. One of the most recent is G. A. Cohen, *Rescuing Justice and Equality* (2008), pp. 187–188.

'solution'. A Pareto-improving contract may not be viable, since the incentive for breaking it can be strong.[18] This may not be the principal argument against seeing a solution to the problem through collusion (the main argument against this alleged resolution may relate to the reasoning behind the two parties offering and accepting such a contract), but it is one argument to be considered before taking up the more serious issues. We have to consider the credibility of such a contract, and the difficulty of ensuring its compliance (i.e. how to make sure that Prude actually reads the book rather than just pretending to).

This is no mean problem but, perhaps more importantly, attempts at enforcing such contracts (for example, the policeman ensuring that Prude is actually engaged in reading the book and is not just turning the pages) in the name of liberty can powerfully – and chillingly – endanger liberty itself. Those who seek a liberal solution that would demand such intrusive policing in personal lives must have a rather odd idea of what a liberal society should be like.

Of course, such enforcement would not be necessary if people were to conform voluntarily to the agreement. If individual preference is taken to determine choice (no variations at all on any other grounds – those discussed in Chapter 8), then this possibility is not open, since Prude will not read the book, given that choice (that is, in the absence of intrusive policing). If, on the other hand, preferences are taken to represent people's *desires* (not necessarily their choices), which is perhaps more sensible in this case, then it is, of course, possible to argue that even though Prude and Lewd both desire to act in a way contrary to the contract, they need not actually act that way, since they have signed a contract and thus have reason to resist being slaves to their desires. But if that question is raised, and actions that go contrary to felt desires are permitted, then we have to ask a prior – and more basic – question for this 'solution by collusion': why should we assume that Prude and Lewd would *choose* to have such a contract in the first place (even though they may *desire* the corresponding outcome – seen simply as a 'culmination outcome')?

It is not at all obvious why Prude and Lewd must go for a peculiarly 'other-regarding' social contract by which Prude agrees to read the book he hates in order to make eager-to-read Lewd refrain from reading it, and Lewd in turn agrees to forgo reading a book he would love to read in order to make reluctant Prude read it instead. If people attach some importance to minding their own business rather than just following their desires, then that odd contract need not in fact materialize (cf. 'I think Ann would be much happier if she divorced Jack, and I wish she would do this – and so let me jump in and tell her to do this'). The good liberal practice of reading what one likes and letting others read what *they* like can perhaps survive the apparent temptations of having this remarkable contract. It is hard to see solution by collusion as a solution at all.

For some inexplicable reason, some authors seem to believe that the issue in question is whether rights are 'alienable' (in the sense of people being permitted to trade away particular rights) and whether the persons involved should be *allowed* to have such a contract.[19] I see no reason why rights of this kind should not in general be taken to be open to contracting and exchange through mutual agreement. Indeed, there can be little doubt that people do not, in general, need anyone else's (or 'the society's') permission to have such a contract. But they do need a reason, which is where the rub is. To offer as a reason, as some have done, the fact that such a contract would be the only way of getting – and sustaining – a Pareto-efficient outcome is to beg the question, since one of the motivations for discussing the impossibility result is precisely to question and assess the priority of Pareto efficiency.

The real issue concerns the adequacy of the reasons for having such a contract in the first place, and then for sticking to it. Of course, no-nonsense maximization of pleasure or desire-fulfilment (ignoring the principle of minding one's own business) could provide *some* reason for seeking or accepting such a contract. But this would also give both Prude and Lewd good reasons for reneging on the contract if signed (since their simple desire orderings indicate that), and in considering the contract, both Lewd and Prude would have to take note of this fact. More importantly, even for desire-based choice, we must distinguish between a desire that someone should act in a particular way (for example, Lewd's desire that Prude should read the book), and a desire for a *contract* enforcing that this person must act in that way (for example, Lewd's wanting Prude to sign a contract binding him to read the book which he would not otherwise read). If outcomes are seen in 'comprehensive' terms, the two objects of desire are not at all the same.\* Indeed, Lewd's general desire that Prude should read the book need not at all entail a desire to have a *contract that would enforce* Prude's reading the book. The introduction of a contract brings in issues that cannot be escaped by just referring to simple desires regarding individual actions without any contracts.

The impossibility of the Paretian liberal, like the much grander impossibility theorem of Arrow, is best seen as a contribution to public discussion, by bringing into focus questions that may not have been raised otherwise. That, as I have argued earlier (in Chapter 4 'Voice and Social Choice'), is one of the major uses of social choice theory in trying to clarify the issues involved and in attempting to encourage public discussion on those issues. Such engagement is central to the approach to justice presented in this work.

## SOCIAL CHOICE VERSUS GAME FORMS

Over thirty years ago, Robert Nozick raised a question of importance both about the impossibility of the Paretian liberal and about the formulation of liberty in social choice theory.

The trouble stems from treating an individual's rights to choose among alternatives as the right to determine the relative ordering of these alternatives within a social ordering . . . A more appropriate view of individual rights is as follows. Individual rights are co-possible; each person may exercise his rights as he chooses. The exercise of these rights fixes some features of the world. Within the constraints of these fixed features, a choice may be made by a social choice mechanism based upon a social ordering; if there are any choices left to make! Rights do not determine a social ordering but instead set the constraints within which a social choice is to be made, by excluding certain alternatives, fixing others, and so on . . . If any patterning is legitimate, it falls *within* the domain of social choice, and hence is constrained by people's rights. How else can we cope with Sen's result?[20]

---

\* The distinction between 'comprehensive' and 'culmination' perspectives, which has been discussed earlier in this book (in the Introduction, but particularly in Chapter 7), is relevant here.

Nozick thus characterizes rights to liberty in terms of giving the individual *control* over certain personal decisions, and 'each person may exercise his right as he chooses'. But there is no guarantee of any outcome – it is only a right to the choice of action.

This entirely process-oriented view of liberty is, in fact, an alternative way of thinking about rights. That line of reasoning generated many echoes and developments in the literature that followed. One source of complexity relates to the problem of interdependence: a person's right to do something may be seen as conditional on some other things happening or not happening. If my right to join others when they sing is to be distinguished from my right to sing no matter what else happens (for example, whether others are singing, praying, eating or lecturing), then the permissible strategies for me must be defined in relation to (in the context of) the strategy choices of others. Social choice formulations can deal with such interdependence easily enough since the rights are characterized with explicit reference to outcomes (linked to the combinations of strategies). To have similar sensitivity, the process-oriented understanding of liberty has tended to incorporate the game-theoretic idea of 'game forms' (abandoning Nozick's attempt at seeing liberty in terms of each person's rights, defined in isolation from each other).[21]

In the game-form formulation, each person has a set of permissible acts or strategies, from which each can choose one. The outcome depends on the choices of acts, or strategies, by everyone. The requirements of liberty are specified in terms of restrictions on permissible choices of acts or strategies (what we can do), but not in terms of acceptable outcomes (what we get). Is this structure robust enough for an adequate specification of liberty? It certainly catches one way in which our liberty to act is often understood. However, liberty and freedom are not concerned only with the respective actions, but also with what emanates from those choices taken together.*

The question of interdependence in characterizing liberty is particularly important for taking note of what may be called 'invasive actions'. Consider a non-smoker's right not to have smoke blown in

---

* The importance of 'social realizations' has already been discussed earlier, particularly in the contrast between *nyaya* and *niti* (Chapters 1–6 and 9).

her face. This is, of course, a right to an outcome, and no understanding of liberty can be adequate if it remains entirely detached from the outcomes that emerge. The game-form formulations have to be worked 'backwards' by moving from acceptable outcomes to the combinations of strategies that would yield one of those outcomes. So the game-form formulations have to get at this problem indirectly. Rather than rejecting a possibility in which the outcome is that smoke is blown in my face, the procedural requirement takes the form of restrictions on strategy choice. We can try out the effectiveness, respectively, of:

- prohibiting smoking if others object,
- banning smoking in the presence of others, or
- forbidding smoking in public places no matter whether others are present or not (so that others do not have to stay away).

We move increasingly to more and more exacting demands on smokers if the less restrictive constraints do not bring about the outcome needed for the realization of the liberty to avoid passive smoking (as has indeed happened in the legislative history of some countries). We do, of course, choose between different 'game forms' here, but the choice of game forms is guided by its effectiveness in bringing about the social realization that is aimed at for the sake of liberty.

There is no doubt that game forms can be characterized in a way that they can take note of interdependence and protect from the invasive actions of others. The characterization of permissible game forms has to be worked out – directly or indirectly – in the light of the outcomes emerging from the combination of different people's strategies. If the driving force behind the choice of game forms is the judgement that smoking is inadmissible if it leads to 'passive smoking' of unwilling victims, or their having to move away in order to avoid passive smoking, then the game-form choices are indeed parasitic on the focus of attention of social choice theory, namely the nature of the social realizations (or comprehensive outcomes) that emerge. We have to consider both the freedom of action and the nature of the consequences and outcomes to have an adequate understanding of liberty.

The upshot of this discussion is that both equality and liberty must be seen as having several dimensions within their spacious contents. We have reason to avoid the adoption of some narrow and unifocal view of equality or of liberty, ignoring all other concerns that these broad values demand. This plurality has to be a part of a theory of justice, which must be alive to several different considerations that each of these grand ideas – liberty and equality – invokes.

## PART IV

# Public Reasoning
# and Democracy

# 15

# Democracy as Public Reason

In Aldous Huxley's novel, *Point Counter Point*, the lead character, Sidney Quarles, goes frequently to London from his country home in Essex, ostensibly to work at the British Museum on democracy in ancient India. 'It's about local government in Maurya times,' he explains to his wife Rachel, referring to the Indian imperial dynasty that ruled the country in the fourth and the third centuries BC. Rachel does not, however, have much difficulty in figuring out that this is an elaborate ploy by Sidney to cheat on her, since his real reason for going to London, she surmises, is to spend time with a new mistress. Aldous Huxley tells us how Rachel Quarles assesses what is going on.

[Sidney's] visits to London had become frequent and prolonged. After the second visit Mrs. Quarles had wondered, sadly, whether Sidney had found another woman. And when, on his return from a third journey and, a few days later, on the eve of a fourth, he began to groan ostentatiously over the vast complexity of the history of democracy among the Ancient Indians, Rachel felt convinced that the woman had been found. She knew Sidney well enough to be certain that, if he had really been reading about the Ancient Indians, he would never have troubled to talk about them over the dinner-table – not at such length, in any case, nor so insistently. Sidney talked for the same reason as the hunted sepia squirts ink, to conceal his movements. Behind the ink-cloud of the Ancient Indians [Sidney] hoped to go jaunting up to town unobserved.[1]

It turns out in Huxley's novel that Rachel Quarles was right. Sidney was squirting ink for exactly the reason she suspected.

The confusion of 'ink-clouds' has an important bearing on the subject of this book. Are we misleading ourselves – perhaps not in quite the same way in which Sidney Quarles wanted to mislead Rachel – in assuming that the experience of democracy is not confined to the West and can be found elsewhere, for example, in ancient India? The belief that democracy has not flourished anywhere in the world other than in the West is widely held and often expressed. And it is also used to explain contemporary events; for example, the blame for the immense difficulties and problems faced in post-intervention Iraq is sometimes put not so much on the peculiar nature of the under-informed and badly reasoned military intervention of 2003, but attri-buted instead to some imagined difficulty that sees democracy and public reasoning as being unsuitable for the cultures and traditions of non-Western countries like Iraq.

The subject of democracy has become severely muddled because of the way the rhetoric surrounding it has been used in recent years. There is, increasingly, an oddly confused dichotomy between those who want to 'impose' democracy on countries in the non-Western world (in these countries' 'own interest', of course) and those who are opposed to such 'imposition' (because of the respect for the countries' 'own ways'). But the entire language of 'imposition', used by both sides, is extraordinarily inappropriate since it makes the implicit assumption that democracy belongs exclusively to the West, taking it to be a quintessentially 'Western' idea which has originated and flourished only in the West.

But that thesis and the pessimism it generates about the possibility of democratic practice in the world would be extremely hard to justify. As it happens, even 'the ink-cloud of the Ancient Indians', as Rachel called them, is not entirely imaginary, since there were, in fact, several experiments in local democracy in ancient India (more on those pres-ently). Indeed, in understanding the roots of democracy in the world, we have to take an interest in the history of people's participation and public reasoning in different parts of the world. We have to look beyond thinking of democracy only in terms of European and Ameri-can evolution. We would fail to understand the pervasive demands for participatory living, on which Aristotle spoke with far-reaching insight, if we take democracy to be a kind of a specialized cultural product of the West.

It cannot, of course, be doubted that the institutional structure of the contemporary practice of democracy is largely the product of European and American experience over the last few centuries.* This is extremely important to recognize since these developments in institutional formats were immensely innovative and ultimately effective. There can be little doubt that there is a major 'Western' achievement here.

And yet, as Alexis de Tocqueville, the great historian of American democracy, noted in the early nineteenth century, while the 'great democratic revolution' occurring then in Europe and America was 'a new thing', it was also an expression of 'the most continuous, ancient, and permanent tendency known to history'.† Even though Tocqueville's own elucidation of this radical claim did not go beyond Europe, or further back than the twelfth century, the general point he was making has a much wider relevance. In assessing the pros and cons of democracy, we have to give an adequate recognition to the attraction of participatory governance that has surfaced and resurfaced with some consistency in different parts of the world. It has not been, to be sure, an irresistible force, but it has persistently challenged the unscrutinized belief that authoritarianism is an immovable object in most parts of the world. Democracy in its elaborate institutional form may be quite new in the world – its practice is hardly more than a couple of centuries old – and yet, as Tocqueville remarked, it gives expression to a tendency in social living that has a much longer and more widespread history. The critics of democracy – no matter how vigorous they may be in their rejection – must find some way of addressing the deep attraction of participatory governance, which is of continuing relevance today, and is hard to eradicate.

* As John Dunn points out in his illuminating book on the institutional history of democracy (*Democracy: A History* (New York: Atlantic Monthly Press, 2005), p. 180):

You can track the progress of representative democracy as a form of government from the 1780s until today, sticking pins into the map to record its advance, and noting not merely the growing homogenization of its institutional formats as the decades go by, but also the cumulative discrediting of the rich variety of other state forms which have competed against it throughout, often with very considerable initial assurance. The state form which advances across this time span was pioneered by Europeans; and it has spread in a world in which first Europe and then the United States wielded quite disproportionate military and economic power.

† Alexis de Tocqueville, *Democracy in America*, translated into English by George Lawrence (Chicago, IL: Encyclopaedia Britannica, 1990), p. 1.

## THE CONTENT OF DEMOCRACY

From earlier chapters of this book, it should be clear how central the role of public reasoning is for the understanding of justice. This recognition takes us to a connection between the idea of justice and the practice of democracy, since in contemporary political philosophy the view that democracy is best seen as 'government by discussion' has gained widespread support. That phrase, as was mentioned in the Introduction, was probably first coined by Walter Bagehot, but it is John Stuart Mill's work that has played a big part in making that perspective better understood and well defended.*

There is, of course, the older – and more formal – view of democracy which characterizes it mainly in terms of elections and ballots, rather than in the broader perspective of government by discussion. And yet, in contemporary political philosophy, the understanding of democracy has broadened vastly, so that democracy is no longer seen just in terms of the demands for *public balloting*, but much more capaciously, in terms of what John Rawls calls 'the exercise of public reason'. Indeed, a large shift in the understanding of democracy has been brought about by the works of Rawls[2] and Habermas,[3] and by a large recent literature on this subject, including the contributions of Bruce Ackerman,[4] Seyla Benhabib,[5] Joshua Cohen,[6] Ronald Dworkin,[7] among others. A similar interpretation of democracy has also come from the writings of the pioneering 'public choice' theorist, James Buchanan.[8]

In his *Theory of Justice*, Rawls puts this focus upfront: 'The definitive idea for deliberative democracy is the idea of deliberation itself. When citizens deliberate, they exchange views and debate their supporting reasons concerning public political questions.'[9]

Habermas's treatment of public reasoning is, in many ways, broader

---

* Clement Attlee invoked that particular description of democracy in what I can only describe as an 'unjustly famous' speech in Oxford in June 1957 when he could not resist the temptation to make a little joke – enjoyable enough, I suppose, when you hear it for the first time – on a really grand subject: 'Democracy means government by discussion, but it is only effective if you can stop people talking' (reported in *The Times*, 15 June 1957).

than Rawls's, as Rawls himself has noted.[10] Democracy is also given a more directly procedural form in Habermas's exposition than in other approaches to democracy, including Rawls's, even though (as argued in Chapter 5) the apparently sharp contrast between Rawlsian and Habermasian uses of procedural features in characterizing the process and outcome of public reasoning may be a little deceptive. However, Habermas has made a truly definitive contribution in clarifying the broad reach of public reasoning and in particular the dual presence in political discourse of both 'moral questions of justice' and 'instrumental questions of power and coercion'.*

In the debates on the characterization of the nature and outcome of public reasoning there has been some misunderstanding of each other's views. For example, Jürgen Habermas remarks that John Rawls's theory 'generates a priority of liberal rights which demotes the democratic process to an inferior status', and includes in his list of rights that liberals want 'liberty of belief and conscience, the protection of life, personal liberty, and property'.† The inclusion of property rights here does not, however, match John Rawls's stated position on this, since a general right to property is not an entitlement that Rawls has, in fact, defended in any of his works of which I am aware.‡

---

* Habermas has also commented illuminatingly on the differences between three conceptually disparate general approaches to the idea and role of public reasoning. He contrasts his 'procedural-deliberative view' with what he describes as the 'liberal' and 'republican' views (see his 'Three Normative Models of Democracy', in Seyla Benhabib (ed.), *Democracy and Difference: Contesting the Boundaries of the Political* (Princeton, NJ: Princeton University Press, 1996)). See also Seyla Benhabib, 'Introduction: The Democratic Moment and the Problem of Difference', in *Democracy and Difference* (1996), and Amy Gutmann and Dennis Thompson, *Why Deliberative Democracy?* (Princeton, NJ: Princeton University Press, 2004).

† Jürgen Habermas, 'Reconciliation through the Public Use of Reason: Remarks on John Rawls's Political Liberalism', *Journal of Philosophy*, 92 (1995), pp. 127–8.

‡ Perhaps Habermas is influenced in his diagnosis by the fact that Rawls makes room for catering to the need for incentives, which could give property rights an important instrumental role. Rawls does allow inequalities in his perfectly just arrangements for reasons of incentives when they enhance the deal the worst-off receive. I have discussed this issue in Chapter 2 ('Rawls and Beyond') in addressing G. A. Cohen's critique (in his book, *Rescuing Justice and Equality*, 2008) of this feature of Rawlsian principles of justice. Whether the acceptance of inequalities on grounds of incentives should have any role in what is claimed to be a perfectly just society is certainly debatable, but it

There are, clearly, many differences in the distinct ways in which the role of public reasoning in politics and discursive ethics can be viewed.* However, the main thesis that I am trying to explore here is not threatened by the existence of these differences. What is more important to note is that the totality of these new contributions has helped to bring about the general recognition that the central issues in a broader understanding of democracy are political participation, dialogue and public interaction. The crucial role of public reasoning in the practice of democracy makes the entire subject of democracy relate closely with the topic that is central to this work, namely justice. If the demands of justice can be assessed only with the help of public reasoning, and if public reasoning is constitutively related to the idea of democracy, then there is an intimate connection between justice and democracy, with shared discursive features.

However, the idea of seeing democracy as 'government by discussion', which is so widely accepted in political philosophy today (though not always by political institutionalists), is sometimes in tension with contemporary discussions on democracy and its role in older – and more rigidly organizational – terms. The *niti*-oriented institutional understanding of democracy, seen in terms just of ballots and elections, is not only traditional but it has been championed by many contemporary political commentators, including Samuel Huntington: 'Elections, open, free and fair, are the essence of democracy, the inescapable sine qua non.'[11] Despite the general transformation in the conceptual understanding of democracy in political philosophy, the history of democracy is often recounted, even now, in rather narrowly organizational terms, focusing particularly on the procedure of balloting and elections.

Ballots do, of course, have a very important role even for the

---

is important to see that Rawls does not support unconditional property rights as a part of a libertarian entitlement, as, for example, Robert Nozick does (*Anarchy, State and Utopia*, 1974).

* See Joshua Cohen, 'Deliberative Democracy and Democratic Legitimacy', in Alan Hamlin and Philip Pettit (eds), *The Good Polity* (Oxford: Blackwell, 1989); Jon Elster (ed.), *Deliberative Democracy* (Cambridge: Cambridge University Press, 1998); Amy Gutmann and Dennis Thompson, *Why Deliberative Democracy?* (Princeton, NJ: Princeton University Press, 2004); James Bohman and William Rehg, *Deliberative Democracy* (Cambridge, MA: MIT Press, 1997).

expression and effectiveness of the process of public reasoning, but they are not the only thing that matters, and they can be seen just as one part – admittedly a very important part – of the way public reason operates in a democratic society. Indeed, the effectiveness of ballots themselves depends crucially on what goes with balloting, such as free speech, access to information and freedom of dissent.* Balloting alone can be thoroughly inadequate on its own, as is abundantly illustrated by the astounding electoral victories of ruling tyrannies in authoritarian regimes in the past as well as those in the present, for example in today's North Korea. The difficulty lies not just in the political and punitive pressure that is brought to bear on voters in the balloting itself, but in the way expressions of public views are thwarted by censorship, informational exclusion and a climate of fear, along with the suppression of political opposition and the independence of the media, and the absence of basic civil rights and political liberties. All this makes it largely redundant for the ruling powers to use much force to ensure conformism in the act of voting itself. Indeed, a great many dictators in the world have achieved gigantic electoral victories even without any overt coercion in the process of voting, mainly through suppressing public discussion and freedom of information, and through generating a climate of apprehension and anxiety.

## THE LIMITED TRADITION OF DEMOCRACY?

Even if it is accepted that, properly understood, democracy is closely linked with the analysis of justice as is being explored in this work, is there not a serious difficulty in thinking of the pervasive and omnipresent idea of justice, which inspires discussion and agitation right across the world, in terms of what is often seen as a quintessentially 'Western' idea in the form of democracy. Are we not, it can be asked, trying in this exercise to focus on a purely Western feature of political

---

* On the importance of freedom of speech and the arguments related to it in the United States, see Anthony Lewis, *Freedom for the Thought That We Hate: A Biography of the First Amendment* (New York: Basic Books, 2007).

organization as a general approach to fairness and justice in the world? If public reasoning is so critically important for the practice of justice, can we even think about justice in the world at large when the art of public reasoning as a part of democracy seems to be, according to common belief, so quintessentially Western and locationally confined? The belief that democracy is basically a Western notion with European – and American – origins is a widespread one, and it does have some apparent plausibility, despite its being ultimately a wrong and superficial diagnosis.

John Rawls and Thomas Nagel may have been discouraged about the possibility of global justice because of the absence of a global sovereign state (as discussed in the Introduction), but is there not another difficulty in trying to see the enhancement of global justice through public discussion *of, for and by* the people of the world? It has been already argued in this work (particularly in Chapters 5 'Impartiality and Objectivity', and 6 'Closed and Open Impartiality') that the demands for open impartiality make the global perspective a necessity for a full consideration of justice anywhere in the contemporary world. If that is correct, would that necessity not, in fact, be impossible to meet if it were to turn out that people of the world fall into rigidly separated groups, many of whom could not be drawn into public reasoning in any way whatsoever? This is a huge question, which despite its extensive empirical correlates, can hardly be avoided in this work on the theory of justice. It is, therefore, important to examine whether the tradition of democracy, either in its largely organizational interpretation in terms of ballots and election, or more generally as 'government by discussion', is quintessentially 'Western' or not.

When democracy is seen in the broader perspective of public reasoning, going well beyond the specific institutional features that have emerged particularly strongly in Europe and America over the last few centuries, we have to reassess the intellectual history of participatory governance in different countries in many parts of the world – not just those in Europe and North America.[12] Cultural separatists, who criticize the claim of democracy to be a universal value, often point to the unique role of ancient Greece, particularly that of ancient Athens, where balloting emerged in a particular form in the sixth century BC.

# THE GLOBAL ORIGINS
# OF DEMOCRACY

Ancient Greece was indeed quite unique.* Its contribution to both the form and the understanding of the content of democracy cannot be overemphasized. But to see that experience as clear evidence that democracy is a quintessentially 'European' or 'Western' idea deserves much more critical scrutiny than it tends to get. It is, for one thing, particularly important to understand that even the success of Athenian democracy turned on the climate of open public discussion, rather than just balloting, and while balloting certainly began in Greece, the tradition of public discussion (very strong in Athens and ancient Greece) has had a much more widespread history.

Even as far balloting is concerned, the tendency to seek backing for a culturally segregationist view of the origins of elections in Europe calls for some further examination. First, there is an elementary difficulty in trying to define civilizations not in terms of the exact history of ideas and actions but in terms of broad regionality, for instance, being 'European' or 'Western', with a grossly aggregative attribution. In this way of looking at civilizational categories, no great difficulty is seen in considering the descendants of, say, Vikings and Visigoths as proper inheritors of the electoral tradition of ancient Greece (since they are part of 'the European stock'), even though ancient Greeks, who were very involved in intellectual interchange with other ancient civilizations to the east or south of Greece (in particular Iran, India

---

* Ancient Greece also had a remarkable combination of circumstances that made the emergence of democratic procedures possible and viable. As John Dunn's penetrating history of democracy brings out, democratic governance 'began as an improvised remedy for a very local Greek difficulty two and half thousands years ago, flourished briefly but scintillatingly, and then faded away almost everywhere for all but two thousand years' (*Democracy: A History* (2005), pp. 13–14). While I am arguing that democracy, broadly understood in terms of public reasoning, did not have such an ephemeral history of rise and fall, Dunn's remark would certainly apply to the formal institutions of democracy that emerged in ancient Greece and were temporarily instituted in a number of countries like Iran, India and Bactria (influenced by the Greek experience – to be discussed presently), but would not re-emerge until much nearer our times.

and Egypt), seem to have taken little interest in chatting up the lively Goths and Visigoths.

The second problem relates to what actually followed the early Greek experience of balloting. While Athens certainly was the pioneer in getting balloting started, many Asian regions used balloting in the centuries that followed, largely under Greek influence. There is no evidence that the Greek experience in electoral governance had much immediate impact in the countries to the west of Greece and Rome, in, say, what is now France or Germany or Britain. In contrast, some of the cities in Asia – in Iran, Bactria and India – incorporated elements of democracy in municipal governance in the centuries following the flowering of Athenian democracy; for example, for several centuries the city of Shushan, or Susa, in South-West Iran, had an elected council, a popular assembly and magistrates who were elected by the assembly.*

The practice of municipal democracy in ancient India is also well recorded. It was to this literature that Sidney Quarles was referring, in his conversations with Rachel, as the subject of his imagined studies in London, though he even quoted the names of the relevant authors on the subject accurately enough.[13] B. R. Ambedkar, who chaired the drafting committee that wrote up the new Indian constitution for adoption by the Constituent Assembly shortly after Indian independence in 1947, wrote fairly extensively on the relevance, if any, of India's ancient experiences in local democracy for the design of a large democracy for the whole of modern India.†

The practice of elections, in fact, has had a considerable history in non-Western societies, but it is the broader view of democracy in terms of public reasoning that makes it abundantly clear that the

---

* See also the various Indian examples of local democratic governance in Radhakumud Mookerji, *Local Government in Ancient India* (1919) (Delhi: Motilal Banarsidas, 1958).

† In fact, after his studies of ancient Indian history in local democracy, Ambedkar saw, eventually, little merit in drawing on that old – and strictly local – experience for devising a constitution for modern Indian democracy. He went on to argue that 'localism' generated 'narrow-mindedness and communalism', and remarked that 'these village republics have been the ruination of India' (see *The Essential Writings of B. R. Ambedkar*, edited by Valerian Rodrigues (Delhi: Oxford University Press, 2002), particularly essay 32: 'Basic Features of the Indian Constitution').

cultural critique of democracy as a purely regional phenomenon fails altogether.[14] While Athens certainly has an excellent record in public discussion, open deliberation also flourished in several other ancient civilizations, sometimes spectacularly so; for example, some of the earliest open general meetings aimed specifically at settling disputes between different points of view, on social and religious matters, took place in India in the so-called Buddhist 'councils', where adherents of different points of view got together to argue out their differences, beginning in the sixth century BC. The first of these councils met in Rajagriha (modern Rajgir) shortly after Gautama Buddha's death, and the second was held, about a hundred years later, in Vaisali. The last one happened in the second century AD in Kashmir.

Emperor Ashoka, who hosted the third and the largest Buddhist Council in the third century BC in Patna (then called Pataliputra), the capital city of the Indian empire, also tried to codify and propagate what were among the earliest formulations of rules for public discussion (some kind of an early version of the nineteenth-century 'Robert's rules of order').* To choose another historical example, in early seventh-century Japan the Buddhist Prince Shotoku, who was Regent to his mother, Empress Suiko, produced the so-called 'constitution of seventeen articles', in 604 AD. The constitution insisted, much in the spirit of the *Magna Carta*, signed six centuries later in 1215 AD: 'Decisions on important matters should not be made by one person alone. They should be discussed with many.'[15] Some commentators have seen in this seventh-century Buddhism-inspired constitution, Japan's 'first step of gradual development toward democracy'.[16] The Constitution of Seventeen Articles went on to explain: 'Nor let us be resentful when others differ from us. For all men have hearts, and each heart has its own leanings. Their right is our wrong, and our right is their wrong.' Indeed, the importance of public discussion is a recurrent theme in the history of many countries in the non-Western world.

The relevance of this global history does not, however, lie in any implicit presumption that we cannot break from history, cannot initiate a departure. Indeed, departures from the past are always

---

* See Chapter 3, 'Institutions and Persons', and also *The Argumentative Indian* (2005).

needed in different ways across the world. We do not have to be born in a country with a long democratic history to choose that path today. The significance of history in this respect lies rather in the more general understanding that established traditions continue to exert some influence on people's ideas, that they can inspire or deter, and they have to be taken into account whether we are moved by them, or wish to resist and transcend them, or (as the Indian poet Rabindranath Tagore discussed with compelling clarity) want to examine and scrutinize what we should take from the past and what we must reject, in the light of our contemporary concerns and priorities.[17]

It is not, therefore, surprising – though it does deserve clearer recognition today – that in the fight for democracy led by visionary and fearless political leaders across the world (such as Sun Yat-sen, Jawaharlal Nehru, Nelson Mandela, Martin Luther King, or Aung San Suu Kyi), an awareness of local as well as world history has played an importantly constructive part. In his autobiography, *Long Walk to Freedom*, Nelson Mandela describes how impressed and influenced he was, as a young boy, by seeing the democratic nature of the proceedings of the local meetings that were held in the regent's house in Mqhekezweni:

Everyone who wanted to speak did so. It was democracy in its purest form. There may have been a hierarchy of importance among the speakers, but everyone was heard, chief and subject, warrior and medicine man, shopkeeper and farmer, landowner and laborer . . . The foundation of self-government was that all men were free to voice their opinions and equal in their value as citizens.[18]

Mandela's understanding of democracy was hardly aided by the political practice that he saw around him in the apartheid state run by people of European origin, who, it is perhaps worth recollecting in this context, used to call themselves by the cultural term 'European' rather than just 'white'. In fact, Pretoria had little to contribute to Mandela's comprehension of democracy. His discernment of democracy came, as we see from his autobiography, from his general ideas about political and social equality, which had global roots, and from his observations of the practice of participatory public discussion that he found in his local town.

## IS THE MIDDLE EAST AN EXCEPTION?

In re-examining the historical background of democratic features in the past, we also have to reassess the history of the Middle East, since there is an often-articulated belief that this block of countries has always been hostile to democracy. That constantly repeated conviction is exasperating for fighters for democracy in the Arab world, but as a piece of historical generalization it is basically nonsense. It is of course true that democracy as an institutional system has not been prominent in the past of the Middle East, but institutional democracy is in fact a very new phenomenon in most parts of the world.

If we look instead for public reasoning and tolerance of different points of view, in line with the broader understanding of democracy that I have been discussing, then the Middle East does have quite a distinguished past. We must not confuse the narrow history of Islamic militancy with the capacious history of the Muslim people and the tradition of political governance by Muslim rulers. When the Jewish philosopher Maimonides was forced to emigrate from Spain in the twelfth century (when more tolerant Muslim regimes had given way to a far less tolerant Islamic regime), he sought shelter not in Europe but in a tolerant Muslim kingdom in the Arab world, and was given an honoured and influential position at the court of Emperor Saladin in Cairo. Saladin was certainly a strong Muslim; indeed, he fought hard for Islam in the Crusades and Richard the Lionheart was one of his distinguished opponents. But it was in Saladin's kingdom where Maimonides found his new base and a renewed voice. Tolerance of dissent is, of course, central to the opportunity to exercise public reasoning, and the tolerant Muslim regimes in their heyday offered a freedom that Inquisition-ridden Europe sometimes withheld.

Maimonides' experience was not, however, exceptional. Indeed, even though the contemporary world is full of examples of conflicts between Muslims and Jews, Muslim rule in the Arab world and in medieval Spain had a long history of integrating Jews as secure members of the social community whose liberties – and sometimes

leadership roles – were respected.* For instance, as Maria Rosa Menocal has noted in her book, *The Ornament of the World*, by the tenth
century the achievement of Cordoba in Muslim-ruled Spain as being
'as serious a contender as Baghdad, perhaps more so, for the title of
most civilized place on earth' was due to the joint influence of Caliph
Abd al-Rahman III and his Jewish vizier, Hasdai ibn Shaprut.[19]

Middle Eastern history and the history of Muslim people also
include a great many accounts of public discussion and political participation through dialogues. In Muslim kingdoms centred around
Cairo, Baghdad and Istanbul, or in Iran, India or for that matter
Spain, there were many champions of public discussion. The extent
of toleration of diversity of views was often exceptional in comparison
with Europe. For example, when in the 1590s the great Mughal
emperor Akbar was making his pronouncements in India on the need
for religious and political toleration, and when he was busy arranging
organized dialogues between holders of different faiths (including
Hindus, Muslims, Christians, Parsees, Jains, Jews and even atheists),
the Inquisitions were still very active in Europe. Giordano Bruno was
burnt at the stake in Rome for heresy in 1600, even when Akbar was
lecturing in Agra on toleration and the need for dialogue across the
borders of religions and ethnicities.

The present-day problems of the Middle East and what is called,
somewhat oversimply, 'the Muslim world', may well be immense, but
a probing assessment of the causation of these problems requires, as
I have argued in my book *Identity and Violence* (2006), a fuller
understanding of the nature and dynamics of identity politics. This
calls for the recognition of the multiple affiliations that people have
other than that of their religion, and the fact that these loyalties can
vary from secular priorities to political interest in exploiting religious
differences. We have to take note also of the dialectical encounters of
the Middle East with its own imperial past and the subjugation that
followed from the dominance of an imperial West – a dominance that

---

* It is important in this context to see how the influence of Islamic intellectual heritage
affected the development of European culture and the emergence of many features
that we now standardly associate with Western civilization. On this, see David Levering
Lewis, *God's Crucible: Islam and the Making of Europe, 570–1215* (New York:
W. W. Norton & Co., 2008).

still has many remaining influences. The illusion of an inescapably non-democratic destiny of the Middle East is both confused and very seriously misleading – perniciously so – as a way of thinking about either world politics or global justice today.

## THE ROLE OF THE PRESS AND THE MEDIA

The thesis that democracy is a Western intellectual inheritance derived from a long and unique past (unmatched anywhere else in the world) does not, therefore, work. It would not survive very well even if we took the rather limited public balloting view of democracy, and it does particularly badly when the history of democracy is seen in terms of public reasoning.

One of the central issues to consider for the advancement of public reasoning in the world is support for a free and independent press, which is often conspicuous by its absence – a situation that can certainly be reversed. And here the traditions established in Europe and America over the last three hundred years have indeed made a gigantic difference. The lessons derived from these traditions have been transformational for the world as a whole, from India to Brazil, and from Japan to South Africa, and the need for a free and vigorous media is being rapidly learned across the globe. What I think is particularly heartening is the speed with which the coverage – and indeed sometimes the culture – of the media can change.*

An unrestrained and healthy media is important for several different reasons, and it is useful to separate out the distinct contributions it can make. The first – and perhaps the most elementary – connection concerns the *direct contribution* of free speech in general and of press freedom in particular to the quality of our lives. We have reason enough to want to communicate with each other and to understand

* On a personal note, I have to say that on my first visit to Thailand in 1964, I could have hardly guessed how the miserable newspaper situation in that country could so rapidly become enriched into what is now one of the most vigorous media traditions in the world, making a huge contribution to the reach of public discussion in that country.

better the world in which we live. Media freedom is critically important for our capability to do this. The absence of a free media and the suppression of people's ability to communicate with each other have the effect of directly reducing the quality of human life, even if the authoritarian country that imposes such suppression happens to be very rich in terms of gross national product.

Second, the press has a major *informational role* in disseminating knowledge and allowing critical scrutiny. The informational function of the press relates not only to specialized reporting (for example on scientific advances or on cultural innovations), but also to keeping people generally informed about what is going on where. Furthermore, investigative journalism can unearth information that would have otherwise gone unnoticed or even unknown.

Third, media freedom has an important *protective function* in giving oice to the neglected and the disadvantaged, which can greatly contribute to human security. The rulers of a country are often insulated, in their own lives, from the misery of common people. They can live through a national calamity, such as a famine or some other disaster, without sharing the fate of its victims. If, however, they have to face public criticism in the media and confront elections with an uncensored press, the rulers have to pay a price too, and this gives them a strong incentive to take timely action to avert such crises. I shall further pursue this question in the next chapter, 'The Practice of Democracy'.

Fourth, informed and unregimented *formation of values* requires openness of communication and argument. The freedom of the press is crucial to this process. Indeed, reasoned value formation is an interactive process, and the press has a major role in making these interactions possible. New standards and priorities (such as the norm of smaller families with less frequent child bearing, or greater recognition of the need for gender equity) emerge through public discourse, and it is public discussion, again, that spreads the new norms across different regions.*

---

* The role of communication and deliberation in social choice was discussed in Chapter 4, 'Voice and Social Choice'. See also Kaushik Basu, *The Retreat of Democracy And Other Itinerant Essays on Globalization, Economics, and India* (Delhi: Permanent Black, 2007).

The relationship between majority rule and the protection of minority rights, both of which are integral parts of democratic practice, is particularly dependent on the formation of tolerant values and priorities. One of the lessons drawn from the social choice result of 'the impossibility of the Paretian liberal', as discussed in Chapter 14 ('Equality and Liberty'), is the crucial relevance of mutually tolerant preferences and choice in making liberty and liberal rights consistent with the priority of majority rule and of being guided by unanimity over particular choices. If a majority is ready to support the rights of minorities, and even of dissenting or discordant individuals, then liberty can be guaranteed without having to restrain majority rule.

Finally, a well-functioning media can play a critically important role in facilitating public reasoning in general, the importance of which for the pursuit of justice has been a recurrent theme in this work. The evaluation needed for the assessment of justice is not just a solitary exercise but one that is inescapably discursive. It is not hard to see why a free, energetic and efficient media can facilitate the needed discursive process significantly. The media is important not only for democracy but for the pursuit of justice in general. 'Discussionless justice' can be an incarcerating idea.

The many-sided relevance of the media connection also brings out the way institutional modifications can change the practice of public reason. The immediacy and strength of public reasoning depends not only on historically inherited traditions and beliefs, but also on the opportunities for discussion and interactions that the institutions and practice provide. The allegedly 'age-old and unshiftable' cultural parameters that are far too often invoked to 'explain', and even justify, the deficiencies in public discussion in a particular country, very often do a much worse job in providing a robust explanation than can be obtained from a fuller understanding of the working of modern authoritarianism – through censorship, regulation of the press, suppression of dissent, banning of opposition parties and the incarceration (or worse) of dissidents. The removal of those barriers is not the least of the contributions that the idea of democracy can make. It is a contribution that is important in itself, but further, if the approach developed in this book is right, it is centrally important for the pursuit of justice as well.

# 16

# The Practice of Democracy

'The Secretary of State for India seems to be a strangely misinformed man,' wrote *The Statesman*, the Calcutta newspaper, in a powerfully worded editorial, published on 16 October 1943.* It went on to say:

Unless the cables are unfair to him, he told Parliament on Thursday that he understood that the weekly death-roll (presumably from starvation) in Bengal including Calcutta was about the 1,000, but that it might be higher. All the publicly available data indicate that it is very much higher; and his great office ought to afford him ample means of discovery.†

Two days later the Governor of Bengal (Sir T. Rutherford) wrote to the Secretary of State for India:

Your statement in the House about the number of deaths, which was presumably based on my communication to the Viceroy, has been severely criticised in some of the papers . . . The full effects of the shortage are now being felt, and I would put the death-roll now at no less than 2,000 a week.

So what was it: 1,000 or 2,000, or something quite different?

---

* In contrast with the rest of this book, this chapter is primarily empirical. An understanding of some of the central issues in political philosophy turn, as I have already discussed, on a plausible reading of the causal connections that influence social realization: the unfolding of *nyaya* from the institutional *niti*s. How democracies have tended to behave, and how the absence of democracy can be assessed, are part of the subject matter of this chapter. We can obtain some insights in examining these *actual* experiences, despite the well-known limitations involved in trying to get general empirical insights from studies of particular experiences and specific cases.

† 'The Death-Roll', editorial, *The Statesman*, 16 October 1943. On this subject, see my *Poverty and Famines: An Essay on Entitlement and Deprivation* (Oxford: Clarendon Press, 1981), which also provides the full references for the citations used here.

The Famine Inquiry Commission that reported on the famine in December 1945 concluded that in the period July–December 1943, 1,304,323 deaths were recorded as against an average of 626,048 in the same period in the previous quinquennium, and it concluded that the number of further deaths due to the famine was over 678,000. That amounts to a weekly death toll not very close to 1,000 or 2,000, but rather larger than 26,000 every week.\*

The Bengal famine of 1943, which I witnessed as a child, was made viable not only by the lack of democracy in colonial India, but also by severe restrictions on reporting and criticism imposed on the Indian press, and the voluntary practice of 'silence' on the famine that the British-owned media chose to follow (as a part of the alleged 'war effort', for fear of aiding the Japanese military forces that were at the door of India, in Burma). The combined effect of imposed and voluntary media silence was to prevent substantial public discussion on the famine in metropolitan Britain, including in Parliament in London, which neither discussed the famine, nor considered the policy needs of dealing with it (that is, not until October 1943 when *The Statesman* forced its hand). There was of course no parliament in India under the British colonial administration.

In fact, governmental policy, far from being helpful, actually exacerbated the famine. There was no official famine relief over the many months in which thousands were dying every week. More than this, the famine was aggravated, first, by the fact that the British India Government in New Delhi had suspended the trade in rice and food grains between the Indian provinces, so that food could not move through legitimate channels of private trade despite the much higher price of food in Bengal. Second, rather than trying to get more food into Bengal from abroad – the New Delhi colonial administration was adamant that it did not want to do that – the official policy took the form of looking for food exports *out of* Bengal over that period.

---

\* In my *Poverty and Famines* (1981), I show that the Famine Inquiry Commission's own estimate of the total death toll from the famine was also a serious underestimation mainly because the increase in mortality caused by the famine remained for a number of years following the starvation because of the ongoing famine-induced epidemics (Appendix D). See also my entry on 'Human Disasters' in *The Oxford Handbook of Medicine* (Oxford: Oxford University Press, 2008).

Indeed, even as late as January 1943, when the famine was about to break, the Viceroy of India told the head of the local Bengal government that he 'simply *must* produce some more rice out of Bengal for Ceylon even if Bengal itself went short!'.[1]

It must be mentioned here, to make any kind of sense of British Indian official thinking on the subject, that these policies were based on the idea that there was no particular decline in food output in Bengal at that time, and 'therefore' a famine 'simply could not occur' there. The government's understanding of the volume of the food output was not altogether wrong, but its theory of famine was disastrously mistaken, since the demand for food had radically expanded, primarily because of the war effort in Bengal, with the arrival of soldiers and other war personnel, new construction and ancillary economic activities associated with the war boom. A very substantial part of the population, mostly in rural areas, with stationary income, was facing much higher food prices, thanks to the demand-fed price rise, and consequently starved. To secure the ability of the vulnerable to buy food, it would have helped to have given them more income and purchasing power, for example through emergency employment or public relief, but help could also have come from having a larger supply of food grains in the region – despite the fact that the crisis was not *caused* by a supply decline, but by a demand rise.

What was extraordinary, even beyond the colonial government's belief in a wrong theory of famine, was New Delhi's inability to notice that so many thousands were actually dying on the streets every day: the officers had to be real 'theorists' to miss the facts on the ground in such a gross way. A democratic system with public criticism and parliamentary pressure would not have allowed the officials, including the Governor of Bengal and the Viceroy of India, to think the way they did.*

A third way in which government policy was counter-productive was its role in the redistribution of food within Bengal. The government bought food at high prices from rural Bengal to run a selective rationing system at controlled prices, specifically for the resident popu-

---

* These issues are discussed in my *Poverty and Famines: An Essay on Entitlement and Deprivation* (1981), Chapter 6.

lation of Calcutta. This was a part of the war effort intended to lessen urban discontent. The most serious consequence of this policy was that the rural population, with their low and stationary income, faced rapidly exploding food prices: the strong outward movement of food from rural Bengal because of the war-fed boom was powerfully reinforced by the government policy of buying dear from rural areas (at 'whatever price') and selling it cheap in Calcutta for a selected population. None of these issues came into parliamentary discussion in any substantive way during the period of news and editorial blackout.

The Bengali newspapers in Calcutta protested as loudly as government censorship permitted – it could not be very loud, allegedly, for reasons of the war and 'fighting morale'. Certainly there was little echo of these native criticisms in London. Responsible public discussion on what to do began in the circles that mattered, in London, only in October 1943, after Ian Stephens, the courageous editor of *The Statesman* of Calcutta (then British owned), decided to break ranks by departing from the voluntary policy of 'silence' and publishing graphic accounts and stinging editorials on 14 and 16 October.* The rebuke to the Secretary of State for India, quoted earlier, was from the second of those two editorials. This was immediately followed by a stir in the governing circles in British India and it also led to serious parliamentary discussions in Westminster in London. This, in turn, quickly resulted in the beginning – at long last – of public relief arrangements in Bengal in November (there had been only private charity earlier on). The famine ended in December, partly because of a new crop, but also, very significantly, because of the relief that was finally available. However, by this time the famine had already killed hundreds of thousands of people.

---

* Ian Stephens's dilemma on the subject, and his ultimate decision to give priority to his role as a journalist, is beautifully discussed in his book *Monsoon Morning* (London: Ernest Benn, 1966). When, later on, I came to know him in the 1970s, it became clear to me very soon how strongly the memory of that difficult decision lived on in his mind. He was, however, rightly proud of the fact that, through his editorial policy, he had saved the lives of a great many people and had managed to stem the tide of the 'death roll'.

# FAMINE PREVENTION AND
# PUBLIC REASONING

It was mentioned in the last chapter that no major famine has ever occurred in a functioning democracy with regular elections, opposition parties, basic freedom of speech and a relatively free media (even when the country is very poor and in a seriously adverse food situation). This understanding has now become fairly widely accepted, even though there was much scepticism about the thesis initially.* This is a simple but rather important illustration of the most elementary aspect of the protective power of political liberty. Though Indian democracy has many imperfections, nevertheless the political incentives generated by it have been adequate to eliminate major famines right from the time of independence. The last substantial famine in India – the Bengal famine – occurred only four years before the Empire ended. The prevalence of famines, which had been a persistent feature of the long history of the British Indian Empire, ended abruptly with the establishment of a democracy after independence.

Despite China's greater success than India's in many economic fields, China – unlike independent India – did have a huge famine, indeed the largest famine in recorded history, in 1958–61, with a mortality count estimated at close to 30 million. Though the famine raged for three years, the government was not pressed to change its disastrous policies: there was, in China, no parliament open for critical dissent, no opposition party and no free press. The history of famines has, in fact, had a peculiarly close connection with authoritarian rules, for example with colonialism (as in British India or Ireland), one-party states (as in the Soviet Union in the 1930s, or in China or Cambodia later on), and military dictatorships (as in Ethiopia or Somalia). The contemporary famine situation in North Korea is a continuing example.[2]

* After my initial presentation of this thesis in 'How Is India Doing?' *New York Review of Books*, 29 (1982), and 'Development: Which Way Now?' *Economic Journal*, 93 (1983), there was a good deal of reprimand from a number of critics (including food experts), and there were strongly worded altercations both in the *New York Review of Books* and in the *Economic and Political Weekly*, following my articles.

The direct penalties of a famine are borne only by the suffering public and not by the ruling government. The rulers never starve. However, when a government is accountable to the public, and when there is free news-reporting and uncensored public criticism, then the government too has an excellent incentive to do its best to eradicate famines.*

Aside from this immediate connection with the political incentive to prevent famines that is embedded in government by discussion, there are two other specific issues here which may be worth noting. First, the proportion of the population affected, or even threatened, by a famine tends to be very small – typically much less than 10 per cent (often much less than that) and hardly ever more than that ratio. So if it were true that only disaffected famine victims vote against a ruling government when a famine rages or threatens, then the government could still be quite secure. What makes a famine such a political disaster for a ruling government is the reach of public reasoning, which moves and energizes a very large proportion of the general public to protest and shout about the 'uncaring' government and to try to bring it down. Public discussion of the nature of the calamity can make the fate of the victims a powerful political issue with far-reaching effects on the climate of media coverage and public discussion, and

* It is worth mentioning here that doubts about the reach of this proposition have sometimes been raised by referring to the fact that there have been famines, or at least conditions approximating a famine, in a few countries that have started having some kind of democratic elections, without the other features that make a democracy accountable. Niger, which had both elections and famines, was given as an alleged counter-example in 2005 by a number of observers. The point to recognize here is, as the *New York Times* noted in an editorial, that the incentive-based connection with famine prevention applies specifically to a *functioning* democracy. Niger did not qualify, since democracy functions not only with the help of elections (which Niger had recently instituted), but also on the basis of other democratic institutions that produce accountability. The *Times* put the basic issue with much clarity: 'Amartya Sen has taught, rightly, that "no famine has ever taken place in the history of the world in a functioning democracy". Functioning is the key word; leaders who are truly accountable to their people have strong incentives to take timely preventative action. Mr Tandeja [the head of the Nigerian government], whom President Bush hailed at the White House this June as an exemplary democrat, clearly needs a refresher course in humane economics and accountable democracy' ('Meanwhile, People Starve', *New York Times*, 14 August 2005).

ultimately on the voting of others – a potential majority.* Not least of the achievements of democracy is its ability to make people take an interest, through public discussion, in each other's predicaments, and to have a better understanding of the lives of others.

The second point concerns the informational role of democracy which goes beyond its incentive function; for example, in the Chinese famine of 1958–61, the failure of the so-called 'Great Leap Forward', involving a drastic expansion of collectivization, was kept a closely guarded secret. There was little public knowledge of the nature, size and reach of the famine within China, or outside it.

Indeed, the lack of a free system of news distribution ultimately misled the government itself, fed by its own propaganda and by rosy reports of local party officials competing for credit in Beijing. The vast number of communes or cooperatives who had failed to produce enough grain were, of course, aware of their own problem. But thanks to the news black-out they did not know anything much about the widespread failure across rural China. No collective farm wanted to acknowledge that it alone had failed, and the government in Beijing was fed rosy reports of great success even from the badly failing collectives. By adding up these numbers, the Chinese authorities mistakenly believed that they had 100 million more metric tons of grain than they actually did, just when the famine was moving towards its peak.[3]

Despite the fact that the Chinese government was quite committed to eliminating hunger in the country, it did not substantially revise its disastrous policies (associated with the ill-advised 'Great Leap Forward') during the three famine years. The non-revision was possible not only because of the lack of a political opposition and the absence of an independent media, but also because the Chinese

---

* All this has obvious connection with the arguments presented in earlier chapters, in particular in Chapters 8, 'Rationality and Other People', and 15, 'Democracy as Public Reason'. The different types of impartial reasons discussed in Chapter 9, 'Plurality of Impartial Reasons', also have relevance to the political engagement that the predicament of famine victims may arouse, involving not only reflections on cooperation and mutual benefit, but also the responsibility of 'effective power' that the clearly fortunate in a famine-threatened country may specifically acknowledge towards the more vulnerable, thanks to public reasoning.

government itself did not see the need to change its policies, partly because it did not have enough information on the extent to which the 'Great Leap Forward' had failed.

It is interesting to note that even Chairman Mao himself, whose radical beliefs had much to do with the initiation of, and unrelenting persistence with, the 'Great Leap Forward', identified one particular role of democracy, once the failure had been belatedly acknowledged. In 1962, just after the famine had killed tens of millions, Mao made the following observation to a gathering of 7,000 cadres of the Communist Party:

Without democracy, you have no understanding of what is happening down below; the general situation will be unclear; you will be unable to collect sufficient opinions from all sides; there can be no communication between top and bottom; top-level organs of leadership will depend on one-sided and incorrect material to decide issues, thus you will find it difficult to avoid being subjectivist; it will be impossible to achieve unity of understanding and unity of action, and impossible to achieve true centralism.[4]

Mao's defence of democracy here is, of course, quite limited. The focus is exclusively on the *informational* side, ignoring its incentive role as well as the intrinsic and constitutive importance of political freedom.* But nevertheless it is extremely interesting that Mao himself acknowledged the extent to which disastrous official policies were caused by the lack of the informational links that more active public reasoning could have provided in averting disasters of the kind that China experienced.

## DEMOCRACY AND DEVELOPMENT

Most champions of democracy have been rather reticent in suggesting that democracy would itself promote development and enhancement of social welfare – they have tended to see them as good but distinctly

---

* On this, see also Ralph Miliband, *Marxism and Politics* (London: Oxford University Press, 1977), pp. 149–50, who provides a remarkably illuminating analysis and assessment of this odd turn in Mao's political thought.

separate and largely independent goals. The detractors of democracy, on the other hand, seemed to have been quite willing to express their diagnosis of what they see as serious tensions between democracy and development. The theorists of the practical split – 'Make up your mind: do you want democracy, or instead, do you want development?' – often came, at least to start with, from East Asian countries, and their voice grew in influence as several of these countries were immensely successful – through the 1970s and 1980s and even later – in promoting economic growth without pursuing democracy. The observation of a handful of such examples led rapidly to something of a general theory: democracies do quite badly in facilitating development, compared with what authoritarian regimes can achieve. Didn't South Korea, Singapore, Taiwan and Hong Kong achieve astonishingly fast economic progress without fulfilling, at least in the early days, the basic requirements of democratic governance? And after the economic reforms in China in 1979, didn't authoritarian China fare a lot better in terms of economic growth than democratic India?

To deal with these issues, we have to pay particular attention to both the content of what can be called development and to the interpretation of democracy (in particular to the respective roles of voting and of public reasoning). The assessment of development cannot be divorced from the lives that people can lead and the real freedom that they enjoy. Development can scarcely be seen merely in terms of enhancement of inanimate objects of convenience, such as a rise in the GNP (or in personal incomes), or industrialization – important as they may be as means to the real ends. Their value must depend on what they do to the lives and freedom of the people involved, which must be central to the idea of development.*

If development is understood in a broader way, with a focus on human lives, then it becomes immediately clear that the relation between development and democracy has to be seen partly in terms of their constitutive connection, rather than only through their external links. Even though the question has often been asked whether political freedom is 'conducive to development', we must not miss the crucial

* This issue received attention in Chapter 11, 'Lives, Freedoms and Capabilities'.

recognition that political liberties and democratic rights are among the 'constituent components' of development. Their relevance for development does not have to be established *indirectly* through their contribution to the growth of GNP.

However, after acknowledging this central connection, we also have to subject democracy to consequential analysis, since there are other kinds of freedoms as well (other than political liberties and civil rights), to which attention must be paid. We must be concerned, for example, with economic poverty. We do, therefore, have reason to be interested in economic growth, even in the rather limited terms of growth of GNP or GDP per head, since raising real income can clear the way to some really important achievements; for example, the general connection between economic growth and poverty removal is by now reasonably well established, supplemented by distributional concerns. Aside from generating income for many people, a process of economic growth also tends to expand the size of public revenue, which can be used for social purposes, such as schooling, medical services and healthcare, and other facilities that directly enhance the lives and capabilities of people. Indeed, sometimes the expansion of public revenue as a result of fast economic growth is much faster than the economic growth itself (for example, in recent years, as the Indian economy has grown at 7, 8 or 9 per cent per annum, the rate of increase of public revenue has been around 9, 10 or 11 per cent). Public revenue creates an opportunity that the government can seize to make the process of economic expansion more equitably shared. This is, of course, only a potential condition, since the actual use of the expanding public revenue is another matter of great importance, but economic growth creates the condition when that choice is responsibly exercised by the government.*

The much-articulated scepticism about the compatibility of democracy and rapid economic growth was based on some selected cross-country comparisons, focusing particularly on the rapidly growing economies of East Asia, on one side, and India, on the other, with its

---

* On important contrasts between different types of uses – and waste – of resources generated by economic growth, see my joint book with Jean Drèze, *Hunger and Public Action* (Oxford: Clarendon Press, 1989).

long history of modest GNP growth of 3 per cent per annum. However, fuller cross-country comparisons, for what they are worth (and they cannot be worth less than the prevailing practice of basing a big conclusion on a handful of selected inter-country contrasts), have not provided any empirical support for the belief that democracy is inimical to economic growth.[5] And while India used to be cited as living proof that democratic countries are destined to grow much more slowly than authoritarian ones, now that the economic growth of India has accelerated remarkably (this began in the 1980s but was firmly consolidated through the economic reforms of the 1990s and has continued since then at a rapid rate), it becomes hard to use India as the quintessential example of the slowness of economic progress under democratic governance. And yet India is no less democratic today than it was in the 1960s or 1970s.* Indeed, the evidence is overwhelming that growth is helped by the supportiveness of a friendly economic climate rather than by the fierceness of a ruthless political system.†

## HUMAN SECURITY AND POLITICAL POWER

Furthermore, we have to go beyond economic growth to understand the fuller demands of development and of the pursuit of social welfare. Attention must be paid to the extensive evidence that democracy and political and civil rights tend to enhance freedoms of other kinds (such as human security) through giving a voice, at least in many circumstances, to the deprived and the vulnerable. That is an important issue, and closely linked with democracy's role in public reasoning and in fostering 'government by discussion'. Democracy's success in preventing famines belongs to democracy's many-sided contributions

---

* India is also a counter-example to the thesis that is sometimes entertained that a country's per capita income has to be reasonably high for the stability of the democratic system.

† What must also be noted here is that, despite the dominance of befuddled economic policies in India for many decades, the democratic system itself allowed – and made way for – some of the necessary reforms that could make economic growth much faster.

in advancing human security, but there are many other fields of application as well.*

The protective power of democracy in providing security is, in fact, much more extensive than famine prevention. The poor in booming South Korea or Indonesia may not have given much thought to democracy when the economic fortunes of all seemed to go up and up together in the 1980s and early 1990s, but when the economic crises came (and divided they fell) in the late 1990s, democracy and political and civil rights were desperately missed by those whose economic means and lives were unusually battered. Democracy suddenly became a central issue in these countries, with South Korea taking a major initiative in that direction.

India has, without doubt, benefited from the protective role of democracy in giving the rulers excellent political incentive to act supportively when natural disasters threaten. However, the practice and reach of democracy can be quite imperfect, as it is in India, despite the achievements that are undoubtedly present. Democracy gives an opportunity to the opposition to press for policy change even when the problem is chronic and has had a long history, rather than being acute and sudden, as in the case of famines. The relative weakness of Indian social policies on school education, basic healthcare, child nutrition, essential land reform and gender equity reflects deficiencies of politically engaged public reasoning and social pressure (including pressure from the opposition), not just inadequacies in the official thinking of the government.† Indeed, India provides an excellent example of both the significant achievements of democracy and its

---

* See the report of the Commission on Human Security, set up jointly by the United Nations and the government of Japan: *Human Security Now* (New York: UN, 2003). I was privileged to chair this commission jointly with the visionary Dr Sadako Ogata, formerly the United Nations High Commissioner for Refugees. See also Mary Kaldor, *Human Security: Reflections on Globalization and Intervention* (Cambridge: Polity Press, 2007).

† The Indian press can also be faulted for the lack of reach in dealing with persistent but not immediately fatal deprivations. For an analysis of this problem from one of the most distinguished editors in India, see N. Ram, 'An Independent Press and Anti-hunger Strategies: The Indian Experience', in Jean Drèze and Amartya Sen (eds), *The Political Economy of Hunger* (Oxford: Clarendon Press, 1990). See also Kaushik Basu, *The Retreat of Democracy* (Delhi: Permanent Black, 2007).

specific failures connected with an inadequate utilization of the opportunities offered by democratic institutions. There is a strong case for going beyond electoral *niti* to democratic *nyaya*.

## DEMOCRACY AND POLICY CHOICE

Only in some parts of India has the urgency of social policies been adequately politicized. The experiences of the state of Kerala provide perhaps the clearest example, where the need for universal education, basic healthcare, elementary gender equity and land reforms has received effective political backing. The explanation encompasses both history and contemporary development: the educational orientation of Kerala's anti-upper-caste movements (of which the current left-wing politics of Kerala is a successor), the early initiatives of the 'native kingdoms' of Travancore and Cochin (which stayed outside the Raj for domestic policies), missionary activities in the spread of education (their effects were not confined only to Christians, who constitute a fifth of the Kerala population), and also a stronger voice for women in family decisions, partly linked to the presence and prominence of matrilineal property rights for a substantial and influential section – the Nairs – of the Hindu community.[6] Over a very long time now Kerala has made good use of political activism and voice to expand the range of social opportunities. The utilization of democratic institutions is certainly not independent of the nature of social conditions.

It is hard to escape the general conclusion that economic performance, social opportunity, political voice and public reasoning are all deeply interrelated. In those fields in which there has recently been a more determined use of political and social voice, there are considerable signs of change. The issue of gender inequality has produced much more political engagement in recent years (often led by women's movements), and this has added to determined political efforts at reducing gender asymmetry in social and economic fields. There is a long history in India of women's prominence in particular areas, including in leadership positions in politics. While those achievements were certainly linked with the voice of women (helped by the opportunities of participatory politics in recent years), their reach has been largely confined to relatively small segments – mostly the more prosperous sections – of the population.* An important feature of the strengthening of the voice of women in contemporary Indian public life is the gradual broadening of this social coverage. India still has a long way to go in removing inequalities in the position of women, but the increasing political involvement in the social role of women has been an important and constructive development in democratic practice in India.

In general, possibilities of public agitation on issues of social inequality and deprivation are now beginning to be more utilized than before, even though engagement on these issues was eclipsed for several years because of the sectarian politics that diverted attention from these concerns. There has been much more action recently in organized movements based broadly on demands for human rights, such as the right to school education, the right to food (and, in particular, to midday school meals), the entitlement to basic healthcare, guarantees of environmental preservation and the right of 'employment guarantee'. These movements serve to focus attention on particular societal failures, partly as a supplement to broad public discussions in the media, but they also provide a politically harder edge to socially important demands.

Democratic freedom can certainly be used to enhance social justice and a better and fairer politics. The process, however, is not automatic and requires activism on the part of politically engaged citizens. While the lessons of empirical experiences studied here have come mainly from Asia, particularly India and China, similar lessons can be drawn for other regions, including the United States and European countries.†

---

* While most of the female political leaders in India have come from the urban elite, there are a few cases of remarkable political success of female leaders of rural low-caste groups, coming from the more affluent sections of those groups.

† Indeed, the practice of democracy remains still quite imperfect in the world's oldest democracy in terms of barriers to participation and the reach of media coverage (even though with Barack Obama's election as President one big barrier to participation seems, at last, to have been breached at the top). On the problems of democratic practice in the USA, see the illuminating book by Ronald Dworkin, *Is Democracy Possible Here? Principles for a New Political Debate* (Princeton, NJ: Princeton University Press, 2006).

## MINORITY RIGHTS AND INCLUSIVE PRIORITIES

I turn, finally, to what is undoubtedly one of the most difficult issues that democracy has to tackle. The recognition that democracy has to be concerned both with majority rule and the rights of minorities is not a new idea, even though (as was discussed in the last chapter), in the organizational context, democracy is frequently seen entirely in terms of balloting and majority rule. A broader understanding of democracy as public reasoning (discussed in the last chapter), which includes the use of ballots but goes much beyond that, can accommodate the importance of minority rights without ignoring majority votes as part of the total structure of democracy. The eighteenth-century pioneer of social choice theory, the Marquis de Condorcet, had warned against 'the maxim, too prevalent among ancient and modern republicans, that the few can legitimately be sacrificed to the many'.[7]

There remains, however, the problem that a ruthless majority that has no compunction in eliminating minority rights would tend to make the society face a hard choice between honouring majority rule and guaranteeing minority rights. The formation of tolerant values is thus quite central to the smooth functioning of a democratic system (as was discussed in Chapter 14).

The issues involved also apply to the role of democracy in preventing sectarian violence. The problem here is more complicated than the easy recognition that democracy can eliminate famines. Even though famine victims form a small proportion of any threatened population, democracy prevents famines because the plight of the minority is politicized by public discussion to generate a huge majority for famine prevention, since the general population has no particular reason to entertain any hardened hostility – or exploitable animosity – towards potential famine victims. The process is far more complicated with sectarian strife when inter-community hostilities can be fanned by extremists through demagoguery.

The role of democracy in preventing community-based violence depends on the ability of inclusive and interactive political processes to subdue the poisonous fanaticism of divisive communal thinking.

This has been an important task in independent India, especially since that multireligious and secular polity was born in a period of huge communal strife and violence in the 1940s, a period that was short in the number of years but long in casting a huge shadow of vulnerability. The problem was explicitly discussed in this form by Mohandas Gandhi, in his clarification of the importance of inclusiveness as an essential part of the democracy sought by the independence movement that he led.[8]

There has been some success in this respect, and the secularism of democratic India has broadly speaking survived intact, despite occasional strains, with mutual tolerance and respect. That survival has not, however, prevented periodic outbursts of sectarian violence, often fed by political groups that benefit from such divisiveness. The effect of sectarian demagoguery can be overcome only through the championing of broader values that go across divisive barriers. The recognition of the multiple identities of each person, of which the religious identity is only one, is crucially important in this respect; for example, Hindus, Muslims, Sikhs and Christians in India not only share a nationality, but, depending on the individual, can share other identities, such as a language, a literature, a profession, a location and many other bases of categorization.* Democratic politics allows the opportunity to discuss these non-sectarian affiliations and their rival claims over religious divisions.† The fact that, after the murderous attacks in Mumbai in November 2008 by terrorists from a Muslim background (and almost certainly of Pakistani ancestry), the much-feared reaction against Indian Muslims did not emerge was to a great extent due to the public discussion that followed the attacks, to which both Muslims and non-Muslims contributed richly. The

* Similarly the Hutu activists who committed dreadful violence against Tutsis in Rwanda in 1994, not only had their divisive Hutu identity, but also shared with Tutsis other identities, such as being Rwandan, African, possibly a Kigalian.
† India, with a population that is more than 80 per cent Hindu, currently has a Sikh prime minister and a leader of the ruling political coalition (and the leading party, Congress) who has a Christian background. Between 2004 and 2007, these two were supplemented by a Muslim president (there were Muslim presidents of India earlier also), so that in that period none of the three principal governing positions of the country was occupied by a member of the majority community – and yet there was no noticeable sense of discontent.

practice of democracy can certainly assist in bringing out a greater recognition of the plural identities of human beings.[9]

And yet communal distinctions, like racial differences, remain open to exploitation by those who want to cultivate discontent and instigate violence, unless the bonds established by national democracies serve as an effective safeguard against this.* Much will depend on the vigour of democratic politics in generating tolerant values, and there is no automatic guarantee of success by the mere existence of democratic institutions. Here an active and energetic media can play an extremely important part, in making the problems, predicaments and humanity of certain groups more understood by other groups.

The success of democracy is not merely a matter of having the most perfect institutional structure that we can think of. It depends inescapably on our actual behaviour patterns and the working of political and social interactions. There is no chance of resting the matter in the 'safe' hands of purely institutional virtuosity. The working of democratic institutions, like that of all other institutions, depends on the activities of human agents in utilizing opportunities for reasonable realization. The practical lessons from these empirical accounts would seem to complement, broadly, the theoretical arguments explored earlier in this book. The conceptual case for invoking *nyaya*, and not just *niti*, in the pursuit of justice is strongly supported by the lessons of the empirical experiences presented here.

* The organized riots in Gujarat in 2002, in which close to 2,000 people, mostly Muslims, died, remains a huge blot in the country's political record, just as the opposition to those events in the rest of India pointed to the strength of secular values in democratic India. There is evidence, based on electoral studies, that this shameful episode did strengthen the electoral support of the secular parties in the 2004 general elections that followed those terrible events.

# 17

## Human Rights and Global Imperatives

There is something very appealing in the idea that every person anywhere in the world, irrespective of citizenship, residence, race, class, caste or community, has some basic rights which others should respect. The big moral appeal of human rights has been used for a variety of purposes, from resisting torture, arbitrary incarceration and racial discrimination to demanding an end to hunger and starvation, and to medical neglect across the globe. At the same time, the basic idea of human rights, which people are supposed to have simply because they are human, is seen by many critics as entirely without any kind of a reasoned foundation. The questions that are recurrently asked are: do these rights exist? Where do they come from?

It is not disputed that the invoking of human rights can be very attractive as a general belief, and it may even be politically effective as rhetoric. Scepticism and anxiety relate to what is thought to be the 'softness' or the 'mushiness' of the conceptual grounding of human rights. Many philosophers and legal theorists see the rhetoric of human rights as just loose talk – well-meaning and perhaps even laudable loose talk – which cannot, it is presumed, have much intellectual strength.

The sharp contrast between the widespread use of the idea of human rights and the intellectual scepticism about its conceptual soundness is not new. The American Declaration of Independence took it to be 'self-evident' that everyone had 'certain inalienable rights', and thirteen years later, in 1789, the French declaration of 'the rights of man' asserted that 'men are born and remain free and equal in rights'.* But

---

* The declaration of the 'rights of man' came out of the radical ideas associated with the French Revolution, a seismic political event which not only reflected growing

355

it did not take Jeremy Bentham long, in his *Anarchical Fallacies* written during 1791-2 and aimed against the French 'rights of man', to propose the total dismissal of all such claims. Bentham insisted that 'natural rights is simple nonsense: natural and imprescriptible rights, rhetorical nonsense, nonsense upon stilts',[1] by which, I take it, he meant some kind of an artificially elevated nonsense.

The dichotomy remains very alive today, and despite persistent use of the idea of human rights in the affairs of the world, there are many who see the idea as no more than 'bawling upon paper' (to use another of Bentham's derisive descriptions). The dismissal of human rights is often comprehensive and aimed against any belief in the existence of rights that people can have simply by virtue of their humanity, rather than those they have contingently on specific qualifications such as citizenship, related to provisions in actual legislation or in the accepted 'common laws'.

Human rights activists are often quite impatient with this intellectual scepticism, perhaps because many of those who invoke human rights are concerned with changing the world rather than interpreting it (to recall a classic distinction made famous by Karl Marx). It is not hard to understand the reluctance of the activists to spend much time in trying to provide conceptual justifications to convince sceptical theorists, given the obvious urgency to respond to terrible deprivations around the world. This proactive stance has had its rewards, since it has allowed the immediate use of the generally appealing idea of human rights to confront intense oppression or great misery, without having to wait for the theoretical air to clear. Nevertheless, conceptual doubts about the idea of human rights must be addressed and its intellectual basis clarified, if it is to command reasoned and sustained loyalty.

---

social tensions but also a deep upheaval of thought. The American Declaration of Independence also reflected a transformation of social and political ideas. 'Government, Jefferson wrote, was self-evidently a mere instrument, more or less useful, by which men, born equal, seek to secure their lives and liberties and their right to pursue happiness; when a government violates these purposes, it is, he said in a phrase that would ring through the palaces of Europe, "the right of people to alter or to abolish it"' (Bernard Bailyn, *Faces of Revolution: Personalities and Themes in the Struggle for American Independence* (New York: Vintage Books, 1992), p. 158).

# WHAT ARE HUMAN RIGHTS?

It is important to consider seriously the questioning of the nature and basis of human rights, and to respond to the long – and well-established – tradition of precipitately dismissing these claims. Bentham's diagnosis that 'the rights of man' are just 'nonsense' (if not 'nonsense upon stilts') is merely a muscular expression of general doubts that are shared – mildly or strongly – by a great many people. The doubts demand serious analysis both for ascertaining the status of human rights and for understanding their relevance to the idea of justice.

What exactly are human rights? Are there, as is often asked, really such things? There are some variations in the ways in which the idea of human rights are invoked by different people. However, we can see the basic concerns behind these articulations by examining not only the contemporary practice of utilizing the concept, but also the history of its use over a very long period. That substantial history includes the invoking of 'inalienable rights' in the American Declaration of Independence and similar affirmations in the French declaration of 'the rights of man' in the eighteenth century, but also the relatively recent adoption by the United Nations of the Universal Declaration of Human Rights in 1948.

The 'existence' of human rights is obviously not like the existence of, say, Big Ben in the middle of London. Nor is it like the existence of a legislated law in the statute book. Proclamations of human rights, even though stated in the form of recognizing the *existence* of things that are called human rights, are really strong ethical pronouncements as to what *should* be done.* They demand acknowledgement of

* The subject of 'fact-value entanglements' in the language we use was discussed in general terms in Chapters 1, 'Reason and Objectivity' and 5, 'Impartiality and Objectivity', and it is important here to see that the force of the assertion about the existence of human rights lies in the recognition of some important freedoms that, it is claimed, should be respected, and correspondingly in the acceptance of obligations by the society, in one way or another, to support and promote these freedoms. I shall have more to say on these ethical connections in what follows. On the methodological issues related to such entanglements, see Hilary Putnam, *The Collapse of the Fact/Value Dichotomy and Other Essays* (Cambridge, MA: Harvard University Press,

imperatives and indicate that something needs to be done for the realization of these recognized freedoms that are identified through these rights. One thing they are not are claims that these human rights are already established *legal* rights, enshrined through legislation or common law (Bentham's confounding of the two different issues will be discussed presently).[2]

If this is the way we understand human rights, then two questions immediately arise, concerning content and viability. The issue of content is the subject of the ethical assertion that is being made through the declaration of a human right. To answer briefly (on the basis of what is theorized and what is practically invoked), the ethical assertion is about the critical importance of certain freedoms (like the freedom from torture, or the freedom to escape starvation) and correspondingly about the need to accept some social obligations to promote or safeguard these freedoms.* Both of these claims – about freedoms and obligations – will have to be examined more fully (at this time I am just identifying the *kind* of claims that the ethics of human rights tries to present).

The second question concerns the viability of the ethical claims that are involved in a declaration of human rights. Like other ethical claims that their proponents promote, there is an implicit presumption in making pronouncements on human rights that the underlying ethical claims will survive open and informed scrutiny. This is where the understanding of what is being discussed here relates to the exercise of 'open impartiality' discussed earlier in this book. Indeed, the invoking of such an interactive process of critical scrutiny, open to argu-

---

2002); see also Willard Van Orman Quine, 'Two Dogmas of Empiricism,' in his *From a Logical Point of View* (Cambridge, MA: Harvard University Press, 1961). Attempts to evade these entanglements have been a source of considerable difficulty in economics, on which see Vivian Walsh, 'Philosophy and Economics', in John Eatwell, Murray Milgate and Peter Newman (eds), *The New Palgrave: A Dictionary of Economics* (London: Macmillan, 1987), pp. 861–9.

* As Judith Blau and Alberto Moncada have pointed out in their powerfully argued book, *Justice in the United States: Human Rights and the US Constitution* (New York: Rowman & Littlefield, 2006), the Declaration of Independence in 1776, with its recognition of certain basic rights, 'was like a cueing card for everything that came next – independence, writing a constitution, and setting up the machinery of governance' (p. 3).

ments coming from others and sensitive to the relevant information that can be obtained, is a central feature of the general framework of ethical and political evaluation already explored in this work. Viability in impartial reasoning is seen, in this approach, as central to the vindication of human rights, even if such reasoning leaves considerable areas of ambiguity and dissonance.* The discipline of scrutiny and viability has to be applied to the specific field of human rights, and I shall return to that issue towards the end of this chapter.

The ethical pronouncements, with distinct political content, that belong to a declaration of human rights may come from persons or from institutions, and they may be presented as individual remarks or as social pronouncements. They can also be rather prominently asserted by particular groups of people charged to examine these issues, such as the drafters of the American Declaration of Independence and of the French rights of man, or by the United Nations committee that authored the Universal Declaration (led by Eleanor Roosevelt). These group articulations may also receive some kind of an institutional ratification, as happened, for example, in the vote in 1948 in the newly established United Nations. But what is being articulated or ratified is an ethical assertion – not a proposition about what is already legally guaranteed.

Indeed, these public articulations of human rights are often invitations to initiate some fresh legislation, rather than relying on what is already seen as legally installed. The framers of the Universal Declaration in 1948 clearly hoped that the articulated recognition of human rights would serve as a kind of a template for new laws that would be enacted to legalize those human rights across the world.† The focus was on fresh legislation, and not just on more humane interpretation of existing legal protections.

* Partial dissonance is not an embarrassment to the approach used in this work for reasons discussed earlier, particularly in the Introduction and in Chapter 4, 'Voice and Social Choice'. It will be further considered in the next and final chapter, 'Justice and the World'.
† Eleanor Roosevelt, in particular, had such expectations when she led the young United Nations to adopt the Universal Declaration in 1948. That extraordinary history of a momentous global pronouncement is beautifully recounted by Mary Ann Glendon, *A World Made New: Eleanor Roosevelt and the Universal Declaration of Human Rights* (New York: Random House, 2001).

Ethical proclamations of human rights are comparable to pronouncements in, say, utilitarian ethics – even though the substantive contents of the articulation of human rights are altogether different from utilitarian claims. Utilitarians want utilities to be taken as the only things that ultimately matter and demand that policies be based on maximizing the sum-total of utilities, whereas human rights advocates want the recognition of the importance of certain freedoms and the acceptance of some social obligations to safeguard them. But even as they differ on what exactly is demanded by ethics, their battle is on the same – and shared – general territory of ethical beliefs and pronouncements. And that is the point at issue here in answering the question: what are human rights?

Thus understood, an assertion of a human right (for example in the form: 'this freedom is important and we must seriously consider what we should do to help each other realize it') can indeed be compared with other ethical proclamations, such as 'happiness is important', or 'autonomy matters', or 'personal liberties must be preserved'. The question, 'Are there really such things as human rights?' is thus comparable to asking, 'Is happiness really important?' or 'Does autonomy or liberty really matter?'* These are eminently discussable ethical questions, and the viability of the particular claims made depends on the scrutiny of what is being asserted (the discipline of investigation and assessment of viability are subjects to which I shall presently return).† The 'proof of existence' that is often demanded from

* However, in seeking answers to these critical questions, we do not have to search for the existence of some ethical 'objects' that are identifiable as human rights. On the general issue of ethical evaluation, see Chapter 1, 'Reason and Objectivity'. See also Hilary Putnam, *Ethics without Ontology* (Cambridge, MA: Harvard University Press, 2004).

† The assertion of the importance of a 'right' must not be confused with the interpretation that Ronald Dworkin chooses, and Thomas Scanlon supports, that a right must, by definition, 'trump' every contrary argument based on 'what would be good to happen' (Dworkin, *Taking Rights Seriously* (Cambridge, MA: Harvard University Press, 1977), and Scanlon, 'Rights and Interests', in Kaushik Basu and Ravi Kanbur (eds), *Arguments for a Better World* (Oxford and New York: Oxford University Press, 2009), pp. 68–9). I would argue that taking rights seriously requires us to recognize that it would be bad – sometimes terrible – if they were violated. This does not imply that the recognition of a claim as a right requires us to assume that it must always overwhelm every other argument in the contrary direction (based, for example, on

human rights activists is comparable to asking for the validation of ethical claims of other types – from the utilitarian to the Rawlsian or Nozickian. This is one way in which the subject of human rights relates closely to the focus of this book, since public scrutiny is central to the approach that is being taken here.

## ETHICS AND LAW

The analogy between articulations of human rights and utilitarian pronouncements as ethical propositions can help to address some of the confusion that has plagued discussions on human rights for a long time. The basic similarity between these two approaches as alternative – but very different – routes to social ethics is easy to see. However, the great founder of modern utilitarianism, Jeremy Bentham, managed to miss the connection altogether in his classic hatchet job on the French declaration of the 'rights of man'. Rather than understanding the perspective of human rights as an ethical approach (an alternative to, and competitive with, his own approach of utilitarianism), Bentham took the appropriate comparison to be that between the respective *legal status* of (1) declarations of human rights, and (2) actually legislated rights. He found, not surprisingly, the former to be essentially lacking in legal standing in the way the latter obviously had.

Armed powerfully with the wrong question and the wrong comparison, Bentham dismissed human rights with admirable swiftness and breathtaking simplicity. '*Right*, the substantive *right*, is the child of law; from *real* laws come *real* rights; but from *imaginary* laws, from "law of nature",' can come, Bentham argued, only '*imaginary* rights'.[3] It is easy to see that Bentham's rejection of the idea of natural 'rights

---

well-being, or a freedom not included in that right). It is perhaps not surprising that the opponents of the idea of human rights often thrust on them remarkably all-conquering pretensions and then dismiss these rights on the grounds that these pretensions are highly implausible. Mary Wollstonecraft and Thomas Paine did not attribute unconditional all-conquering pretensions to the rights of human beings; nor do most of the people today who can be seen as human rights activists. They do, however, insist that human rights be taken seriously and be included among the powerful determinants of action, rather than being ignored or easily overwhelmed.

of man' depends entirely on the rhetoric of privileged use of the term 'right'.

Bentham simply postulated that for a claim to count as a right, it must have legal force, and any other use of the term 'right' – no matter how common – is simply mistaken. However, in so far as human rights are meant to be significant ethical claims, the pointer to the fact that they do not necessarily have legal force is as obvious as it is irrelevant to the nature of these claims.[4] The appropriate comparison is, surely, between a utility-based ethics (as championed by Bentham himself), which sees fundamental ethical importance in utilities but none – at least directly – in freedoms and liberties, and a human rights ethics that makes room for the basic importance of rights seen in terms of freedoms and corresponding obligations (as the advocates of 'rights of man' did).*

Just as utilitarian ethical reasoning takes the form of insisting that the utilities of the relevant persons must be taken into account in deciding what should be done, the human rights approach demands that the acknowledged rights of everyone, in the form of respecting freedoms and corresponding obligations, must be given ethical recognition. The relevant comparison lies in this important contrast, *not* in differentiating the legal force of legislated rights (for which Bentham's phrase 'the child of law' is an appropriate description) from the obvious absence of any legal standing generated by the *ethical* recognition of rights without any legislation or legal reinterpretation. Indeed, even as Bentham, the obsessive slayer of what he took to be legal pretensions, was busy writing down his dismissal of the 'rights of man' in 1791–2, the reach and range of ethical understanding of rights, based on the value of human freedom, were being powerfully explored by Thomas Paine's *Rights of Man* (1791, 1792), and by Mary Wollstonecraft's *A Vindication of the Rights of Men* (1790)

---

* The importance of freedoms and rights can of course be combined with giving weight to well-being, on which see Chapter 13, 'Happiness, Well-being and Capabilities'. However, in incorporating the priorities of utility and liberty in ethical reasoning, some consistency problems can arise, which have to be specifically addressed. That issue was discussed in Chapter 14, 'Equality and Liberty'; see also my *Collective Choice and Social Welfare* (1970), Chapter 6, and Kotaro Suzumura, 'Welfare, Rights and Social Choice Procedures', *Analyse & Kritik*, 18 (1996).

and *A Vindication of the Rights of Woman: with Strictures on Political and Moral Subjects* (1792).[5]

An ethical understanding of human rights clearly goes against seeing them as legal demands, and also against taking them to be, as in Bentham's view, legal pretensions. Ethical and legal rights do, of course, have motivational connections. There is, in fact, a different approach that is also law-oriented and which avoids Bentham's misapprehension, and sees the recognition of human rights as moral propositions that can serve as grounds for legislation. In a justly famous essay 'Are There Any Natural Rights?', published in 1955, Herbert Hart has argued that people 'speak of their moral rights mainly when advocating their incorporation in a legal system'.[6] He added that the concept of a right 'belongs to that branch of morality which is specifically concerned to determine when one person's freedom may be limited by another's and so to determine what actions may appropriately be made the subject of coercive legal rules'. Whereas Bentham saw rights as a 'child of law', Hart's view takes the form of seeing human rights as, in effect, *parents of law*: they motivate specific legislations.*

Hart is clearly right – there can be little doubt that the idea of moral rights can serve, and has often served in practice, as the basis of new legislation. It has frequently been utilized in this way, and this is indeed an important use of claims of human rights.† Whether or not the language of human rights is employed, claims that certain freedoms should be respected, and if possible guaranteed, have been the basis of powerful and effective political agitation in the past, for example in the suffragist movement that demanded voting rights for women, ultimately with success. Providing inspiration for legislation is certainly one way in which the ethical force of human rights has been constructively deployed, and Hart's qualified defence of the idea

---

* Joseph Raz has developed this perspective of seeing human rights as moral bases of legal initiatives. See his largely critical but ultimately constructive essay ('Human Rights without Foundations', forthcoming in Samantha Besson and John Tasioulas (eds), *The Philosophy of International Law* (Oxford: Oxford University Press, 2009)).
† That, for example, is precisely the way the diagnosis of inalienable rights was invoked in the American Declaration of Independence and reflected in the subsequent legislation, a route that has been well trodden in the legislative history of many countries in the world.

and usefulness of human rights in this specific context has been both illuminating and powerfully influential.* Many actual laws have been enacted by individual states, or by associations of states, which gave legal force to certain rights seen as basic human rights; for example, the European Court of Human Rights (ECHR), established in 1950 (following the European Convention), can consider cases brought by individuals from the signatory states against violations of human rights. This has been supplemented, for example, in the United Kingdom, by the Human Rights Act of 1998, aimed at incorporating the main provisions of the European Convention into domestic law, with the ECHR trying to ensure 'just satisfaction' of these provisions in domestic judgments. The 'legislative route' has indeed had much active use.

## BEYOND THE LEGISLATIVE ROUTE

We can nevertheless ask whether this is all there is to human rights. It is, in fact, important to see that the idea of human rights can be – and is – also used in several other ways as well, that is, other than motivating legislation. To acknowledge that the recognition of human rights can inspire fresh legislation aimed at those rights is not the same thing as taking the relevance of human rights to lie *exclusively* in determining what should 'appropriately be made the subject of coercive legal rules', and it would be particularly confusing to make that into the *definition* of human rights. Indeed, if human rights are seen as powerful moral claims, as Hart himself suggests by seeing them as 'moral rights', then surely we have reason for some catholicity in considering different avenues for promoting these moral claims. The ways and means of advancing the ethics of human rights need not be confined only to making new laws (even though sometimes legislation may turn out to be the right way to proceed); for example, social monitoring and other activist support provided by such organizations as Human Rights Watch, Amnesty International, OXFAM, Médecins

* On the enormous influence of Tom Paine on the emergence of a US public policy for poverty removal, see Gareth Stedman Jones, *An End to Poverty* (New York: Columbia University Press, 2005). See also Judith Blau and Alberto Moncada, *Justice in the United States* (2006).

sans Frontières, Save the Children, the Red Cross, or Action Aid (to consider many different types of NGOs) can help to advance the effective reach of acknowledged human rights. In many contexts, legislation may not, in fact, be involved at all.

There is an interesting question about the appropriate domain of the legislative route. It is sometimes presumed that if an unlegislated human right is important, then it would be best to try to legislate it into a precisely specified legal right. This may, however, be a mistake. For example, recognizing and defending a wife's right to have an effective voice in family decisions, often denied in traditionally sexist societies, may well be extremely important. And yet the advocates of this right, who emphasize, correctly, its far-reaching ethical and political relevance, could quite possibly agree that it is not sensible to make this human right into (in Herbert Hart's language) a 'coercive legal rule' (perhaps with the result that a husband would be taken in custody if he were to fail to consult his wife). The necessary changes would have to be brought about in other ways, including media exposure and criticism as well as public debates and agitation.* Because of the importance of communication, advocacy, exposure and informed public discussion, human rights can have influence without necessarily depending on coercive legislation.

Similarly, the ethical importance of a stammerer's liberty not to be slighted or ridiculed in public meetings may well be very important and demand protection, but this is not likely to be a good subject for punitive legislation (with fines or imprisonment of the badly behaved) to suppress the violation of the freedom of speech of the afflicted person. The protection of that human right would have to be sought elsewhere, for example through the influence of education and public discussion on civility and social conduct.† The effectiveness of the human rights perspective does not rest on seeing it invariably in terms of putative proposals for legislation.

In the approach pursued in this work, human rights are ethical

---

* This recognition would not have come as a surprise to Mary Wollstonecraft, who discussed a variety of ways in which women's rights could be advanced (*A Vindication of the Rights of Woman*, 1792).

† See Drucilla Cornell's illuminating discussion of the far-reaching role of civility and related values in *Defending Ideals* (New York: Routledge, 2004).

claims constitutively linked with the importance of human freedom, and the robustness of an argument that a particular claim can be seen as a human right has to be assessed through the scrutiny of public reasoning, involving open impartiality. Human rights can serve as the motivation for many different activities, from legislation and implementation of appropriate laws to enabling help from other people and public agitation against rights violations.* The different activities can contribute – separately and together – to advancing the realization of important human freedoms. It is perhaps important to emphasize that not only are there several ways of safeguarding and promoting human rights other than legislation, these different routes have considerable complementarity; for example, for effective enforcement of new human rights laws, public monitoring and pressure can make a considerable difference. The ethics of human rights can be made more effective through a variety of interrelated instruments and a versatility of ways and means. This is one of the reasons why it is important to give the general ethical status of human rights its due, rather than locking up the concept of human rights prematurely within the narrow box of legislation – real or ideal.

## RIGHTS AS FREEDOMS

Since declarations of human rights are, I have argued, ethical affirmations of the need to pay appropriate attention to the significance of freedoms incorporated in the formulation of human rights, an appropriate starting point for investigating the relevance of human

* Following the Universal Declaration of Human Rights in 1948, there have been many other declarations, often pioneered by the United Nations, varying from the Convention on the Prevention and Punishment of the Crime of Genocide, signed in 1951, and the International Covenant on Civil and Political Rights and on Economic, Social and Cultural Rights in 1966, to the Declaration on the Right to Development, signed in 1986. The approach is motivated by the idea that the ethical force of human rights is made more powerful in practice through giving it social recognition and an acknowledged status, even when no enforcement is instituted. On these issues, see also Arjun Sengupta, 'Realizing the Right to Development', *Development and Change*, 31 (2000) and 'The Human Right to Development', *Oxford Development Studies*, 32 (2004).

rights must be the importance of the freedoms underlying those rights. The importance of freedoms provides a foundational reason not only for affirming our own rights and liberties, but also for taking an interest in the freedoms and rights of others – going well beyond the pleasures and desire-fulfilment on which utilitarians concentrate.* Bentham's ground for choosing utility as the basis of ethical evaluation, which was more declaratory than justificatory, has to be contrasted and comparatively assessed with the reasons for focusing on freedoms.[7]

For a freedom to be included as a part of a human right, it clearly must be important enough to provide reasons for others to pay serious attention to it. There must be some 'threshold conditions' of relevance, including the importance of the freedom and the possibility of influencing its realization, for it to plausibly figure within the spectrum of human rights. In so far as some agreement is needed for the social framework of human rights, the agreement that would be sought is not only whether some particular freedom of a particular person has any ethical importance at all, but also whether the relevance of that freedom meets the threshold condition of having sufficient social importance to be included as a part of the human rights of that person, and correspondingly to generate obligations for others to see how they can help the person to realize those freedoms, a subject that will be more fully discussed presently.

The threshold condition may prevent, for a variety of reasons, particular freedoms from being the subject matter of human rights. To illustrate, it is not hard to argue that considerable importance should be attached to all five of the following freedoms of a person – let us call her Rehana:

(1) Rehana's freedom not to be assaulted;
(2) her freedom to be guaranteed some basic medical attention for a serious health problem;
(3) her freedom not to be called up regularly and at odd hours by her neighbours whom she detests;
(4) her freedom to achieve tranquillity, which is important for Rehana's good life;
(5) her 'freedom from fear' of some kind of detrimental action by

* The contrast was examined in Chapter 13, 'Happiness, Well-being and Capabilities'.

others (going beyond the freedom from the detrimental actions themselves).

Even though all five may be important in one way or another, it is not altogether implausible to argue that the first (the freedom not to be assaulted) is good subject matter for a human right, as is the second (the freedom to receive basic medical attention), but the third (the freedom not to be called up too often and too disturbingly by unloved neighbours) is not, in general, reason enough to cross the threshold of social relevance to qualify as a human right. In contrast, the fourth (the freedom to achieve tranquillity), while quite possibly extremely important for Rehana, may be too inward-looking and beyond the effective reach of social policies to be good subject matter for a human right. The exclusion of the right to tranquillity relates more to the content of that freedom and the difficulty of influencing it through social help, rather than to any presumption that it is not really important for Rehana.

The fifth alternative, involving fear of negative action by others, cannot really be sensibly judged without examining the basis of that fear, and how that can be removed. Some fears may, of course, be entirely cogent, such as the fear of the finiteness of life as a human predicament. Others may be hard to justify on reasoned grounds, and as Robert Goodin and Frank Jackson argue in their important essay 'Freedom from Fear', before determining whether we should 'rationally fear' something, we ought to 'ascertain the likelihood of that possibility, which might turn out to be very remote'.* Goodin and Jackson are right to conclude that 'freedom from fear' seen as 'being free from undue influences that irrationally frighten us, is . . . a genuinely important but genuinely elusive social goal'.[8] And yet freedom from fear can be something that a person has reason to want and that others – or the society – may have good reason to try to support,

---

* Goodin and Jackson cite former Vice President Dick Cheney's 'one percent doctrine' in this context: 'if there was even a one percent chance of terrorists getting a weapon of mass destruction – and there has been a small probability of such an occurrence for some time – the United States must now act as if it were a certainty' (Robert E. Goodin and Frank Jackson, 'Freedom from Fear', *Philosophy and Public Affairs*, 35 (2007), p. 249). See also Ron Suskind, *The One Percent Doctrine: Deep Inside America's Pursuit of Its Enemies Since 9/11* (New York: Simon & Schuster, 2006).

whether or not that fear is particularly rational. Panic attacks of mentally impaired persons certainly demand attention for medical reasons, and there is quite plausibly an argument for medical facilities in these cases, from the perspective of human rights: the irrationality of such fear need not exclude it from consideration in the rights perspective since the fear and suffering are genuine and may not be removable by the solitary efforts of the medically ill.

There can even be a reasonable case for placing elimination of the fear of terrorism within the concerns of human rights, even if the fears were stronger than probability statistics would justify. There is something to be concerned about in a general climate of fear, even if a fear of terrorist violence may be exaggerated in the aftermath of what happened in New York in 2001 or in London in 2005, or in Mumbai in 2008.* What makes sense from the perspective of human rights in the fifth case is open to scrutiny and assessment, and much would depend on the characterization of the necessary contingencies, in particular whether society or the state can help to eliminate these fears in a way that an individual acting separately cannot, no matter how rational he or she may try to be.†

---

* The trouble with Cheney's 'one percent doctrine' does not lie in the irrationality of fearing something terrible that may have only a 1 per cent chance, but in treating it as if 'it were a certainty', which is clearly irrational and does not lead to a particularly good way of deciding what should be done, especially by the state.

† The possibility of a person's freedom being compromised by interference of the state raises a different kind of question in the perspective of the 'republican' view of freedom, defended by Philip Pettit (*Republicanism: A Theory of Freedom and Government*, Oxford: Clarendon Press, 1997); it is also very similar to the 'Neo-Roman' view discussed by Quentin Skinner (*Liberty before Liberalism*, Cambridge: Cambridge University Press, 1998). That way of seeing the content of freedom does not turn pivotally on the high likelihood of state intervention but on the mere *possibility* of such interference which makes the liberties of the individuals contingent on the will of others. I have resisted the argument that this is the central content of freedom, though I have argued for making room for it within the broad spectrum of different aspects of freedom (see Chapter 14, 'Equality and Liberty'). As was also discussed earlier, whatever support Thomas Hobbes might have given to the republican view did in fact disappear in his later writings in the evolution of his theory of freedom; on this, see Quentin Skinner, *Hobbes and Republican Liberty* (Cambridge: Cambridge University Press, 2008). See also Richard Tuck, *Hobbes* (Oxford: Oxford University Press, 1989), and jointly edited with M. Silverthorne, *Hobbes: On the Citizen* (Cambridge: Cambridge University Press, 1998).

Obviously, we can have debates on how the threshold of relevance should be determined, and on whether a particular freedom crosses that threshold or not. The analyses of thresholds, related to the seriousness and social relevance of particular freedoms, has a significant place in the assessment of human rights. The possibility of disagreement always exists in pronouncements about human rights, and critical examination is part of what can be called the discipline of human rights. Indeed, even the viability of claims about human rights, which will be discussed presently, is closely linked with impartial scrutiny.

## OPPORTUNITY AND PROCESS ASPECTS OF FREEDOM

I turn now to a different distinction in the idea of freedom that may be of relevance to the theory of human rights. I have discussed earlier, particularly in Chapter 11 ('Lives, Freedoms and Capabilities'), the importance of the distinction between the 'opportunity aspect' and the 'process aspect' of freedom, and have pointed to the complex issues involved in assessing each aspect.[9] An example, a variation of the one discussed in Chapter 11,[10] can help to bring out the *separate* (though not necessarily independent) relevance of both substantive opportunities and the actual processes involved in a person's freedom. Consider a young person, let us call her Sula, who decides that she would like to go out dancing with a friend in the evening. To take care of some considerations that are not central to the issues involved here (but which could make the discussion unnecessarily complex), it is assumed that there are no particular safety risks involved in her going out, and that she has critically reflected on this decision and judged that going out would be sensible (indeed, as she sees it, the 'ideal' thing to do).

Now consider the threat of a violation of this freedom if some authoritarian guardians of society decide that she must not go dancing ('it is most unseemly'), and force her, in one way or another, to stay indoors. To see that there are two distinct issues involved in this one violation, consider an alternative case in which the authoritarian bosses decide that she must – absolutely *must* – go out ('you are expelled for the evening – stay away from us this evening – we are entertaining some important guests who would be upset by your behaviour and outlandish look'). There is clearly a violation of free-dom even in this case, and yet Sula is being forced to do something that she would have chosen to do anyway (she has to go out to go dancing), and this is readily seen when we compare the two alterna-tives: 'choosing freely to go out' and 'being forced to go out'. The latter involves an immediate violation of the 'process aspect' of Sula's freedom, since an action is being forced on her, even though it is an action she would have also freely chosen ('imagine spending time with those pompous guests, rather than dancing with Bob'). The opportunity aspect is affected too, though in an indirect way, since a plausible accounting of opportunities can include having options and Sula can *inter alia* include valuing free choice (an issue that was discussed in Chapter 11, 'Lives, Freedoms and Capabilities').

However, the violation of the opportunity aspect would be more substantial and manifest if Sula were not only forced to do something chosen by another, but in fact forced to do something she would not otherwise choose to do. The comparison between 'being forced to go out' when she would have chosen to go out anyway, and being forced to stay at home with boring guests, brings out this contrast, which lies primarily in the opportunity aspect, rather than in the process aspect. In being forced to stay at home to listen to pontificating bankers, Sula loses freedom in two different ways, related respectively to being forced to do something with no freedom of choice, *and* being obliged in particular to do something she would not choose to do.

Both processes and opportunities can figure in human rights. For the opportunity aspect of freedom, the idea of 'capability' – the real opportunity to achieve valuable functionings – would typically be a good way of formalizing freedoms, but issues related to the process aspect of freedom demand that we go beyond seeing freedoms only in terms of capabilities. A denial of 'due process' in being, say, imprisoned without a proper trial can be the subject matter of human rights – no matter whether the outcome of a fair trial could be expected to be any different or not.

## PERFECT AND IMPERFECT OBLIGATIONS

In the general approach being outlined here, the significance of rights relates ultimately to the importance of freedom including its opportunity aspect and the process aspect. What about the duties of others that may be associated with these rights? We can, again, proceed from the importance of freedoms, but now look at consequential connections that relate freedoms to obligations. If freedoms are seen as important (in line with what has been discussed earlier in the book), people have reason to ask what they should do to help each other in defending or promoting their respective freedoms. Since violation – or non-realization – of the freedoms underlying significant rights are bad things to happen (or bad social realizations), even others who are not themselves causing the violation, but who are in a position to help, have a reason to consider what they should do in this case.[11]

However, the move from a *reason* for action (to help another person), which is straightforward enough in a consequence-sensitive ethical system, to an actual *duty* to undertake that action is neither simple, nor sensibly covered under just one straightforward formula. Possible variations of reasoning can be entertained here, including the assessment of how – and how strongly – a person must take a reason for action for it to serve as the basis of a possible duty. There is, related to this question, the issue of sympathy, which makes other people's concerns – and the freedom to pursue them – among one's own derivative involvements. The reach and force of sympathy must be part of the conceptual underpinning of human rights. However, sympathy in the form of feeling other people's pain is not really essential in being able to see reasons to help a person in pain (or suffering from any other serious adversity or deprivation).*

The basic general obligation here must be to consider seriously what one can reasonably do to help the realization of another person's

---

* Adam Smith's distinction between helping others on grounds of 'sympathy' and doing the same because of 'generosity' or 'public spirit' is relevant here (*The Theory of Moral Sentiments*, 1759, 1790). On the distinction, see also Chapter 8, 'Rationality and Other People'.

freedom, taking note of its importance and influenceability, and of one's own circumstances and likely effectiveness. There are, of course, ambiguities here and scope for disagreement, but it does make a substantial difference in determining what one should do to acknowledge an obligation to consider this argument seriously. The necessity to ask that question (rather than to proceed on the possibly comforting assumption that we owe nothing to each other) can be the beginning of a more comprehensive line of ethical reasoning, and the territory of human rights belongs there. The reasoning cannot, however, end there. Given any person's limited abilities and reach, and the priorities between different types of obligations as well as the demands of other – non-deontological – concerns one may reasonably have, there is serious practical reasoning to be undertaken, in which one's various obligations (including imperfect obligations) must, directly or indirectly, figure.*

The recognition of human rights is not an insistence that everyone rises to help prevent any violation of any human right no matter where it occurs. It is, rather, an acknowledgement that if one is in a position to do something effective in preventing the violation of such a right, then one does have a good reason to do just that – a reason that must be taken into account in deciding what should be done. It is still possible that other obligations, or non-obligational concerns, may overwhelm the reason for the particular action in question, but the reason is not simply brushed away as being 'none of one's business'. There is a universal ethical demand here, but not one that automatically identifies contingency-free, ready-made actions.

The choice of actions related to these connections must allow for considerable variation, depending on the choice of priorities and weights as well as evaluative frameworks. There can also be some

---

* The importance of obligations related to one's power and effectiveness was discussed in Chapter 9, 'Plurality of Impartial Reasons', and 13, 'Happiness, Well-being and Capabilities'. This takes us well beyond obligations related to imagined 'social contracts' which are typically seen as being confined to people in one's own community or polity, rather than applying also to others outside these boundaries. On the general issue of global inclusiveness, without ignoring foreigners, or alternatively, without having to opt for some mechanical formula of what should be done for foreigners, see Kwame Anthony Appiah's illuminating discussion in *Cosmopolitanism: Ethics in a World of Strangers* (New York: W. W. Norton & Co., 2006), Chapter 10.

diversity in the way the causal analysis is pursued, particularly in dealing with actions that may be undertaken by other people who are also in a position to help or harm. There can, therefore, be much variation and possibly even some ambiguity in the specification of duties. However, the presence of some ambiguity in an idea is not a reason for dismissing the cogency of it. Ambiguity in the application of an otherwise significant concept is a reason for incorporating appropriate incompletenesses and allowable variations in the understanding of that concept itself (as I have argued in *Inequality Reexamined*, 1992).*

Indeed, loosely specified obligations must not be confused with no obligations at all. They belong, rather, to an important category of duties, as was mentioned earlier, which Immanuel Kant called 'imperfect obligations', and which can coexist with other – more fully specified – imperatives of 'perfect obligations'.[12] An example can help to illustrate the distinction between (as well as the dual presence of) different kinds of obligations. Consider a real-life case that occurred in Queens in New York in 1964: a woman, called Catherine (Kitty) Genovese, was repeatedly and then fatally assaulted in full view of others watching the event from their apartments, but her cries for assistance were ignored by the observers.† It is plausible to argue that three terrible things happened there, which are distinct but interrelated:

(1) *the woman's freedom* not to be assaulted was violated (this is, of course, the primary issue here);

(2) *the assaulter's duty* not to attack and murder was violated (a breach of a 'perfect obligation'); and

(3) *the others' duty* to provide reasonable help to a person facing

---

* See my *Inequality Reexamined* (Cambridge, MA: Harvard University Press, and Oxford: Clarendon Press, 1992), pp. 46–9, 131–5. This issue is also addressed in my 'Maximization and the Act of Choice', *Econometrica*, 65 (1997), reprinted in *Rationality and Freedom* (Cambridge, MA: Harvard University Press, 2002).

† One spectator from an apartment above did shout to the assailant to 'let that girl alone', but the help provided did not go beyond that solitary and very distant effort, and the police were not called until long after the assault. For a powerful discussion of the incident and the moral and psychological issues involved in it, see Philip Bobbitt, *The Shield of Achilles: War, Peace and the Course of History* (New York: Knopf, 2002), Chapter 15, 'The Kitty Genovese Incident and the War in Bosnia'.

assault and murder was also violated (a transgression of an 'imperfect' obligation).

These failings are interrelated, and bring out a complex pattern of correspondence of rights and duties in a structured ethics, which can contribute to explicating the evaluative framework of human rights.* The human rights perspective demands engagement with these diverse concerns.†

The presumed precision of legal rights is often contrasted with inescapable ambiguities in the ethical claims of human rights. This contrast, however, is not in itself a great embarrassment for ethical claims, including those of imperfect obligations, since a framework of normative reasoning can sensibly allow variations that cannot be easily accommodated in fully specified legal requirements. As Aristotle remarked in the *Nicomachean Ethics*, we have 'to look for precision in each class of things just so far as the nature of the subject admits'.[13]

Imperfect obligations, along with the inescapable ambiguities involved in that idea, can be avoided only if the rest of humanity – other than those directly involved – are exempted from any responsibility to try to do what they reasonably can to help. While that kind of general immunity might seem reasonable as far as *legal* requirements are concerned, the case for such impunity in the *ethical* domain would be hard to justify. As it happens, in the laws of some countries, there is even a legal demand to provide reasonable help to third parties; for example, in France there is provision for 'criminal liability of omissions' in the failure to provide reasonable help to others suffering from particular types of transgressions. Not surprisingly, ambiguities in the application of such laws have proved to be quite substantial

---

* In this analysis I do not go into the distinction between agent-specific and agent-neutral moral evaluations. The present line of characterization can be further extended through making room for position-specific assessments, as was discussed in Chapter 10, 'Realizations, Consequences and Agency'. See also my 'Rights and Agency', *Philosophy and Public Affairs*, 11 (1982), and 'Positional Objectivity', *Philosophy and Public Affairs*, 22 (1993).

† The obligational failure of the passive observers of Kitty Genovese's violation and murder relates to the diagnosis that it would have been reasonable for them to do something to help, including calling the police without delay. This did not happen: no one came out to scare away the assaulter and the police were called after – indeed, long after – the event.

and have been the subject of some legal discussion in recent years.[14] The ambiguity of duties of this type – whether in ethics or in law – would be difficult to avoid if the third-party obligations of others in general are given some room.

## FREEDOM AND INTERESTS

A pronouncement of human rights, as interpreted here, is an assertion of the importance of the freedoms that are identified and acclaimed in the formulation of the rights in question. For example, when the human right of a person not to be tortured is acknowledged, the importance of freedom from torture is reaffirmed and acclaimed for everyone,* and with this the confirmation of the need for others to consider what they can reasonably do to secure freedom from torture for all. For a would-be torturer, the demand is obviously quite straightforward: to refrain and desist (this is clearly a 'perfect obligation'). For others, too, there are responsibilities, even though they are less specific and generally consist of trying to do what one reasonably can in the circumstances (this would fall in the broad category of 'imperfect obligations'). The perfectly specified demand not to torture anyone is supplemented by the more general – and less exactly specified – requirement to consider the ways and means through which torture can be prevented and then to decide what one should, in this particular case, reasonably do.[15]

There is an interesting and important issue here concerning the competing claims of freedoms and interests as the basis of human rights. In contrast with the focus on freedoms here, Joseph Raz has developed, particularly in his insightful book, *The Morality of Freedom*, a powerful, interest-based theory of human rights: 'Rights ground requirements for action in the interest of other beings.'[16] I find Raz's approach attractive, not just because he is an old friend, from

---

* As Charles Beitz has pointed out, human rights play 'the role of a moral touchstone – a standard of assessment and criticism for domestic institutions, a standard of aspiration for their reform, and increasingly a standard of evaluation for the policies and practices of international economic and political institutions' ('Human Rights as a Common Concern', *American Political Science Review*, 95 (2001), p. 269).

whom, in discussions over a decade in Oxford (1977–87), I have learned a great deal, but mainly because he sketches out a line of reasoning that seems to have much understandable appeal.* The question must, however, be asked, whether the focus on the *interests* of different people as the foundational basis of rights, attractive as it is, is adequate for a theory of rights in general and human rights in particular. And, related to that question, we also have to ask: is the contrast between the perspective of freedom and that of interest significant?

There is certainly something of a contrast here. I have already touched on the profound importance of this contrast in general in a context very different from that of human rights. To consider an example discussed in Chapter 8,† the person sitting in a window seat finds a strong enough reason to pull the window shade down (thereby sacrificing his own enjoyment of the sun) to allow his neighbour to play a silly computer game that he wants to play. The reason involved, as seen by the occupant of the window seat, was not the 'interest' of

---

* For a similar claim, see also Thomas Scanlon, 'Rights and Interests', in Kaushik Basu and Ravi Kanbur (eds), *Arguments for a Better World* (2009). On a related, but different, point of disagreement with Scanlon from the same essay, I take the opportunity here of noting that there is some misinterpretation in his belief that if he were to accept my argument for the need to 'weigh' different claims based on rights, then what would be 'needed is a *ranking of rights*, which determines which right is to prevail in cases of conflict' (p. 76, italics added). The mathematics of weighing allows various weighting procedures, taking note of intensities, circumstances and consequences, without making us go for a straightforward 'lexical' priority of one type of right over another in all cases. This issue has been discussed earlier in Chapter 2, 'Rawls and Beyond' in the context of commenting on Rawls's choice of lexical priority for liberty (in every case against every contrary concern), rather than more sophisticated forms of weighting that could recognize the strong and special importance of liberty, without ignoring everything that competes with it. The point here also relates to Herbert Hart's argument that the claims of liberty may sensibly be outweighed if the exercise of the liberty involved leads to very unfavourable consequences for the well-being of people, even though liberty may win in other cases against considerations of well-being. Non-lexical weighting systems can accommodate the fairly common understanding that the conflict between competing concerns related to rights need not be resolved by pure 'typology' and a contextless 'ranking of rights' that is completely innocent of intensities and consequences. See also S. R. Osmani, 'The Sen System of Social Evaluation' in the same book, *Arguments for a Better World*.
† See Chapter 8, 'Rationality and Other People', pp. 192–3.

the game maniac (indeed, the window-seat occupant did not think the move enhanced the game-player's interest at all, quite the contrary), but the game enthusiast's 'freedom' to do what he wanted very much to do (whether or not it served his interest, as seen by the window-seat occupant or the game-player himself). The contrast between freedom and interest can be quite significant.

Now consider a different example – more in line with the kind of cases that figure in Raz's investigation of rights. A non-Londoner's freedom to travel to London to join a peaceful demonstration there (against, say, the 2003 US-led military intervention in Iraq) could be violated through some policy of exclusion by which the aspiring demonstrator could be prevented from joining in (this is an entirely hypothetical example; there was no such exclusion). If such a restriction were to be imposed, it would be manifestly a violation of the *freedom* of the excluded person (who does want to demonstrate), and correspondingly a violation of something in the person's *rights* if rights were to incorporate such freedoms. There is a direct connection in the reasoning here.

If, however, rights are grounded only on 'interests' (as opposed to 'freedoms') of the person involved, we shall have to consider whether it is in that person's *interest* to join such a demonstration about Iraq. And if the answer turns out to be that while it is a political priority of the potential demonstrator in question, it does not really serve his own 'interest' much or at all to join in the organized protesting, then the freedom to demonstrate in London could not be readily included within the orbit of human rights if they have to be based on the person's interest. If the interest-based understanding of rights were to be accepted, then the status of freedom as the basis of the human right to demonstrate would surely be undermined. If, on the other hand, freedoms are accepted as important because they give the person involved the liberty to choose (no matter whether he chooses to pursue personal interest or something very different) and lead his life in terms of his own priorities (whether interest-oriented or not), then an interest-based perspective on human rights must, ultimately, be inadequate.*

---

* As Richard Tuck has plausibly argued, 'one of the striking differences between a rights theory and Utilitarianism is that the ascription of a right to someone does not

Having said this, however, I must also note that it is possible to define 'interest' in such an expansive – and capacious – way that it encompasses all the concerns that a person chooses to pursue, irrespective of motivation. Indeed, in ordinary language, a violation of a person's freedom of choice is often identified with going against the person's interest.* If such a commodious view is taken of what counts as interest, then the gap between interests and freedoms would be, to that extent, removed.† If that proves to be the right way of seeing Raz's thesis, that would make our respective approaches to rights, to a great extent, congruent.

## THE PLAUSIBILITY OF ECONOMIC AND SOCIAL RIGHTS

I turn now from a general analysis of human rights to the analysis of some specific types of claims to be included within the category of human rights. There is a particular question about the inclusion of the so-called 'economic and social rights' and what are sometimes called 'welfare rights'.‡ These rights, which are seen by their proponents as

---

require us to make any estimate of the person's inner condition'. Tuck goes on to explain: 'If he has a right to stand in Trafalgar Square, it does not matter whether he gets pleasure from the act or a kind of Dostoevskian sense of tragedy; it does not even matter whether he chooses to perform the act on any particular occasion or not (compare Hobbes, for whom it does not matter, strictly, whether people do always seek to preserve themselves)' ('The Dangers of Natural Rights', *Harvard Journal of Law and Public Policy*, 20 (Summer 1997), pp. 689–90).

* I have argued against the reasoning behind that identification not only in Chapter 8, 'Rationality and Other People', but also in Chapters 9, 'Plurality of Impartial Reasons' and 13, 'Happiness, Well-being and Capabilities'.

† Indeed, Joseph Raz himself discusses the extensive connections between the notions of interests and freedoms, in his *Morality of Freedom* (1986), and even though I see a real distinction between the two, I am not trying to assess here how much of a difference there is between the implications of the two distinct ideas.

‡ The use of the word 'welfare' here is much narrower and more specific than its use as a synonym for well-being in general (as the term was used in the context of the discussion of the relevance of happiness or well-being in the assessment of justice (see Chapter 13, 'Happiness, Well-being and Capabilities'). 'Welfare rights' refer typically to entitlements to pensions, unemployment benefits and other such specific public provisions aimed at curtailing certain identified economic and social deprivations, and

important 'second generation' rights, such as a common entitlement to subsistence or to medical care, have mostly been added relatively recently to earlier enunciations of human rights, thereby vastly expanding the domain of human rights.[17] Even though these rights did not figure in the classic presentations of rights of human beings in, say, the American Declaration of Independence, or French 'rights of man', they are very much a part of the contemporary domain of what Cass Sunstein calls the 'rights revolution'.[18]

A big departure came in this area with the Universal Declaration of Human Rights in 1948. The new proclamation reflected a transformation in radical social thought in the changing world of the twentieth century. The contrast with the earlier proclamations is sharp indeed. It may be recollected that even President Abraham Lincoln had not initially demanded political and social rights for the slaves – only some minimal rights, concerning life, liberty and fruits of labour. The UN Declaration takes a much larger list of freedoms and claims under its protective umbrella. This includes not only basic political rights, but the right to work, the right to education, protection against unemployment and poverty, the right to join trade unions and even the right to just and favourable remuneration. This is quite a radical departure from the confined limits of the American Declaration of 1776 or the French affirmation of 1789.

The global politics of justice in the latter half of the twentieth century became more and more involved with these second-generation rights. The nature of global dialogue and of the types of reasoning entertained in the new era has come to reflect a much broader reading of agencies and the content of global responsibilities.[19] As Brian Barry has argued, 'the Universal Declaration of Human Rights has implications – and very important ones – for the international community as a whole, not just for individual states'.* The removal of global poverty

_____

the list of deprivations to be covered can be extended to include illiteracy and preventable ill-health.

* Brian Barry, *Why Social Justice Matters* (London: Polity Press, 2005), p. 28. Barry goes on to identify what he argues are the implications of this momentous recognition: 'If governments simply do not have the means of supplying everyone with such things as adequate nutrition and housing, pure drinking water, sanitation and a generally healthy environment, education and medical care, then the wealthy countries, individu-

and other economic and social deprivations has thus come to centre-stage in the global engagement with human rights, sometimes led by philosophers, such as Thomas Pogge.[20] The rapidly expanding interest on this subject has also had an impact on the demands of policy reforms. Indeed, as Deen Chatterjee has argued, 'the global recognition of endemic poverty and systemic inequity as serious human rights concerns has put pressure on individual countries for internal democratic reforms and made vivid the need for more just and effective international institutional directives'.[21] The second-generation rights have become a significant influence on the agenda of institutional reforms for the fulfilment of 'imperfect' global obligations, which have been explicitly but more often implicitly acknowledged.

The inclusion of second-generation rights makes it possible to integrate ethical issues underlying general ideas of global development with the demands of deliberative democracy, both of which connect with human rights and quite often with an understanding of the importance of advancing human capabilities. In his far-reaching contribution to this integration in *Ethics of Global Development: Agency, Capability, and Deliberative Democracy*, David Crocker points out that because agency and valuable capabilities are 'the basis for human rights, social justice, and both individual and collective duties, a development ethic will also examine how a globalized world is a help or a hindrance as individuals and institutions fulfil their moral obligation to respect rights'. He goes on to argue that 'the long-term goal of good and just development – whether national or global – must be to secure an adequate level of agency and morally basic capabilities for everyone in the world – regardless of nationality, ethnicity, religion, age, gender, or sexual preference'.[22] It is only with the inclusion of second-generation rights that this kind of a radical proposal for extended integration becomes possible, *without* taking us beyond the human rights framework.[23]

These newer inclusions of human rights, however, have been subjected to more specialized disputation, and the reasoning behind such rejection has been powerfully presented by a number of political

---

ally or in any combination, have an obligation to ensure that, by one means or another, the resources are forthcoming' (p. 28).

theorists and philosophers. The objections are not confined to the use of economic and social rights across the globe, and are intended to apply to the viability of these rights even within the limits of any particular nation. Two of the most powerful rejections have come from Maurice Cranston and Onora O'Neill.[24] I should hasten to explain that the arguments against the inclusion of these freedoms under human rights do not typically spring from ignoring their importance. Indeed, O'Neill's analysis of the philosophical issues – to a great extent along Kantian lines, involving poverty and hunger in the world – provides a far-reaching investigation of the momentous importance of these problems.[25] Rather, the proposed exclusions from the domain of human rights are related to the interpretation of the content and reach of the idea of human rights favoured by these critics, including O'Neill.

There are, in fact, two specific lines of reproach, which I shall call the 'institutionalization critique' and the 'feasibility critique'. The institutionalization critique, which is aimed particularly at economic and social rights, relates to the belief that real rights must involve an exact correspondence with precisely formulated correlate duties. Such a correspondence, it is argued, would exist only when a right is institutionalized. Onora O'Neill has presented the following criticism with clarity and force:

Unfortunately much writing and rhetoric on rights heedlessly proclaims universal rights to goods or services, and in particular 'welfare rights', as well as to other social, economic and cultural rights that are prominent in international Charters and Declarations, without showing what connects each presumed right-holder to some specified obligation-bearer(s), which leaves the content of these supposed rights wholly obscure . . . Some advocates of universal economic, social and cultural rights go no further than to emphasize that they *can* be institutionalized, which is true. But the point of difference is that they *must* be institutionalized: if they are not there is no right.[26]

In responding to this criticism, we have to invoke the understanding, already discussed, that obligations can be both perfect and imperfect. Even the classical 'first-generation' rights, like freedom from assault, can be seen as imposing imperfect obligations on others, as was illustrated with the example of the case of assault on Kitty Genovese in

public view in New York. Economic and social rights may similarly call for both perfect and imperfect obligations. There is a large area of fruitful public discussion, and possibly effective pressure, concerning what a particular society or a state – even an impoverished one – can do to prevent violations of certain basic economic or social rights (associated with, say, the prevalence of famines, or chronic under-nourishment, or absence of medical care).

Indeed, the supportive activities of social organizations are often aimed precisely at institutional change, and the activities are plausibly seen as part of imperfect obligations that individuals and groups have in a society where basic human rights are violated. Onora O'Neill is, of course, correct to see the importance of institutions for the realization of 'welfare rights' (and even for economic and social rights in general), but the ethical significance of these rights provides good grounds for seeking realization through their work in pressing for, or contributing to, changes in institutions as well as social attitudes. This can be done, for example, through agitation for new legislation, or through helping to generate greater awareness of the seriousness of the problem.* To deny the ethical status of these claims would be to ignore the reasoning that fires these constructive activities, including working for institutional changes of the kind that O'Neill would like, with good reason, to have for the realization of what the activists see as human rights.

The 'feasibility critique', which is not unrelated to the institutionalization critique, proceeds from the argument that even with the best of efforts, it may not be feasible to realize many of the alleged economic and social rights for all. This is an empirical observation of some interest on its own, but it is made into a criticism of the acceptance of these claimed rights on the basis of the presumption, largely undefended, that to be coherent human rights must be wholly accomplishable for all. If this presumption were accepted, that would have the effect of immediately putting many so-called economic and social

* The role of public discussion and the media in helping to bring about a reduction or removal of social and economic deprivations was discussed in Chapters 15, 'Democracy as Public Reason', and 16, 'The Practice of Democracy'.

rights outside the domain of possible human rights, especially in poorer societies. Maurice Cranston puts the argument thus:

The traditional political and civil rights are not difficult to institute. For the most part, they require governments, and other people generally, to leave a man alone ... The problems posed by claims to economic and social rights, however, are of another order altogether. How can the governments of those parts of Asia, Africa, and South America, where industrialization has hardly begun, be reasonably called upon to provide social security and holidays with pay for millions of people who inhabit those places and multiply so swiftly?[27]

Is this apparently plausible critique persuasive? I would argue that it is based on a confounding of the content of what an ethically acknowledged right must demand. Just as utilitarians want to pursue maximization of utilities and the viability of that approach is not compromised by the fact that there always remains scope for further improvement in utility achievements, human rights advocates want the *recognized* human rights to be maximally *realized*.[28] The viability of this approach does not crumble merely because further social changes may be needed at any point of time to make more and more of these acknowledged rights fully realizable and actually realized.*

Indeed, if feasibility were a necessary condition for people to have any rights, then not just social and economic rights, but all rights – even the right to liberty – would be nonsensical, given the infeasibility of ensuring the life and liberty of all against transgression. To guarantee that every person is 'left alone' has never been particularly easy (contrary to Cranston's claim). We cannot prevent the occurrence of murder somewhere or other every day. Nor, with the best of efforts, can we stop all mass killings, like those in Rwanda in 1994, or in New York on 11 September 2001, or in London, Madrid, Bali and Mumbai more recently. The confusion in dismissing claims to human rights on grounds of incomplete feasibility is that a not fully realized right is still a right, calling for remedial action. Non-realization does not, in itself, make a claimed right a non-right. Rather, it motivates further

---

* Affirmation of human rights is a call to action – a call for social change – and it is not parasitic on pre-existing feasibility. On this, see my 'Rights as Goals', in S. Guest and A. Milne (eds), *Equality and Discrimination: Essays in Freedom and Justice* (Stuttgart: Franz Steiner, 1985).

social action. The exclusion of all economic and social rights from the inner sanctum of human rights, keeping the space reserved only for liberty and other first-generation rights, attempts to draw a line in the sand that is hard to sustain.

## SCRUTINY, VIABILITY AND USE

I turn now to the postponed question about the viability of human rights. How can we judge the acceptability of claims to human rights and assess the challenges they may face? How would such a disputation – or a defence – proceed? To some extent, I have already answered the question indirectly, through defining human rights (or, perhaps more accurately, articulating the implicit definition behind the use of human rights) in a certain way. Like other ethical propositions that claim acceptability under impartial scrutiny, there is an implicit presumption in making pronouncements on human rights that the cogency of the underlying ethical claims would survive open and informed scrutiny. This involves the invoking of an interactive process of critical scrutiny with open impartiality (including being open to information coming *inter alia* from other societies and to arguments coming from far as well as near), which allows disputations on the content and reach of putative human rights.*

A claim that a certain freedom is important enough to be seen as a human right is also a claim that reasoned scrutiny would sustain that judgement. Such sustaining may indeed take place in many cases, but not whenever such claims are made. Sometimes we may be quite close to a general agreement, without getting universal acceptance. The advocates of particular human rights can be involved in active work to get their basic ideas accepted as widely as possible. No one, of course, expects that there will be complete unanimity in what everyone in the world actually wants, and there is little hope that, say, a dedicated racist or sexist will be invariably reformed by the force of public

---

* See the earlier discussion of public reasoning and open impartiality in Chapters 1, 'Reason and Objectivity', 5, 'Impartiality and Objectivity', and 6, 'Closed and Open Impartiality'.

argument. What sustainability of a judgement demands is a general appreciation of the reach of reasoning in favour of those rights, if and when others try to scrutinize the claims on an impartial basis.

In practice we do not, of course, have any actual worldwide undertaking of public scrutiny of putative human rights. Actions are undertaken on the basis of a general belief that if such impartial scrutiny were to occur, the claims made would be sustained. In the absence of powerful contrary arguments coming from well-informed and reflective critics, a presumption of sustainability tends to be made.[29] It is on that basis that many societies have introduced fresh human rights legislation and given power and voice to the advocates of human rights to particular freedoms, including non-discrimination between members of different races or between women and men, or the basic liberty to have reasonable freedom of speech. Advocates of the recognition of a wider class of human rights will tend, of course, to press for more, and the pursuit of human rights is understandably a continuing and interactive process.*

It must, however, be recognized that even with agreement on the affirmation of human rights, there can still be serious debate, particularly in the case of imperfect obligations, on the ways in which the attention that is owed to human rights should be best directed. There can also be debate on how the different types of human rights should be weighed against each other and their respective demands integrated together, and on how the claims of human rights should be consolidated with other evaluative concerns that may also deserve ethical attention.[30] The acceptance of a class of human rights will nevertheless still leave room for further discussion, disputation and argument – that is indeed the nature of the discipline.

The viability of ethical claims in the form of a declaration of human rights is ultimately dependent on the presumption of the claims' survivability in unobstructed discussion. Indeed, it is extremely important to understand this connection between human rights and public

---

* The Universal Declaration of Human Rights by the United Nations has been quite pivotal in bringing discussion and debate to a very important subject, and its impact on both reasoning and actions in the world has been quite remarkable. I have examined the achievements of that visionary move in my essay, 'The Power of a Declaration: Making Human Rights Real', *The New Republic*, 240 (4 February 2009).

reasoning, especially in relation to the demands of objectivity discussed in a more general context earlier in this work (particularly in Chapters 1 and 4–9). It can be reasonably argued that any general plausibility that these ethical claims – or their rejection – have is dependent on their survival when they encounter unobstructed discussion and scrutiny, along with adequately wide informational availability.

The force of a claim for a human right would indeed be seriously undermined if it were possible to show that it is unlikely to survive open public scrutiny. However, contrary to a commonly offered reason for scepticism and rejection of the idea of human rights, the case for it cannot be discarded simply by pointing to the fact – a much-invoked fact – that in repressive regimes across the globe, which do not allow open public discussion, or do not permit free access to information about the world outside the country, many of these human rights do not acquire serious public standing. The fact that monitoring of violations of human rights and the procedure of 'naming and shaming' can be so effective (at least, in putting the violators on the defensive) is some indication of the reach of public reasoning when information becomes available and ethical arguments are allowed rather than suppressed. Uncurbed critical scrutiny is essential for dismissal as well as for justification.

# 18

# Justice and the World

In the troubled English summer of 1816, James Mill, the utilitarian philosopher, wrote to David Ricardo, the great political economist of his time, about the effects of the drought on agricultural output. Mill was worried about the misery that would be an unavoidable result of the drought, 'the thought of which makes the flesh creep on one's bones – one third of the people must die'. If Mill's fatalism about famines and drought was striking, so was his faith in the demands of a rather simple version of utilitarian justice, geared only to reducing suffering. 'It would be a blessing,' Mill wrote, 'to take them [the starving population] into the streets and high ways, and cut their throats as we do with the pigs.' Ricardo expressed considerable sympathy for Mill's line of exasperated thought, and like Mill (James Mill, I hasten to emphasize, not John Stuart) expressed his disdain for social agitators who try to sow discontent with the established order by telling people, wrongly, that the government can help them. Ricardo wrote to Mill that he was 'sorry to see a disposition to inflame the minds of the lower orders by persuading them that legislation can afford them any relief'.[1]

David Ricardo's denunciation of inflammatory protests is understandable given his – and Mill's – belief that people threatened by famine resulting from the crop failure of 1816 could not, in any way, be saved. The general approach of this book is, however, inimical to that reproach. It is important to understand the reasons for this divergence.

First, what tends 'to inflame the minds' of suffering humanity cannot but be of immediate interest both to policy-making and to the diagnosis of injustice. A sense of injustice must be examined even if it turns out to be erroneously based, and it must, of course, be thoroughly pursued if it is well founded. And we cannot be sure whether it is erroneous or well founded without some investigation.* However, since injustices relate, often enough, to hardy social divisions, linked with divisions of class, gender, rank, location, religion, community and other established barriers, it is often difficult to surmount those barriers to have an objective analysis of the contrast between what is happening and what could have happened – a contrast that is central to the advancement of justice. We have to go through doubts, questions, arguments and scrutiny to move towards conclusions about whether and how justice can be advanced. An approach to justice that is particularly involved with the diagnoses of injustice, as this work is, must allow note to be taken of 'inflamed minds' as a prelude to critical scrutiny. Outrage can be used to motivate, rather than to replace, reasoning.

Second, even though David Ricardo was perhaps the most distinguished economist in Britain of his time, the arguments of those whom he took to be mere instigators of protest did not deserve such prompt dismissal. Those who were encouraging the people threatened by starvation to believe that government legislation and policy can mitigate hunger were actually more right than was Ricardo in his pessimism about the possibility of effective social relief. Indeed, good public policy can eliminate the incidence of starvation altogether. Close investigation of famines has brought out their easy preventability and the results support the pleading of the protesters, rather than upholding the formulaic – and somewhat lazy – dismissal by pillars of the establishment of the possibility of relief. A proper economic understanding of the causation and preventability of famines, with appropriate consideration of the diversity of the economic and political causes involved, shows the naivety of a mechanically food-based view of starvation, as recent economic investigations have shown.†

---

* On the relation between inadequately examined theories and their possibly dire consequences, which is a central issue in development analysis, see Sabina Alkire, 'Development: A Misconceived Theory Can Kill', in Christopher W. Morris, *Amartya Sen*, Contemporary Philosophy in Focus series (Cambridge: Cambridge University Press, forthcoming in 2009).
† The connection between famines and failures of entitlement to food (as opposed to food shortage per se) is analysed in my *Poverty and Famines: An Essay on Entitlement*

A famine is the result of many people not having enough food to eat, and it is, by itself, no evidence of there being not enough food to eat.[2] People who lose out altogether in the food battle, for one reason or another, can be given more market command rapidly enough, through various income-generation measures, including public employment, thus achieving a less unequal distribution of food in the economy (a means of famine prevention that is often used now – from India to Africa). The point here is not merely that David Ricardo's pessimism was unjustified, but also that contrary arguments cannot be sensibly dismissed without serious engagement.* There is a requirement for public reasoning, rather than prompt rejection of contrary beliefs, no matter how implausible those beliefs might initially look and how voluble the crude and rough protests might appear. Open-minded engagement in public reasoning is quite central to the pursuit of justice.

## WRATH AND REASONING

Resistance to injustice typically draws on both indignation and argument. Frustration and ire can help to motivate us, and yet ultimately we have to rely, for both assessment and for effectiveness, on reasoned scrutiny to obtain a plausible and sustainable understanding of the basis of those complaints (if any) and what can be done to address the underlying problems.

---

and Deprivation (Oxford: Clarendon Press, 1981). The ways and means of recreating lost food entitlements, for example through public work programmes, are also explored in my joint book with Jean Drèze, Hunger and Public Action (Oxford: Clarendon Press, 1989). There are many recent cases across the world in which severe food supply decline has been prevented from causing starvation through public policy that gives the most vulnerable an entitlement to minimally necessary food. The 'inflamed' minds of 'the lower orders' got things more nearly right than did the refined intellects of Ricardo and Mill.

* Based on empirical studies of actual experiences across the world, the effectiveness of well-thought-out public policy in removing 'unfreedoms' of various kinds, including the unfreedom of starvation, is discussed in my Development as Freedom (New York: Knopf, 1999). See also Dan Banik, Starvation and India's Democracy (London: Routledge, 2007).

The dual functions of indignation and reasoning are well illustrated by the attempts of Mary Wollstonecraft, the pioneering feminist thinker, to achieve a 'vindication of the rights of woman'.* There is plentiful expression of anger and exasperation in Wollstonecraft's discussion of the need for a radical rejection of the subjugation of women:

Let woman share the rights and she will emulate the virtues of man; for she must grow more perfect when emancipated, or justify the authority that chains such a weak being to her duty. – If the latter, it will be expedient to open a fresh trade with Russia for whips; a present which a father should always make to his son-in-law on his wedding day, that a husband may keep his whole family in order by the same means; and without any violation of justice reign, wielding this sceptre, sole master of his house, because he is the only being in it who has reason.[3]

In her two books on rights of men and women, Wollstonecraft's anger is not aimed only at inequities suffered by women; it is directed also at the treatment of other deprived groups of people, for example slaves in the United States and elsewhere.† And yet her classic writings are, ultimately, based on a strong appeal to reason. Angry rhetoric is consistently followed by reasoned arguments that Wollstonecraft wants her opponents to consider. In her letter to M. Talleyrand-Périgord, to whom her book, *A Vindication of the Rights of Woman*, is addressed, Wollstonecraft concludes by reaffirming her strong confidence in relying on reason:

I wish, Sir, to set some investigations of this kind afloat in France; and should they lead to a confirmation of my principles, when your [French] constitution is revised the Rights of Woman may be respected, if it be fully proved that reason calls for this respect, and loudly demands JUSTICE for one half of the human race.[4]

* I have discussed, and made considerable use of, Wollstonecraft's works earlier in this book. See also my discussion of some of her works in 'Mary, Mary, Quite Contrary: Mary Wollstonecraft and Contemporary Social Sciences', *Feminist Economics*, 11 (March 2005).
† Wollstonecraft's angry critique of Edmund Burke for ignoring the issue of slavery in supporting the freedom of independence-seeking white Americans was discussed in Chapter 5, 'Impartiality and Objectivity'.

The role and reach of reason are not undermined by the indignation that leads us to an investigation of the ideas underlying the nature and basis of the persistent inequities which characterized the world in which Wollstonecraft lived in the eighteenth century, as they do also the world in which we live today. While Wollstonecraft is quite remarkable in combining wrath and reasoning in the same work (indeed, alongside each other), even pure expressions of discontent and disappointment can make their own contributions to public reasoning if they are followed by investigation (perhaps undertaken by others) of whatever reasonable basis there might be for the indignation.

The appeal to reason in public, on which Mary Wollstonecraft insists, is an important feature of the approach to justice I have been trying to present in this book. Understanding the demands of justice is not any more of a solitarist exercise than any other discipline of human understanding.* When we try to determine how justice can be advanced, there is a basic need for public reasoning, involving arguments coming from different quarters and divergent perspectives. An engagement with contrary arguments does not, however, imply that we must expect to be able to settle the conflicting reasons in all cases and arrive at agreed positions on every issue. Complete resolution is neither a requirement of a person's own rationality, nor is it a condition of reasonable social choice, including a reason-based theory of justice.†

## JUSTICE BEING SEEN TO BE DONE

A preliminary question may be asked: why should a publicly reasoned agreement be seen as having any particular status in the soundness of a theory of justice? When Mary Wollstonecraft expressed the hope to

* As was discussed in Chapter 5, communication and discourse have significant roles to play in the understanding and assessment of moral and political claims. On this, see also Jürgen Habermas, *Justification and Application: Remarks on Discourse Ethics*, translated by Ciaran Cronin (Cambridge, MA: MIT Press, 1993).
† The demands of rationality and reasonableness were examined in Chapters 8, 'Rationality and Other People', and 9, 'Plurality of Impartial Reasons'.

There are indeed schools of thought which insist, explicitly or by implication, that all the distinct values must be reduced ultimately to a single source of importance. To some extent that search is fed by fear and panic about what is called non-commensurability – that is, irreducible diversity between distinct objects of value. This anxiety, based on the presumption of some alleged barriers to judging the relative importance of distinct objects, overlooks the fact that nearly all appraisals undertaken as a part of normal living involve prioritiz-ation and weighing of distinct concerns, and that there is nothing particularly special in the recognition that evaluation has to grapple with competing priorities.* The fact that we understand perfectly clearly that apples are not oranges, and that their virtues as food vary in different dimensions – from pleasure to nutrition – does not keep us transfixed with indecision every time we face a choice between the two in deciding what to eat. Those who are insistent that human beings cannot cope with determining what to do unless all values are somehow reduced to no more than one, are evidently comfortable with counting ('is it more or is it less?') but not with judgement ('is this more important than the other?').

The plurality of reasons that a theory of justice has to accommodate relates not only to the diversity of objects of value that the theory recognizes as significant, but also to the type of concerns for which the theory may make room, for example, on the importance of differ-ent kinds of equality or liberty.† Judgements about justice have to take on board the task of accommodating different kinds of reasons and evaluative concerns. The recognition that we can often prioritize and order the relative importance of competing considerations does not, however, indicate that all alternative scenarios can always be completely ordered, even by the same person. A person may have clear views on some rankings and yet not be sure enough about some other comparisons. The fact that a person can reason his or her way

---

David Hume, given the latter's proto-utilitarian inclinations. Bentham would, of course, fit the description more easily than Hume.
* This question was discussed in Chapter 11, 'Lives, Freedoms and Capabilities', in the specific context of evaluating the relative importance of distinct capabilities.
† The inescapable pluralities within the broad ideas of equality and liberty were examined in Chapter 14, 'Equality and Liberty'.

into rejecting slavery or the subjugation of women does not indicate that the same person must be able to decide with certainty whether a 40 per cent top rate of income tax would be better than – or more just than – a top rate of 39 per cent. Reasoned conclusions can easily take the form of partial rankings, and, as has been discussed earlier, there is nothing particularly defeatist in that acknowledgement.

## IMPARTIAL REASONING AND PARTIAL ORDERINGS

If incomplete resolution can be a part of the discipline of an individual's evaluative assessment, it plays an even more prominent part in what public reasoning can be expected to yield. When dealing with a group, there is need for accommodation not only of different individuals' respective partial rankings, but also of the extent of incompleteness that may exist in a shared partial ranking on which different individuals can reasonably agree.* It was Mary Wollstonecraft's claim that if and when people examine with impartiality the reasons for respecting women's basic freedoms, they will agree that 'reason calls for this respect'. The actual disagreements that exist may be removed through reasoning, helped by questioning established prejudices, vested interests and unexamined preconceptions. Many such agreements of real significance can be reached, but this is not to claim that every conceivable problem of social choice can be settled this way.

Plurality of reasons can sometimes pose no problem for a definitive decision, whereas in other cases it can pose a serious challenge. The case of the three children with claims on a flute, discussed in the Introduction, illustrated the possibility of an impasse in trying to decide what would be the just thing to do. But the acceptance of a diversity of considerations does not entail that an impasse would necessarily arise. Even in the case of the three children, it may turn out that the child who has made the flute, Carla, is also the poorest, or the only one who knows how to play the flute. Or it might be the

* This issue was discussed in Chapter 4, 'Voice and Social Choice'.

case that the deprivation of the poorest child, Bob, is so extreme, and his dependence on something to play with so important for a plausible life, that the poverty-based argument might come to dominate the judgement of justice. There can be a congruence of different reasons in many particular cases. The idea of justice does, it would seem, include cases of different types, with easy resolution in some instances and very hard decisional problems in others.

One implication of this line of reasoning is the recognition that a broad theory of justice that makes room for non-congruent consider-ations *within* the body of that broad theory need not thereby make itself incoherent, or unmanageable, or useless. Definite conclusions can emerge despite the plurality.* When the competing concerns reflected in that plurality have far-reaching merits, on the relative strength of which we remain partially undecided, then it would make good sense to try to see how far we can go even without resolving completely the problems of relative weights.† And sometimes we can go far enough for the theory to be of very considerable use in applica-tion, without sacrificing any of the rigorous demands of each compet-ing line of argument.

The competing criteria will yield different rankings of alternatives, with some shared elements and some divergent ones. The intersection – or the shared elements of the rankings – of the diverse orderings generated by the different priorities will yield a partial ordering that ranks some alternatives against each other with great clarity and internal consistency, while failing altogether to rank other pairs of

---

* This issue relates closely to the tendency of 'participants in legal controversies to try to produce incompletely theorized agreements on particular outcomes', as Cass Sunstein has discussed illuminatingly in his far-reaching essay, 'Incompletely Theorized Agreements', *Harvard Law Review*, 108 (May 1995). While Sunstein focuses on the possibility of a practical agreement without a consensus on the theory that lies behind that choice (and this is indeed an important issue in legal as well as non-legal decisions), I am trying to clarify a related but somewhat different question. It is being argued here that considerable heterogeneity of perspectives can be accommodated internally *within* a capacious theory, generating partially complete rankings which help to separate out plausible decisions (if not 'the best' decision) from clearly rejected pro-posals.

† The acceptance of an unresolvable diversity of views is, however, a last resort, rather than a first option, since all disagreements need to be critically examined and assessed first, as was discussed in Chapter 1, 'Reason and Objectivity'.

alternatives.* The commonality of the shared partial ranking can then be seen as the definitive outcome of that broad theory. Definitive conclusions are of use as and when they emerge, without there being any necessity to look for something of a guarantee that a 'best' or a 'right' choice must invariably emerge in every case in which we are tempted to invoke the idea of justice.

The basic issue here, which is simple enough when shorn of the analytical formalities, is the need to recognize that a complete theory of justice may well yield an incomplete ranking of alternative courses of decision, and that an agreed partial ranking will speak unambiguously in some cases and hold its silence in others. When Condorcet and Smith argued that the abolition of slavery would make the world far less unjust, they were asserting the possibility of ranking the world with and without slavery, in favour of the latter, that is, showing the superiority – and greater justice – of a world without slavery. In asserting such a conclusion they were not also making the further claim that all the alternatives that can be generated by variations of institutions and policies can be fully ranked against each other. Slavery as an institution can be assessed without evaluating – with the same definitiveness – all the other institutional choices the world faces. We do not live in an 'all or nothing' world.

It is important to emphasize, particularly to avoid a possible misunderstanding, that the agreed acceptance that is sought is not exactly the same thing as complete unanimity of different persons' *actual* preference rankings over the domain of the reasoned partial ordering. There is no presumption here that every slave-owner must opt for renunciation of his rights over other human beings – rights that are given to him by the established laws of the land. The claim that Smith or Condorcet or Wollstonecraft made was, rather, that arguments in defence of slavery would be overwhelmed by the case for abolition, given the requirements of public reasoning and the demands of impar-

* There are well-defined mathematical resolutions in the identification of the domain of clear-cut decisions when the intersection that emerges from surviving plural criteria has incompleteness, on which see my *Collective Choice and Social Welfare* (San Francisco, CA: Holden-Day, 1970; republished, Amsterdam: North-Holland, 1979); also 'Interpersonal Aggregation and Partial Comparability', *Econometrica*, 38 (1970), and 'Maximization and the Act of Choice', *Econometrica*, 65 (1997).

tiality. The elements of congruence of surviving impartial reasonings form the basis of a partial ordering underlying the claims of manifest enhancement of justice (as was discussed earlier). The basis of a partial ordering aimed at comparisons of justice is the congruence of the conclusions of impartial reasonings, which is not the same thing as the requirement of complete agreement of the personal preferences entertained by different individuals.*

## THE REACH OF PARTIAL RESOLUTIONS

To be useful, a social ranking must have some substantive coverage, but need not be complete. A theory of justice has to rely fundamentally on partial orderings based on the intersection – or commonality – of distinct rankings drawing on different reasons of justice that can all survive the scrutiny of public reasoning. In the particular example of the three approaches to allocating the flute (discussed in the Introduction), it is quite possible that no unanimity may emerge at all in the rankings between those three alternatives. If we are specifically concerned with a choice between precisely those three alternatives, we shall not be able to obtain help from a ranking that is incomplete in that choice.

On the other hand, there are a great many choices in which a partial ordering with specific gaps could give us a great deal of guidance. If, for example, through critical scrutiny of reasons of justice, we can place an alternative $x$ above both $y$ and $z$, without being able to rank $y$ and $z$ against each other, we can comfortably go for $x$, without having to resolve the dispute between $y$ and $z$. If we are less lucky, and scrutiny of reasons of justice does not yield a ranking between $x$ and $y$, but places both $x$ and $y$ above $z$, then we do not have a specific

* There is clearly a connection here with the distinction between the demands of 'rationality' and those of 'reasonableness' discussed in Chapters 8, 'Rationality and Other People' and 9, 'Plurality of Impartial Reasons'. That distinction has Rawlsian roots, but in its use here there is more acceptance of surviving plurality of impartial reasons than is accommodated in the Rawlsian principles of justice (as was discussed in Chapter 2, 'Rawls and Beyond').

choice that emerges from considerations of justice alone. And yet reasons of justice would still guide us to reject and shun altogether the alternative $z$, which is clearly inferior to both $x$ and $y$.

Partial orderings of this kind can have quite a significant reach; for example, if it is agreed that the status quo in the United States, which does not come anywhere close to universal medical coverage, is distinctly less just than a number of specific alternatives which offer different schemes of coverage for all, then on the grounds of justice we can reject the status quo of non-universal coverage, even if reasons of justice do not fully rank the alternatives that are all superior to the status quo. We have excellent reason to scrutinize and critically examine the arguments based on considerations of justice to see how far we can extend the partial ordering that emanates from that perspective. We have no great reason to turn down the help we get from the partial ordering that we end up with, even if it leaves some choices beyond reach. In the case of healthcare, we would have reason enough to press for universal medical care coverage through one of the specified ways, even if we are unable to agree on other issues of social choice.*

## A COMPARATIVE FRAMEWORK

Debates about justice – if they are going to relate to practicalities – cannot but be about comparisons. We do not abstain from comparisons even if we are unable to identify the perfectly just. For example, it may well turn out that the introduction of social policies that eliminate widespread hunger, or remove rampant illiteracy, can be endorsed by a reasoned agreement that it would be an advancement

---

* Rational choice would demand that one of the superior – but mutually unranked – alternatives be chosen, rather than sticking to the distinctly inferior status quo as a result of indecision regarding precisely which superior alternative is to be adopted. There is a lesson here from the old story of Buridan's ass that failed to determine which of two haystacks in front of it was the better one, and died of starvation thanks to indefinite dithering. The demands of reasoning and rationality with incomplete orderings are discussed in my 'Maximization and the Act of Choice', *Econometrica*, 65 (1997), and *Rationality and Freedom* (Cambridge, MA: Harvard University Press, 2002).

of justice. But the implementation of such policies could still leave out many improvements that we can propose individually and even accept socially. The identification of the transcendental requirements of a fully just society, if it were possible to make such an identification, would of course have a great many other demands on how to idealize an actual society – whether or not such changes could actually be implemented. Justice-enhancing changes or reforms demand comparative assessments, not simply an immaculate identification of '*the* just society' (or 'the just institutions').

If the reasoning here is right, an approach to justice can be both entirely acceptable in theory and eminently useable in practice, even without its being able to identify the demands of perfectly just societies (or the exact nature of 'just institutions'). The approach can include the understanding that different reasonable and impartial judges could sensibly differ on the identification – and even on the existence – of a transcendental alternative. Perhaps more importantly, the approach can recognize – and allow – the possibility that even a specific individual may not be fully resolved on the comparisons between the different alternatives, if he or she is unable to jettison, through critical scrutiny, every competing consideration save one.

Justice is an immensely important idea that has moved people in the past and will continue to move people in the future. And reasoning and critical scrutiny can indeed offer much to extend the reach and to sharpen the content of this momentous concept. And yet it would be a mistake to expect that every decisional problem for which the idea of justice might conceivably be relevant would, in fact, be resolved through reasoned scrutiny. And it would also be a mistake to assume, as was discussed earlier, that since not all disputes can be resolved through critical scrutiny, we do not have secure enough grounds to use the idea of justice in those cases in which reasoned scrutiny yields a conclusive judgement. We go as far as we reasonably can.

## JUSTICE AND OPEN IMPARTIALITY

A question that remains is the reach and coverage of the reasonable evaluations that come from many different sides and many different lands. Is the exercise of impartiality – or fairness – to be confined within the borders of a country with a shared sovereignty, or within a culture with shared attitudes and priorities? That issue, discussed earlier (in Chapters 5–9), can be usefully recapitulated, given its importance to the approach to justice presented in this book.

There are two principal grounds for requiring that the encounter of public reasoning about justice should go beyond the boundaries of a state or a region, and these are based respectively on the relevance of other people's *interests* for the sake of avoiding bias and being fair to others, and on the pertinence of other people's *perspectives* to broaden our own investigation of relevant principles, for the sake of avoiding under-scrutinized parochialism of values and presumptions in the local community.*

The first ground, related to the interdependence of interests, is easy enough to appreciate in the world in which we live. How America responds to the barbarity of 9/11 in New York affects the lives of many hundreds of millions elsewhere in the world – in Afghanistan and Iraq, of course, but also well beyond these direct fields of American action.† Similarly, how America succeeds in managing its present economic crisis (the crisis of 2008–9 that is unfolding as this book is being completed) will have a profound effect on other countries that have trade and financial relations with America and still others who have business relations with those who have commerce with America.

---

* These issues were discussed in Chapters 5, 'Impartiality and Objectivity', and 6, 'Closed and Open Impartiality'.

† We live today in a phase of world history that is peculiarly interconnected through war as well as peace. Indeed, as Eric Hobsbawm has noted, 'it would be easier to write about the subject of war and peace in the twentieth century if the difference between the two remained as clear-cut as it was supposed to be at the beginning of the century' (Hobsbawm, *Globalization, Democracy and Terrorism* (London: Little, Brown & Co., 2007), p. 19). See also Geir Lundestad and Olav Njølstad (eds), *War and Peace in the 20th Century and Beyond* (London: World Scientific, 2002), and Chris Patten, *What Next? Surviving the Twenty-first Century* (London: Allen Lane, 2008).

Further, AIDS and other epidemics have moved from country to country, and from continent to continent; equally, the medicines developed and produced in some parts of the world are important for the lives and freedoms of people far away. Many other avenues of interdependence can also be readily identified.

The interdependences also include the impact of a sense of injustice in one country on lives and freedom in others. 'Injustice anywhere is a threat to justice everywhere,' said Dr Martin Luther King, Jr., in April 1963, in a letter from Birmingham jail.* Discontent based on injustice in one country can rapidly spread to other lands: our 'neighbourhoods' now effectively extend across the world.† Our involvement with others through trade and communication is remarkably extensive in the contemporary world, and further, our global contacts, in terms of literary, artistic and scientific endeavour, make it hard for us to expect that an adequate consideration of diverse interests or concerns can be plausibly confined to the citizenry of any given country, ignoring all others.


## NON-PAROCHIALISM AS A
## REQUIREMENT OF JUSTICE

In addition to the global features of interdependent interests, there is a second ground – that of avoidance of the trap of parochialism – for accepting the necessity of taking an 'open' approach to examining the demands of impartiality. If the discussion of the demands of justice is confined to a particular locality – a country or even a larger region – there is a possible danger of ignoring or neglecting many challenging counter-arguments that might not have come up in local political debates, or been accommodated in the discourses confined to the local culture, but which are eminently worth considering, in an impartial perspective. It is this limitation of reliance on parochial reasoning, linked with national traditions and regional understandings, that

* For the background to King's judgement on the relevance of global justice for local justice, see *The Autobiography of Martin Luther King, Jr.*, edited by Clayborne Carson (New York: Werner Books, 2001).
† This has been discussed in Chapter 7, 'Position, Relevance and Illusion'.

Adam Smith wanted to resist. He did so by using the device of the impartial spectator, in the form of a thought-experiment that asked what would a particular practice or procedure look like to a disinterested person – from far or near.*

Smith was particularly concerned about avoiding the grip of parochialism in jurisprudence and moral and political reasoning. In a chapter entitled 'On the Influence of Custom and Fashion upon the Sentiments of Moral Approbation and Disapprobation', he gives various examples of how discussions confined within a given society can be incarcerated within a seriously narrow understanding.

> ... the murder of new-born infants was a practice allowed of in almost all the states of Greece, even among the polite and civilized Athenians; and whenever the circumstances of the parent rendered it inconvenient to bring up the child, to abandon it to hunger, or to wild beasts, was regarded without blame or censure ... Uninterrupted custom had by this time so thoroughly authorized the practice, that not only the loose maxims of the world tolerated this barbarous prerogative, but even the doctrine of philosophers, which ought to have been more just and accurate, was led away by the established custom, and upon this as upon many other occasions, instead of censuring, supported the horrible abuse, by far-fetched considerations of public utility. Aristotle talks of it as of what the magistrate ought upon many occasions to encourage. The humane Plato is of the same opinion, and, with all that love of mankind which seems to animate all his writings, nowhere marks this practice with disapprobation.[5]

Adam Smith's insistence that we must *inter alia* view our sentiments from 'a certain distance from us' is thus motivated by the objective of scrutinizing not only the influence of vested interests, but also the captivating hold of entrenched traditions and customs.

While Smith's example of infanticide remains sadly apposite today,

---

* Smith's approach of the impartial spectator was examined in Chapter 6, 'Closed and Open Impartiality'. It is important to recognize that the device of the impartial spectator is used by Smith to open up questioning, rather than close down a debate with a formulaic answer allegedly derived from the impartial spectator seen as a definitive arbitrator. For Smith, the impartial spectator, who raises a great many relevant questions, is a part of the discipline of impartial reasoning, and it is in that sense that the idea has been used in this work.

though only in a few societies, some of his other examples have relevance to many other contemporary societies as well. This applies, for instance, to his insistence that 'the eyes of the rest of mankind' must be invoked to understand whether 'a punishment appears equitable'.[6] I suppose even the practice of lynching of identified 'miscreants' appeared to be perfectly just and equitable to the strong-armed enforcers of order and decency in the American South, not very long ago.* Even today, scrutiny from a 'distance' may be useful for practices as different as the stoning of adulterous women in the Taliban's Afghanistan, selective abortion of female foetuses in China, Korea and parts of India,† and widespread use of capital punishment in China, or for that matter in the United States (with or without the celebratory public jubilations that are not entirely unknown in some parts of the country).‡ Closed impartiality lacks something of the quality that makes impartiality – and fairness – so central to the idea of justice.

The relevance of distant perspectives has a clear bearing on some current debates in the United States, for example that in the Supreme Court in 2005, on the appropriateness of death sentence for crimes committed in a person's juvenile years. The demands of justice being seen to be done, even in a country like the United States cannot entirely neglect the understanding that may be generated by asking questions about how the problem is assessed in other countries in the world, from Europe and Brazil to India and Japan. The majority judgment of the Court, as it happens, was against the use of the death sentence for a crime that was committed in juvenile years, even

* See, for example, Walter Johnson's study of the ideas surrounding slave markets in the south of the United States: *Soul by Soul: Life inside the Antebellum Slave Market* (Cambridge, MA: Harvard University Press, 1999).
† On this, see my 'The Many Faces of Gender Inequality', *The New Republic*, 522 (17 September 2001), and *Frontline*, 18 (2001).
‡ Amnesty International reports that of the 2,390 people known to have been executed in 2008, 1,718 were in China, followed by Iran (346), Saudi Arabia (102), the United States (37) and Pakistan (36). In the whole of the two continents of North and South America, there is 'only one state – the United States – [that] consistently executes' ('Report Says Executions Doubled Worldwide', *New York Times*, 25 March 2009).

though the execution would take place after the person had reached adulthood.*

With the change in the composition of the US Supreme Court, this judgment may no longer be easy to sustain. In an explicit statement at his confirmation hearing, the current Chief Justice, John G. Roberts, Jr., has expressed his agreement with the minority opinion of the court, which would have allowed execution for a murder committed by a minor person once he or she had reached adulthood: 'If we're relying on a decision from a German judge about what our Constitution means, no president accountable to the people appointed that judge . . . And yet he's playing a role in shaping the law that binds the people in this country.'[7] To this, Justice Ginsburg, who voted with the majority of the Supreme Court at the time of the judgment, has responded: 'Why shouldn't we look to the wisdom of a judge from abroad with at least as much ease as we would read a law review article written by a professor?'[8]

General wisdom, including its connection with law, is certainly one issue, and Ginsburg is right to think that it can come from abroad as well as home.† But there is a more specific point of relevance to the debate, made by Adam Smith, that distant judgments are particularly important to consider and scrutinize in order to avoid being trapped in local or national parochialism. It is for that reason that Smith argued for taking note of what is seen by 'the eyes of the rest of mankind'. In denying the appropriateness of capital punishment in the case of murder committed by a minor, the majority in the Supreme Court did not simply 'defer to like-minded foreigners' (as Justice Scalia, who wrote a dissenting note at the time of the court judgment, suggested). Scrutiny from 'a distance' can be very useful in order to arrive at grounded but open-minded judgements, taking note of

* *Roper* v. *Simmons*, 543 U.S. 551, 2005.
† Unlike some of the US Supreme Court judges, who took the view that it would be wrong to pay attention to foreigners and their evaluations in making legal judgments in the United States, civil society in America is not insistent on ignoring the ideas of foreigners (from Jesus Christ to Mohandas Gandhi and Nelson Mandela) that have a bearing on the demands of law and justice today. It is quite a specialized thesis to assert that while it was OK for Jefferson to be influenced by the arguments of foreigners, the ears should now be closed to arguments presented outside the United States.

questions that consideration of non-local perspectives can help to generate (as Smith discussed in some detail).

Indeed, the apparent cogency of parochial values often turns on the lack of knowledge of what has proved feasible in the experiences of other people. The inertial defence of infanticide in ancient Greece, on which Smith wrote, was clearly influenced by the lack of knowledge of other societies in which infanticide is ruled out and yet which do not crumble into chaos and crisis as a result. Despite the undoubted importance of 'local knowledge', global knowledge has some value too, and can contribute to the debates on local values and practices.

To listen to distant voices, which is part of Adam Smith's exercise of invoking the 'impartial spectator', does not require us to be respectful of every argument that may come from abroad. Willingness to consider an argument proposed elsewhere is very far from a predisposition to accept all such proposals. We may reject a great many of the proposed arguments – sometimes even all of them – and yet there would remain particular cases of reasoning that could make us reconsider our own understandings and views, linked with the experiences and conventions entrenched in a country, or in a culture. Arguments that may first appear to be 'outlandish' (especially when they do actually come, initially, from other lands) may help to enrich our thinking if we try to engage with the reasoning behind these locally atypical contentions. Many people in the USA or China may not be impressed by the mere fact that many other countries – the bulk of Europe for example – do not allow capital punishment. And yet if reasons are important, there would be, in general, a strong case for examining the justificatory arguments against capital punishment that are used elsewhere.*

---

* There would, of course, be a similar case for continuing to examine the arguments in favour of using capital punishment that may emanate from the USA or China, or any other country that makes substantial use of that system of punishment.

## JUSTICE, DEMOCRACY AND
## GLOBAL REASONING

Giving serious consideration to distinct and contrary arguments and analyses coming from different quarters is a participatory process that has much in common with the working of democracy through public reasoning, which was explored earlier.* The two are not of course the same, since democracy is concerned with a political assessment – leading us (in this interpretation) to 'government by discussion' – whereas undertaking non-self-centred and non-parochial scrutiny through paying attention to distant perspectives may be largely motivated by the demands of objectivity. And yet there are common features, and indeed, even the demands of democracy can be (at least in one interpretation) seen as ways of enhancing the objectivity of the political process.† It can be asked, in this context, what the implications of these recognitions are for the demands of global justice and also for the nature and requirements of global democracy.

The point is often made, with evident plausibility, that, for the foreseeable future, it is really impossible to have a global state, and therefore *a fortiori* a global democratic state. This is indeed so, and yet if democracy is seen in terms of public reasoning, then the practice of global democracy need not be put in indefinite cold storage. Voices that can make a difference come from several sources, including global institutions as well as less formal communications and exchanges. These articulations are not, of course, perfect for the purpose of global arguments, but they do exist and actually operate with some effectiveness, and they can be made more effective through supporting the institutions that help the dissemination of information and enhance the opportunities for discussions across borders. The plurality of sources enriches the reach of global democracy seen in this light.‡

* See Chapters 15, 'Democracy as Public Reason', 16, 'The Practice of Democracy', and 17, 'Human Rights and Global Imperatives'.
† See Chapter 15, 'Democracy as Public Reason'.
‡ Just as in the assessment of justice, in which the case for comparisons is strong (as has been argued throughout this work), for democracy too the central question is not so much the characterization of an imagined perfect democracy (even if there could

Many institutions have a role here, including the United Nations and the institutions associated with it, but there is also the committed work of citizens' organizations, of many NGOs and of parts of the news media. There is also an important role for the initiatives taken by a great many individual activists, working together. Washington and London may have been irritated by the widely dispersed criticism of the Coalition strategy in Iraq, just as Paris or Tokyo may be appalled by the spectacular vilification of global business in parts of the so-called 'anti-globalization' protests – one of the most globalized movements in the world today. The points that the protesters make are not invariably sensible (sometimes not at all), but many of them do ask very relevant questions and thus contribute constructively to public reasoning.

The distribution of the benefits of global relations depends not only on domestic policies, but also on a variety of international social arrangements, including trade agreements, patent laws, global health initiatives, international educational provisions, facilities for techno-logical dissemination, ecological and environmental restraint, treat-ment of accumulated debts (often incurred by irresponsible military rulers of the past), and the restraining of conflicts and local wars. These are all eminently discussable issues which could be fruitful subjects for global dialogue, including criticisms coming from far as well as near.*

Active public agitation, news commentary and open discussion are

---

be agreement on what it would be like), but how the reach and vigour of democracy can be enhanced. See also Chapters 15, 'Democracy as Public Reason', and 16, 'The Practice of Democracy'.

* The global reach of voices coming from previously ignored nations is also much larger now in what Fareed Zakaria calls 'the post-American world' at a time when a 'great transformation is taking place around the world' (Zakaria, *The Post-American World* (New York: W. W. Norton & Co., 2008), p. 1). That is certainly an important change, but there also remains the need to go beyond voices coming from countries with recent economic success (including, in different ways, China, Brazil, India and others), which speak more forcefully now, but often do not represent the concerns and views of people in countries with lesser economic stride (including much of Africa and parts of Latin America). There is also the need, in any country, to go beyond the voices of governments, military leaders, business tycoons and others in commanding positions, who tend to get an easy hearing across borders, and to pay attention to the civil societies and less powerful people in different countries around the world.

among the ways in which global democracy can be pursued, even without waiting for the global state. The challenge today is the strengthening of this already functioning participatory process, on which the pursuit of global justice will to a great extent depend. It is not a negligible cause.

## SOCIAL CONTRACT VERSUS SOCIAL CHOICE

If the reliance on public reasoning is an important aspect of the approach to justice presented in this work, so is the form in which questions of justice are asked. There is a strong case, I have argued, for replacing what I have been calling transcendental institutionalism – that underlies most of the mainstream approaches to justice in contemporary political philosophy, including John Rawls's theory of justice as fairness – by focusing questions of justice, first, on assessments of social realizations, that is, on what actually happens (rather than merely on the appraisal of institutions and arrangements); and second, on comparative issues of enhancement of justice (rather than trying to identify perfectly just arrangements). That programme, which was outlined in the Introduction, has been followed throughout the book, making use of the demands of impartiality in open public reasoning.

The approach developed in this book is much influenced by the tradition of social choice theory (initiated by Condorcet in the eighteenth century and firmly established by Kenneth Arrow in our own time), and concentrates, as the discipline of social choice does, on making evaluative comparisons over distinct social realizations.* In

* The pioneering contribution to modern social choice theory was undoubtedly Kenneth Arrow's path-breaking book *Social Choice and Individual Values* (New York: John Wiley, 1951). But the elegance and reach of Arrow's astonishing 'impossibility theorem' presented in that book inclined many readers to assume that social choice theory must be forever preoccupied with tackling 'impossibilities' regarding rational social choice. In fact, the framework used by Arrow, with some small but effective extensions, can be the basis of constructive social analysis as well (on this see my *Collective Choice and Social Welfare* (San Francisco, CA: Holden-Day, 1970; republished, Amsterdam: North-Holland, 1979)). The usability and contribution of

this respect, the approach here also has important similarities with the works of Adam Smith, Jeremy Bentham, John Stuart Mill and Karl Marx, among others.*

While the roots of the approach go back to the Enlightenment, there is a significant contrast with another tradition particularly cultivated over that period – the discipline of reasoning about justice in terms of the idea of a social contract. The contractarian tradition goes back at least to Thomas Hobbes, but also had major contributions from Locke, Rousseau and Kant, and in our time from leading philosophical theorists from Rawls to Nozick, Gauthier, Dworkin and others. In opting for the social choice approach rather than that of the social contract, it is not of course my intention to deny the understanding and illumination that have been generated by the latter approach to justice. However, enlightening as the social contract tradition is, I have argued that its limitations in providing an underpinning for a theory of justice with adequate reach are so strong that it ultimately serves partly as a barrier to practical reason on justice.

The theory of justice, which is most widely used now and which has served as the point of departure for this work is, of course, the theory of 'justice as fairness' presented by John Rawls. Even though Rawls's broad political analysis has many other elements, his justice as fairness has the characteristics of being directly concerned only with the identification of just institutions. There is a transcendentalism here, even though (as was discussed earlier) Rawls made deeply enlightening observations on comparative issues and also tried to take note of possible disagreements on the nature of a perfectly just society.†

Rawls focused on institutions as the subject matter of his principles of justice. His concentration on institutional choice does not, however, reflect his lack of interest in social realizations. The social realizations

---

social choice theory for the analysis of justice was discussed in Chapter 4, 'Voice and Social Choice'.

\* I have also discussed earlier the similarity between the approach here and the long Indian tradition of seeing justice as *nyaya* (concentrating on comprehensive outcomes), rather than as *niti* (focusing on arrangements and institutions). On this, see the Introduction and also Chapter 3, 'Institutions and Persons'.

† See the discussion on this in the Introduction and in Chapter 2, 'Rawls and Beyond'.

are assumed in Rawls's 'justice as fairness' to be determined by a combination of just institutions and fully compliant behaviour by all to make a predictable transition from institutions to states of affairs. This is related to Rawls's attempt at getting to a perfectly just society with a combination of ideal institutions and corresponding ideal behaviour.* In a world where those extremely demanding behavioural assumptions do not hold, the institutional choices made will tend not to deliver the kind of society that would have strong claims to being seen as perfectly just.

## DIFFERENCES AND COMMONALITIES

In a memorable observation in the *Leviathan*, Thomas Hobbes noted that the lives of people were 'nasty, brutish and short'. That was a good starting point for a theory of justice in 1651, and I am afraid it is a still good starting point for a theory of justice today, since the lives of so many people across the world have exactly those dire features, despite the substantial material progress of others. Indeed, a good deal of the theory presented here has been directly concerned with people's lives and capabilities, and the deprivation and suppression suffered.† Even though Hobbes moved on from his powerful characterization of human deprivation to the idealist approach of a social contract (the limitations of which I have tried to discuss), there can be little doubt about the life-enhancing motivations that inspired

---

* There is, however, some lacuna here (as was discussed earlier) since Rawls does not demand sufficiently selfless behaviour to make it redundant to accommodate inequalities for the sake of incentives. This is so despite his evident egalitarianism, which would make us think that he would have found a society without incentive-relative inequality to have a better claim to be seen as perfectly just. By restraining his behavioural demands in line with allowing incentive-based inequalities (on which G. A. Cohen has complained with reason), Rawls makes a compromise towards pragmatism at the cost of an imaginary ideal. But questions of realism arise with the other demanding behavioural assumptions that Rawls does in fact make. The issue was discussed in Chapter 2, 'Rawls and Beyond'.

† See Chapter 11, 'Lives, Freedoms and Capabilities', but also Chapters 10, 'Realizations, Consequences and Agency', 12, 'Capabilities and Resources', 13, 'Happiness, Well-being and Capabilities', and 14, 'Equality and Liberty'.

Hobbes. Much the same thing can be said about the theories of justice of Rawls or Dworkin or Nagel today, for example, even though formally they have anchored their principles of justice to certain arrangements and rules (thereby going in the direction of *niti*, rather than *nyaya*), rather than directly to social realizations and human lives and freedoms. The connections between the disparate theories of justice have to be firmly noted since, in the debates about different theories, the focus tends to be on differences rather than on similarities.*

As this book is completed, I realize that I too have largely succumbed to the analytical temptation to concentrate on distinctions and to highlight contrasts. And yet there is an important shared involvement in being concerned with justice in the first place. No matter where our theories of justice take us, we all have reasons to be grateful for the recent intellectual animation around them, which has been, to a great extent, initiated and inspired by John Rawls's pioneering move in this field, beginning with his outstanding paper in 1958 ('Justice as Fairness').

Philosophy can – and does – produce extraordinarily interesting and important work on a variety of subjects that have nothing to do with the deprivations and inequities and unfreedoms of human lives. This is as it should be, and there is much to rejoice in the expansion and consolidation of the horizon of our understanding in every field of human curiosity. However, philosophy can also play a part in bringing more discipline and greater reach to reflections on values and priorities as well as on the denials, subjugations and humiliations from which human beings suffer across the world. A shared commitment of

---

* For example, while I find Barbara Herman's excellent arguments on the reach and importance of what she calls 'moral literacy' to be extremely illuminating, I cannot but resist her claim that 'most of what is required of us individually in this way of helping strangers falls under the general obligation to support just institutions' (Herman, *Moral Literacy* (Cambridge, MA: Harvard University Press, 2007), p. 223). One could hope that strangers badly in need would have some direct claim to just consideration by others at home and abroad, not merely through 'the obligation to support just institutions', particularly when just institutions are derived from 'an approximately Kantian or liberal account of social justice, based in something like a nation or a state' (Herman, p. 222). The limitations of an institution-focused view of justice with direct reach only within a nation or a state was discussed in the Introduction, and also in Chapters 2–7.

theories of justice is to take these issues seriously and to see what they can do in terms of practical reasoning about justice and injustice in the world. If epistemic curiosity about the world is one tendency that many people have, concern about goodness, rightness and justness also has a powerful presence – manifest or latent – in our minds. Distinct theories of justice may compete in finding the right use of that concern, but they share the significant feature of being involved in the same pursuit.

Many years ago, in a justly famous paper called 'What Is It Like to Be a Bat?', Thomas Nagel presented some foundational ideas on the mind–body problem.* The pursuit of a theory of justice has something to do with a similar question: *what is it like to be a human being?* In his paper, Nagel too was actually involved with human beings, and only very marginally with bats. He argued powerfully against the cogency of understanding consciousness and mental phenomena by trying to see them in terms of the corresponding physical phenomena (as is attempted by many scientists and some philosophers), and in particular, he differentiated the nature of consciousness from the connections – causal or associative – that may link it to bodily operations.† Those distinctions remain, and my reason for asking what it is like to be a human being is different – it relates to the feelings, concerns and mental abilities that we share as human beings.

In arguing that the pursuit of a theory of justice has something to do with the kind of creatures we human beings are, it is not at all my contention that debates between theories of justice can be plausibly settled by going back to features of human nature, rather to note the fact that a number of different theories of justice share some common presumptions about what it is like to be a human being. We could have been creatures incapable of sympathy, unmoved by the pain and

---

* Thomas Nagel, 'What Is It Like to Be a Bat?' *The Philosophical Review*, 83 (1974).
† Cf. Michael Polanyi's argument that an understanding of operations at a 'higher' level cannot be accounted for by the laws governing its particulars forming a 'lower' level, and his disputation of 'the predominant view of biologists – that a mechanical explanation of living functions amounts to their explanation in terms of physics and chemistry' (*The Tacit Dimension* (London: Routledge & Kegan Paul, 1967; republished with a Foreword by Amartya Sen, Chicago, IL: University of Chicago Press, 2009), pp. 41–2).

humiliation of others, uncaring of freedom, and – no less significant – unable to reason, argue, disagree and concur. The strong presence of these features in human lives does not tell us a great deal about which particular theory of justice should be chosen, but it does indicate that the general pursuit of justice might be hard to eradicate in human society, even though we can go about that pursuit in different ways.

I have made considerable use of the existence of the human faculties just mentioned (for example, the ability to sympathize and to reason) in developing my argument, and so have others in presenting their theories of justice. There is no automatic settlement of differences between distinct theories here, but it is comforting to think that not only do proponents of different theories of justice share a common pursuit, they also make use of common human features that figure in the reasoning underlying their respective approaches. Because of these basic human abilities – to understand, to sympathize, to argue – people need not be inescapably doomed to isolated lives without communication and collaboration. It is bad enough that the world in which we live has so much deprivation of one kind or another (from being hungry to being tyrannized); it would be even more terrible if we were not able to communicate, respond and altercate.

When Hobbes referred to the dire state of human beings in having 'nasty, brutish and short' lives, he also pointed, in the same sentence, to the disturbing adversity of being 'solitary'. Escape from isolation may not only be important for the quality of human life, it can also contribute powerfully to understanding and responding to the other deprivations from which human beings suffer. There is surely a basic strength here which is complementary to the engagement in which theories of justice are involved.

# Notes

## PREFACE

1. Charles Dickens, *Great Expectations* (1860–61) (London: Penguin, 2003), Chapter 8, p. 63.
2. The critically important role of a sense of injustice has been well discussed by Judith N. Shklar, *The Faces of Injustice* (New Haven: Yale University Press, 1992).
3. John Rawls, *A Theory of Justice* (Cambridge, MA: Harvard University Press, 1971). He develops – and to some extent broadens – his analysis of justice in his later publications, beginning with *Political Liberalism* (New York: Columbia University Press, 1993).
4. John Rawls, 'Justice as Fairness', *Philosophical Review*, 67 (1958).
5. Christine Korsgaard, *Creating the Kingdom of Ends* (Cambridge: Cambridge University Press, 1996), p. 3. See also Onora O'Neill, *Acting on Principle – An Essay on Kantian Ethics* (New York: Columbia University Press, 1975), and A. Reath, C. Korsgaard and B. Herman (eds), *Reclaiming the History of Ethics* (Cambridge: Cambridge University Press, 1997).
6. Kwame Anthony Appiah, 'Sen's Identities', in Kaushik Basu and Ravi Kanbur (eds), *Arguments for a Better World: Essays in Honor of Amartya Sen*, vol. I (Oxford and New York: Oxford University Press, 2009), p. 488.

## INTRODUCTION

1. *The Works of the Right Honourable Edmund Burke*, vol. X (London: John C. Nimmo, 1899), pp. 144–5.
2. The remark was made by William Murray, 1st Earl of Mansfield, as cited in John Campbell, *The Lives of the Chief Justices in England: From the Norman Conquest to the Death of Lord Mansfield* (London: John Murray, 1949–57), vol. 2, Chapter 40, p. 572.

3. See Thomas Hobbes, *Leviathan*, edited by Richard Tuck (Cambridge: Cambridge University Press, 1991); John Locke, *Two Treatises of Government*, edited by Peter Laslett (Cambridge: Cambridge University Press, 1988); Jean-Jacques Rousseau, *The Social Contract*, translated by Maurice Cranston (Harmondsworth: Penguin, 1968); Immanuel Kant, *Principles of the Metaphysics of Ethics*, translated by T. K. Abbott, 3rd edn (London: Longmans, 1907).

4. See John Rawls, *The Law of Peoples* (Cambridge, MA: Harvard University Press, 1999), pp. 137, 141.

5. See Thomas Scanlon, *What We Owe to Each Other* (Cambridge, MA: Harvard University Press, 1998).

6. These issues are discussed more fully in my paper, 'What Do We Want from a Theory of Justice?', *Journal of Philosophy*, 103 (May 2006). On related questions, see also Joshua Cohen and Charles Sabel, 'Extra Rempublicam Nulla Justitia?', and A. L. Julius, 'Nagel's Atlas', *Philosophy and Public Affairs*, 34 (Spring 2006).

7. See particularly J.-C. de Borda, 'Mémoire sur les élections au scrutin', *Mémoires de l'Académie Royale des Sciences* (1781); Marquis de Condorcet, *Essai sur l'application de l'analyse à la probabilité des decisions rendues à la pluralité des voix* (Paris: L'Imprimerie Royale, 1785).

8. Kenneth J. Arrow, *Social Choice and Individual Values* (New York: Wiley, 1951; 2nd edn, 1963).

9. Amartya Sen, 'Maximization and the Act of Choice', *Econometrica*, 65 (1997).

10. T. S. Eliot, 'The Dry Salvages' in *Four Quartets* (London: Faber and Faber, 1944), pp. 29–31.

11. Amartya Sen, *The Argumentative Indian* (London and Delhi: Penguin, 2005).

12. I shall return to this issue in Chapter 10, 'Realizations, Consequences and Agency'.

13. See Thomas Nagel, 'The Problem of Global Justice', *Philosophy and Public Affairs*, 33 (2005), p. 115.

14. Ibid., pp. 130–33, 146–7.

15. See John Rawls, *The Law of Peoples* (Cambridge, MA: Harvard University Press, 1999).

16. Seamus Heaney, *The Cure at Troy: A Version of Sophocles' Philoctetes* (London: Faber and Faber, 1991).

## I REASON AND OBJECTIVITY

1. See Brian F. McGuinness (ed.), *Letters from Ludwig Wittgenstein, With a Memoir* (Oxford: Blackwell, 1967), pp. 4–5.

2. See, for example, Thomas Schelling, *Choice and Consequence* (Cambridge, MA: Harvard University Press, 1984); Matthew Rabin, 'A Perspective on Psychology and Economics,' *European Economic Review*, 46 (2002); Jean Tirole, 'Rational Irrationality: Some Economics of Self-Management', *European Economic Review*, 46 (2002); Roland Benabou and Jean Tirole, 'Intrinsic and Extrinsic Motivation', *Review of Economic Studies*, 70 (2003); E. Fehr and U. Fischbacher, 'The Nature of Human Altruism', *Nature*, 425 (2003).

3. Different ways of thinking about smart behaviour are considered in Essays 1–6 in my *Rationality and Freedom* (Cambridge, MA: Harvard University Press, 2002).

4. On this and related issues, see Thomas Nagel, *The Possibility of Altruism* (Oxford: Clarendon Press, 1970); Amartya Sen, 'Behaviour and the Concept of Preference', *Economica*, 40 (1973), and 'Rational Fools: A Critique of the Behavioral Foundations of Economic Theory', *Philosophy and Public Affairs*, 6 (1977), both included in *Choice, Welfare and Measurement* (Oxford: Blackwell, 1982, and Cambridge, MA: Harvard University Press, 1997); George Akerlof, *An Economic Theorist's Book of Tales* (Cambridge: Cambridge University Press, 1984); Derek Parfit, *Reasons and Persons* (Oxford: Clarendon Press, 1984); Jon Elster, *The Cement of Society* (Cambridge: Cambridge University Press, 1989).

5. Thomas Scanlon, *What We Owe to Each Other* (Cambridge, MA: Harvard University Press, 1998).

6. See Isaiah Berlin: *Against the Current: Essays in the History of Ideas*, Henry Hardy (ed.) (London: Hogarth Press, 1979); Henry Hardy (ed.), *The Crooked Timber of Humanity: Chapters in the History of Ideas* (London: John Murray, 1990); Henry Hardy (ed.), *Freedom and Its Betrayal: Six Enemies of Human Liberty* (Princeton, NJ: Princeton University Press, 2002); Henry Hardy (ed.), *Three Critics of the Enlightenment: Vico, Hamann, Herder* (London: Pimlico, 2000).

7. See Jonathan Glover, *Humanity: A Moral History of the Twentieth Century* (London: Jonathan Cape, 1999), pp. 6–7.

8. Ibid., p. 310.

9. Ibid., p. 313.

10. The discussion that follows draws on my review essay of Jonathan

Glover's book, 'The Reach of Reason: East and West', in the *New York Review of Books*, 47 (20 July 2000); republished, slightly revised, in *The Argumentative Indian* (London: Penguin, 2005), essay 13.

11. See Glover, *Humanity: A Moral History of the Twentieth Century* (1999), p. 40.

12. Ibid., p. 7.

13. Translation from Vincent Smith, *Akbar: the Great Mogul* (Oxford: Clarendon Press, 1917), p. 257.

14. See Irfan Habib (ed.), *Akbar and His India* (Delhi and New York: Oxford University Press, 1997) for a collection of fine essays investigating the beliefs and policies of Akbar as well as the influences that led him to his heterodox position, including the priority of reason over tradition.

15. For this and other references to policy decisions based on Akbar's reasoning, see the fine discussion in Shireen Moosvi, *Episodes in the Life of Akbar: Contemporary Records and Reminiscences* (New Delhi: National Book Trust, 1994), from which the particular translations of Akbar's statements used here are also taken.

16. See M. Athar Ali, 'The Perception of India in Akbar and Abul Fazl', in Habib (ed.), *Akbar and His India* (1997), p. 220.

17. Hilary Putnam, *Ethics without Ontology* (Cambridge, MA: Harvard University Press 2004), p. 75.

18. John Rawls, *Political Liberalism* (New York: Columbia University Press, 1993), pp. 110, 119. See also his *Justice as Fairness: A Restatement*, edited by Erin Kelly (Cambridge, MA: Harvard University Press, 2001).

19. Jürgen Habermas, 'Reconciliation through the Public Use of Reason: Remarks on John Rawls's Political Liberalism', *Journal of Philosophy*, 92 (March 1995); see also John Rawls's response, 'Reply to Habermas', *Journal of Philosophy*, 92 (1995).

20. See my 'The Reach of Reason: East and West', *New York Review of Books*, 47 (20 July 2000); 'Open and Closed Impartiality' *Journal of Philosophy*, 99 (2002); *The Argumentative Indian* (London: Penguin, 2005); *Identity and Violence: The Illusion of Destiny* (New York: W. W. Norton & Co., and London: Penguin, 2006).

21. See particularly Nicholas Stern, *The Economics of Climate Change: The Stern Review* (Cambridge: Cambridge University Press, 2007). There is a vast literature – and some debate – on this subject now. The investigation of human culpability in environmental decline goes back a long time. An insightful assessment of the early literature on this can be found in Mark Sagoff, *The Economy of the Earth: Philosophy, Law and the Environment* (Cambridge: Cambridge University Press, 1988).

22. See also Martha C. Nussbaum, *Upheavals of Thought: The Intelligence of Emotions* (Cambridge: Cambridge University Press, 2001).

23. David Hume, *Enquiries concerning the Human Understanding and concerning the Principles of Morals*, edited by L. E. Selby-Bigge (Oxford: Clarendon Press, 1962), p. 172.

24. Adam Smith, *The Theory of Moral Sentiments* (London: T. Cadell, 1790; republished Oxford: Clarendon Press, 1976), pp. 319–20.

## 2 RAWLS AND BEYOND

1. See Rawls, 'Outline of a Decision Procedure for Ethics', *Philosophical Review*, 60 (1951); 'Two Concepts of Rules', *Philosophical Review*, 64 (1955), and 'Justice as Fairness', *Philosophical Review*, 67 (1958). They are included in Samuel Freedman (ed.), *John Rawls: Collected Papers* (Cambridge, MA: Harvard University Press, 1999). See also John Rawls, *Justice as Fairness: A Restatement*, edited by Erin Kelly (Cambridge, MA: Harvard University Press, 2001).

2. John Rawls, *A Theory of Justice* (Cambridge, MA: Harvard University Press, 1971). See also his *Political Liberalism* (New York: Columbia University Press, 1993); *Justice as Fairness: A Restatement* (2001).

3. Rawlsian ideas on justice did, in turn, deeply influence welfare economics; see E. S. Phelps (ed.), *Economic Justice* (Harmondsworth: Penguin, 1973), and 'Recent Developments in Welfare Economics: Justice et équité', in Michael Intriligator, (ed.), *Frontiers of Quantitative Economics*, vol. III (Amsterdam: North-Holland, 1977).

4. Scepticism about Rawls's claim regarding the exact contractarian outcome of the original position can be raised on other grounds as well. Economists and decision theorists in particular have tended to be sceptical of Rawls's conclusion about the plausibility of the outcome that he predicts in the original position, particularly the likelihood of the 'maximin' solution being chosen, on which Rawls's 'Difference Principle' can be seen to be based. On particular reasons for scepticism about Rawls's conclusion, see Kenneth Arrow, *Social Choice and Justice: Collected Papers of Kenneth J. Arrow*, vol. I (Cambridge, MA: Harvard University Press, 1983). Edmund Phelps has pioneered the extensive use of Rawlsian rules of justice in economic analysis, though he too has expressed considerable scepticism about Rawls's derivations; see E. S. Phelps (ed.), *Economic Justice* (1973); and his *Studies in Macroeconomic Theory, II: Redistribution and Growth* (New York: Academic Press, 1980).

5. Immanuel Kant, *Fundamental Principles of the Metaphysics of Ethics*, translated by T. K. Abbott, 3rd edn (London: Longmans, 1907), p. 66. For the demands of Kantian reasoning see, among others, Barbara Herman, *Morality as Rationality: A Study of Kant's Ethics* (New York: Garland Publishing, 1990).

6. Rawls, *Justice as Fairness: A Restatement* (2001), pp. 133–4.

7. Rawls, *A Theory of Justice* (1971), pp. 60–65.

8. On related issues, see also Liam Murphy and Thomas Nagel, *The Myth of Ownership* (New York: Oxford University Press, 2002).

9. See G. A. Cohen, *Rescuing Justice and Equality* (Cambridge, MA: Harvard University Press, 2008). See also Amartya Sen, 'Merit and Justice', in Kenneth Arrow, Samuel Bowles and Steven Durlauf (eds), *Meritocracy and Economic Inequality* (Princeton, NJ: Princeton University Press, 2000).

10. Rawls, *Political Liberalism* (1993), p. 110.

11. I have discussed the limitations of the leading versions of 'rational choice theory' in my *Rationality and Freedom* (Cambridge, MA: Harvard University Press, 2002), particularly in the introductory essay 1, and also in essays 3–5.

12. See, particularly, Rawls, *Political Liberalism*, pp. 48–54.

13. The priority of liberty plays an important part in the result derived in my 'The Impossibility of a Paretian Liberal', *Journal of Political Economy*, 78 (1970). John Rawls comments illuminatingly on this connection in his essay, 'Social Unity and Primary Goods', in Amartya Sen and Bernard Williams (eds), *Utilitarianism and Beyond* (Cambridge: Cambridge University Press, 1982). I shall discuss the issue more fully in Chapter 16.

14. The allocational criterion of 'lexicographic maximin' is used in Rawls's 'Difference Principle', which involves giving priority to the worst-off people – judged in terms of the index of holdings of primary goods – in each respective conglomeration. When the worst-off people in two different conglomerations are equally well off, then it is the position of the second worst-off group that becomes the focus of attention, and so on. For those who are interested in the formal structure of this criterion, an easy statement and motivating discussion can be found in my *Collective Choice and Social Welfare* (1970); see also Phelps, *Economic Justice* (1973), and Anthony Atkinson, *The Economics of Inequality* (Oxford: Clarendon Press, 1975).

15. This issue is discussed also in my essay 'Justice: Means versus Freedoms', *Philosophy and Public Affairs*, 19 (Spring 1990).

16. Herbert Hart, 'Rawls on Liberty and Its Priority', *University of Chicago Law Review*, 40 (1973).

17. See Rawls, *Political Liberalism* (1993), chapter VIII. There are also

qualifications to the priority of liberty in his first book, *A Theory of Justice* (1971), pp. 132, 217–18.

18. John Rawls, *Political Liberalism* (1993), p. 23.

19. Samuel Freedman, 'Introduction: John Rawls – An Overview', in Samuel Freedman (ed.), *The Cambridge Companion to Rawls* (Cambridge: Cambridge University Press, 2003), pp. 3–4.

20. Immanuel Kant, *Critique of Practical Reason* (1788), English translation by L. W. Beck (New York: Liberal Arts Press, 1956).

21. John Rawls, *A Theory of Justice* (1971), p. viii.

22. Rawls, *Justice as Fairness: A Restatement* (2001), pp. 95–6. Indeed, that was the principal point of departure to which Rawls drew explicit attention in his pioneering essay, 'Justice as Fairness', *Philosophical Review*, 67 (1958).

23. See Thomas W. Pogge (ed.), *Global Justice* (Oxford: Blackwell, 2001).


## 3 INSTITUTIONS AND PERSONS

1. Italics added. These statements of Ashoka occur in Edict XII (on 'Toleration') at Erragudi; I am using here the translation presented by Vincent A. Smith in *Asoka: The Buddhist Emperor of India* (Oxford: Clarendon Press, 1909), pp. 170–71, except for some very minor emendations based on the original Sanskrit text).

2. On Ashoka's life, see Romila Thapar, *Asoka and the Decline of the Mauryas* (Oxford: Oxford University Press, 1961); Upindar Singh, *A History of Ancient and Medieval India: From the Stone Age to the 12th Century* (New Delhi: Pearson Education, 2008).

3. On the last point, see also Bruce Rich's excellent book, *To Uphold the World: The Message of Ashoka and Kautilya for the 21st Century* (New Delhi: Penguin, 2008), Chapter 8.

4. Rawls, *Justice as Fairness: A Restatement*, edited by Erin Kelly (Cambridge, MA: Harvard University Press, 2001), pp. 42–3.

5. On this question, see Anthony Laden, 'Games, Fairness, and Rawls's "A Theory of Justice"', *Philosophy and Public Affairs*, 20 (1991).

6. Rawls, *Political Liberalism*, p. 50.

7. Ibid., p. 86.

8. John Kenneth Galbraith, *American Capitalism: The Concept of Countervailing Power* (Boston, MA: Houghton Mifflin, 1952; London: Hamish Hamilton, 1954; revised edn, 1957). See also Richard Parker, *John Kenneth Galbraith: His Life, His Politics, His Economics* (New York: Farrar, Straus &

NOTES TO PP. 81–93

Giroux, 2005); republished as *John Kenneth Galbraith: A Twentieth-Century Life* (Chicago, IL: University of Chicago Press, 2007).

9. Some of the reasons for this variance between rigidly institutional visions and actual realizations are discussed in my *Development as Freedom* (New York: Knopf, and Oxford: Oxford University Press, 1999).

10. David Gauthier, *Morals by Agreement* (Oxford: Clarendon Press, 1986), Chapter IV ('The Market: Freedom from Morality').

11. See Robert Nozick, *Anarchy, State and Utopia* (Oxford: Blackwell, 1974).

## 4 VOICE AND SOCIAL CHOICE

1. For the source material on this and other related conversations, see my *The Argumentative Indian* (London: Allen Lane, and New York: Farrar, Straus & Giroux, 2005).

2. See Peter Green, *Alexander of Macedon, 356–323 B.C.: A Historical Biography* (Berkeley, CA: University of California Press, 1992), p. 428.

3. J.-C. de Borda, 'Mémoire sur les élections au scrutin', *Mémoires de l'Académie Royale des Sciences* (1781); Marquis de Condorcet, *Essai sur l'application de l'analyse à la probabilité des decisions rendues à la pluralité des voix* (Paris: L'Imprimerie Royale, 1785).

4. See C. L. Dodgson, *A Method of Taking Votes on More Than Two Issues* (Oxford: Clarendon Press, 1876), and *The Principles of Parliamentary Representation* (London: Harrison, 1951).

5. The classic book of social choice theory is the remarkable monograph of Kenneth Arrow, based on his Ph.D. dissertation, *Social Choice and Individual Values* (New York: Wiley, 1951; 2nd edn, 1963).

6. Arrow, *Social Choice and Individual Values* (1951, 1963). For explications of the result in informal as well as mathematical terms, see my *Collective Choice and Social Welfare* (San Francisco, CA: Holden-Day, 1970; republished, Amsterdam: North-Holland, 1979).

7. There were a number of impossibility results involving variations of the axioms used by Arrow and showing other conflicts of apparently sensible demands on rational social choice; see my *Collective Choice and Social Welfare* (1970); Peter C. Fishburn, *The Theory of Social Choice* (Princeton, NJ: Princeton University Press, 1973); Jerry Kelly, *Arrow Impossibility Theorems* (New York: Academic Press, 1978); Kotaro Suzumura, *Rational Choice, Collective Decisions, and Social Welfare* (Cambridge: Cambridge University Press, 1983); Prasanta K. Pattanaik and Maurice Salles (eds),

*Social Choice and Welfare* (Amsterdam: North-Holland, 1983); Thomas Schwartz, *The Logic of Collective Choice* (New York: Columbia University Press, 1986), among many other contributions. Fine introductory discussions can be found in Jerry Kelly, *Social Choice Theory: An Introduction* (Berlin: Springer Verlag, 1987); Wulf Gaertner, *A Primer in Social Choice Theory* (Oxford: Oxford University Press, 2006).

8. This was also one of the principal issues discussed in my Nobel Lecture in 1998, 'The Possibility of Social Choice' (1999). See also Marc Fleurbaey, 'Social Choice and Just Institutions; New Perspectives', *Economics and Philosophy*, 23 (March 2007).

9. Interpersonal comparisons of various types can be fully axiomatized and exactly incorporated in social choice procedures, and various constructive possibilities can be devised and used: see my *Collective Choice and Social Welfare* (1970), *Choice, Welfare and Measurement* (1982), and 'Social Choice Theory' in *Handbook of Mathematical Economics* (1986). The literature on this subject is quite large, and includes, among other contributions, Peter J. Hammond, 'Equity, Arrow's Conditions and Rawls' Difference Principle', *Econometrica*, 44 (1976); Claude d'Aspremont and Louis Gevers, 'Equity and the Informational Basis of Collective Choice', *Review of Economic Studies*, 44 (1977); Kenneth J. Arrow, 'Extended Sympathy and the Possibility of Social Choice', *American Economic Review*, 67 (1977); Eric Maskin, 'A Theorem on Utilitarianism', *Review of Economic Studies*, 45 (1978); Louis Gevers, 'On Interpersonal Comparability and Social Welfare Orderings', *Econometrica*, 47 (1979); Eric Maskin, 'Decision-making under Ignorance with Implications for Social Choice', *Theory and Decision*, 11 (1979); Kevin W. S. Roberts, 'Possibility Theorems with Interpersonally Comparable Welfare Levels', and 'Interpersonal Comparability and Social Choice Theory', *Review of Economic Studies*, 47 (1980); Kotaro Suzumura, *Rational Choice, Collective Decisions, and Social Welfare* (Cambridge: Cambridge University Press, 1983); Charles Blackorby, David Donaldson, and John Weymark, 'Social Choice with Interpersonal Utility Comparisons: A Diagrammatic Introduction', *International Economic Review*, 25 (1984); Claude d'Aspremont, 'Axioms for Social Welfare Ordering', in Leonid Hurwicz, David Schmeidler and Hugo Sonnenschein (eds), *Social Goals and Social Organization* (Cambridge: Cambridge University Press, 1985); to mention just a few of this large body of constructive literature.

10. Kenneth J. Arrow, 'Extended Sympathy and the Possibility of Social Choice', *American Economic Review*, 67 (1977).

11. See Marie-Jean-Antoine-Nicolas de Caritat, Marquis de Condorcet, *Esquisse d'un tableau historique des progrès de l'esprit humain* (1793). Later

included in *Œuvres de Condorcet*, vol. 6 (Paris: Firmin Didot Frères, 1847; republished, Stuttgart: Friedrich Frommann Verlag, 1968).

12. On this, see my Nobel Lecture in December 1998, 'The Possibility of Social Choice', *American Economic Review*, 89 (1999). See also Marc Fleurbaey and Philippe Mongin, 'The News of the Death of Welfare Economies Is Greatly Exaggerated', *Social Choice and Welfare*, 25 (2005).

13. Sometimes the formulations of social choice theory specify the outcomes not as rankings of social states but as 'choice functions' that tell us what the choosable alternatives are in each possible set. While the choice functional format may look quite remote from the relational formulation, they are, in fact, analytically linked with each other, and we can identify the implicit rankings that lie behind the respective choice functions; on this see my *Choice, Welfare and Measurement* (Oxford: Blackwell, 1982, and Cambridge, MA: Harvard University Press, 1997), essays 1 and 8, and *Rationality and Freedom* (Cambridge, MA: Harvard University Press, 2002), essays 3, 4 and 7, and the literature – I fear rather large – cited there.

14. Robert Nozick, *Anarchy, State and Utopia* (Oxford: Blackwell, 1974), p. 28.

15. On this, see my *Collective Choice and Social Welfare* (San Francisco, CA: Holden-Day, 1970; republished, Amsterdam: North-Holland, 1979), Chapter 9.

16. Indeed, even in social choice theory, where the analytical framework is firmly relational and altogether geared to comparative judgements, the actual investigations of 'social justice' have been closely linked with the identification of transcendental justice (often in the Rawlsian mould). The hold of the transcendental format is almost ubiquitous in academic investigations of the demands of justice and, despite having a broader analytical base, social choice theory has not escaped the influence of transcendentalism in the choice of problems that have been investigated in detail.

17. The formal characteristics of 'intersection partial orderings' are discussed in my *On Economic Inequality* (Oxford: Clarendon Press, 1973; enlarged edition, with an addendum written jointly with James Foster, 1997).

18. See also my *Collective Choice and Social Welfare* (1970).

19. See Herbert Simon, *Models of Man* (New York: Wiley, 1957), and *Models of Thought* (New Haven: Yale University Press, 1979).

20. This is part of the typology of social choice problems discussed in my essay, 'Social Choice Theory: A Re-examination', *Econometrica*, 45 (1977), republished in *Choice, Welfare and Measurement* (1982; 1997).

21. The issue of membership entitlement is the principal focus of the important analysis of judgement aggregation presented by Christian List and Philip

Pettit, 'Aggregating Sets of Judgments: An Impossibility Result', *Economics and Philosophy*, 18 (2002).

22. See the references cited in note 9 of this chapter.

23. The result was included in my *Collective Choice and Social Welfare* (1970), Chapter 6, and also in 'The Impossibility of a Paretian Liberal', *Journal of Political Economy*, 78 (1970). It will be briefly discussed in Chapter 14, 'Equality and Liberty'.

24. The contributions include, among many others, Allan Gibbard, 'A Pareto-Consistent Libertarian Claim', *Journal of Economic Theory*, 7 (1974); Peter Bernholz, 'Is a Paretian Liberal Really Impossible?' *Public Choice*, 20 (1974); Christian Seidl, 'On Liberal Values', *Zeitschrift für Nationalökonomie*, 35 (1975); Julian Blau, 'Liberal Values and Independence', *Review of Economic Studies*, 42 (1975); Donald E. Campbell, 'Democratic Preference Functions', *Journal of Economic Theory*, 12 (1976); Jerry S. Kelly, 'Rights-Exercising and a Pareto-Consistent Libertarian Claim', *Journal of Economic Theory*, 13 (1976); Michael J. Farrell, 'Liberalism in the Theory of Social Choice', *Review of Economic Studies*, 43 (1976); John A. Ferejohn, 'The Distribution of Rights in Society', in Hans W. Gottinger and Werner Leinfellner (eds), *Decision Theory and Social Ethics* (Boston: Reidel, 1978); Jonathan Barnes, 'Freedom, Rationality and Paradox', *Canadian Journal of Philosophy*, 10 (1980); Peter Hammond, 'Liberalism, Independent Rights and the Pareto Principle', in L. J. Cohen, H. Pfeiffer and K. Podewski (eds), *Logic, Methodology and the Philosophy of Sciences, II* (Amsterdam: North-Holland, 1982); Kotaro Suzumura, 'On the Consistency of Libertarian Claims', *Review of Economic Studies*, 45 (1978); Wulf Gaertner and L. Krüger, 'Self-supporting Preferences and Individual Rights: The Possibility of Paretian Libertarianism', *Economica*, 48 (1981); Kotaro Suzumura, *Rational Choice, Collective Decisions and Social Welfare* (1983); Kaushik Basu, 'The Right to Give up Rights', *Economica*, 51 (1984); John L. Wriglesworth, *Libertarian Conflicts in Social Choice* (Cambridge: Cambridge University Press, 1985); Jonathan M. Riley, *Liberal Utilitarianism* (Cambridge: Cambridge University Press, 1987); Dennis Mueller, *Public Choice II* (New York: Cambridge University Press, 1989). See also the special issue on 'the liberal paradox' of *Analyse & Kritik*, 18 (1996), with contributions from a large number of authors interested in the subject, and also a response from me.

25. I have tried to discuss this connection in 'Minimal Liberty', *Economica* 59 (1992), and in 'Rationality and Social Choice', Presidential Address to the American Economic Association, published in *American Economic Review*, 85 (1995), reprinted in my *Rationality and Freedom* (2002). See also Seidl, 'On Liberal Values' (1975).

26. See Philippe Mongin, 'Value Judgments and Value Neutrality in Economics', *Economica*, 73 (2006); Marc Fleurbaey, Maurice Salles and John Weymark (eds), *Justice, Political Liberalism and Utilitarianism* (Cambridge: Cambridge University Press, 2008).

27. On this, see my 'Fertility and Coercion', *University of Chicago Law Review*, 63 (Summer 1996); also *Development as Freedom* (New York: Knopf, 1999).

## 5 IMPARTIALITY AND OBJECTIVITY

1. Wollstonecraft, in Sylvana Tomaselli (ed.), *A Vindication of the Rights of Men and A Vindication of the Rights of Woman* (Cambridge: Cambridge University Press, 1995, p. 13.

2. Mary Wollstonecraft, *A Vindication of the Rights of Woman: with Strictures on Political and Moral Subjects* (1792); included in the volume edited by Sylvana Tomaselli, 1995.

3. Immanuel Kant, *Fundamental Principles of the Metaphysics of Ethics*, translated by T. K. Abbott, 3rd edn (London: Longmans, 1907), p. 66.

4. Henry Sidgwick, *The Methods of Ethics* (London: Macmillan, 1907; New York: Dover, 1966), Preface to the 6th edition, p. xvii.

5. Vivian Walsh, 'Sen after Putnam', *Review of Political Economy*, 15 (2003), p. 331.

6. Antonio Gramsci, *Letters from Prison*, translated and edited by Lynne Lawner (London: Jonathan Cape, 1975), p. 324. See also Quintin Hoare and Geoffrey Nowell Smith (eds), *Selections from the Prison Notebooks of Antonio Gramsci* (London: Lawrence and Wishart, 1971).

7. Amartya Sen, 'Sraffa, Wittgenstein, and Gramsci', *Journal of Economic Literature*, 41 (2003).

8. Ludwig Wittgenstein, *Philosophical Investigations* (Oxford: Blackwell, 1953, 2nd edn, 1958).

9. In his insightful analysis of the influence of Sraffa, along with that of Freud, on Wittgenstein's later philosophy, Brian McGuinness points out the impact on Wittgenstein of 'the ethnological or anthropological way of looking at things that came to him from the economist Sraffa'. See Brian McGuinness (ed.), *Wittgenstein and His Times* (Oxford: Blackwell, 1982), pp. 36–9.

10. Rawls, *Political Liberalism* (1993), p. 119. Even though Rawls's language seems to partition people into reasonable and unreasonable people, this does not restrict the reach of his criterion to cover all persons to the extent that

they are willing to engage in public discussion, examine arguments and evidences offered, and reason about them in an open-minded way (on this see Chapter 1).

11. Adam Smith, *The Theory of Moral Sentiments* (1759; revised edn, 1790; republished, Oxford: Clarendon Press, 1976).

## 6 CLOSED AND OPEN IMPARTIALITY

1. Adam Smith, *The Theory of Moral Sentiments* (London: T. Cadell, extended version, 1790; republished, Oxford: Clarendon Press, 1976), III, i, 2; the extended version occurs in the sixth edition. On the points of emphasis see the discussion in D. D. Raphael, 'The Impartial Spectator', in Andrew S. Skinner and Thomas Wilson (eds), *Essays on Adam Smith* (Oxford: Clarendon Press, 1975), pp. 88–90. On the centrality of these issues in the Enlightenment perspectives, particularly in the works of Smith and Condorcet, see Emma Rothschild, *Economic Sentiments: Smith, Condorcet and the Enlightenment* (Cambridge, MA: Harvard University Press, 2001).

2. See Raphael and Macfie, 'Introduction', in Smith, *The Theory of Moral Sentiments* (republished 1976), p. 31.

3. Adam Smith, *The Theory of Moral Sentiments*, III, 1, 2, in the 1975 reprint, p. 110.

4. *A Theory of Justice* (1971), pp. 516–17.

5. Ibid., p. 517.

6. Smith, *The Theory of Moral Sentiments*, III, 1, 2, p. 110.

7. On this, see my *Identity and Violence: The Illusion of Destiny* (New York: W. W. Norton & Co., and London: Penguin, 2006).

8. Rawls, *Political Liberalism* (1993), p. 23.

9. Rawls, 'Reply to Alexander and Musgrave', in *John Rawls: Collected Papers*, p. 249. See also Tony Laden, 'Games, Fairness and Rawls's *A Theory of Justice*', *Philosophy and Public Affairs*, 20 (1991).

10. *A Theory of Justice* (1971), pp. 516–17; more extensively, see section 78 in *A Theory of Justice*, pp. 513–20, and *Political Liberalism* (1993). pp. 110–16.

11. Rawls, *A Theory of Justice*, pp. 22–3, footnote 9.

12. Smith, *The Theory of Moral Sentiments*, VII, ii, 2, 14, p. 299.

13. In the argument that follows I draw on an earlier analysis I presented in 'Open and Closed Impartiality', *Journal of Philosophy*, 99 (September 2002).

14. This is not to deny the possible existence of what topologists would call a 'fixed point' (with suitable assumptions regarding continuity) such that the

decisions of a given focal group lead exactly back to the same focal group (however unlikely that congruence might be). But the problem of possible inconsistency cannot be ruled out, to say the least, in general when decisions to be taken by a focal group influence the composition of the focal group itself.

15. I have tried to identify these issues in 'Global Justice: Beyond International Equity', in Inga Kaul, I. Grunberg and M. A. Stern (eds), *Global Public Goods: International Cooperation in the 21st Century* (Oxford: Oxford University Press, 1999), and also in 'Justice across Borders', in Pablo De Greiff and Ciaran Cronin (eds) *Global Justice and Transnational Politics* (Cambridge, MA: MIT Press, 2002), originally presented as a lecture for the Centennial Year Celebrations of the De Paul University in Chicago in September 1998.

16. John Rawls, 'The Law of Peoples', in Stephen Shute and Susan Hurley (eds), *On Human Rights* (New York: Basic Books, 1993), and *The Law of Peoples* (Cambridge, MA: Harvard University Press, 1999).

17. See Charles R. Beitz, *Political Theory and International Relations* (Princeton, NJ: Princeton University Press, 1979); Brian Barry, *Theories of Justice*, vol. 1 (Berkeley, CA: University of California Press, 1989); Thomas Pogge, *Realizing Rawls* (Ithaca, NY: Cornell University Press, 1989); Thomas Pogge (ed.), *Global Justice* (Oxford: Blackwell, 2001); Deen Chatterjee (ed.), *The Ethics of Assistance: Morality and the Distant Needy* (Cambridge: Cambridge University Press, 2004); Thomas Pogge and Sanjay Reddy, *How Not to Count the Poor* (New York: Columbia University Press, 2005).

18. See Kenneth Arrow, Amartya Sen and Kotaro Suzumura (eds), *Social Choice Re-examined* (Amsterdam: Elsevier, 1997). See also Isaac Levi, *Hard Choices* (Cambridge: Cambridge University Press, 1986).

19. On this, see Derek Parfit, *Reasons and Persons* (Oxford: Clarendon Press, 1984). Parfit's general point has a bearing on 'inclusionary incoherence', though he does not discuss it specifically.

20. See David Hume, 'On the Original Contract', republished in David Hume, *Selected Essays*, edited by Stephen Copley and Andrew Edgar (Oxford: Oxford University Press, 1996), p. 279.

21. Rawls, 'Justice as Fairness: Political Not Metaphysical', *Collected Papers*, p. 401.

22. Rawls, 'Reply to Alexander and Musgrave', *Collected Papers*, p. 249.

## 7 POSITION, RELEVANCE AND ILLUSION

1. William Shakespeare, *King Lear*, IV.6.150-54.
2. Thomas Nagel, *The View from Nowhere* (New York: Oxford University Press, 1986), p. 5.
3. See *Alberuni's India*, edited by A. T. Embree (New York: W. W. Norton & Co., 1971), p. 111.
4. G. A. Cohen, *Karl Marx's Theory of History: A Defence* (Oxford: Clarendon Press, 1978), pp. 328-9.
5. I have discussed these issues in my 'Gender and Cooperative Conflict', in Irene Tinker (ed.), *Persistent Inequalities* (New York: Oxford University Press, 1990). See also my 'Many Faces of Gender Inequality', *New Republic* (2001) and *Frontline* (2001).
6. David Hume, *An Enquiry Concerning the Principles of Morals* (1777; republished, La Salle, Ill: Open Court, 1966), p. 25.

## 8 RATIONALITY AND OTHER PEOPLE

1. Jon Elster, *Reason and Rationality* (Princeton, NJ, and Oxford: Princeton University Press, 2008), p. 2. In this small book Jon Elster provides a remarkably engaging account of the connection between reasoning and rationality, a subject in which Elster has himself made outstanding contributions. He also critically surveys the literature on this subject.
2. Bounded rationality has been particularly studied by Herbert Simon, 'A Behavioral Model of Rational Choice', *Quarterly Journal of Economics*, 69 (1955), and *Models of Thought* (New Haven: Yale University Press, 1979).
3. See Daniel Kahneman, P. Slovik, and A. Tversky, *Judgement under Uncertainty: Heuristics and Biases* (Cambridge: Cambridge University Press, 1982). See also B. P. Stigum and F. Wenstøp (eds), *Foundations of Utility and Risk Theory with Applications* (Dordrecht: Reidel, 1983); Isaac Levi, *Hard Choices* (Cambridge: Cambridge University Press, 1986); L. Daboni, A. Montesano and M. Lines, *Recent Developments in the Foundations of Utility and Risk Theory* (Dordrecht: Reidel, 1986); Richard Thaler, *Quasi-Rational Economics* (New York: Russell Sage Foundation, 1991); Daniel McFadden, 'Rationality for Economists', *Journal of Risk and Uncertainty*, 19 (1999).
4. See Adam Smith, *The Theory of Moral Sentiments* (1759, 1790); republished and edited by D. D. Raphael and A. L. Macfie (Oxford: Clarendon Press, 1976); Thomas Schelling, *Choice and Consequence* (Cambridge, MA:

Harvard University Press, 1984), Chapters 3 ('The Intimate Contest of Self-Command') and 4 ('Ethics, Law and the Exercise of Self-Command').

5. Many of these departures can be made to fit into a general pattern of behaviour that Richard Thaler calls 'quasi-rational' (see his *Quasi-Rational Economics* (New York: Russell Sage Foundation, 1991).

6. See Milton Friedman, *Essays in Positive Economics* (Chicago, IL: University of Chicago Press, 1953).

7. Amartya Sen, 'The Discipline of Economics', *Economica*, 75 (November 2008).

8. On this and related issues, see Donald Davidson, *Essays on Actions and Events* (Oxford: Oxford University Press, 2nd edn, 2001).

9. The demands of rationality as well as departures from rationality can take many different forms, which I have tried to address in several essays included in *Rationality and Freedom* (Cambridge, MA: Harvard University Press, 2002).

10. *Rationality and Freedom* (Cambridge, MA: Harvard University Press, 2002).

11. See John Broome, 'Choice and Value in Economics', *Oxford Economic Papers*, 30 (1978); Amartya Sen, *Choice, Welfare and Measurement* (Oxford: Blackwell, 1982; Cambridge, MA: Harvard University Press, 1997).

12. F. Y. Edgeworth, *Mathematical Psychics: An Essay on the Application of Mathematics to the Moral Sciences* (London: C. K. Paul, 1881), pp. 16, 104.

13. *The Theory of Moral Sentiments* (1770, 1790), p. 191 (in the 1976 edition, Clarendon Press, Oxford).

14. Ibid., pp. 190–92.

15. Ibid., p. 189.

16. See George Stigler, 'Smith's Travel on the Ship of State', in A. S. Skinner and T. Wilson (eds), *Essays on Adam Smith* (Oxford: Clarendon Press, 1975), particularly p. 237, and 'Economics or Ethics?', in S. McMurrin (ed.), *Tanner Lectures on Human Values*, vol. II (Cambridge: Cambridge University Press, 1981), particularly p. 176.

17. See, however, Geoffrey Brennan and Loran Lomasky, 'The Impartial Spectator Goes to Washington: Towards a Smithian Model of Electoral Politics', *Economics and Philosophy*, vol. 1 (1985); Patricia H. Werhane, *Adam Smith and His Legacy for Modern Capitalism* (New York: Oxford University Press, 1991); Emma Rothschild, 'Adam Smith and Conservative Economics', *Economic History Review*, vol. 45 (February 1992); Emma Rothschild, *Economic Sentiments* (Cambridge, MA: Harvard University Press, 2001).

18. Stephen Leacock, *Hellements of Hickonomics* (New York: Dodd, Mead & Co, 1936), p. 75; see also my *On Ethics and Economics* (Oxford: Blackwell, 1987), Chapter 1.

19. This issue of misinterpretation is more fully discussed in my 'Adam Smith's Prudence', in S. Lal and F. Stewart (eds), *Theory and Reality in Development* (London: Macmillan, 1986); *On Ethics and Economics* (Oxford: Blackwell, 1987).

20. Adam Smith, *An Inquiry into the Nature and Causes of the Wealth of Nations* (in the 1976 reprint, pp. 26–7).

21. *The Theory of Moral Sentiments*, p. 192.

22. Ibid., p. 162.

23. *Choice, Welfare and Measurement* (1982), pp. 7–8.

24. Gary S. Becker, *The Economic Approach to Human Behavior* (Chicago, IL: University of Chicago Press, 1976), p. 14; and *Accounting for Tastes* (Cambridge, MA: Harvard University Press, 1996).

## 9 PLURALITY OF IMPARTIAL REASONS

1. See John Rawls, *Justice as Fairness: A Restatement*, edited by Erin Kelly (Cambridge, MA: Harvard University Press, 2001), pp. 5–8.

2. Thomas Scanlon, *What We Owe to Each Other* (1998), p. 5; see also his 'Contractualism and Utilitarianism', in Amartya Sen and Bernard Williams (eds), *Utilitarianism and Beyond* (Cambridge: Cambridge University Press, 1982).

3. Rawls, *Justice as Fairness: A Restatement*, p. 6.

4. See, for example, M. Sagoff, *The Economy of the Earth: Philosophy, Law, and the Environment* (Cambridge: Cambridge University Press, 1988); Bruno S. Frey, 'Does Monitoring Increase Work Effort? The Rivalry with Trust and Loyalty', *Economic Inquiry*, 31 (1993); David M. Gordon, 'Bosses of Different Stripes: A Cross-Sectional Perspective on Monitoring and Supervision', *American Economic Review*, 84 (1994); Elinor Ostrom, 'Collective Action and the Evolution of Social Norms', *Journal of Economic Perspectives*, 14 (Summer 2000); Andrew Dobson, *Citizenship and the Environment* (Oxford: Oxford University Press, 2003); Barry Holden, *Democracy and Global Warming* (London: Continuum International Publishing Group, 2002).

5. See, for example, Elinor Ostrom, 'Collective Action and the Evolution of Social Norms' (2000).

6. The classic English translation of *Sutta-Nipata* can be found in F. Max Muller (ed.), *The Sacred Books of the East*, vol. X, Part II, *The Sutta-Nipata*:

*A Collection of Discourses*, translated by V. Fausboll (Oxford: Clarendon Press, 1881). A later translation is *The Sutta-Nipata*, translated by H. Saddhatissa (London: Curzon Press, 1985).

7. See also my essays, 'Elements of a Theory of Human Rights', *Philosophy and Public Affairs*, 32 (2004), and 'Human Rights and the Limits of Law', *Cardozo Law Journal*, 27 (April 2006).

## 10 REALIZATIONS, CONSEQUENCES AND AGENCY

1. In collaboration with Swami Prabhavananda (Madras: Sri Ramakrishna Math, 1989).

2. T. S. Eliot, 'The Dry Salvages', in *Four Quartets* (London: Faber & Faber, 1944), pp. 29–31.

3. See Len Giovannitti and Fred Freed, *The Decision to Drop the Bomb* (London: Methuen, 1957).

4. On the integration of procedures in the evaluation of consequences, see the illuminating paper of Kotaro Suzumura, 'Consequences, Opportunities, and Procedures', *Social Choice and Welfare*, 16 (1999).

5. On these and related issues, see also my essays, 'Rights and Agency', *Philosophy and Public Affairs*, 11 (Winter 1982), and 'Evaluator Relativity and Consequential Evaluation', *Philosophy and Public Affairs*, 12 (Spring 1983); the latter also responds to an interesting critique of Donald H. Regan, 'Against Evaluator Relativity: A Response to Sen', in the same number of the journal.

## 11 LIVES, FREEDOMS AND CAPABILITIES

1. I have tried to pursue this more direct approach in a series of publications that followed my initial move towards a capability-based approach in my 1979 Tanner Lecture, published as 'Equality of What?' in S. McMurrin, *Tanner Lectures on Human Values*, vol. I (Cambridge: Cambridge University Press, and Salt Lake City, UT: University of Utah Press, 1980). See my *Commodities and Capabilities* (Amsterdam: North-Holland, 1985, and Delhi: Oxford University Press, 1987); *The Standard of Living*, edited by G. Hawthorne (Cambridge: Cambridge University Press, 1987); *Development as Freedom* (New York: Knopf, 1999). See also the jointly edited volume with Martha Nussbaum, *The Quality of Life* (Oxford: Clarendon Press, 1993).

2. See William Petty's *Political Arithmetick*, which was written around 1676

but published in 1691; see C. H. Hull (ed.), *The Economic Writings of Sir William Petty* (Cambridge: Cambridge University Press, 1899), vol. I, p. 312. I have discussed the nature of the debates involved among the early estimators of national income and living standards in my 1985 Tanner Lectures, published, along with comments from others (Bernard Williams, John Muellbauer, Ravi Kanbur and Keith Hart), in *The Standard of Living*, edited by Geoffrey Hawthorn (Cambridge: Cambridge University Press, 1987).

3. These and other related comparisons are discussed in my book *Development as Freedom* (New York: Knopf, 1999), Chapters 1 and 4. See also my 'The Economics of Life and Death', *Scientific American*, 266 (1993); 'Demography and Welfare Economics', *Empirica*, 22 (1995); and 'Mortality as an Indicator of Economic Success and Failure', *Economic Journal*, 108 (1998).

4. One of the pioneering statistical analyses of the policy relevance of this distinction came from Sudhir Anand and Martin Ravallion, 'Human Development in Poor Countries: On the Role of Private Incomes and Public Services', *Journal of Economic Perspectives*, 7 (1993).

5. This question is examined in my *Development as Freedom* (1999); *The Argumentative Indian* (London and Delhi: Penguin, and New York: FSG, 2005); and *Identity and Violence: The Illusion of Destiny* (New York: W. W. Norton & Co., and London and Delhi: Allen Lane, 2006). See also my essay 'Human Rights and Asian Values', *New Republic*, 14 and 21 July 1997.

6. That narrow view of opportunity – focusing only on the culmination outcome – has some following in the traditional economic theory of behaviour and choice, particularly in the 'revealed preference approach' (even though that theory, pioneered by Paul Samuelson, is not particularly addressed to evaluating or assessing freedom). For example, in the revealed preference approach, the opportunity of choosing from the so-called 'budget set' (that is to choose one commodity bundle from the set of alternative bundles that are all within the person's total budget) would be valued exactly at the value of the *chosen* element of that set. Nothing would be lost in this 'thin' view of opportunity, if the budget set is somehow cut down, so long as the previously chosen element remains available for choice. The relevance of the process of choice, as a contrast, is investigated in my essay, 'Maximization and the Act of Choice', *Econometrica*, 65 (1997).

7. There is a similar issue of informational choice even within the idea of freedom, which is associated with many distinct features, as I have tried to discuss in my Kenneth Arrow Lectures, included in *Rationality and Freedom* (Cambridge, MA: Harvard University Press, 2002), Chapters 20–22. Indeed, even in assessing the opportunity aspect of freedom, distinct ways of doing the accounting can make a substantial difference. While my own approach,

related to the reasoning in social choice theory, has been to do the assessment taking significant note of the exact preferences of an individual, there are other interesting explorations of evaluation in terms of the 'range' of the options available, for example, in some contributions, counting the number of alternatives a person can choose from. On various issues involved in this question, see also Patrick Suppes, 'Maximizing Freedom of Decision: An Axiomatic Approach', in G. Feiwel (ed.), *Arrow and the Foundations of Economic Policy* (London: Macmillan, 1987); Prasanta Pattanaik and Yongsheng Xu, 'On Ranking Opportunity Sets in Terms of Choice', *Recherches économique de Louvain*, 56 (1990); Hillel Steiner, 'Putting Rights in Their Place', *Recherches économique de Louvain*, 56 (1990); Ian Carter, 'International Comparison of Freedom', in *Economics and Philosophy*, 11 (1995), and *A Measure of Freedom* (Oxford: Clarendon Press, 1999); Robert Sugden, 'A Metric of Opportunity', *Economics and Philosophy*, 14 (1998).

8. See particularly Martha Nussbaum, 'Nature, Function and Capability: Aristotle on Political Distribution', *Oxford Studies in Ancient Philosophy*, supplementary volume, 1988; 'Human Functioning and Social Justice', *Political Theory*, 20 (1992); Nussbaum and Jonathan Glover (eds), *Women, Culture and Development* (Oxford: Clarendon Press, 1995).

9. An illuminating and wide-ranging introduction to the approach can be found in Sabina Alkire's *Valuing Freedoms: Sen's Capability Approach and Poverty Reduction* (Oxford and New York: Oxford University Press, 2002).

10. See the collection of essays in Flavio Comim, Mozaffar Qizilbash and Sabina Alkire (eds), *The Capability Approach: Concepts, Measures and Applications* (Cambridge: Cambridge University Press, 2008); Reiko Gotoh and Paul Dumouchel (eds), *Against Injustice: The New Economics of Amartya Sen* (Cambridge: Cambridge University Press, 2009); Ingrid Robeyns and Harry Brighouse (eds), *Measuring Justice: Primary Goods and Capabilities* (Cambridge: Cambridge University Press, 2009); Kaushik Basu and Ravi Kanbur (eds), *Arguments for a Better World: In Honor of Amartya Sen* (Oxford and New York: Oxford University Press, 2009), which is a larger collection but several of the essays deal directly with the capability perspective, including the papers of Bina Agarwal, Paul Anand (and Cristina Santos and Ron Smith), Amiya Kumar Bagchi, Lincoln C. Chen, Kanchan Chopra, James Foster and Christopher Handy, Sakiko Fukuda-Parr, Jocelyn Kynch, Enrica Chiappero-Martinetti, S. R. Osmani, Mozaffar Qizilbash, Sanjay G. Reddy (and Sujata Visaria and Muhammad Asali), Ingrid Robeyns, and Rehman Sobhan; some of the other essays also have an indirect bearing on the subject. See also, among other writings in this astonishingly fast-growing literature: Marko Ahtisaari, 'Amartya Sen's Capability Approach to the

Standard of Living', mimeographed, Columbia University Press, 1991; Sabina Alkire, *Valuing Freedoms: Sen's Capability Approach and Poverty Reduction* (Oxford: Clarendon Press, 2002); 'Why the Capability Approach?' *Journal of Human Development and Capabilities*, 6 (March 2005); 'Choosing Dimensions: The Capability Approach and Multidimensional Poverty' in Nanak Kakwani and Jacques Silber (eds), *The Many Dimensions of Poverty* (Basingstoke: Palgrave Macmillan, 2008); Anthony B. Atkinson, 'Capabilities, Exclusion, and the Supply of Goods', in Kaushik Basu, Prasanta Pattanaik and Kotaro Suzumura (eds), *Choice, Welfare, and Development* (Oxford: Oxford University Press, 1995); Kaushik Basu, 'Functioning and Capabilities', in Kenneth Arrow, Amartya Sen and Kotaro Suzumura (eds), *The Handbook of Social Choice Theory*, vol. II (Amsterdam: North-Holland, forthcoming); Enrica Chiappero-Martinetti, 'A New Approach to Evaluation of Well-being and Poverty by Fuzzy Set Theory', *Giornale degli Economisti*, 53 (1994); 'A Multidimensional Assessment of Well-being Based on Sen's Functioning Theory', *Rivista Internazionale di Scienze Sociali*, 2 (2000); 'An Analytical Framework for Conceptualizing Poverty and Re-examining the Capability Approach', *Journal of Socio-Economics*, 36 (2007); David Crocker, 'Functioning and Capability: The Foundations of Sen's and Nussbaum's Development Ethic', *Political Theory*, 20 (1992); *Ethics of Global Development: Agency, Capability and Deliberative Democracy* (Cambridge: Cambridge University Press, 2008); Reiko Gotoh, 'The Capability Theory and Welfare Reform', *Pacific Economic Review*, 6 (2001); 'Justice and Public Reciprocity', in Gotoh and Dumouchel, *Against Injustice* (2009); Kakwani and Silber (eds), *The Many Dimensions of Poverty* (2008); Mozaffar Qizilbash, 'Capabilities, Well-being and Human Development: A Survey', *Journal of Development Studies*, 33 (1996); 'Capability, Happiness and Adaptation in Sen and J. S. Mill', *Utilitas*, 18 (2006); Ingrid Robeyns, 'The Capability Approach: A Theoretical Survey', *Journal of Human Development*, 6 (2005); 'The Capability Approach in Practice', *Journal of Political Philosophy*, 17 (2006); Jennifer Prah Ruger, 'Health and Social Justice', *Lancet*, 364 (2004); 'Health, Capability and Justice: Toward a New Paradigm of Health Ethics, Policy and Law', *Cornell Journal of Law and Public Policy*, 15 (2006); *Health and Social Justice* (Oxford and New York: Oxford University Press, forthcoming 2009); Robert Sugden, 'Welfare, Resources and Capabilities: A Review of Inequality Reexamined by Amartya Sen', *Journal of Economic Literature*, 31 (1993).
11. See Richard A. Arneson, 'Equality and Equality of Opportunity for Welfare', *Philosophical Studies*, 56 (1989), and G. A. Cohen, 'Equality of What? On Welfare, Goods and Capabilities', in Martha Nussbaum and

Amartya Sen (eds), *The Quality of Life* (Oxford: Oxford University Press, 1993). See also Paul Streeten, *Development Perspectives* (London: Macmillan, 1981) and Frances Stewart, *Planning to Meet Basic Needs* (London: Macmillan, 1985).

12. This was called 'elementary evaluation' in my first book on the capability approach: *Commodities and Capabilities* (1985).

13. See Isaiah Berlin, *The Proper Study of Mankind*, edited by Henry Hardy and Roger Hausheer (London: Chatto & Windus, 1997) and *Liberty*, edited by Henry Hardy (Oxford: Oxford University Press, 2002); Bernard Williams, 'A Critique of Utilitarianism', in J. J. C. Smart and Bernard Williams, *Utilitarianism: For and Against* (Cambridge: Cambridge University Press, 1973), and Bernard Williams, *Ethics and the Limits of Philosophy* (Cambridge, MA: Harvard University Press, 1985).

14. T. S. Eliot, *Four Quartets* (London: Faber and Faber, 1944), p. 8.

15. I have discussed this question in 'Incompleteness and Reasoned Choice', *Synthese*, 140 (2004).

16. Frances Stewart and Séverine Deneulin, 'Amartya Sen's Contribution to Development Thinking', *Studies in Comparative International Development*, 37 (2002).

17. Karl Marx, *Economic and Philosophical Manuscripts of 1844* (Moscow: Progress Publishers, 1959), p. 104. See also Jon Elster, *Making Sense of Marx* (Cambridge: Cambridge University Press, 1985).

18. Karl Marx, *The Critique of the Gotha Programme* (1875; London: Lawrence and Wishart, 1938), pp. 21–3.

19. The Brundtland Report is the report produced by the World Commission on Environment and Development, chaired by Gro Brundtland (the former Prime Minister of Norway, and later the Director-General of the World Health Organization): *Our Common Future* (New York: Oxford University Press, 1987).

20. Robert Solow, *An Almost Practical Step toward Sustainability* (Washington, DC: Resources for the Future, 1992).

## 12 CAPABILITIES AND RESOURCES

1. Aristotle, *Nicomachean Ethics*, translated by D. Ross (Oxford: Oxford University Press, revised edn, 1980), Book I, section 5, p. 7.

2. See, among other writings on this important subject, Robert Putnam, *Bowling Alone: Collapse and Revival of American Community* (New York: Simon & Schuster, 2000).

3. On this see my 'Poor, Relatively Speaking', *Oxford Economic Papers*, 35 (1983), included in *Resources, Values and Development* (Cambridge, MA: Harvard University Press, 1984) Also, Dorothy Wedderburn, *The Aged in the Welfare State* (London: Bell, 1961), and J. Palmer, T. Smeeding and B. Torrey, *The Vulnerable: America's Young and Old in the Industrial World* (Washington, DC: Urban Institute Press, 1988).

4. On this, see my *Development as Freedom* (New York: Knopf, 1999), Chapters 8 and 9, and the literature cited there. Two of the pioneering contributions in this area are Pranab Bardhan, 'On Life and Death Questions', *Economic and Political Weekly*, 9 (1974), and Lincoln Chen, E. Huq and S. D'Souza, 'Sex Bias in the Family Allocation of Food and Health Care in Rural Bangladesh', *Population and Development Review*, 7 (1981). See also my joint paper with Jocelyn Kynch, 'Indian Women: Well-being and Survival', *Cambridge Journal of Economics*, 7 (1983), and jointly with Jean Drèze, *India: Economic Development and Social Opportunity* (New Delhi and Oxford: Oxford University Press, 1995), and *India: Development and Participation* (Delhi and Oxford: Oxford University Press, 2002).

5. These estimates come from the World Bank.

6. Wiebke Kuklys, *Amartya Sen's Capability Approach: Theoretical Insights and Empirical Applications* (New York: Springer-Verlag, 2005).

7. Thomas Pogge has made important contributions on this line; see particularly his *World Poverty and Human Rights: Cosmopolitan Responsibilities and Reforms* (Cambridge: Polity Press, 2002; 2nd edn, 2008).

8. Thomas Pogge, 'A Critique of the Capability Approach', in Harry Brighouse and Ingrid Robeyns (eds), *Measuring Justice: Primary Goods and Capabilities* (Cambridge: Cambridge University Press, forthcoming).

9. Elizabeth Anderson, 'Justifying the Capabilities Approach to Justice', in Brighouse and Robeyns (eds) *Measuring Justice: Primary Goods and Capabilities* (forthcoming). On related issues, see also her 'What Is the Point of Equality?' *Ethics*, 109 (1999).

10. See Kenneth Arrow and Frank Hahn, *General Competitive Analysis* (San Francisco, CA: Holden-Day, 1971; Amsterdam: North-Holland, 1979); George Akerlof, 'The Market for "Lemons": Quality Uncertainty and the Market Mechanism', *Quarterly Journal of Economics*, 84 (1970); Joseph Stiglitz and M. E. Rothschild, 'Equilibrium in Competitive Insurance Markets', *Quarterly Journal of Economics*, 90 (1976); among many other important contributions in this area.

## 13 HAPPINESS, WELL-BEING AND CAPABILITIES

1. See John E. Roemer, *Theories of Distributive Justice* (Cambridge, MA: Harvard University Press 1996). In this closely argued critique of different theories of justice, Roemer presents his reasoned assessment of some of the major approaches to the theory of justice in contemporary political philosophy and welfare economics.

2. Richard Easterlin, 'Will Raising the Income of All Increase the Happiness of All?', *Journal of Economic Behaviour and Organization*, 27 (1995). See also Easterlin's far-reaching analysis of the dissonance between income and happiness, and about ways and means of advancing happiness, both with the help of raising levels of income and through other means, 'Income and Happiness: Towards a Unified Theory', *Economic Journal*, 111 (2001). See also Bernard M. S. van Praag and Ada Ferrer-i-Carbonell, *Happiness Quantified: A Satisfaction Calculus Approach* (Oxford: Oxford University Press, 2004).

3. Tibor Scitovsky, *The Joyless Economy* (London: Oxford University Press, 1976).

4. Richard Layard, *Happiness: Lessons from a New Science* (London and New York: Penguin, 2005), p. 3.

5. Ibid., p. 113.

6. Ibid.

7. See Robert Nozick, *Anarchy, State and Utopia* (New York: Basic Books, 1974); Ronald Dworkin, *Sovereign Virtue: The Theory and Practice of Equality* (Cambridge, MA: Harvard University Press, 2002).

8. Lionel Robbins, 'Interpersonal Comparisons of Utility: A Comment', *Economic Journal*, 48 (1938).

9. Kenneth J. Arrow, *Social Choice and Individual Values* (New York: Wiley, 1951; 2nd edn, 1963).

10. Ibid. p. 9.

11. On this issue, see also my *Choice, Welfare and Measurement* (Oxford: Blackwell, 1982; Cambridge, MA: Harvard University Press, 1997), and 'Social Choice Theory', in K. J. Arrow and M. Intriligator (eds), *Handbook of Mathematical Economics* (Amsterdam: North-Holland, 1986).

12. Layard, *Happiness: Lessons from a New Science* (2005). See also Daniel Kahneman, 'Objective Happiness', in Daniel Kahneman and N. Schwartz (eds), *Well-being: The Foundations of Hedonic Psychology* (New York: Russell Sage Foundation, 1999), and Alan Krueger and Daniel Kahneman, 'Developments in the Measurement of Subjective Well-being', *Journal of Economic Perspectives*, 20 (2006). On related issues, see van Praag and

Carbonell, *Happiness Quantified: A Satisfaction Calculus Approach* (2004).

13. Layard, *Happiness* (2005), p. 4.

14. I have discussed this issue more fully elsewhere, in particular in 'Economic Progress and Health', with Sudhir Anand, in D. A. Leon and G. Walt (eds), *Poverty, Inequality and Health* (Oxford: Oxford University Press, 2000); and 'Health Achievement and Equity: External and Internal Perspectives', in Sudhir Anand, Fabienne Peter and Amartya Sen (eds), *Public Health, Ethics and Equity* (Oxford: Oxford University Press, 2004).

15. See, particularly, Arthur Kleinman, *The Illness Narratives: Suffering, Healing and the Human Condition* (New York: Basic Books, 1988) and *Writing at the Margin: Discourse between Anthropology and Medicine* (Berkeley, CA: University of California Press, 1995).

16. I discussed the distinctions between these four categories in my 1984 Dewey Lectures: 'Well-being, Agency and Freedom: The Dewey Lectures 1984', *Journal of Philosophy*, 82 (1985). The distinctions and their disparate relevance have been further pursued in my book, *Inequality Reexamined* (Cambridge, MA: Harvard University Press, and Oxford: Oxford University Press, 1992).

## 14 EQUALITY AND LIBERTY

1. *Inequality Reexamined* (Cambridge, MA: Harvard University Press, and Oxford: Oxford University Press, 1992).

2. See Robert Nozick, 'Distributive Justice', *Philosophy and Public Affairs*, 3 (1973), and *Anarchy, State and Utopia* (Oxford: Blackwell, 1974); James Buchanan, *Liberty, Market and the State* (Brighton: Wheatsheaf Books, 1986), and 'The Ethical Limits of Taxation', *Scandinavian Journal of Economics*, 86 (1984). See also James Buchanan and Gordon Tullock, *The Calculus of Consent* (Ann Arbor, MI: University of Michigan Press, 1962).

3. Richard Hare, *Moral Thinking: Its Level, Method and Point* (Oxford: Clarendon Press, 1981), p. 26; John Harsanyi, 'Morality and the Theory of Rational Behaviour', in Amartya Sen and Bernard Williams (eds), *Utilitarianism and Beyond* (Cambridge: Cambridge University Press, 1982), p. 47.

4. William Letwin (ed.), *Against Equality: Readings on Economic and Social Policy* (London: Macmillan, 1983).

5. Harry Frankfurt, 'Equality as a Moral Ideal', in Letwin (ed.), *Against Equality* (1983), p. 21.

6. In his engaging and stronlgly worded attack on mainstream political philosophy, Raymond Geuss points to the important fact that in many

theories of justice in the past, the need for unequal treatment is enshrined, rather than shunned: 'The Roman legal code conceptualized with firm and unwavering clarity the almost universally shared "intuition" that to treat a slave as if he or she had any entitlements would be a gross violation of the basic principles of justice' (Geuss, *Philosophy and Real Politics* (Princeton, NJ: Princeton University Press, 2008), p. 74). Geuss's point is well taken (and his analysis of the relevance of disparities of power points to a significant issue), but it is also particularly important to distinguish between that kind of rejection of equality as a principle and Frankfurt's argument against equality in some narrowly characterized space for the sake of other impartial values, including equality in what he would consider to be a more significant space.

7. The Marxian perspective on this is well developed in Maurice Dobb's classic writings: *Political Economy and Capitalism* (London: Routledge, 1937), and *Theories of Value and Distribution since Adam Smith: Ideology and Economic Theory* (Cambridge: Cambridge University Press, 1973). See also G. A. Cohen's contributions: *Karl Marx's Theory of History: A Defence* (Oxford: Clarendon Press, 1978), and *History, Labour and Freedom: Themes from Marx* (Oxford: Clarendon Press, 1988). I have attempted to scrutinize the labour theory of value in terms of its descriptive and evaluative contents in 'On the Labour Theory of Value: Some Methodological Issues', *Cambridge Journal of Economics*, 2 (1978).

8. On this, see my 'Liberty and Social Choice', *Journal of Philosophy*, 80 (1983), and *Inequality Reexamined* (Oxford: Clarendon Press, and Cambridge, MA: Harvard University Press, 1992).

9. A discussion of this kind of 'effectiveness' and its pervasive relevance in modern society can be found in my 'Liberty as Control: An Appraisal', *Midwest Studies in Philosophy*, 7 (1982).

10. John Stuart Mill, *On Liberty* (London: Longman, Roberts and Green, 1869). See also Friedrich Hayek, *The Constitution of Liberty* (Chicago, IL: University of Chicago Press, 1960).

11. See Philip Pettit, 'Liberalism and Republicanism', *Australasian Journal of Political Science*, 28 (1993); *Republicanism: A Theory of Freedom and Government* (Oxford: Clarendon Press, 1997); and *A Theory of Freedom* (Cambridge: Polity Press, 2001); and Quentin Skinner, *Liberty before Liberalism* (Cambridge: Cambridge University Press, 1998).

12. This plurality was defended in my 1984 Dewey Lectures, published as 'Well-being, Agency and Freedom: The Dewey Lectures 1984', *Journal of Philosophy*, 82 (1985); see particularly the third lecture.

13. This was presented in my 'The Impossibility of a Paretian Liberal', *Journal*

NOTES TO PP. 310-315

*of Political Economy*, 78 (1970), and in *Collective Choice and Social Welfare* (San Francisco, CA: Holden-Day, 1970, and Amsterdam: North-Holland, 1979), Chapter 6.

14. See particularly Christian Seidl, 'On Liberal Values', *Zeitschrift für Nationalökonomie*, 35 (1975).

15. See Kotaro Suzumura, 'On the Consistency of Libertarian Claims', *Review of Economic Studies*, 45 (1978); and Peter Hammond, 'Liberalism, Independent Rights and the Pareto Principle', in J. Cohen, (ed.), *Proceedings of the 6th International Congress of Logic, Methodology and Philosophy of Science* (Dordrecht: Reidel, 1981), and 'Utilitarianism, Uncertainty and Information', in Amartya Sen and Bernard Williams (eds), *Utilitarianism and Beyond* (Cambridge: Cambridge University Press, 1982).

16. See Julian Blau, 'Liberal Values and Independence', *Review of Economic Studies*, 42 (1975); Michael J. Farrell, 'Liberalism in the Theory of Social Choice', *Review of Economic Studies*, 43 (1976); Wulf Gaertner and Lorenz Kruger, 'Self-Supporting Preferences and Individual Rights: The Possibility of a Paretian Liberal', *Economica*, 48 (1981).

17. In what follows, I have used my discussion of this issue in 'Minimal Liberty', *Economica*, 59 (1992).

18. See Roy Gardner, 'The Strategic Inconsistency of Paretian Liberalism', *Public Choice*, 35 (1980); Friedrich Breyer and Roy Gardner, 'Liberal Paradox, Game Equilibrium and Gibbard Optimum', *Public Choice*, 35 (1980); Kaushik Basu, 'The Right to Give up Rights', *Economica*, 51 (1984).

19. See Brian Barry, 'Lady Chatterley's Lover and Doctor Fischer's Bomb Party: liberalism, Pareto optimality, and the problem of objectionable preferences', in Jon Elster and A. Hylland (eds), *Foundations of Social Choice Theory* (Cambridge: Cambridge University Press, 1986); and R. Hardin, *Morality within the Limits of Reason* (Chicago, IL: University of Chicago Press, 1988).

20. Robert Nozick, *Anarchy, State and Utopia* (New York: Basic Books, 1974), pp. 165-6. The result referred to is the impossibility of the Paretian liberal.

21. See particularly Peter Gardenfors, 'Rights, Games and Social Choice', *Nous*, 15 (1981); Robert Sugden, *The Political Economy of Public Choice* (Oxford: Martin Robertson, 1981), and 'Liberty, Preference and Choice', *Economics and Philosophy*, 1 (1985); Wulf Gaertner, Prasanta Pattanaik and Kotaro Suzumura, 'Individual Rights Revisited', *Economica*, 59 (1992).

## 15 DEMOCRACY AS PUBLIC REASON

1. Aldous Huxley, *Point Counter Point* (London: Vintage, 2004), pp. 343–4.
2. See particularly Rawls, *A Theory of Justice* (1971), and *Political Liberalism* (1993).
3. Jürgen Habermas, *The Structural Transformation of the Public Sphere* (Cambridge, MA: MIT Press, 1989); *The Theory of Communicative Action* (Boston, MA: Beacon Press, 1984), and *Moral Consciousness and Communicative Action* (Cambridge, MA: MIT Press, 1990).
4. The so-called liberal theory of public reasoning has been very powerfully championed by Bruce Ackerman, *Social Justice in the Liberal State* (New Haven: Yale University Press, 1980). See also his spiritedly argumentative essay, 'Why Dialogue?', *Journal of Philosophy*, 86 (1989).
5. Seyla Benhabib, *Another Cosmopolitanism* (New York: Oxford University Press, 2006), including her exchanges with Bonnie Honig, Will Kymlicka and Jeremy Waldron. See also Seyla Benhabib (ed.), *Democracy and Difference* (Princeton, NJ: Princeton University Press, 1996). On related matters, see also Elizabeth Anderson, *Value in Ethics and Economics* (Cambridge, MA: Harvard University Press, 1993).
6. See Joshua Cohen and Joel Rogers (eds), *On Democracy* (London: Penguin, 1983), and *Associations and Democracy* (London: Verso, 1995).
7. Ronald Dworkin, *Is Democracy Possible Here? Principles for a New Political Debate* (Princeton, NJ: Princeton University Press, 2006).
8. James Buchanan, 'Social Choice, Democracy and Free Markets', *Journal of Political Economy*, 62 (1954). See also James Buchanan and Gordon Tullock, *The Calculus of Consent* (Ann Arbor, MI: University of Michigan Press, 1962).
9. John Rawls, *Collected Papers* (Cambridge, MA: Harvard University Press, 1999), pp. 579–80. See also his *A Theory of Justice* (1971), *Political Liberalism* (1993), and *Justice as Fairness: A Restatement* (2001).
10. John Rawls, 'Reply to Habermas', *Journal of Philosophy*, 92 (March 1995).
11. Samuel Huntington, *The Third Wave: Democratization in the Late Twentieth Century* (Norman, OK, and London: University of Oklahoma Press, 1991), p. 9.
12. I have discussed these broader connections in 'Democracy as a Universal Value', *Journal of Democracy*, 10 (1999); 'Democracy and Its Global Roots', *New Republic*, 6 October 2003; *Identity and Violence: The Illusion*

*of Destiny* (New York: W. W. Norton & Co., and London and Delhi: Penguin, 2006), pp. 51-5.

13. Aldous Huxley himself was evidently quite familiar with this literature on ancient Indian experiments in urban democracy, as is evident from books that Sidney Quarles cites to his wife as objects of his study in his proposed visit to the Library of the British Museum.

14. This issue is more fully treated in my books, *The Argumentative Indian* (London and Delhi: Penguin, and New York: Farrar, Straus and Giroux, 2005), and *Identity and Violence: The Illusion of Destiny* (New York: W. W. Norton & Co., and London: Penguin, 2006).

15. For a fuller discussion of these traditions, with the references to the source material, see *The Argumentative Indian* (2005) and *Identity and Violence* (2006).

16. See Nakamura Hajime, 'Basic Features of the Legal, Political, and Economic Thought of Japan', in Charles A. Moore (ed.), *The Japanese Mind: Essentials of Japanese Philosophy and Culture* (Tokyo: Tuttle, 1973), p. 144.

17. See Ramachandra Guha, 'Arguments with Sen: Arguments about India', *Economic and Political Weekly*, 40 (2005), and Amartya Sen, 'Our Past and Our Present', *Economic and Political Weekly*, 41 (2006).

18. Nelson Mandela, *Long Walk to Freedom* (Boston, MA, and London: Little, Brown & Co., 1994), p. 21.

19. Maria Rosa Menocal, *The Ornament of the World: How Muslims, Jews, and Christians Created a Culture of Tolerance in Medieval Spain* (Boston, MA, and London: Little, Brown & Co., 2002), p. 86.


## 16 THE PRACTICE OF DEMOCRACY

1. For the sources of this and other citations on the Bengal famine, see my *Poverty and Famines* (1981), Chapter 9 and Appendix D.

2. On the North Korean famines, including the connection with authoritarian rule, see Andrew S. Natsios, *The Great North Korean Famine* (Washington, DC: Institute of Peace Press, 2002), and Stephan Haggard and Marcus Noland, *Famine in North Korea: Markets, Aid, and Reform* (New York: Columbia University Press, 2007).

3. See T. P. Bernstein, 'Stalinism, Famine, and Chinese Peasants', *Theory and Society*, 13 (1984), p. 13. See also Carl Riskin, *China's Political Economy* (Oxford: Clarendon Press, 1987).

4. Quoted in Mao Tse-tung, *Mao Tse-tung Unrehearsed, Talks and Letters:*

*1956–71*, edited by Stuart Schram (Harmondsworth: Penguin, 1974), pp. 277–8.

5. See, for example, Adam Przeworski et al., *Sustainable Democracy* (Cambridge: Cambridge University Press, 1995); Robert J. Barro, *Getting It Right: Markets and Choices in a Free Society* (Cambridge, MA: MIT Press, 1996).

6. On these issues, see my *Development as Freedom* (New York: Knopf, and Oxford: Oxford University Press, 1999). Also, Robin Jeffrey, *Politics, Women, and Well-being: How Kerala Became a 'Model'* (Cambridge: Cambridge University Press, 1992); V. K. Ramachandran, 'Kerala's Development Achievements', in Jean Drèze and Amartya Sen (eds), *Indian Development: Selected Regional Perspectives* (Oxford and Delhi: Oxford University Press, 1996).

7. Condorcet, *Essai sur l'application de l'analyse à la probabilité des decisions rendues à la pluralité des voix* (1785; New York: Chelsea House, 1972), in *Œuvres de Condorcet*, edited by A. Condorcet O'Conner and M. F. Arago (Paris: Firmin Didot, 1847–49), vol. 6, pp. 176–7. See also the discussion on this and related issues in Emma Rothschild, *Economic Sentiments: Smith, Condorcet and the Enlightenment* (Cambridge, MA: Harvard University Press, 2001), chapter 6.

8. Gandhi wrote on this subject; see *The Collected Works of Mahatma Gandhi* (New Delhi: Government of India, 1960). See also my *Identity and Violence: The Illusion of Destiny* (New York: W. W. Norton & Co., and London and Delhi: Allen Lane, 2006), especially pp. 165–9.

9. On this see my *Identity and Violence: The Illusion of Destiny* (2006).


## 17 HUMAN RIGHTS AND GLOBAL IMPERATIVES

1. Jeremy Bentham, *Anarchical Fallacies; Being an Examination of the Declaration of Rights Issued during the French Revolution* (1792); republished in J. Bowring (ed.), *The Works of Jeremy Bentham*, vol. II (Edinburgh: William Tait, 1843), p. 501.

2. Discussion and defence of this claim can be found in my 'Elements of a Theory of Human Rights', *Philosophy and Public Affairs*, 32 (2004), and 'Human Rights and the Limits of Law', *Cardozo Law Journal*, 27 (April 2006). Those essays also present a general framework for the basis, reach and implications of seeing rights as, ultimately, ethical claims satisfying the basic demands of impartial reasoning.

3. Bentham, *Anarchical Fallacies* (1792); in *The Works of Jeremy Bentham*, vol. II, p. 523.

4. Accepting a general contrast between the respective categories of ethical assertions and legal pronouncements does not, of course, deny the possibility that ethical views may contribute to the interpretation and substantive content of laws. The recognition of that possibility may go against a strictly positivist theory of law (on which see Ronald Dworkin, *A Matter of Principle*, Cambridge, MA: Harvard University Press, 1985). But it does not obliterate the considerable difference that exists between primarily ethical claims and principally legal proclamations.

5. Thomas Paine, *The Rights of Man: Being an Answer to Mr Burke's Attack on the French Revolution* (1791); second part, *Combining Principle and Practice* (1792); republished, *The Rights of Man* (London: Dent, and New York: Dutton, 1906). Mary Wollstonecraft, *A Vindication of the Rights of Men, in a Letter to the Right Honourable Edmund Burke; occasioned by his Reflections on the Revolution in France* (1790) and *A Vindication of the Rights of Woman: with Strictures on Political and Moral Subjects* (1792); both included in Mary Wollstonecraft, *A Vindication of the Rights of Men and A Vindication of the Rights of Woman*, edited by Sylvana Tomaselli (Cambridge: Cambridge University Press, 1995).

6. H. L. A. Hart, 'Are There Any Natural Rights?', *The Philosophical Review*, 64 (April 1955), reprinted in Jeremy Waldron (ed.), *Theories of Rights* (Oxford: Oxford University Press, 1984), p. 79.

7. See also my 'Well-being, Agency and Freedom: The Dewey Lectures 1984', *Journal of Philosophy*, 82 (April 1985); *Inequality Reexamined* (Cambridge, MA: Harvard University Press, and Oxford: Clarendon Press, 1992); and *Development as Freedom* (New York: Knopf, 1999).

8. Robert E. Goodin and Frank Jackson, 'Freedom from Fear', *Philosophy and Public Affairs*, 35 (2007), p. 250.

9. For a fuller exploration of the distinction and its far-reaching implications, see my Kenneth Arrow Lectures, 'Freedom and Social Choice', included in my *Rationality and Freedom* (Cambridge, MA: Harvard University Press, 2002), essays 20–22.

10. See Chapter 11.

11. The relevance of a consequence-sensitive framework for this type of ethical reasoning is investigated in my essay 'Rights and Agency', *Philosophy and Public Affairs*, 11 (1982), 'Positional Objectivity', *Philosophy and Public Affairs*, 22 (1993), and 'Consequential Evaluation and Practical Reason', *Journal of Philosophy*, 97 (2000).

12. Immanuel Kant, *Groundwork of the Metaphysics of Morals* (1785); republished edn (Cambridge: Cambridge University Press, 1998), and

*Critique of Practical Reason* (1788); republished edn (Cambridge: Cambridge University Press, 1997).

13. Aristotle, *The Nicomachean Ethics*, translated by William David Ross (Oxford: Oxford University Press, 1998), p. 3.

14. On this, see Andrew Ashworth and Eva Steiner, 'Criminal Omissions and Public Duties: The French Experience', *Legal Studies*, 10 (1990); Glanville Williams, 'Criminal Omissions: The Conventional View', *Law Quarterly Review*, 107 (1991).

15. The connection of rights with obligations – both imperfect and perfect – was briefly explored and scrutinized in an earlier paper, 'Consequential Evaluation and Practical Reason', *Journal of Philosophy*, 97 (September 2000), and in the introductory chapter to the United Nations' *Human Development Report 2000* (New York: UNDP, 2000), which was based on an essay I wrote for that special issue, 'Human Rights and Human Development'.

16. Joseph Raz, *The Morality of Freedom* (Oxford: Clarendon Press, 1986), p. 180.

17. See Ivan Hare, 'Social Rights as Fundamental Human Rights', in Bob Hepple (ed.), *Social and Labour Rights in Global Context* (Cambridge University Press, 2002).

18. Cass R. Sunstein, *After the Rights Revolution; Reconceiving the Regulatory State* (Cambridge, MA: Harvard University Press, 1990).

19. See, for example, Andrew Kuper's analysis of *Democracy Beyond Borders: Justice and Representation in Global Institutions* (New York and Oxford: Oxford University Press, 2004); see also the collection of essays edited by him, *Global Responsibilities: Who Must Deliver on Human Rights?* (New York and London: Routledge, 2005).

20. The works of Thomas Pogge, along with those of his collaborators, have opened up many areas of policy analysis broadly based on the idea of human rights and the demands of justice. See particularly Thomas Pogge, *World Poverty and Human Rights: Cosmopolitan Responsibilities and Reforms* (Cambridge: Polity Press, 2002; 2nd edn, 2008); Andreas Føllesdal and Thomas Pogge (eds), *Real World Justice* (Berlin: Springer, 2005); Thomas Pogge and Sanjay Reddy, *How Not to Count the Poor* (New York: Columbia University Press, 2005); Robert Goodin, Philip Pettit and Thomas Pogge (eds), *A Companion to Contemporary Political Philosophy* (Oxford: Blackwell, 2007); Elke Mack, Thomas Pogge, Michael Schramm and Stephan Klasen (eds), *Absolute Poverty and Global Justice: Empirical Data – Moral Theories – Realizations* (Aldershot: Ashgate, 2009).

21. Deen Chatterjee, *Democracy in a Global World: Human Rights and*

*Political Participation in the 21st Century* (London: Rowman & Littlefield, 2008), p. 2.

22. David Crocker, *Ethics of Global Development: Agency, Capability, and Deliberative Democracy* (Cambridge: Cambridge University Press, 2008), pp. 389–90.

23. See also Christian Barry and Sanjay Reddy, *International Trade and Labor Standards* (New York: Columbia University Press, 2008).

24. See Maurice Cranston, 'Are There Any Human Rights?' *Daedalus*, 112 (Fall 1983), and Onora O'Neill, *Towards Justice and Virtue* (Cambridge: Cambridge University Press, 1996).

25. Onora O'Neill, *Faces of Hunger: An Essay on Poverty, Justice and Development* (London: Allen & Unwin, 1986).

26. O'Neill, *Towards Justice and Virtue* (1996), pp. 131–2. See also her *Bounds of Justice* (Cambridge: Cambridge University Press, 2000).

27. Maurice Cranston, 'Are There Any Human Rights?' (1983), p. 13.

28. This issue is forcefully discussed by Bernardo Kliksberg, *Towards an Intelligent State* (Amsterdam: IOS Press, 2001).

29. On this, see my 'Elements of a Theory of Human Rights', *Philosophy and Public Affairs*, 32 (2004).

30. Some of the foundational issues are discussed by John Mackie, 'Can There Be a Rights-based Moral Theory?', *Midwest Studies in Philosophy*, 3 (1978).

## 18 JUSTICE AND THE WORLD

1. See J. C. Jacquemin, 'Politique de stabilisation par les investissements publics', unpublished Ph.D. thesis for the University of Namur, Belgium, 1985. Jean Drèze and I have discussed different aspects of this correspondence in *Hunger and Public Action* (Oxford: Clarendon Press, 1989), pp. 65–8.

2. See also 'Famine, Poverty, and Property Rights', in Christopher W. Morris (ed.), *Amartya Sen*, Contemporary Philosophy in Focus series (Cambridge: Cambridge University Press, forthcoming 2009).

3. Mary Wollstonecraft, *A Vindication of the Rights of Woman* (1792); in Sylvana Tomaselli (ed.), *A Vindication of the Rights of Men and A Vindication of the Rights of Woman* (Cambridge: Cambridge University Press, 1995), p. 294.

4. *A Vindication of the Rights of Woman* (1792), in Tomaselli (ed.) (1995), p. 70.

5. Smith, *The Theory of Moral Sentiments*, V. 2. 15, p. 210.

6. Adam Smith, *Lectures on Jurisprudence*, edited by R. L. Meek, D. D. Raphael and P. G. Stein (Oxford: Clarendon Press, 1978; reprinted, Indianapolis, IN: Liberty Press, 1982), p. 104.
7. Quoted in 'Ginsburg Shares Views on Influence of Foreign Law on Her Court, and Vice and Versa', *New York Times*, 12 April 2009, p. 14,
8. *New York Times*, 12 April 2009.

# Name Index

# Subject Index

accountability *see* responsibilities

achievements and opportunity 235–43, 236, 287

Afghanistan 149–50, 192, 402, 405

Africa xi, 48, 116, 166, 257, 335, 343, 353, 384, 390, 409

agencies 19, 23, 142, 184, 214, 215–9, 220–21, 231, 249–50, 254, 286–90, 297–8, 375, 380–381, 434, 437, 441, 442, 449

agency freedom 19, 249–50, 271, 286–90, 297–8

agent relativity 161, 168, 169, 221

Akbar, Indian emperor, on the priority of reason 37–9, 49, 51

Alberuni (Iranian mathematician) on debates in ancient Indian astronomy 158–9

al-Qaeda 3

America *see* United States

anger, the role of 195, 390–92

Arab history 247, 333–5

Aristotle's *Nicomachean Ethics* and *Politics* 91, 253, 375, 438, 448

Arrow's impossibility theorem (General Possibility Theorem) 92–3, 110, 279–81, 314, 410

Aryabhata (Indian mathematician) on projections and astronomy 158–9

Ashoka, Indian emperor, on tolerance and dialogue 69, 75–7, 76, 228, 331

atrocities 34, 35, 36, 49, 384

Austria 33, 77

balloting *see* voting and elections

Bastille, fall of vii, 1, 114

behaviour
  actual ix, xi, 6–7, 10, 67–9, 79, 176–8, 204, 268, 354
  assumed 8, 32–33, 67–9, 178–83, 184–5, 188–90, 203–5
  weakness of will 176–8

Bentham, Jeremy, on natural and human rights 356, 361–2, 363
  *see also* utilitarianism

*Bhagavadgita* (*Gita*) 23–4, 208–17, 210, 212, 213

bounded rationality 108, 176

Brazil 335, 405, 409

Brundtland Commission on sustainable development 248–50, 251–2

Buddha and Buddhism xiv, 77, 87, 205–6, 225, 251, 331

Burke, Edmund
  on the American War of Independence 114, 115–16
  on the French Revolution 114–15
  his impeachment of Warren Hastings 1–2, 31
  on liberty 114–15, 116
  on plural grounding 1–2, 4
  Wollstonecraft on 115, 116, 122, 161